MARY LINCOLN DEMYSTIFIED

Mary Lincoln Demystified

Frequently Asked Questions about Abraham's Wife

DONNA D. MCCREARY

Southern Illinois University Press
Carbondale

Southern Illinois University Press
www.siupress.com

24 24 23 22   4 3 2 1

Cover illustration: Mary Lincoln, from a steel engraving created by
William Sartain of Philadelphia, circa 1861 (cropped and tinted).
Author's collection.

Library of Congress Cataloging-in-Publication Data
Names: McCreary, Donna D., author.
Title: Mary Lincoln demystified: frequently asked questions
about Abraham's wife / Donna D. McCreary.
Description: Carbondale: Southern Illinois University Press, [2022] |
Includes bibliographical references and index.
Identifiers: LCCN 2022026171 (print) | LCCN 2022026172 (ebook) |
ISBN 9780809338696 (paperback) | ISBN 9780809338702 (ebook)
Subjects: LCSH: Lincoln, Mary Todd, 1818–1882—Miscellanea. |
Presidents' spouses—United States—Biography—Miscellanea.
Classification: LCC E457.25.L55 M383 2022 (print) |
LCC E457.25.L55 (ebook) | DDC 973.7/092 [B]—dc23/eng/20220603
LC record available at https://lccn.loc.gov/2022026171
LC ebook record available at https://lccn.loc.gov/2022026172

SIU
Southern Illinois University System

To my parents, Donald and Helen,
who always inspire me to do my best.

CONTENTS

Galleries follow pages 110 and 156

PREFACE

$\mathscr{M}$y parents believed family vacations should be entertaining and educational, and so it was that at the age of ten, I had my first encounter with Mary Lincoln. She was a simulacrum at the American History Wax Museum in Gatlinburg, Tennessee. Before this trip from my home in Clarksville, Indiana to Tennessee, I had, on a Florida beach trip, visited Castillo de San Marcos in Saint Augustine. A journey to the Pacific Ocean and Disneyland had incorporated stops at Roy Rogers Museum, National Cowboy and Western Heritage Museum, historic Dodge City, and Old Town Albuquerque. My family's excursion to the Blue Ridge Mountains encompassed visits at tourist attractions, such as Ruby Falls and Lookout Mountain near Chattanooga, Tennessee, where nature, history, and legend blend together to create an American panorama that inspired my innocent imagination.

By the time I stood eye-to-eye with Mary, I was an experienced American historical traveler. I had seen an extensive number of historic sites, been jolted by a variety of rides at multiple theme parks, journeyed countless historic trails, and walked an immense number of hallowed paths where Lincoln had once sojourned.

Throughout all those experiences, however, it was Mary Lincoln who always fascinated me. My school library offered a few titles about her, and I read, and often reread, them all. Whether it was a book for juvenile readers or historical fiction, if the book focused on Mary, I read it. I was not looking for Abraham Lincoln; I was searching for the love story between a wealthy, well-educated, upper-class society girl and her lanky, poor, homely beau. Her family's disapproval of her marital choice made the story more exhilarating to me. When reading *I, Mary* by Ruth Painter Randall, I felt the love story leap from the pages to fulfill my quest for romance. Here was the well-bred aristocratic young girl who fell in love with a poor boy. It was *Cinderella* reversed. I read every Mary Lincoln book in the school library and in the children's section of the public library in our community.

By the time I stood in front of the wax tableau of Lincoln's assassination, I thought I knew Lincoln and his wife. I was wrong. Once I began to read adult biographies, I realized how little I truly knew about Mary and her family. The more I read, the more questions I had.

In 1991, I was invited to attend a performance by Jim Getty, who was scheduled to appear as Abraham Lincoln at the Presbyterian Church in Madison, Indiana. Mary's half-sister Emilie, and Mary's stepmother, Elizabeth ("Betsy") had moved to Madison in 1866. While Emilie provided an income for the family by teaching piano and playing the organ at the Christ Episcopal Church on Mulberry Street, Betsy fit into Madison society and attended church services at the Madison Presbyterian Church on Broadway. Madison was the perfect location for me to meet a Lincoln presenter.

Before his performance, Mr. Getty and I met and discussed the Lincolns. We mulled over the basic fact-versus-fiction stories that circulate throughout historical organizations. We wondered at the similarities in our personal histories and interests—both had some theater background; both taught college courses; both had a lifelong interest in at least one of the members of the Lincoln household. At the end of our conversation, Mr. Getty offered me a challenge—the prospect of telling Mary's story in the same manner that he told Abraham's.

The idea intrigued me.

So, I spent the next eighteen months finding and reading every biography available about Mary Lincoln. I began by rereading some of the books I had devoured in my youth to refresh my knowledge and prepare to search deeper into the personal story of the characters. I purchased and read Jean Baker's *Mary Todd Lincoln: A Biography*; Gerry Van der Heuvel's *Crowns of Thorns and Glory*; and *The Insanity File*, by Mark Neely Jr. and R. Gerald McMurtry. I fell in love with the writings of such authors as William Townsend, Katherine Helm, and W. A. Evans. I kept notebooks filled with anecdotes about Mary, trying to separate fact, fiction, myth, legend, and wild tale.

Even after learning parts of Mary's story, I still had much work to do. If I were going to fulfill Mr. Getty's challenge, I could not simply learn about Mary and tell her story—I had to become Mary on stage. I had to learn her history, come to know her family, understand her society, feel her emotions, and become her voice. To do all of this required understanding her personality and knowing her passions, so I needed to turn to her own writings. Mary's letters had been compiled by Justin G. Turner and his daughter-in-law Linda Turner. Reading Mary's letters gave me her sound—her tone. Other authors helped me understand Mary's love for her family and her world. But to understand her so deeply that an audience could be transported to her era, I had to use Mary's own words in my scripts.

Theater is not just auditory; it is also visual. Therefore, I had to fashion clothing, find or make props, create sets, and block out my movements. I wanted every detail seen and heard by the audience to carry them to 1865.

I performed first in Madison, Indiana, for a Civil War Round Table. After the show, I returned to the stage to answer questions about Mary and her family. Since I was in a city where members of the Todd family had lived, I was glad I had been able to study the family and could respond to the questions knowledgeably. As I packed props, an audience member approached me about bringing a stage show to the local library. A spark had been lit, and slowly I began to build a business of being Mary.

Over the next few decades, I wrote five scripts: two one-woman productions and three two-person scripts using a readers' theater format. During the process of writing and re-writing, my research methods grew more sophisticated. Instead of reading magazine articles and books by others about Mary and Abraham, I found myself going to research libraries and archives to dig into original source material for details that could not be found in secondary sources. In other words, I searched for the deeper story.

After a few years of performing stage shows, I had the opportunity to participate in the *History Alive!* programs sponsored by the Indiana Humanities Council. These programs would be hosted by elementary schools throughout the state. Participation in the program required writing lesson plans and study guides for teachers as well as activity pages for the students. Most importantly, participation required being able to answer the students' questions at the end of each program.

It is true: Kids ask the darndest things. The first question, from a fourth-grade boy, was "Mrs. Lincoln, what is your favorite food?" I told a story about strawberry parties and explained how just about anything can be made from a strawberry.

The boy's question inspired me to search for recipes of foods that Abraham and Mary ate. Soon, I collected enough recipes to write a book, *Lincoln's Table*. After its publication, I was able to share recipes with the faculty of schools that sponsored *History Alive!*, and their students were able to share a taste of history.

Throughout the years, I have enjoyed my journey with Mary and her family. Researching the Todds allowed me to meet several family members and friends. One of the most interesting people was a dear woman named Mary

Genevieve Townsend Murphy, the daughter of Lincoln scholar William H. Townsend. She owned the last home that had been owned by Emilie Todd Helm and her children. Mrs. Murphy allowed me to peruse the letters and documents that the Helm family had left in the house. This collection included several letters written between the Helms and their cousin, Robert Todd Lincoln. I marveled at the Todd family history that Emilie had compiled. I was amazed at the vast number of items that had belonged to the family, and I was mesmerized by the portraits the talented Katherine Helm had painted. Mrs. Murphy has since passed away, and the items have been separated and moved to various museums and historic sites. I shall always be grateful for those moments I sat in the parlor and listened to Mrs. Murphy tell stories about her days of knowing Emilie and her family. My visits with Mrs. Murphy always made me want to learn more about Mary Lincoln. Just as Jim Getty had given me a challenge, Mrs. Murphy encouraged me to "continue to tell the story of Mary and the Todds."

I have set aside my stage shows and now focus on lecturing and writing, and just as I always returned to the stage after a performance to allow an audience to ask questions, I continue to entertain questions at public appearances. This book is a collection of the questions I have been asked—some by serious adults, some by innocent children. All of the questions were asked with sincerity and a desire to understand one of America's more controversial figures.

My desire is that as you read these pages, your own questions are answered, and you come to better understand Mary Lincoln and her love story.

MARY LINCOLN DEMYSTIFIED

Introduction

*O*ften, a scholar's favorite part of a lecture is the question-and-answer session that follows. It allows the speaker an opportunity to delve deeper into a topic that an audience member finds interesting, and often inspires the speaker to dig deeper into archives to find answers. Depending on the question, an answer may be a short simple sentence, or it may begin a conversation which needs exploration for further understanding.

When performing a one-woman (or two-person) stage play as Mary Lincoln, I found that the question-and-answer session allowed me to engage with ideas that could not be covered within the time frame of a script. For example, one of the shows, *Lincoln's Christmas*, had a distinct date: December 24, 1864. Our script allowed us to concentrate on events that happened up to that date. Our "Abraham and Mary" described visiting hospitals, talking to nurses, and caring for their children—including their thoughts on both Robert's desire to enter the Civil War and the war itself. We were able to focus on a conversation between a husband and wife as they prepared for a Christmas meal and discussed their hopes for the new year. During the Q&A, the audience's questions often covered just about everything except Christmas 1864. The audience members asked: How long did Mary live after Lincoln's death? What happened to Robert? Are there any living descendants? Did Mary remarry? A play gave the audience just enough information to want to know more. Only one of my shows, *Mary, the Widow of Lincoln*, followed Mary to the end of her life. Afterward, the audience often wanted to know about Mary as a person. Who was her family? What did she study in school? What were her religious beliefs? What type of mother was she? Was she insane? Was she a shrew?

I sought to answer as many questions as I could. During my research travels, I made several trips to the Lincoln Museum in Fort Wayne, Indiana where I

met their Lincoln scholar, Dr. Gerald Prokopowicz. Museum visitors asked
him a variety of questions about Lincoln. Some of the questions were funny
and lighthearted; others were thought provoking. Prokopowicz collected the
questions and published them in *Did Lincoln Own Slaves? And Other Frequently Asked Questions about Abraham Lincoln* (New York, Pantheon, 2008).
His purpose was to answer questions which were asked by the public, not
historians. After the release of his book, he and I discussed a book with a
similar purpose: to answer questions about Mary Lincoln asked by the public.
His book includes a few questions about Mary, but no one had ever tackled
answering a collection of questions that focused on Mary. This book came
out of our discussion.

Mary has been called the First Lady of Controversy. This moniker comes from
the variety of stories that have circulated about her since Abraham became
the Republican candidate in 1860. Was Mary a Confederate spy? Why did
she purchase one thousand dollars' worth of mourning clothing before her
husband's death? Did she believe in ghosts? Those answering these questions
have offered different versions of the truth. Often, their answers are simply
incorrect. Rumors, untruths, incorrect information, and lies have been told
and written about Mary for generations. My purpose here is to present both
sides and examine the documentation that explains Mary's actions and truths.

My journey led me not only to answer questions asked by audience members, but also those that I wondered about myself. As I moved away from
performance work and more into developing lectures, I often sought the trivia
that do not fit neatly into the narrative of a biography. Lists of Mary's siblings,
her servants, African Americans she knew, and the names of her friends often
do not fit into a life story. Most of the biographies about Mary also get bogged
down with details about Abraham. While it is impossible to tell Mary's life
story without including Abraham, this Q&A book places the focus on Mary
and allows the reader to quickly find answers without searching through a
narrative.

I need to state up front that I do lean toward an empathetic and sympathetic
view of Mary. Having presented as Mary for decades, I have developed an
understanding of Mary as a mother, a wife, and a woman. When a historian
answers questions after performances and lectures, it is their responsibility
to explain Mary's story. For those who answer questions in first person as
the historical figure, as I have, the ability to think quickly, and in character,
is crucial to the performance. Of course, "Mary" would be sympathetic to

herself and defensive of her actions. Some of this perspective does carry over into the answers presented in the book, but I have presented evidence for both sides of issues.

This book is divided into ten chapters. The first five chapters are presented in chronological order and can be considered a biography of Mary presented through questions. Chapters are dedicated to her girlhood in Lexington, Kentucky; her adulthood in Springfield, Illinois; the First Lady years in Washington; the death of her husband, and her widowhood of self-exile. Chapter four is dedicated to Lincoln's assassination, since it is the single most traumatic day of Mary's life. Countless books have been written about this one night. For Mary, the event deserves a chapter of its own.

The rest of the chapters delve into various aspects of Mary's life. By addressing these topics in a Q&A format, I can incorporate detailed information that may not be appropriate in a narrative biography. For example, lists of hired girls and servants, the enslaved persons owned by the Todd family, and the proper birth order of Mary's siblings, are well suited for a Q&A format.

Chapter six looks at the facts of the insanity trial and investigates whether Mary suffered from mental illness. Historians will never agree on Mary's mental health, so my purpose is to present the evidence and allow readers to draw their own conclusions.

Mary's family relationships were dramatic, ranging between periods of sheer delight and friendship, distrust and dismay, to dependence and support. Chapter seven delves into these complicated relationships and explains Mary's ever-changing relationships with them.

Chapter eight looks at Mary's relations with the African American community in her youth and in her adult life. While historians have written about Abraham's feelings on slavery and race relations, other than her relationship with Elizabeth Keckly,[1] Mary's thoughts have been, in the main, ignored. But they need to be interrogated. Mary grew up in a slave-holding family. She hired African American servants both in Springfield and Washington. Mary developed friendships with African American men and women.

Chapter nine examines Mary's personality and habits. In today's world of social media and celebrity infatuation, people want to know personal tidbits about historical figures as well.

The final chapter is a look at Lincoln descendants, the family legacy, and Mary's place in history. These questions are those that one can never answer when presenting a historical figure but are often asked either after the curtain has fallen, or after a lecture.

The three appendixes offer information which helps the reader understand those people who were in Mary's life: her friends, and her family. Often, names within a family are repeated. Having a list of them helps sort them out. The last appendix is a timeline for Mary. Knowing where she was, or what she was doing on a (given) day, helps readers understand the requirements of a First Lady. Seeing how much she traveled during her widowhood allows one to understand why she felt she lived in a land among strangers.

When writing a biography, authors usually take a stand on one side of an issue, such as "Was Mary Lincoln insane?" My purpose is to explain both sides by presenting the facts. Yes, she was declared insane in a court of law, but she was released from a sanitarium four months later. I have always wanted to know the details of the story. While most biographers may be happy stating that one of Mary's beaux was the grandson of Patrick Henry, I searched until I found his name. This book includes this and other pieces of trivia that will give a better understanding of who Mary was as a woman.

And Mary was a complicated woman—an enigma. She was a loving daughter, a devoted wife, a compassionate mother, a controversial First Lady, and an eccentric recluse. Her complex life offers many questions. Some of the answers can be found here.

CHAPTER ONE

Mary Grows Up in the Bluegrass:
The Lexington Years, 1818 to 1835

[Y]et the memory of earlier years and the memory of those who were
so kind to me in my desolate childhood is ever remembered by me.
— Mary Lincoln to Eliza Stuart Steele, May 23, 1871

*M*ary Lincoln once referred to her childhood as "desolate." However,
"desolate" is not the word her friends and family would have used when describing Mary's early years. They found her to be a vivacious, lively, high-
spirited, quick-tempered girl surrounded by a large family and a wide circle of
friends. Yet in the loneliness of her later years, Mary remembered, and often
dwelled upon the sadness and tragedies she experienced as a child. Her mother
died before Mary's seventh birthday. Her father remarried hastily, even by the
standards of the time. Mary's relationship with her stepmother was a mixture
of respect, turmoil, and conflict. Mary was emotionally close to her father,
but he was not always available as his business took him as far away as New
Orleans. When home, he served as Clerk for the Kentucky House of Representatives and was often either away from home or too busy for his children.

Many authors have emphasized these elements of Mary's young life to either
win sympathy for her, or to provide a childhood basis for later erratic behavior,
and possible mental instability. Yet, these childhood traumas—which were
far from uncommon in the early nineteenth century—are only part of her
formative years. Mary's childhood also included a father who doted on her
and occasionally spoiled her. Mary maintained close relationships with other
girls her age, both family and non-family members. She was born into a family
whose name carried great respect in Kentucky and the young republic.

Elizabeth Humphreys Norris (Mary's step-cousin) explained their girlhood by writing "children had few privileges & led very dull lives."[1] They did not believe their lives were interesting enough to record for prosperity. Neither Mary nor her friends nor her family members kept diaries during those early years; at least, no journals have survived. What is known of Mary's childhood world, her experiences and personality traits, has been culled from newspaper clippings, court records, wills, a few family letters, and recollections from her contemporaries. Most of those stories were written down years after Mary's death leaving no one to question, or correct, failing memories of her girlhood companions.

Frequently asked questions about Mary's childhood revolve around her place in the Todd family and her relations with her father, mother, stepmother, siblings and half-siblings; her education; and her religious background. Mainly, people wonder if there was anything unique in the childhood of a little Bluegrass girl which emboldened her to declare she would one day marry a president of the United States.

Birth and Order

When and where was Mary born?

Mary's maternal grandmother, Elizabeth Parker (called Widow Parker) owned a home and large lot at 511 West Short Street in Lexington. When Robert Smith Todd married Eliza Parker, they built a brick home on the front corner of this property. While no one can be sure whether Mary was born in this home, or in the home of her grandmother next door, it is believed that on December 13, 1818, Mary was born in the home of her parents at 509 West Short Street.

Sadly, this home no longer exists; it was partially destroyed by fire in the latter part of the nineteenth century. In 1887 the home was purchased by St. Paul's Catholic Church and torn down by local contractors Albert Howard and George Clark. They salvaged the bricks, stairway, windows, and doors, using them to construct the two-story gatehouse at the entrance to Calvary Cemetery on West Main Street in Lexington.[2]

What is Mary's connection to the house in Lexington that is a museum?

What is now known as the Mary Todd Lincoln House was built between 1803 and 1806 for William Palmateer, who operated an inn named the

Sign of the Green Tree. Palmateer lost the house to foreclosure in 1832, at which time the building was purchased in a commissioner's sale by Mary's father, Robert Smith Todd, who needed a larger home for his expanding family. Mary lived there until she moved to Springfield, Illinois in 1839, but spent much of that time at a boarding school. The Lincolns visited this home while en route to Washington when Abraham was elected to Congress in 1847. It was the first time Mary had visited her family in Lexington since her marriage in 1842. This museum is located at 578 West Main Street in Lexington.[3]

Was Mary named after anyone particular?

Mary was named after her mother's older (and only) sister, Mary Ann Parker Richardson.[4]

Was Mary an only child? What was her birth order?

Mary Ann Todd was the fourth child and third daughter of Robert Smith Todd and Eliza Parker.

Historian and author Jean Baker wrote, "Eliza Todd was pregnant within a few months of Mary Ann's birth." She claimed that Eliza "nursed Mary Ann so rarely as to remain fertile and thus lost her only means of natural contraception," and that in 1819, "Mary lost any particularity when Levi was born."[5] Actually, Levi, who was named after his paternal grandfather, was born June 25, 1817, and thus was one-and-a-half years older than Mary. If anyone was abruptly weaned it was Levi. Of course, mothers can nurse more than one child at a time, and the practice of using a wet nurse, especially in families with enslaved servants, was common. It is presumptuous to assume Eliza neither nursed her own children nor nursed more than one child at a time. It is also erroneous to say Eliza could not have been nursing children because she became pregnant. Nursing a child may hinder pregnancy, but it does not prevent it.

Young Mary enjoyed being the youngest child for nearly 2½ years until May 1821 when Robert Parker Todd was born. When baby Robert died in July 1823, Mary once again took her position as the youngest child—a position she held until Ann's birth in 1824.[6]

When Emilie Todd Helm, Mary's half-sister, compiled a genealogy of the Todd clan, she deliberately created confusion. Practicing the adage, "A woman's age is a changeable number," Emilie did all she could to obscure the ladies' ages. While Emilie often did list children in the order of their birth, she divided them—first the boys, and then the girls. Making the genealogy more confusing, she omitted dates, leaving it to readers and future historians to determine the correct birth order. Emilie appears to have deliberately given her daughter Katherine Helm misinformation when Katherine wrote her biography *Mary, Wife of Lincoln*. Katherine stated that Elizabeth was "about sixteen" when she married Ninian Wirt Edwards and moved to Springfield. In truth, Elizabeth was nineteen when she married.[7]

Even census takers could not obtain correct ages for the Todd sisters. In Kentucky, Mary's stepmother Elizabeth Humphreys Todd not only forgot her own age, but also the ages of her daughters.[8]

After moving to Springfield, Illinois, Elizabeth, Frances, Mary, and Ann all seemed to have "forgotten" their correct ages. Their ages were incorrectly given to census takers, and when interviewed by William Herndon in 1866, Mary incorrectly gave her birth year as 1823. This confusing habit was carried to the grave by at least one of the Todd women: The tombstone of Mary's sister Frances Wallace, who is buried in Springfield, indicates Frances was born in 1817; in fact, she was born in 1815. Why the incorrect date?[9] Apparently, once Frances had established a later birth date, nothing, not even death, would reveal the truth.

How many children were in the Todd family?
Robert Smith Todd was the father of sixteen children. He and his first wife, Eliza Parker, were the parents of seven children. One died as a toddler; six lived to adulthood. Robert and his second wife, Elizabeth Humphreys, had nine children. Eight of them lived to adulthood; one died as an infant.

What existing documents reveal the actual birth dates of the Todd children?
Emilie may have tried to hide the ages of the women, but on her application to join the Daughters of the American Revolution, she had to be truthful.[10] Death records, cemetery records, court records and wills, newspaper announcements for births and funerals, family letters, and family Bibles help establish a correct birth order list. (For more information about the Todd children, and a list of Mary's siblings, see appendix 1.)

The Todd Family

Were Mary's parents cousins?

Robert and Eliza were related, but not as closely as some have speculated. They shared a common great-grandfather, Robert Todd (often referred to as Robert the Emigrant). Mary's father was descended through David, a son of Robert the Emigrant and his first wife Ann Smith. Eliza was descended through Mary, a daughter born of Robert's second wife, Isabella Bodley Hamilton. Thus, Mary's parents were half-second cousins.[11]

When did Mary's mother die?

Eliza died on July 5, 1825, one day after giving birth to her seventh child, a son named George Rogers Clark Todd. She was 30 years old. Her funeral was held in the family home the following day.[12]

When did Mary's father remarry?

On November 1, 1826, Robert married Elizabeth "Betsy" L. Humphreys at her mother's home in Frankfort, Kentucky. Betsy was the daughter of Dr. Alexander Humphreys and his wife Mary Brown.[13]

How did the Todd family obtain its wealth?

The first Todd family members in America were farmers in Montgomery County, Pennsylvania. A family of property, their wealth quickly grew, and the men were soon educated to be doctors, lawyers, and clergymen. Several of Mary's ancestors served during the American Revolutionary War and attained ranks as high as major general in the state forces.[14]

Her paternal grandfather, Levi Todd studied law and was a surveyor. He served as a lieutenant under General George Rogers Clark during the latter part of the Revolutionary war. After the war, Levi was the first elected clerk of Fayette County, Kentucky, a position he held until his death in 1807. Levi raised his family on a farm just outside Lexington's city limits that he dubbed Ellerslie after the Scottish town that was the Todds' ancestral home. Levi left an estate worth nearly one hundred thousand dollars, including 21 enslaved persons. After his death, he was awarded 2,156 acres of land in Indiana under the Clark Grant for his service during the Revolutionary War. This land was given to his children who increased their own wealth by selling it.[15]

Robert Smith Todd inherited Plot #46 in the Clark's Grant. This area contained 500 acres and was valued at $2,210. Robert also inherited part of a lot in Lexington that was located on High Street and ran halfway back to Main Street.[16]

What did Mary's father do for a living?

Robert Smith Todd studied law at Transylvania University but never practiced professionally. His varied career included being part owner of a cotton factory; owning a successful grocery, and serving as president of the Lexington Branch of the Bank of Kentucky. He was also captain of a militia company (though one-third of his men never showed up for muster), and he enlisted in the 5th Regiment of Kentucky Volunteers in the War of 1812.[17] His political career included serving as a state senator, a member of the Fayette Fiscal Court, a city councilman for Lexington, Clerk of the Session for the Kentucky State House of Representatives, and a member of the Kentucky State House of Representatives.[18]

What was Mary's relationship with her father?

Some historians believe that Mary suffered from abandonment issues from her father, stating that he was not available to his children due to the amount of time he spent in the state capital of Frankfort on business (and apparently his time courting Elizabeth Humphreys).[19] However, despite his frequent travels Mr. Todd seemingly was adored by his children; at least it is fair to say that he adored Mary and she idolized him. He showered her with gifts such as fabric for a new dress when her feelings had been hurt, a new pony, and the newest, fanciest imported doll he could find. When his eldest daughters moved to Springfield, Illinois, he visited them. After Mary gave birth to one of his namesakes (Levi had earlier named a son for their father) Robert visited his daughters again. During this trip, he aided Lincoln's finances by giving him business and providing money to Mary every month to help pay for domestic help. If Robert Todd showed love by giving gifts and money, then Robert loved his daughter.[20]

What was the significance of the pony Robert Smith Todd purchased for Mary?

Mary wanted a new pony—specifically, the white dancing pony that belonged to a group of "strolling players" who had been stranded in

Lexington. Robert Smith Todd purchased it for his daughter. The only documentation for this is found in Katherine Helm's book; Katherine likely heard the story from her mother, who must have heard it from other family members—since Mary was 18 years old when Emilie was born, Emilie witnessed none of the events described by Katherine. The story Katherine wrote is filled with dialogue that no family member was present to hear. Did Katherine invent the dialogue to move the story's plot, or is the dialogue part of the family legend? Perhaps a bit of both.

The story is that when Robert Smith Todd was away on business in Frankfort, his wife Betsy was not feeling well. Sally, the Todds' enslaved nurse, gave Mary permission to ride the pony for a little while in front of the house, but Mary took off down the dusty road to Ashland, the home of family friend Henry Clay, Speaker of the U.S. House of Representatives. Upon arrival, she knocked on the door and requested an immediate audience with Mr. Clay. The butler said, "Mr. Clay is entertaining five or six fine gentlemen."

Mary insisted that Mr. Clay come to the door. The servant went into the house, and returned saying that Mr. Clay wished to be excused, for he was entertaining "distinguished strangers." At that, Mary announced, "I can't help that. I've come all the way out to Ashland to show Mr. Clay my new pony. You go right back and tell him that Mary Todd would like him to step out here for a moment." The butler did so, and Mr. Clay quickly came to the doorway.

Mary had come for a reason. Still sitting on her pony when Mr. Clay came out onto the driveway, Mary said, "Look Mr. Clay—my new pony. Father bought him from those strolling players that were stranded here last week. He can dance—Look!" She touched the pony with a whip, and the pony reared up gracefully on his hind legs to dance. Mary continued, "Mr. Clay, my father says you are the best judge of horse-flesh in Fayette County. What do you think about this pony?"

"He seems as spirited as his present diminutive jockey. I am sure nothing can outdistance him." Mr. Clay lifted Mary off the pony and invited her to dinner.

When Mrs. Clay saw Mary, she gave her a letter from a relative to give to Betsy. Mary enjoyed her dinner and the political discussion at the table. She entered the conversation by saying "Mr. Clay, my father says you will be the next President of the United States. I wish I could go to Washington and live in the White House. I begged my father to be

President but he only laughed and said he would rather see you be than to be President himself. He must like you more than he does himself. My father is a very, very peculiar man, Mr. Clay. I don't think he really wants to be President."

Mr. Clay replied, "If I am ever President I shall expect Mary Todd to be one of my first guests. Will you come?"

Mary's response: "If you were not already married, I would wait for you."

Katherine Helm used this story to speculate that perhaps this adventure was when the seed of ambition to grow up to be mistress in the White House was planted in Mary's mind. According to family legend (or at least according to Helm) Mary often said "she would marry a President of the United States."[21]

Author and historian William A. Evans saw the incident as an example of "impatience of oppositions and restraint."[22] Perhaps it is neither; however, it does give some insight into Mary's world. If the story is true, it is evidence that she was loved, spoiled, and pampered by her father. She was a "daddy's girl." There is no mention of his purchasing something from the strolling players for other children. Mary wanted the pony; Mary got the pony.[23]

What was the connection between the Todd family and Henry Clay?

The Clays and the Todds were political allies, but more importantly, the families were friends. If the pony story contains any truth, it depicts the close friendship between the two families. When telling the story, Emilie included the fact that Mrs. Clay had a message from Betsy's uncle Mr. James Brown and wanted it taken to Betsy. This indicates the friendly connections were family wide. The husbands were friends as well as political allies. Lively dinner table discussion about politics occurred in both homes. Mr. Clay knew Mary well enough to know she could hold her own in adult conversation, and he knew her family well enough to know the women as well as the men discussed politics.

Mary probably had a school-girl crush on Henry Clay; at the least, she admired him greatly. At the time of the "dancing pony story," Mary was 13 years old—too old to be considered a "girl" and too young to be considered a "woman." Girls of her age were beginning to think about beaux and what type of man would make a good husband. Mary was already demonstrating her attraction to men who showed great intellect and professional ambition, and who were politically motivated. Years later, Mary's friendship and admiration of Henry Clay drew her closer to Abraham Lincoln, who also admired Henry Clay. As a young wife, Mary was able to introduce her husband to Mr. Clay. This action thrilled Lincoln and gave Mary a great sense of joy.

What were the Todds'/Mary's religious beliefs?

They were members of the Presbyterian Church. Several men in the Todd family were ordained Presbyterian ministers including Robert Stuart who was married to Mary's aunt Hannah Todd. The extended family clan included a great, great-uncle, Reverend John Todd, who was ordained by the Hanover Presbytery. He helped establish Hampden-Sydney College in Virginia and served as a trustee. He later helped obtain the charter for Transylvania College (later Transylvania University). His son, Parson John Todd, followed in his father's footsteps and established Presbyterian churches and schools in Southern Indiana, including Hanover College.[24]

What church did the family attend?

They attended what became Second Presbyterian Church, in Lexington, Kentucky. It began in 1813 when James McChord, a minister of the Associate Reformed Presbyterian Church, started preaching at the home of Dr. T. S. Bell. In 1814, Rev. McChord published a treatise on the nature of the church. His work was condemned by the Associate Reformed Presbytery; he, therefore, sent a "declinature of their authority, and connected himself with the West Lexington Presbytery."[25] Those who had been meeting at Dr. Bell's home formed the Market Street Church in 1815 with fifteen members. Robert Smith Todd was a signer of the church's constitution.

Reverend McChord served as the pastor until 1819. When he died suddenly in 1820, his remains were buried under the church pulpit and a marble memorial tablet hung on the wall. In 1823, to further memorialize the pastor, the church was renamed McChord Presbyterian Church. However, this name did not last long. Thinking it inappropriate to name a church after an individual, the congregation settled upon the name Second Presbyterian in 1828.

A new building was erected on October 31, 1847. A few weeks later, Abraham and Mary Lincoln attended a Thanksgiving service there led by Rev. John H. Brown D.D. This building was destroyed by fire in 1917, but the congregation rebuilt it and it is still active.[26]

Education and Enlightment

Did Mary ever attend Transylvania University as a student, or did she ever climb a tree, sit outside a window, or hide in the attic to hear lectures?

Mary never attended classes at Transylvania University, nor did she eavesdrop on classes while her brothers attended.

In 1780, the Virginia Legislature, led by Governor Thomas Jefferson, issued a charge to establish an institution of higher learning in Kentucky which was then part of Virginia territory. Established by a group of Presbyterian clergy, Transylvania (which is Latin for "across the woods") became the first college west of the Allegheny Mountains. The first chairman of the Board of Trustees, Reverend David Rice, held classes in his cabin near Danville (Boyle County), Kentucky. Later, the school was given College Lot, now known as Gratz Park, to relocate to Lexington. General Levi Todd, Mary's grandfather, was an early trustee of Transylvania. His sons, John, David, Samuel, Roger North, and Robert Smith Todd studied there. Students studied disciplines such as medicine, law, divinity, arts, and science.

By 1818, Transylvania had a new president, Horace Holley. His Unitarian beliefs were predominant throughout the school, and the Presbyterian influence was quickly waning. By the time the children of Robert Smith Todd were ready to attend, a rift had developed between the Todd family and the overseers at Transylvania and sons were sent to other colleges including Centre College in Danville, Kentucky, which still maintains its affiliation with the Presbyterian Church.

Mary's younger brother George Rogers Clark Todd did attend Transylvania for additional schooling after graduating from Centre College and earned a medical degree in 1848. By then, Mary was a wife and mother in Springfield. Even when she visited Lexington in 1847, she would not have been sneaking around windows or hiding in attics to hear lectures.[27]

Where did Mary attend school?

Her first years of education were received at Dr. John Ward's Shelby Female Academy which was later called the Young Ladies Seminary.

The school was located at 190 Market Street, which was at the southeast corner of Market and Second Street. Tuition was forty-four dollars per year. Dr. Ward was the rector of Christ Episcopal Church; he was known to be kindly and scholarly, as well as a strict disciplinarian.[28] He believed in coeducation at a time when most schoolmasters did not and educated about 120 boys and girls from some of the most prominent Lexington families. Mary attended Dr. Ward's school from 1826 to 1832.[29]

In the fall of 1832, Mary was enrolled at Mentelle's for Young Ladies, where she boarded from Monday morning until Friday afternoon each week. August Waldermarde Mentelle had left his homeland in France in 1789 to seek a trade or profession in America. Four years later, his soon-to-be-wife, Charlotte Victorie LeClere, joined him. They couple married in Ohio.[30] After a brief stay in Ohio, the Mentelles arrived in Lexington in 1798 and soon advertised a French School at Transylvania Seminary and a dancing school on Saturday nights. Mary Owen *Todd*[31] Russell (a first cousin to Mary's father) turned over a home and five acres of land to the Mentelles, and they named the property Rose Hill. By 1820, their boarding school was opened.[32] Mary continued her education with Madame Mentelle until 1836.

How much education did Mary receive? Why did she attend school for so long?

It is generally believed Mary had twelve years of formal education. She studied six years with Dr. Ward, four years at Mentelle's, and according to some, an additional two years with Dr. Ward.[33]

Her level of education was, in part, because of her religious background. In the 1820s, Presbyterian clergy began speaking about the importance of a woman's position in society. At the Presbyterian Church, the Todds and their fellow congregants would have heard ministers discuss the need to educate young girls and develop their useful minds. An educated woman was more likely to attract a potential husband from a higher social plane, thus ensuring a life of financial security. She had the ability to be a true helpmate to her spouse, the ability to manage household servants and accounts, and the ability to help educate her children. An educated woman could read and teach Scriptures to the children.[34]

Whether Mary had eleven years, or twelve years, of education, she was, as described by Elizabeth Humphreys, "far advanced over girls of her age in education."[35]

Mary excelled in school. Years later, a fellow classmate described Mary as "one of the brightest girls in Madame Mentelle's school; always had the highest marks and took the biggest prizes."[36]

What subjects would Mary have studied in school?

Dr. John Ward emphasized the character traits obedience, duty, and dependability, and he believed that discipline was a foundation of education. His class studies included fundamentals such as grammar, geography, arithmetic, reading, and writing. He followed the popular educational theory that memory worked best when strengthened by use. Lessons were memorized, and in the summer, history recitations began at 5 a.m.

Madame Charlotte Mentelle advertised in the newspapers that students entrusted to her care would receive "a truly useful & Solid English Education in all its branches." The study of the French language was optional.[37] Even though every school mistress chose her own curriculum based on her own talents, parents expected their children to be taught skills that would enable them to function well as an adult. Nineteenth-century English education usually included spelling, reading, writing, geography, grammar, and arithmetic. Classes in scripture verses, sewing, household duties, knitting, music, and dancing were often added according to the talents of the school mistress.[38]

Tuition at Mentelle's was $120 per year. For this sum students were taught social manners and graces. They learned dancing, singing, the art of conversation, and letter writing. Those students who studied French were expected to "acquire a proficiency in speaking and reading French." While at the school, students could speak no English—only French. Mary learned to speak and read the purest Parisian.[39] On winter evenings, Monsieur Mentelle played his violin while Madame instructed the girls in "the latest and most fashionable Cotillions, Round & Hop Waltzes, Hornpipes, Galopades, Mohawks, Spanish, Scottish, Polis, Tyrolienne dances and the beautiful Circassian Circle."[40] During summer months, the girls enjoyed a variety of games. Reading was always encouraged. It was during her years at Mentelle's that Mary developed a love for theatre as she performed in plays written by Racine, Corneille, and Molière. [41]

The summer after graduating from Mentelle's, Mary visited Springfield, Illinois to see her sisters Elizabeth and Frances. When she came back to Lexington, she returned to Dr. John Ward's Academy. In an 1866 interview with William Herndon, Mary said that she studied with Dr. Ward for two years, finishing her formal education in 1839. What she studied at this time is not known, nor is it known if she boarded at the school or lived in her father's home.[42]

Did Mary learn to speak French at Mentelle's, or did she know the language before attending?

She was exposed to the French language before attending. Her older sisters, Elizabeth and Frances, learned French as young girls and continued to speak some French when entertaining in Springfield. Mary's step-grandmother, Mary Brown Humphreys, was well enough educated in the language to read the writings of Voltaire in French. Mary Todd may have become fluent in the language at Mentelle's, but she surely had some exposure to the language prior to her enrollment at school.[43]

Childhood Activities

What did Mary and her friends do for fun and entertainment?"

According to Mary's cousin, Margaret *Stuart* Woodrow, Mary spent many holidays and frequent visits with the Stuart family at their home, Walnut Hill. There, the girls enjoyed horseback riding; both rode well. During warm weather, there were picnics to attend. The winter months brought sleigh rides, and long evening talks by the fire.[44]

Mary also enjoyed reading plays and poetry. Her father had an extensive personal library in which Mary would have found a variety of books to study and enjoy. Also available to Mary was the public library which offered more than 2,000 titles, a selection so diverse that visitor Timothy Flint wrote, "Lexington has taken on the tone of a literary place, claiming to be the 'Athens of the West,' while Cincinnati was 'struggling to be its Corinth.'"[45]

Did Mary make her own clothing as a child?

There is one story of Mary trying to make a hoop skirt to wear to Sunday School. The story, as is the case in many oral histories, has been changed by historians over the years. To find the truth, we must examine the oldest known version of the story. In this case, Katherine Helm was the first to record the tale, using letters from her cousin,

Elizabeth Humphreys Norris, to develop her story. Elizabeth was one of three young nieces of Betsy who came to stay with the Todd family after the death of their parents. Although closer in age to Mary's sister Frances, Elizabeth enjoyed Mary's companionship more. At the time of this incident, the Todd family lived on Short Street, on the corner lot of their Grandmother Parker.

In 1829 when Mary was ten years of age, she longed for a new dress—something more in fashion and more grown-up than her long and narrow white dress, which was reserved for Sunday wear. In her letter Elizabeth explained that "hoops were worn by grown people." Katherine Helm wrote that Mary wanted a "lovely bouffant summer dress that puffed and swayed so entrancingly on the hoop-skirted ladies of the period."

Since Helm did not explain the fashion of the period, most historians and readers have conjured an image of Mary wearing a steel-cage crinoline hoop skirt as a ten-year-old child. Luckily, Elizabeth Humphreys explained the fashion in her letter. She explained that it was "not such as the regular steel that came in at a later date, but homemade affairs with small reeds, basted on the inside of the skirts, such as milliners used in drawn-silk bonnets." This alters the story slightly. Mary was trying to create what she had witnessed her stepmother—or maybe an enslaved sewing woman—accomplish: the small reeds were hand sewn into the hemline of a skirt. Mary's plan was to use willow branches since they are small and flexible. However, her plan failed because milliners' reeds are the same size for their entire length, and willow wands are not. Cousin Elizabeth had joined Mary in her plan to make a fashionable adult-style dress. As hard as they tried, when the two girls finished their skirts, "they bulged in front and at the back, while they fell in at the sides—the narrow white dresses stretched over them to their utmost extent." Still, the girls thought they looked lovely, and tried to sneak out the front door to head to church before anyone saw them. Mary was out on the street and Elizabeth was just about to reach the front door when Elizabeth Humphreys Todd saw her. Quickly calling Mary back into the house, Mrs. Todd looked them over and then said "What frights you are. Take those things off and then go to Sunday school." Mary "gave the finest exhibition of temper" and thought she had been badly treated. While Elizabeth was also angry, she only muttered to herself while Mary freely gave vent to her feelings.

Years later, Elizabeth wrote that they had been a burlesque on vanity—"two of the most grotesque figures"—and that it had been a blessing their display was confined to the house, for (as she wrote to Emily Todd Helm) "if we had got into the McChord church which we were so anxious to do, the congregation would have been convulsed with laughter and your mother too much mortified to lift up her head."

In her book, Katherine Helm explains that this story became a standing joke in the family. The boys would tease and present the girls with switches and make flourishing bows and insulting suggestions as to how switches should be applied. Mary had created a spectacle, and her family would not let her forget it.[46]

Did Mary dance?

Yes, Mary was a graceful dancer. While Mary was a student at Madame Mentelle's, evenings were often spent dancing. Dancing was a popular pastime among Lexington's aristocratic social schedule. One reporter commented that the balls and assemblies in Lexington were "conducted with as much grace and ease as they are anywhere else." Monsieur Giron, the city's most prominent baker, maintained a confectionary shop at 125 North Mill Street. There, he created beautiful "iced cakes decorated with garlands of pink sugar roses." Above his shop was a large beautifully decorated ballroom where young belles and their handsome beaux could dance and enjoy pastries and sweets from his shop.[47]

Did Mary hide from Native Americans or have a fear of them?

There is a story that she did.

Mary was playing with several other children (probably her siblings and cousins) while visiting an aunt who lived in the country. These children had all heard the tales of kinsmen who had either been killed or captured while fighting during the wars with Native Americans. When the children glanced out a window and saw a group of Native Americans walking by, they became frightened and scampered to find hiding places. Mary "ran to the great open fireplace before which was a fire screen and crept behind it, but this seemed too big a place for such a little slender body, so she dashed out to seek another hiding place."[48] As all the other children were hidden, Mary could not find a suitable spot, so she stood in the center of the room, turned her hope to Heaven, and cried, "Hide

me, oh, my Savior, hide."[49] There have been no recollections as to what
happened next, or why the Native Americans were near the window.

Did Mary have political aspirations as a child?

As a woman/girl of her time, Mary would not have considered holding
a political office herself. However, even as a child Mary expressed an
interest in politics and attended political rallies and parades. During
a visit to Lexington, Mary inquired about an old friend, Ann B. Mary
explained that when they were children, the two girls had quarreled at
a political parade because Ann thought that Andrew Jackson was better looking than his political opponent Henry Clay and Mary's father
combined into one. Mary's temper was aroused, and she "threatened that
after the election General Jackson would never smile again."[50]

CHAPTER TWO

Wife, Mother, and Friend:
The Springfield Years, 1835 to February 1861

You will think, we have enlarged *our borders*, since you were here.
—Mary Lincoln to Emilie Todd Helm, February 16, 1857

*M*ary Lincoln's move from Lexington to Springfield ushered in the happiest era of her life. Her courtship and marriage, the births of her children, and the political rise of her husband filled the years with joy and contentment. In 1857, Mary wrote to her half-sister, Emilie Todd Helm, hoping that by now Emilie had become "a *happy, laughing, loving* mama."[1] Her words describe her own life in Springfield. During these years, Mary experienced sorrows too, including the deaths of her son little Eddy Lincoln, her father, and her beloved grandmother, just to name a few. But she was able to cope with these events because she was uplifted by the love and support of friends and family. More than fifty members of the Todd clan living in Springfield surrounded Mary during these years. On occasion, they brought Mary turmoil and conflict. Still, they were family. When tragedy struck, the Todds comforted the Lincolns, and when joy was abundant, the family celebrated together.

When Mary first arrived in Springfield, she was a young belle, and often the center of attention. Her life was a whirlwind of fun social activities. After her marriage, she focused on raising her boys, caring for her home, and being a helpmate to her husband. Mary enjoyed reading newspapers from various parts of the country to keep abreast of social and political issues, and she surrounded herself with good books, music, and literature.

Mary's social circle expanded as she encouraged Lincoln's political ambitions. The couple developed friendships among the elite in local, state, and national politics. It was a heady time of possibilities, capped by Lincoln's election to the presidency.

Mary's letters, and those written by family and friends during her time in Springfield, make vivid the life of a young wife and mother. During the nineteenth century, people often wrote long, gossip-filled letters containing the latest social and local news. They read newspaper notices about social gatherings, local entertainment, weather, crimes, and tragic events like fires. These newspapers depict daily life in towns such as Springfield. During the years the Lincolns lived in Springfield, it grew from a small prairie town to a center of commerce. Public documents such as deeds, census records, vital records, and cemetery records, illustrate the growth of the city and the influence its citizens had on national events.

Questions about Mary during this period include those about her courtship and marriage, her children, her daily life, and the events and development of Springfield.

As a Belle in Springfield Society

When did Mary first arrive in Springfield? Where did she live?

Mary's first visit to Springfield was in 1835 when she came with her sister Frances to visit their sister Elizabeth and brother-in-law Ninian Wirt Edwards. During this trip, Mary and Frances witnessed a sales transaction between Ninian and Samuel Wiggins. It is unknown how long Mary stayed during this visit or if Frances returned to Lexington with her.[2]

As a member of an aristocratic family, Ninian was well educated, well mannered, and politically connected. His father had an illustrious political career, having served as the governor of the Illinois Territory (1809–1818); as a United States Senator (1818–1824); and as the third governor of the state of Illinois (1826–1830). Ninian, the type of man Robert Smith Todd desired his daughters to marry, had begun courting Elizabeth Todd when they were both teenagers. On February 16, 1832, during his final year as a law student at Transylvania, Ninian and Elizabeth were wed. At first the newlyweds lived with the bride's family in Lexington, and after Ninian's studies were completed in 1833, the couple moved to Belleville, Illinois to help take care of Ninian's recently widowed mother. By 1835, Ninian and Elizabeth had moved to Springfield.[3]

As the eldest sister and a maternal figure for her younger siblings, Elizabeth felt it was her duty to bring her sisters from Kentucky to Illinois for the purpose of finding suitable husbands. This enabled Elizabeth to have family near her not just for social reasons but also for female support during times of need.

Perhaps it was during the 1835 visit that Elizabeth was successful in helping Frances meet and find a suitable husband. In any case, after Frances was successfully wed, Elizabeth was determined to help Mary find a spouse. At Elizabeth's request, Mary returned to Springfield for a three month visit in the summer of 1837. She moved there permanently in October 1839. By this time, Elizabeth was the mother of a toddler, was expecting another child, and needed her younger sister's support. After Mary's arrival, the Edwards began introducing her to Springfield society and to the city's most eligible bachelors. Mary Todd became one of the most desirable belles in Springfield.[4]

Had many of Mary's relatives moved to Springfield from Kentucky?

In addition to her two eldest sisters, Elizabeth and Frances, Mary's uncle Dr. John Todd and his family, who lived near the Edwardses on "Aristocracy Hill," and her cousins Stephan Trigg Logan and John Todd Stuart had established residence in the town.

Both Logan and Stuart practiced law with Abraham Lincoln prior to his marriage to Mary. John Todd Stuart had met Lincoln during the Black Hawk War and the two men became friends. Stuart thought that Lincoln needed a profession other than shopkeeper and surveyor that would provide a more stable income and would better suit his intellectual abilities. Stuart encouraged Lincoln to study law. He loaned Lincoln his law books, and in 1837, Lincoln became Stuart's junior law partner. The firm lasted until 1841. From that time until 1843, Lincoln and Logan shared law offices.

The Todd family continued to settle in Springfield. Other relatives included a younger sister, nieces, and cousins. Babies were born into the families nearly every year. By 1855, Mrs. John Todd Stuart described a "little family gathering" that included nearly 50 or 60 people.[5]

What were some of the compliments said about Mary?

James C. Conkling, who later married Mary's friend Mercy Levering, wrote of Mary, "She was the very creature of excitement you know and never enjoys herself more than when in society and surrounded by a company of merry friends."[6] Ninian Edwards described Mary by saying, "Mary could make a bishop forget his prayers."[7] Ninian's sister-in-law, Helen found Mary to be a charming young lady and said of her, "The sunshine in her heart was reflected in her face."[8] Matilda Edwards, a cousin to Ninian, found Mary to be "a very lovely and sprightly girl."[9]

Did Mary have many friends when she first came to Springfield?

Yes. Mary and her friends were young, energetic, single people who gathered in the Edwards's parlor, read poetry, discussed politics, and gossiped about the activities of the city. Frequently they journeyed on excursions to nearby cities and traveled to the countryside for picnics. They called themselves the "coterie," but many others in town referred to them as the "Edwards's clique." (A coterie is a group of close friends with a unifying common interest or purpose.) Mary found her closest friends and her beaus within the group. Those associated with the coterie included: Mercy Levering, Matilda Edwards, Julia Jayne, Ann Caesaria Rodney, Sarah Dunlap, James C. Conkling, Joshua Speed, Lyman Trumbull, Edward Baker, John J. Hardin, James Shields, Edwin Webb, Stephen A. Douglas, and Abraham Lincoln.[10]

What did Mary do for fun and entertainment?

According to family members, Mary could recite "page after page of classic poetry" and she enjoyed "nothing better."[11] She and her friends went on picnics, attended church events, participated in charitable work, visited with one another, attended dances and parties, and other activities that engage the thoughts and time of young people. They attended concerts and theatrical productions and went to dances.

The young women of Springfield amused themselves by being silly with their friends. Family stories include the time that Mary and her friend Jane Huntington dressed as beggars and visited their friends.[12]

One excursion gave Mary and her friends great amusement and led to the creation of a poem they enjoyed. During the winter of 1839–1840, a continuous rain caused Springfield's streets to become muddier than usual. Helen Edwards described them as having "no sidewalks, and the mud so thick it was hard for the stage to pull through."[13] Travel was difficult in the mire and walking nearly impossible. Feeling they had been cooped up for too long, Mary and her friend Mercy Levering wanted to

WIFE, MOTHER, AND FRIEND

go downtown. Mary devised a plan, and the girls set off with a bundle of shingles. One by one, the girls tossed the shingles into the mud to create a path of steppingstones en route to their destination.

According to the story, when it was time to return home, a local man, Ellis Hart, offered Mary a ride in a two-wheeled dray. She plopped onto the back of the cart and was driven to the Edwards's home. Since a dray was normally used to haul things such as lumber or beer barrels, heads must have turned to see Mary Todd in a dray! This would have been considered unladylike. The story did not mention how Mercy arrived home. Most likely, she waited for a proper carriage to taxi her out of the mud.

Shortly after the incident, Dr. Elias H. Merryman wrote a poem that circulated among Mary's friends, including Mercy Levering. Dr. Merryman and Mary's other friends must have teased her for some time over the incident. Mercy's copy was given to the Illinois State Historical Society in 1923; they published it in the same year.

Riding On a Dray

As I walked out on Monday last
A wet and muddy day
'Twas there I saw a pretty lass
A riding on a dray, a riding on a dray.
Quoth I sweet lass, what do you do there
Said she good lack a day
I had no coach to take me home
So I'm riding on a dray.
Up flew windows, out popped heads,
To see the Lady gay
In silken cloak and feathers white
A riding on a dray.
At length arrived at Edwards' gate
Hart backed the usual way
And taking out the iron pin
He rolled her off the dray.
When safely landed on her feet
Said she what is to pay
Quoth Hart I cannot charge you aught
For riding on my dray.[14]

Did she date Stephen Douglas? Were they engaged? Did she date other men?

Yes, Mary and Douglas courted. One amusing story about their court-ship has survived. One afternoon when Douglas came to call, he found Mary sitting on the front porch weaving together flowers to wear in her hair. When Douglas asked if he could accompany Mary on a stroll, she agreed with the condition that he wear the woven flowers on his head. Douglas obliged her request and the two strolled through town.

It is not clear if they were engaged, but likely the answer is no. Years later, after Mary's death, several people interviewed by the press and by William Herndon said the couple had been engaged, or at least that the family favored an engagement between the two. Mary Virginia Stuart, the wife of Mary's cousin John Todd Stuart, claimed that she had be-lieved Mary would marry Douglas. When questioned about him, Mary replied, "I liked him well enough, but that was all."[15]

While visiting her uncle Judge David Todd in Missouri, Mary was courted by an eligible bachelor named James Winston. The relationship may have been serious. Mary wrote to her friend Mercy, "If you conclude to settle in Missouri, *I will do so too.*" Mary explained that her suitor could not bear to hear of her returning to Illinois. She further stated that he was, "an agreeable lawyer & grandson of *Patrick Henry—what an honor!* Shall never survive it—I wish you could see him, the most perfect original I had ever met." It is not known if members of the Todd family found Winston to be a suitable beau for Mary. Even though she felt honored to be courted by him, she continued her letter, "I love him not, & my hand will never be given, where my heart is not."[16]

By the fall of 1840, Mary had returned to Springfield and had attracted the attention of Representative Joseph Gillespie.[17] It is unknown if Mary felt any attraction toward him.

Mary was also courted by Edwin Webb, a widower with two small children whom Mary referred to as "two sweet little objections." Al-though Mary and Edwin's names were linked together for several months in 1841, by June, Mary wrote that she "deeply regretted that his constant visits, attentions && should have given room for remarks." Edwin was nearly twenty years older than Mary, and she was not interested in marrying a middle-aged man with children.[18]

Rumors also paired Mary with James Shields, and it is possible that on first meeting her, William Herndon was a bit smitten.

Relationship and Marriage with Abraham Lincoln

When and where did she meet Abraham?

Many believe that Abraham and Mary first met at "the grand cotillion in honor of the completion of the New (Illinois) Capitol building" held on December 16, 1839. Caroline Owsley Brown (the second wife of Christopher Columbus Brown, whose first wife was Bettie Stuart, daughter of John Todd Stuart), who knew the Lincoln family and was related to the Todds through marriage, claimed they met at a dance held at the old Mansion House in Rochester. Others just say that they met at a party. Oral history and Todd family legend places their meeting at the home of Mary's sister, Elizabeth Edwards. Wherever they met, one thing is certain—there was music and dancing. Abraham spied a vision wearing pink and white billowing masses of lace and organdy. He approached Mary for a dance saying, "Miss Todd, I want to dance with you the worst way." Afterwards, Mary turned to a cousin and said, "And he certainly did."[19]

What first attracted Mary to Mr. Lincoln?

Reportedly, Mary once said, "I would rather marry a good man—a man of mind—with a hope and bright prospects ahead for position—fame & power than to marry all of the houses—gold & bones in the world."[20] She found Lincoln to be a man of mind—and with a mind much like hers.

According to Katherine Helm, it was Mary's cousin John Todd Stuart who told Mary of Lincoln's intellectual ability. Stuart told of Lincoln's mastery of the law and his insight concerning justice. He described Lincoln's interest in literature and his ability to quote from the Bible, Shakespeare, Robert Burns, and other authors. Mary was intrigued with the stories Stuart told her about Lincoln. Once she met Lincoln, she found the stories to be true, and she was smitten.[21]

One of the family legends revealing Mary's interest in Lincoln was told by Katherine Helm. Apparently, Mary's cousin Stephen T. Logan was teasing her about how many beaux she kept busy. He jokingly said, "I hear the Yankee, the Irishman, and our rough diamond from Kentucky were here last night. How many more have you on the string, Mary." Mary inquisitively asked which one he feared the most. Logan replied that perhaps he would have to welcome a Yankee into the family.

"Never," she replied. "The Yankee, as you call Mr. Douglas, differs from me too widely in politics. We would quarrel about Henry Clay.

And Jimmy Shields, the Irishman, has too lately kissed the Blarney Stone for me to believe he really means half of his compliments, and the rough diamond . . . ." Her voice trailed off. Logan quickly interrupted stating that Lincoln was too rough.

Dreamily, Mary responded, "To polish a stone like that would be the task of a lifetime, but what a joy to see the beauty and brilliance shine out more clearly each day!"

According to Helm, Elizabeth Edwards was quick to interject that Mary was not truly considering Lincoln as a mate, but others in the family believed she was considering him.[22]

Their common interests, a love for theatre, Shakespeare, literature, poetry, and politics, drew Abraham and Mary together. They sat talking for hours on a sofa in the Edwards's parlor. Elizabeth described the scene by saying, "He was charmed with Mary's wit and fascinated with her quick sagacity—her will—her nature—and Culture . . . Lincoln would listen & gaze on her as if drawn by some Superior power, irresistible so."[23]

Did Lincoln travel to Missouri to visit Mary while she was visiting her family?

It may be true that the superior, irresistible, power which Elizabeth spoke of drew Lincoln to Missouri, although several historians doubt the story. In June 1840, Mary's uncle Judge David Todd attended the Young Men's Whig convention held in Springfield. When he returned to Columbia, Missouri, he escorted Mary to his home for an extended visit of nearly three months. During Mary's visit, the Whigs of Central Missouri had a large political meeting in Rocheport, which is near Columbia. Her uncle Judge David Todd had been elected as Circuit Judge, and his brother Roger North Todd had been elected as Circuit Clerk. Four steamboat loads of loyal Whigs traveled up the Missouri River to attend. Mary, her Missouri relatives, and ten thousand others gathered in Rocheport for the three-day meeting beginning on June 18 to listen to great orators and enjoy the picnic atmosphere. According to Todd family lore, Abraham Lincoln arranged to travel to Rocheport planning to attend the rally and visit Miss Todd.

Most historians doubt the tale because Lincoln argued his first case in the Illinois Supreme Court on June 18. The following day, he was still in Springfield conducting business, and therefore, could not have been in Missouri. However, according to a descendent of Roger North

Todd, Lincoln was in Missouri. He claimed that he heard the tales of
Lincoln coming to visit Mary from several family members and the
minister of the Columbia Presbyterian Church. According to the Todd
family, the steamboat on which Lincoln traveled ran upon a sand bar
in the Missouri River. By the time Lincoln arrived in Rocheport on
Saturday, the meeting was over. He then traveled to Columbia to visit
Mary. Family members, and the minister, claim that the following day,
Lincoln sat with Mary in the Todd family pew at the Columbia Presbyterian Church.[24]

**What was the "fatal first of January?" Is that the day Lincoln left
Mary at the altar? What caused their breakup?**

January 1, 1841 was a day Lincoln would never forget. The problem is that
no one knows exactly why Lincoln would never forget it. On March 27,
1842, Lincoln wrote to his friend Joshua Speed: "I am not going beyond
the truth, when I tell you, that the short space it took me to read your
last letter, gave me more pleasure, than the total sum of all I have enjoyed
since that fatal first of Jany.'41."[25] Some historians believe that Lincoln
was referring to the day that Speed left Springfield and returned to
Kentucky. Herndon and other historians believe Lincoln was referring
to a broken engagement with Mary where he had left his "bride" at the
altar. The story was repeated in the novel, *Lincoln's Mary and the Babies*,
published in 1929, and has since been depicted in novels and films so
frequently that it has become a popular myth that often finds its way
into history books and then back into popular culture.

Author and historian W. A. Evans believed an engagement had been
broken, but that no one had been left at the altar. He based his theory
on the knowledge that, "there was never a license, nor an assembly of
preacher and guests."[26] Dr. Louis A. Warren also disputed the theory,
stating the story of Mary being left at the altar with no bridegroom was
"a gross fabrication."[27] No printed invitations were known to have been
printed, a marriage license was never secured, and there are no diary
entries or interviews with disappointed wedding guests who mentioned a
reluctant bridegroom. Surely if a wedding had been planned, there would
be evidence. Members of Mary's family, including her sisters Frances
Wallace and Emilie Todd Helm, her cousins Elizabeth Todd Grimsley
and Mrs. John Todd Stuart; and friends Mrs. Joshua Speed and Mrs.
B.T. Edwards all disputed the story of a runaway groom. In 1895, Frances

Wallace reported, "There never was but one wedding arranged between Mary and Mr. Lincoln, and that was the time they were married."[28]

It was Mary's sister, Elizabeth Edwards, who mentioned the incident to Herndon during an interview believed to have been held on January 10, 1866—just months after the president's death. Elizabeth mentioned a broken engagement. She claimed, "Every thing was ready & prepared for the marriage—Even to the Supper &c—Mr. L failed to meet his Engagement."[29] It is unclear whether Elizabeth meant that the wedding was planned when the engagement was broken, or if she meant Mary was left at the altar. More than a decade later during her next interview with Herndon, Elizabeth was not as chatty, but did add another detail. She said that the "arrangements for the wedding had been made—even the cakes had been baked—but L. failed to appear."[30] Ninian was with Elizabeth during this interview, and he cautioned her about saying too much to a reporter. Elizabeth and Ninian's final interview with Herndon occurred in 1887—five years after Mary's death. By this time, Elizabeth's story was completely different. There was neither a mention of Mary having been left at the altar, nor was there a mention of a baked cake and a prepared meal. Elizabeth insisted the engagement was broken because Mary flirted with Stephen A. Douglas.[31]

Katherine Helm, Mary's niece, supported this theory by explaining that Lincoln had forgotten a date to escort Mary to a party. When Lincoln finally arrived, he found Mary dancing with Douglas. Thinking he could not support her in the fashion in which she was accustomed, and knowing that Douglas could, Lincoln left the party believing Mary had made her choice. The following day was New Year's Day and there was a large family gathering at the Edwards home. Lincoln came to tell Mary that their relationship was over. According to Helm, Mary stamped her foot and cried, "Go, and never, never, never come back."[32]

Several family members believed the breakup was due to disapproval of the marriage by the Todd/Edwards family. Albert S. Edwards, the son of Ninian and Elizabeth Edwards, stated that during the years 1841 and 1842, "My mother did what she could to break up the match."[33] Helm claimed the same, saying that the family believed, "Although Mr. Lincoln was honorable, able, and popular, his future, they said, was nebulous, his family relations were on a different social plane. His education had been desultory. He had no culture, he was ignorant of social forms and custom, he was indifferent to social position."[34]

In several versions of the breakup story, one of the betrothed had to write a letter to the other releasing them from the engagement. According to Mary Virginia Stuart, the wife of Mary Lincoln's cousin John Todd Stuart, Ninian Edwards opposed the union because Lincoln was poor with no prospects. As Mary's guardian, he insisted that Mary write a letter to Lincoln, breaking the engagement.[35]

According to Joshua Speed, Lincoln wrote a letter to Mary ending the relationship and planned to have someone else deliver it. Speed encouraged Lincoln to see Mary personally in order to break the engagement.[36]

Even if there is any truth to the story, breaking the engagement did not take place on January 1, for Mary was out of town on a trip to Jacksonville, Illinois and did not return until three days later.[37]

There are no words on the matter from either Abraham or Mary, so the truth will always be unknown. Whatever the cause, something happened between Abraham and Mary that caused them to stop talking to one another for over a year.

Though almost no one now believes that Mary was left the altar, it is true that her younger sister was. Is it possible that Elizabeth confused the family stories? Mary's sister Ann was left at the altar when her groom, Clark M. Smith, failed to show due to an illness. According to Springfield gossip, Ann planned an elaborate wedding, "but at the appointed time, instead of the groom, the intelligence reached her that he was sick." Ann learned "that Mr. Smith's health was very delicate & fearing she would be a young widow, she had declined marrying him." Smith had recovered by the following Sunday and came to Springfield to claim his bride. The wedding was quickly thrown together, with "Ann hardly giving her sisters time to dress for the occasion."[38]

How did they reconcile?

With the help of friends, the two lovers were reunited. According to Elizabeth Keckly, Mary's seamstress in Washington, Mary had flirted with Douglas only to encourage Lincoln to propose marriage. Mary's plan had been to be coy and refuse Lincoln the first time he proposed, but to accept a second proposal. She thought her plan had succeeded, but in fact it went terribly wrong. When Mary rejected the offer of marriage, instead of proposing again, Lincoln fell into a great depression. Lincoln's friend and physician, Dr. Anson G. Henry, found his patient in great emotional and mental anguish over the breakup. Fearing that

Lincoln was suicidal, Henry informed Mary of her beau's condition. Mary assured Dr. Henry that she truly loved Lincoln. Dr. Henry relayed the message to Lincoln, who was successful in his second attempt at a proposal. According to Keckly, she heard all of this directly from Mary and Dr. Henry. Elizabeth Edwards confirmed that Dr. Henry was instrumental in reuniting the couple, but she said nothing of Mary's plan to accept a second proposal.[39]

Another key player in the Lincoln engagement story was Mrs. Simeon Francis, whose husband was the editor of the *Sangamon Journal*. She was able to invite both Abraham and Mary to her home without them expecting one another's presence. At last, the two were face to face and able to discuss their relationship![40]

Caroline Brown added another character to the varying sagas of the love story when she reported that Mr. Legh Kimball, who lived with the Edwards family, frequently drove Mary to the Francis home to meet Lincoln. After several such meetings, the couple was engaged again.[41]

A completely different story of reconciliation featured Martinette Hardin, who married Alexander McKee on September 27, 1842 in Jacksonville, Illinois. Fifty years after her wedding, and long after Lincoln and Mary were deceased, Martinette claimed Lincoln and Mary separately attended her wedding. Part of the wedding festivities included a carriage ride of pairs (several carriages, each seating one man and one woman). Abraham and Mary were placed in the same carriage thus giving the couple an opportunity to reunite.[42]

Did Lincoln fight a duel for Mary's honor?

Lincoln almost fought a duel to defend Mary's honor. The political atmosphere in Illinois became heated when the Illinois State Bank declared bankruptcy and was forced to close. State officials mandated the taxes and other debts could only be paid with either gold or silver, and not the state's own paper currency. The problem was that most citizens did not have a pile of gold or silver lying around their homes.

To generate support for a state bank and to have a little political "fun," Lincoln wrote a series of letters to the editor of the *Sangamon Journal* that were filled with political satire and written in the style and language of a backwoods woman named "Aunt Rebecca" who resided in the fictitious community, "Lost Township." Mary and her friends joined in the fun and wrote their own letters in the series too. At first, the letters simply poked fun of James Shields, the Illinois State Auditor, accusing him of dishonesty over his plan for the state to refuse its own paper money as payment for taxes and other debts. In one of the "Aunt Rebecca" letters, Shields was challenged to a duel at five paces with cow chips, and the letter questioned whether Shield would show up wearing pantaloons or petticoats. Shields demanded the newspaper's editor, Simeon Frances, reveal the true author's identity. Frances sought Lincoln for advice, and Lincoln took responsibility for all of the "Aunt Rebecca" letters, even those written by Mary. Shields challenged Lincoln to a duel.

Another letter appeared in the newspaper (supposedly written by Mary) stating, "I hear the way of these fire-eaters is to give the challenged party the choice of weapons, which being the case, I'll tell you in confidence that I never fight with anything but broomsticks or hot water or a shovelful of coals, the former of which, being somewhat like a shillalah (sic), may not be objectionable to him. I will give him choice, however, in one thing, and that is, whether when we fight, I shall wear breeches or he petticoats, for I presume that change is sufficient to place us on an equality."[43] This enraged Shields.

As the challenged party, it fell to Lincoln to select the weapon. He chose cavalry broadswords because they were long and heavy. The swords were procured in Jacksonville and brought to the duel, held at Bloody Island near Alton, Illinois on September 22, 1842. Lincoln's friend and second in the duel, Dr. Merriman, was a splendid swordsman and trained Lincoln in the finer details of using the weapon.[44] With his long arms and extended height, Lincoln was able to raise his sword high over his head and lop off a tree branch proving to Shields who would win if they fought: Shields realized that before he could get close enough to draw blood, Lincoln would be able to split him from the crown of his head to the end of his spine. Shields, however, was scrappy and he was offended; he still planned to duel with Lincoln. John J. Hardin arrived after furiously paddling his canoe to the island, and let the men know that they were both "damned fools." With the help of their friends, Lincoln and Shields were able to reach an understanding, climbed aboard Chapman's ferry boat, and returned to Springfield as friends. Years later at a White House function when asked about the duel, Lincoln replied that if the guest wished to remain his friend, he would never mention the duel again.[45]

How old was Mary when she married Lincoln? Was this considered late to marry?

When Mary and Abraham were married; she was just shy of her twenty-fourth birthday.

Mary never explained why she married at the age she did; though there are many possible reasons. First, it was actually normal for urban, educated women to marry later than their rural counterparts. Second, due to the lack of medical facilities and knowledge, many young wives died during childbirth. Both Mary and Lincoln had lost loved ones during a childbirth accident. Mary's mother had died from "childbed fevers." When it was time for Lincoln's sister, Sarah, to deliver her baby, there was a complication, and both Sarah and the baby died. To avoid such a fate themselves, some women waited a few years before they married. Finally, others simply waited longer to marry because they enjoyed the freedom and social life allowed to one without the responsibilities of raising a family and running a household.

When and where did they marry?

Early one November morning, Ninian Edwards saw Lincoln on a Springfield street. Lincoln informed Edwards the wedding was to be held that very night at the home of Rev. Charles Dresser. Edwards insisted, however, as Mary's guardian, that the wedding take place in his home.

There are discrepancies as to when this encounter between Lincoln and Edwards occurred. According to Helm, Elizabeth was responsible for providing supper for the Episcopal sewing circle that evening, and she had already ordered the food. The sewing circle could make other plans, and Elizabeth could use the prepared meal for the wedding supper. Mary did not find these arrangements suitable for her nuptial dinner, so Uncle John Todd was sent to inform Lincoln the wedding would be held the following evening.[46] However, according to Helen Edwards, Ninian's sister-in-law, the wedding was held the same day the family learned of the marital plans. Ninian Edwards rushed to his brother's home and invited the family to the evening wedding. He explained that he had met Lincoln a few moments before and had just learned of the wedding arrangements. Ninian Edwards shared that his wife was angry because she did not have time to prepare a proper wedding feast. Elizabeth said, "Mary, you have not given me much time to prepare for this evening. I guess I shall have to send to old Dickey's for some of his gingerbread and beer." Mary, feeling hurt over past comments made about Lincoln, retorted, "Well, that will be good enough for plebeians, I suppose."[47]

Their sister Frances Wallace also told of Elizabeth's disappointment regarding the short notice. Lincoln and Mary were on the front porch of the Edwards's home when they informed Elizabeth they were going to be married that evening. Ever the elegant hostess, Elizabeth, with the help of her sister Frances, managed to provide her sister with a wedding that was considered "a pretty one, simple yet impressive." The cake was still warm when it was served to those gathered.[48] The bride wore a simple white muslin dress when she married Lincoln on November 4, 1842 at the home of Ninian and Elizabeth Edwards. Rev. Charles Dresser officiated the ceremony.[49]

Did Mary's family attend the wedding? Who were the wedding guests?

Yes. Henry Rankin recorded the wedding guests as Benjamin and Helen Edwards; Major John Todd Stuart and his wife Mary Virginia; Dr. John Todd, his wife Elizabeth, and at least some of their children; Dr. William and Frances Wallace; and Ninian and Elizabeth Edwards.[50] Other recorded guests include James H. Matheny who served as the best man and Beverly Powell who also stood up with Lincoln.[51] Mary's bridesmaids were Julia Jayne, Ann Rodney, and Mary's cousin Elizabeth Todd.[52] Rankin may have included Elizabeth when he listed Dr. John Todd's family members. Another wedding guest was Judge Thomas C. Browne. During the ceremony when Lincoln placed the ring on Mary's finger and said, "With this ring I thee endow with all my goods, chattels, land and tenements," Browne allegedly blurted out, "God Almighty, Lincoln, the statute fixes all that."[53]

Was Mary pregnant when they married?

Probably not. Mary's first child, Robert, was born on August 1, 1842. He was likely a wedding night, or honeymoon, baby.

It is rumored that Stephen A. Douglas was the father of Robert Lincoln. They did resemble one another. So, did Lincoln marry her to save her reputation?

No, this is untrue. This ridiculous story was written by Charles J. Bauer in his book, *The Lincoln-Douglas Triangle - with Naughty Mary Lincoln, Seduced by latest Paris Fashions*. (1980).

Did Mary beat Abraham with a broom or knife? Did she hit him with a piece of firewood? Was she abusive toward her husband?

According to William Herndon and Jesse Weik, Abraham Lincoln was a victim of spousal abuse. In 1886, Weik interviewed Margaret Ryan who claimed to have lived with the Lincolns for two years, up until February 1860, while she worked for the family. Supposedly, she witnessed Mary toss a piece of firewood at Lincoln which struck him on the face and cut his nose. Apparently, Lincoln was wounded badly enough to have been seen about town the next day with a bandage on his face. Another recollection of Ryan's was seeing Mary wielding a broom and chasing a half-dressed Lincoln out of the house. Ryan also claimed to have visited Lincoln on April 14, 1865 at which time he gave her a basket of fruit, a pass to return home, and instructions to return the next day at which time he would give her money to purchase clothing for her children.[54]

However, according to historian Richard Miller, Ryan was a fraud. No documentation exists to prove that Margaret Ryan ever worked for the Lincoln family, and nothing supports her claim to have visited the White House. Ryan claimed Lincoln hired her during one of Mary's pregnancies while he traveled to Jacksonville, yet Mary was not pregnant during the period Ryan says she lived with the family.[55] Herndon interviewed Stephen Whitehurst who claimed to have seen Mary chasing Lincoln with a butcher knife—or some woman chasing a man. While Whitehurst viewed the incident as a threat to Lincoln's life and an embarrassment, a man named Barrett who had also allegedly witnessed the scene thought the Lincolns were having a bit of fun.[56] It is possible that Whitehurst exaggerated the story to embarrass Lincoln. Whitehurst edited the *Springfield Conservative*—a proslavery, pro-Whig, anti-Republican newspaper. This alleged incident between Mary and Lincoln occurred in 1856 or 1857. Hence, the root of the tale may have been more political fodder than matrimonial commentary.

How did Mary and Abraham settle their martial disagreements?

Lincoln often found that a good walk and a few hours at his law office gave them time to sort out their differences. Mary often could not control her high temper; however, according to family members, Mary's "little temper was soon over." Katherine Helm wrote of an incident when Mary became angry with Abraham, and a family member soothed her by saying, "Mary, if I had a husband with a mind such as yours has I would not care what he did." These words were soothing to Mary who agreed with her relative, and said, "It is a foolish . . . a very small thing to complain of."[57]

Did Mary and Abraham love one another?

Yes, they did. Despite their faults, their tempers, their mood swings, their tragedies, the Lincolns maintained a loving marriage for twenty-two years. Elizabeth Edwards described Lincoln's being attracted by the charm of Mary's wit and being "fascinated with her quick sagacity—her will—her nature—and Culture." When interviewed by William Herndon, Elizabeth said, "I have happened in the room where they were sitting often . . . Lincoln would listen & gaze on her as if drawn by some Superior power, irresistible."[58]

Few letters between the Lincolns exist today. Most of them were destroyed either by Lincoln and Mary, or by Robert after his mother's death. The remaining letters were written when Lincoln served in the U.S. House of Representatives and Mary enjoyed an extended visit with her family in Lexington, and are filled with stories about the boys, family gossip, and a longing for the two of them to be together. Lincoln had thought that Mary and the children were a hinderance to him while they were in Washington. But now, that he found himself alone, he admitted that business had "grown exceedingly tasteless" to him. He wrote to his wife, "I hate to stay in this old room by myself."[59] Mary responded, "how much, I wish instead of writing, *we* were together this evening, I feel very sad away from you."[60]

During her younger sister Emilie's six-month visit to Springfield, she spent many days with the Lincolns. She noticed that Mary watched for her husband to return home from the office. When she spied him coming up the street, Mary would "meet him at the gate and they would walk to the front door swinging hands and joking like two children." Emilie commented to others, "and, oh, how she did love this man!"[61]

Even during the turmoil of the Civil War, onlookers saw evidence of their love. One friend described Lincoln's expression as "the pleasing look of Abraham Lincoln for her whom he so loved." Another Washington socialite told the story of attending a White House event and catching Lincoln glancing at his wife instead of paying attention to the conversation. Lincoln laughed and said, "My wife is as handsome as when she was a girl, and I, a poor nobody then, fell in love with her; and what is more, I have never fallen out."[62]

As a widow, Mary wrote effusive praise for her husband. She referred to Lincoln as her "great & glorious husband, always a 'World above them all." She wrote of her husband, "who loved me so devotedly and whom I idolized."[63] One of the most loving tributes to her husband that Mary wrote was shared with her dear friend, Sally Orne in 1869. While reflecting on her marriage, Mary penned, "Always—lover—husband—father & all all to me—Truly my all."[64]

Did the Lincolns have nicknames for one another?

Lincoln was known to refer to Mary as "Molly" as did their other friends. After the birth of their first son, Mary became "Mother." Lincoln had other pet names for his wife. He would playfully call her "Puss," or refer to her as his "child-wife,' or "little woman." Mary used the monikers "Father" or "Mr. Lincoln" when referring to Lincoln. It is impossible to know if they used other terms of endearment in private.[65]

Did the Lincolns drink alcohol?

When the members of the Republican Presidential Nomination Notification Committee arrived in Springfield on May 19, 1860 to inform Lincoln that he had won the Republican nomination, Mary had sandwiches, cakes, and drinks ready. It had been discussed with friends that some members of the delegation supported the Temperance Movement and would be offended if hard liquor was served. The committee enjoyed dinner prior to their arrival at the Lincoln's home at eight p.m., and since an assortment of liquors had been available during that meal, Mary chose to served ice water. It was a political, rather than a personal, decision; however, due to the warmth of the evening, it was a welcome choice. After the evening, Lincoln wrote, "Having kept house sixteen years, and having never held the 'cup' to the lips of my friends there, my judgement was that I should not, in my new position, change my habits in this respect."[66]

On other occasions, alcohol was served. In the autumn of 1859, the Burnett House of Cincinnati sent a bill to Lincoln for "whisky, brandy, and cigars" which was expected to have been enjoyed by members of the local Republican committee as well as the Lincolns. After the election, a delegation of political friends, including Mr. Seward, came from

Chicago and brought wines for the celebration. Mr. Lincoln reportedly said, "No boys, water has been good enough so far." There were times in Springfield when the Lincolns purchased rum from the Smith store, but it is not clear if it was used for preserving fruit, baking, medicinal purpose, or personal enjoyment.[67]

Excessive alcohol consumption was one of the faults in people that Mary could not tolerate. She spoke harshly of those who abused hard liquor and shied away from those whom she considered "drinking men." Mary disapproved of William Herndon because of his drinking habit and once referred to him as her husband's "crazy drinking law partner."[68]

William Herndon wrote a good deal about the Lincolns' marriage— where did the stories originate? Did Herndon have letters from those who supposedly witnessed the Lincolns' personal outbursts, or was it speculation on his part? Were all of Herndon's sources credible?

William Herndon met Abraham Lincoln during their bachelor days. For over two decades, Herndon personally observed the Lincoln family. As Lincoln's law partner for seventeen years, Herndon witnessed Lincoln's successes and defeats, his marital quibbles and joys with Mary, and his permissive parenting of his young sons.

After Lincoln's assassination, Herndon began to write his recollections of Lincoln and the family. Traveling to Kentucky, Indiana, and throughout Illinois, he spent the next two years, interviewing people who had known the Lincolns: family members, work associates, fellow politicians, neighbors, friends, and servants. If Herndon could not meet with an individual personally, he sent others to obtain their testimony about Lincoln.[69]

Historians often trust Herndon's sources as "gospel." However, some recent research indicates that while most people were honest in their comments, some may have lied to Herndon just to be included in "Lincoln mania." One such person was Margaret Ryan. As historians continue to research stories, it is possible others will also be proven to be false witnesses.

Was Mary afraid to be at home alone with the children when Lincoln was away on business?

Lincoln, and several other lawyers, traveled the Eighth Judicial Circuit twice a year, often being away from home for as many as eleven weeks at a time. While Lincoln was away, Mary was home with boys and had to make the parenting decisions herself. She also had to do the shopping and deal with the hired help, repairmen, and any family crisis which might occur during Lincoln's absence. Mary's nerves sometimes got the best of her. She was fearful of strangers, robbers, thunderstorms, and something happening to the children. The male visitors who came to call upon the hired girls sometimes made Mary anxious.

To ease her fears, Mary would often have a relative or friend stay at the house; sometimes she would pay a neighbor's child to sleep in the back room or the loft. James Gourley claimed that Mary invited him to sleep in the same bed with her and Robert. Even though such circumstances would not have indicated a sexual relationship, it is doubtful Mary asked a man to sleep in her bed although she may have asked him to stay in the house. Gourley easily could have been confused. During his 1866 interview with Herndon, Gourley made several strange comments, including describing Mary by saying, "She is no prostitute—a good woman."[70]

As a Political Wife

Did Mary help or hurt Lincoln's political career?

The idea of a "power couple" is not necessarily modern—Julius Caesar and Cleopatra VII are considered the first successful power couple. Others appear throughout history, and as more women are elected, or appointed, to leadership roles in government, more married couples will be classified as political power couples. Mary Lincoln was raised in a home filled with political interests and discussions. It is generally believed that she shared a passion for politics with her father and enjoyed nothing more than a good political discussion. Politics is one of the things that drew her into Lincoln's world and gave them a common interest throughout their marriage.

Mary Lincoln biographer Catherine Clinton claimed that Mary was Lincoln's "political adviser all the way through." Clinton is not alone in her thoughts. In her 1990 speech titled, "Parallel Lives: Abraham and Mary Lincoln," historian Jean Baker stated that "Mary broke the rules governing middle-class female behavior to participate in her husband's political career." Baker also claimed, "He read all his speeches to her."[71]

The issue with this image of Mary is that there is no historical documentation to support it. In his essay titled, "The Reports of the Lincolns'

Political Partnership," author Michael Burkhimer explained, "One looks in vain in the historical records for any evidence for this and other times Lincoln supposedly went over his speeches with Mary."[72] In none of Mary's letters did she ever mention that she wrote, edited, or helped write any of Lincoln's speeches. Yet, Baker claimed Mary helped her husband's career during the summer of 1850 by writing to Lincoln's friends and allies.[73]

Abraham and Mary shared political ambition for his career. According to Elizabeth Edwards, even as a girl, Mary claimed she would marry a president.[74] Lincoln had a political career prior to meeting Mary, and he had his own ambitions. While politics interested both, and Mary supported her husband's career, the two did not always agree. In 1856, Mary wrote to her sister Emilie about their husbands' "taste for politics." She explained that Lincoln supported John C. Frémont, but that her, "weak woman's heart was too Southern in feeling, to sympathise (*sic*) with any but Fillmore."[75]

Mary did help her husband's career in the same way that many Victorian wives helped their husbands: She entertained well. According to Philip Wheelock Ayres, whose family lived across the street from the Lincolns, Mary was a true helpmate. In an interview he stated, "In the numerous political gatherings at Mr. Lincoln's house, Mrs. Lincoln was a very great help to her husband. A lady of refined tastes, with a large social experience, and with considerable political insight, she carried the social end of the campaign admirably".[76]

What political party did Mary favor?

Mary was not a member of any political party because women did not have voting rights. However, she aligned herself with the Whigs, the political party of her father and husband. When Lincoln became a presidential candidate for the Republican Party in 1860, Mary considered herself a Republican.

Did Mary travel to Washington with Lincoln when he was elected to the U.S. House of Representatives?

In August 1847, as the Whig candidate, Lincoln won the election for the Seventh Congressional District earning him a seat in the 30th Congress. Mary and the two boys, Robert and Eddy, accompanied Lincoln on the journey to Washington.

What arrangements were made for their home while they were away?

On October 23, Lincoln signed a one-year lease with Cornelius Ludlum. Beginning November 1, 1847, Ludlum and his family would pay $90 to rent the home for the year. The Lincolns reserved the north upstairs room to store their furniture. In 1848 the house was rented to Mason Brayman and his family.[77]

What route did they take? How did they travel?

On October 25, the family boarded a stagecoach headed toward St. Louis. This part of the journey would have taken two days with a stop along the way in Jacksonville and/or White Hall. It is not known exactly where the Lincolns stopped, but they probably stopped at White Hall. From there, the stage continued to Alton. A ferry boat would take the travelers across the Mississippi River into St. Louis. There they met their old friend, Joshua F. Speed, at the Scott Hotel on the corner of Third and Market Streets. From St. Louis, the Lincolns boarded a steamboat and traveled down the Mississippi River to Cairo where the Ohio River and the Mississippi River connect. The steamboat turned east, pushing against the Ohio's current to the Kentucky River in Carrollton, Kentucky. Most likely, they boarded a smaller vessel in Carrollton and traveled upriver along the Kentucky River to Frankfort. Once in Frankfort, they could board a train on the Lexington and Ohio Railroad, finishing their excursion to Lexington, Kentucky. After a week of traveling, on November 2, the family reached their destination—the Todd home in Lexington, Kentucky.[78]

Was traveling with the children difficult?

Abraham and Mary probably found traveling with the children no more difficult than outings in Springfield. However, at least one passenger on the train to Lexington found the boys trying. The passenger was Joseph Humphreys, a nephew of Betsy Todd. Humphreys had the misfortune of traveling on the same train as the Lincolns, but he did not know who they were. Being alone, and having no luggage to retrieve, he arrived at the Todd home exasperated from his journey. He told his aunt that he "was never so glad to get off a train in my life. There were two lively youngsters on board who kept the whole train in turmoil, and their long-legged father, instead of spanking the brats, looked pleased as Punch and aided and abetted the older one in mischief." Just then, the young man looked out the parlor window and saw the father and his "lively youngsters" getting out of the Todd carriage. "Good Lord, there they are now." Panicked, he left the home from another door, vanished, and did not return during the Lincolns' visit.[79]

What impression did the Todd family have when they first saw Mary and family?

Emilie Todd Helm told her daughter the story of meeting the family: The weather was chilly, and the Todds gathered in patriarchal style near the front door to greet the Lincolns. Mary entered with Eddy in her arms. Lincoln followed, holding little Robert. As Lincoln put the child on the floor, Emilie took one look at Mary's tall husband and feared he might be the giant from Jack and the Beanstalk. She clung to her mother and tried to hide behind her skirts. Lincoln greeted all of the adults, saw Emilie hiding, picked her up in his arms, and said, "So this is little sister." Emilie's fears of the giant disappeared, and from then on, Lincoln referred to her as "Little Sister."[80]

Did they do anything special while visiting the family?

Mary's father, Robert Todd, was the vice-chairman of an event held on November 13 where Henry Clay gave a speech denouncing the Mexican War as an act of aggression instigated by President Polk. It is believed that Lincoln was present at the speech and met his political idol.[81]

The Lincoln family attended a special Thanksgiving service at the Second Presbyterian Church led by Rev. John Howe Brown, D.D. Ten years later, Dr. Brown became the minister at the First Presbyterian Church in Springfield where the Lincolns attended worship services.[82]

Most importantly to Mary, she was able to introduce her husband and children to family members who lived in and around Lexington.

How long did the the Lincolns stay in Lexington?

On November 25, three weeks after their arrival, the Lincolns bid farewell to the Todds. The trip to Washington lasted another week.[83]

Where did they stay in Washington?

When the family first arrived on Thursday evening, December 2, 1847, they took rooms in Browns' Indian Queen Hotel on Pennsylvania

Avenue. Their stay was brief, only a day or so, until they could find permanent lodging. Boarding houses that served as lodging for members of Congress filled the streets of Capitol Hill. The Lincolns chose an establishment operated by Mrs. Anna G. Sprigg that was located directly across the street from the U.S. Capitol Building. The building was the fourth in a row of houses known as "Carroll Row." Politics surely dominated the conversation as all the male lodgers were Whigs. Dr. Samuel Busey, a fellow lodger, commented that, "Mrs. Lincoln, with the eldest son, was at the house for a time, but was so retiring that she was rarely seen except at meals." Dr. Busey failed to mention Eddy's presence, but he did notice Robert, "a bright boy about four years old," who "seemed to have his way." Most likely, Mary was busy with both of her young sons and had little time for socialization.

Mrs. Sprigg provided lodging and meals. One of her lodgers recalled that her table featured such items as "Graham bread, corn bread, great pitchers of milk. Mush we have always once and generally twice a day; apples always once a day; at dinner potatoes, turnips, parsnips, spinnage (sic) with eggs, almonds, raisins, figs, and bread; the puddings, pies, cakes, etc."[84] During his first few months at the White House, Lincoln, remembering Mrs. Sprigg fondly, recommended her for a position she wanted. Mary wrote kindly of Mrs. Sprigg and added her own recommendation when she wrote to Caleb B. Smith, Secretary of the Interior: "We boarded some months, with Mrs. Sprigg, & found her a most estimable lady & would esteem it a personal favor, if her request, could be granted."[85]

What did Mary do in Washington? Was she active in the political world of the city?

Mary was mostly busy with her two little boys, but she did manage some social life. Lincoln and Douglas were the Illinois managers for a ball held to raise funds for the Washington Monument Association. Mary probably attended the event. Her love for music and social activity would have drawn her to attend public social ceremonies and music concerts with her husband. In Washington, the Lincolns had more hotel venues, theatres, markets, and restaurants available to them than in Springfield. Whether or not they attended is unknown, but they did have opportunity.[86]

Did Mary stay in Washington during Lincoln's entire term?

Mary spent the winter months in Washington, but by April 1848, she and the boys had returned to Kentucky. It is unclear why Mary decided to return to Kentucky. It is possible she found Washington's living conditions unsuitable for her children. The city was described as "an ill-contrived, ill-arranged, rambling, scrambling village."[87] Sanitary conditions were primitive; livestock roamed the city; and the streets were unpaved. A visit to Kentucky would provide the children with fresh healthy air to breathe and more freedom to play than a boarding house.

However, Lincoln's letter to his wife provides a few other reasons Mary may have been eager to return to Kentucky. He found her and the boys a distraction to his work. Two young, undisciplined boys often demand their father's attention; naturally, Bobby and Eddy would have wanted their father to play with them, tell them stories, and accompany them in some sort of mischief, just as he had done at home in Springfield. After a long day of chasing after the boys and caring for them, Mary was ready for adult conversation and attention from her husband. Lincoln probably felt that as an elected servant of the people, his primary focus should be work. Lincoln's letter reveals that perhaps he suggested she visit her family. Feeling a few pangs of regret over the decision, he lovingly wrote to her, "In this troublesome world, we are never quite satisfied. When you were here, I thought you hindered me some in attending to business; but now, having nothing but business . . . it has grown exceedingly tasteless to me. I hate to sit down and direct documents, and I hate to stay in this old room by myself."

Lincoln's letter also indicates that Mary may have had several disagreements with other boarders at Mrs. Sprigg's. This bickering could have easily hindered Lincoln from attending to business just as much as his lively boys. Whatever the cause of the strife, Lincoln felt compelled to let Mary know that, "All the house—or rather, all with whom you were on decided good terms—send their love to you. The others say nothing."[88]

During her visit to Kentucky, Mary and the boys spent part of their time in Lexington, and part of it at the Todd summer home, "Buena Vista," located near Frankfort. The letters between the couple are filled with stories about the children and other family members. Lincoln told about some of the events in Washington, and Mary kept her husband informed about the family gossip. There were family members in

Springfield who were not well. She planned to take the children to the country for two or three weeks for it "will doubtless benefit the children." She wrote that Uncle James Parker would be traveling to Philadelphia and that she would like to join him since she was "so very fond of sight-seeing." She teased her husband about an opportunity to "carry on quite a flirtation" with her old beau Mr. Webb.[89]

Lincoln's next surviving letter indicates that Mary had requested to return to Washington, and Lincoln asked, "Will you be a *good girl* in all things, if I consent. Then come along, and that as *soon* as possible." Knowing Mary did not have enough money to make the trip, Lincoln requested that her Uncle James pay the travel expenses for which he would be reimbursed.[90]

For whatever reason, Mary did not return to Washington. She stayed in Kentucky where she continued to visit with family, and where the family's enslaved people could help care for the children. In August, Howe's Great Circus and Collection of World Curiosities came to Lexington. They paraded down Main Street in front of the Todd home, delighting Robert and Eddy who had never seen such creatures as Syrian camels and wild beasts of the African jungles.[91]

Did Mary return directly to Springfield and wait for Lincoln's term to end?

No. Congress had a break during the fall at which time most members of Congress returned home. Sometime prior to September, Mary and the boys traveled to Washington to meet Lincoln. He had scheduled several campaign speeches through the New England states for the Whig party. The family left Washington on September 9, and Mary was finally going to do some sightseeing. They traveled to Boston, New York City, and Albany. They arrived in Buffalo on September 25. They boarded the *Globe* side-wheel steamer on September 28. The boat stopped in Milwaukee, and on October 5 the Lincoln family registered at the Sherman House Hotel in Chicago where Lincoln gave a speech. By October 10, they returned to Springfield.[92]

Did Mary return to Washington with Lincoln during the second part of his congressional term?

No. Upon returning from their trip to New England and Niagara, Mary and the boys rented a room at the Globe Tavern until May 1849. The home was still rented to C. Ludlum.[93]

What did Mary think about Lincoln being offered the governorship of Oregon Territory in 1849?

According to Herndon, Mary's response was to "put her foot squarely down on it with a firm and emphatic No."[94] Mary probably had several reasons she did not want to move to Oregon. Her life was in Springfield where she was surrounded by friends and family. Her family was also going through a difficult time. Her father suddenly passed away in July, and her husband was the legal counsel representing Mary and her sisters in Springfield in litigation in Lexington, Kentucky. Before his death, Robert Smith Todd had filed suit to recover the property of his cousin, Mary Todd Russell, who had conveyed the land to her then husband, Robert Wickliffe.

The Todd family often found itself engaged in a lawsuit, and in addition to the battle over ancestral Todd land, another court battle had begun. Robert Smith Todd's will had been signed by only one witness. Mary's youngest full brother George contested the will causing the Todd home and all its contents, including the enslaved persons, to be sold at auction. These legal proceedings required Lincoln's attention, so in mid-October the Lincoln family once again traveled to Lexington and remained until mid-November. Lincoln read that he had been offered the Oregon governorship in the newspapers. He quickly declined the position.[95]

How did Mary respond to Lincoln's defeat for the U.S. Senate seat in 1855?

Lincoln won the election in November 1854 for a seat in the Illinois State House of Representatives. However, he had other plans; he longed to be a U.S. Senator. On February 8, 1855, the Illinois legislature assembled to elect their senator. The voting began with Lincoln in the lead with forty-five votes, but he fell short of the needed fifty-one votes. James Shield was second with forty-one, and trailing was Lyman Trumbull with only five votes. As the voting continued, it became clear to Lincoln that he could not win. Not wanting Shields to win the seat, Lincoln threw his support to Trumbull, who became the next U.S. Senator from Illinois. The next day, Lincoln wrote to E. B. Washburne stating, "The agony is over at last, and the result you doubt less know." He described the particulars of the voting to his friend and explained how a man so far in the lead could lose the election on the tenth ballot.[96]

Mary's half-sister Emilie was visiting Springfield from Lexington, Kentucky and was at the State House to witness the proceedings. She wrote, "I remember how indignant we were that our man was not the chosen one. We feared it would be a terrible blow to Mary, but if she was disappointed, she kept it strictly to herself."[97] This claim by Emilie ignored Mary's response to Mrs. Lyman Trumbull: The former Miss Julia Jayne, who had been Mary's best friend and a bridesmaid, was forever shunned by Mary.

Did Mary attend any of Lincoln's political speeches that were not held in Springfield?

During the next few years, Lincoln traveled making political speeches in support of other candidates. He made several speeches on behalf of John C. Frémont, the Republican candidate for president. There is no documentation that Mary attended any of the speeches. The only mention Mary made of the campaign, or the election, was in her letter to Emilie. Mary's support for Millard Fillmore rather than Frémont was due to his immigration policy. He was anti-immigrant and anti-Catholic and wanted American businesses to not offer them jobs. Mary explained to Emilie that she found Fillmore "made so good a President & is so just a man & feels the *necessity* of keeping foreigners, within bounds."[98] Mary, who like many homemakers was having difficulties finding dependable hired help, thought the influx of immigrants was affecting the quality of servants.

Did Mary attend the Lincoln/Douglas debates?

When Lincoln was selected as the Republican candidate for the U.S. Senate in 1858, Mary would have been proud of her husband's accomplishments. There are no written records from Mary detailing her thoughts. However, Lincoln told a journalist: "Mary insists that I am going to be a Senator and President of the United States, too."[99]

Mary attended the seventh and final debate which was held in Alton, Illinois.

On October 15, 1858, the Sangamon-Alton Railroad offered half-price tickets from Springfield to Alton so Lincoln's friends and neighbors could more easily attend the debate. Mary and Robert boarded the special train to travel to Alton. Robert was a member of the Springfield Cadets, a group of young men who marched in parades and attended other special events. They had been invited to participate in the ceremonies in Alton. Mary would have been proud of her son attired in his cadet uniform consisting of a dark blue coat, white pants, and a glazed cap.[100] Among a crowd of 6,000 people, Mary was able to hear her husband, the "tall Kentuckian" debate her old beau, "The Little Giant."

As a Mother

How many children did Mary have?

Abraham and Mary had four sons.

Robert Todd Lincoln (August 1, 1843–July 26, 1926), who was nicknamed "Bobby" as a youth, was named after Mary's father, Robert Smith Todd. Robert was the only son to live to adulthood. He was an attorney and businessman in Chicago and the attorney for the Pullman Car Company, later serving as their president. Robert served as Secretary of War for Presidents Garfield and Arthur and as Minister to Great Britain for President Hayes. Robert died of a cerebral hemorrhage.

Edward Baker Lincoln (March 10, 1846–February 1, 1850) was called "Eddy" and was named after Edward Baker, a friend of the Lincoln family. He died of "consumption," which was probably tuberculosis.

William Wallace Lincoln (December 21, 1850–February 20, 1862) was called "Willie." Most likely, Willie was named after Mary's brother-in-law, William Wallace. However, there is a slight possibility that he was also named after the Scottish hero of the same name. There are many men in the Todd family named William Wallace. Willie died of "bilious fever" or typhoid fever.

Thomas Lincoln (April 4, 1853–July 15, 1871) was called "Tadpole" or "Tad" for short. He was given his nickname by his father, who proclaimed the newborn's head was so large that he looked like a tadpole. The boy was named after Lincoln's father, Thomas Lincoln. Tad loved animals and was a fearless rider. Even when he was a young boy, he would gallop on his pony at such speeds that his legs stuck out horizontally from the saddle.[101] Tad died of pneumonia.

Who helped Mary when Robert was born?

Robert was born at the Globe Tavern. Years later, Mary wrote of the blessed day by saying, "*Twenty six* years ago my beloved husband, was bending over me at the birth of your husband, with all the affectionate

devotion, which a human being is capable of."[102] Mary obviously meant
that Abraham came into her room after Robert was born, perhaps even
after the baby had been cleaned, for it would have been unusual for
Lincoln to have been present in the room during the actual delivery. It is
unclear whether there was a doctor or midwife present during Robert's
birth. If author James A. Gilmore's notes can be trusted, there was a
doctor present. According to Gilmore, years later, Lincoln said, "When
my wife had her first baby, the doctor from time to time reported to
me that everything was going on as well as could be expected under
the circumstances. That satisfied me *he* was doing his best but still I
felt anxious to hear the first squall. It came at last, and I felt mightily
relieved."[103] After Robert's birth, Mrs. Albert Taylor Bledsoe, another
lodger at the Globe, came to Mary's aid every day for several weeks.
She made Mary comfortable, tidied the room, and washed and dressed
little Robert. Mrs. Bledsoe's daughter, six-year-old Sophie, was allowed
to take the newborn outside for fresh air.[104] In addition to Mrs. Bledsoe
and Sophie, one of Elizabeth's servants, a young girl named Hepsey,
claimed to have been sent to help Mary with the baby.

Did Mary have difficult pregnancies?

After Willie's birth, Lincoln declined a request to visit his dying father
by explaining that he could not leave home, for "My own wife is sick-
abed (It is a case of baby-sickness, and I suppose is not dangerous)." It is
unclear what ailed Mary. She only referenced her illness following Tad's
birth when she wrote, "Since the birth of my youngest son, for about
twelve years I have been more or less a sufferer."[105]

How did Mary tend to her children when they were ill?

Mary followed whatever practices were prescribed by a physician. When
Robert was an infant, he suffered from "summer complaint" which was
an acute form of diarrhea caused by bacterial contamination in food. It
mostly affected infants and children during the hot summer months,
when improperly washed fresh fruits and vegetables and the lack of
refrigeration caused bacteria to grow in food and on food preparation
surfaces. Of course, the Victorian housewife knew nothing of bacteria
lurking on food, and Victorian physicians did not have the best cures
for such an ailment. It was thought that the best cure was to keep the
child in motion. Every morning, when the temperatures were still cool,

Mary was found around town riding in a buggy with Robert propped on a pillow. Mrs. George Huntington's daughter Alice suffered from the same ailment. The two mothers would meet on the streets, stop for a few moments and compare their babies' conditions.[106]

Did Mary attend Eddy Lincoln's funeral?

Eddy was the only member of the Lincoln family to die in the Lincoln Home. Since there are no public mentions of his funeral in the newspapers and no church records that mention Eddy's funeral, it is thought his funeral was held in the Lincolns' home. It is not recorded if Mary attended the funeral. However, based on other examples of family funerals, it is believed she remained in her room during the service as a sign of deep mourning.

Did Mary host birthday parties for her children?

Yes, she held at least one birthday party for Willie. In a letter dated January 1, 1860, written to Hannah Shearer, Mary told her friend about Willie's ninth birthday party which apparently, had been promised to the boy for a while. Mary hosted a party for Willie on the December 21 in which "some 50 or 60 boys & girls attended the gala." Mary claimed that birthday parties are "nonsensical affairs," but it is doubtful that she held a party for Willie without hosting a party at some time for Tad.[107]

Did Mary teach her children at home, or send them to school?

When the Lincoln boys were young, Springfield did not have a public-school system. There were about twenty small private schools in the city. The boys' earliest education began at home where Mary read to them. Emilie Helm recalled Mary reading *Lady of the Lake* by Sir Walter Scott to the boys. Regular readings included scriptures, poetry, and literature, including the works of William Shakespeare. The Illinois State Library offered a variety of reading material. As a teenager, Robert borrowed twenty-eight different titles from the library including the works of Charles Dickens, Washington Irving, and Sir Walter Scott. It is quite possible that his younger brothers enjoyed some of Robert's selections such as *Frankenstein* and *The Hunchback of Notre Dame*.[108] Robert was fluent in both spoken and written French; it is probable that he learned some French from his mother. Robert's formal education began in 1849 when he first attended a "slipper school." These were schools where the teacher used a slipper or hand to spank misbehaving children. Robert attended for less than a year.

With a lack of public education, churches often provided learning opportunities for children. One such establishment was a subscription school, Springfield Academy, run by Abel W. Estabrook who was affiliated with the Presbyterian Church. Beginning at the age of seven, Robert attended for the next three years. Reports indicate that Robert was an excellent student.

In the fall of 1853, Robert attended Illinois State University, the former Literary and Theological Institute of the Evangelical Lutheran Church in Hillsboro, Illinois. In 1852, the board of trustees was persuaded to move to Springfield and change the school's name. Upon graduation, Robert failed to be admitted into Harvard University, so he enrolled in Phillips Exeter Academy, in New Hampshire, to prepare for college. He finished his studies there in 1860 and enrolled in Harvard University. During most of the Civil War, Robert made his home in Cambridge, Massachusetts where he thrived as a college student. He graduated in 1864.

Eddy died young and never attended school. Willie and Tad's educations would have begun in the same manner as Robert's, with Mary reading to them. Not much is known about how much time the two younger boys spent in classrooms. Author Ruth Randall claimed that Willie and Tad were students of Miss Corcoran; other reports indicate they were educated by Reva Springer. What is known is that Willie was a student of Hester Watson who was a private tutor and whose family owned the large confectionary in town. She later married Charles Reeves and the couple moved to Cleveland, Ohio where Hester died. Willie, and probably Tad, studied piano under the direction of Mrs. Charlotte Marsh in her studio on the west side of the city square. She shared a studio with her husband who was a photographer, who had the distinction of taking five photographs of Lincoln in 1860 after the nomination.

By 1857, the city's public schools were opened, with one school located in each ward. It is probable that the younger Lincoln boys attended.

In the White House, the younger boys studied with Alexander Williamson, a private tutor. After Willie's death, Tad seemed to take little interest in school. When Tad and his mother lived in Germany, Tad studied at Dr. Johann Heinrich Hohagen's Private Institute.[109]

How did Mary discipline the children? Did she whip or spank her boys?

In an 1846 letter to Joshua Speed, Lincoln referred to Bob's punishment when he ran away. Lincoln wrote, "Since I began this letter a messenger came to tell me, Bob was lost; but by the time I reached the house, his mother had found him, and had him whiped (*sic*) . . . and, by now, very likely he is run away again."[110] From Lincoln's phrasing, it is unclear if Mary spanked Robert, or if someone else punished the boy for her. The mysterious Margaret Ryan who may, or may not, have worked for the Lincolns, claimed that Mary "would whip Bob a good deal"—but she either embellished or fabricated her statement.[111] Years later, Mary described her disciplining methods as, "I have never whipped a child— In the first place, *they*, never required it, a gentle, loving word, was all sufficient with them—and if *I* have erred, it has been, in being too indulgent."[112]

Other adults who encountered the Lincoln boys would have willingly agreed that both Lincolns were too indulgent when it came to the children. Joseph Gillespie wrote that Lincoln "was the most indulgent parent I ever knew. His children literally ran over him."[113]

In addition to Joseph Humphreys, who had the misfortune of encountering the Lincoln boys while riding the train to Frankfort, Kentucky, William Herndon frequently encountered the shenanigans of the two younger boys. He complained that on Sundays while Mary attended church, Lincoln would often bring Willie and Tad to the office and turn them loose to create chaos. Herndon stated that the boys "soon gutted the room, gutted the shelves of books, rifled the drawers, and riddled boxes, battered the points of my gold pens against the stairs, turned over inkstands on the papers, scattered letters over the office, and danced over them and the like." Herndon was not accustomed to children behaving in such a manner and expressed his displeasure by declaring he wanted to "wring the necks of these brats and pitch them out of the windows."[114]

Friends and family members alike chimed in on the Lincolns' style of parenting. When Frances Wallace witnessed Lincoln carrying his "well-grown son halfway to the office," she said, "Why, Mr. Lincoln put down that great big boy. He's big enough to walk" Lincoln replied, "Oh, don't you think his little feet get too tired?"[115]

A few years later, when the boys were wreaking havoc in the White House, Mary maintained that the children should be allowed to have a good time.[116]

What types of choices did Mary have to make when Abraham was away on business?

Mary would have made the type of decisions a single parent would make today. It was her responsibility to run the household, do the marketing, care for and discipline the children, and handle any situation that occurred while her husband was away.

As a Citizen in the Community

Did Mary participate in any type of charity work? Did she belong to a Sewing Circle?

Springfield ladies participated in sewing circles, church fundraisers—it was said that the foundations of several of the churches were built on the baked goods of Springfield's ladies. Ruth Stanton, who had worked for the Lincolns when she was a teenager, recalled that, "Every Thursday the sewing society of the Episcopal Church would meet at Mrs. Lincoln's home and make clothes for the very poor people."[117]

It is not known if they met in other locations on other evenings. It is possible the ladies met in various homes. Elizabeth Black wrote in her diary of taking her work to Mrs. Lincoln's home, and of visiting other women from the Presbyterian congregation. Mary and her friend Elizabeth both attended the Presbyterian Church, and it is possible the two friends and others also had a sewing circle or ladies' aid society organized through the Presbyterian Church.[118]

Did Mary have a lavish wardrobe while living in Springfield?

Mary was raised as a member of the social plane where ladies were concerned about the width of their ribbons, the length of their skirts, and the latest Parisian fashions. As the wife of a successful attorney and sometimes politician, she would have dressed her best. For the Victorians, especially Victorian women, fashion ruled their lifestyle.[119] How a lady walked, sat, stood, moved, and behaved was controlled by her dress and undergarments. A boned corset "extended not only over the bosom, but also over the abdomen and back down to the hips, thus controlling a woman's posture and ability to lean over.[120] Tight, skin-hugging sleeves prevented her from raising her arms to do chores. Women's clothing shut them away from others and protected them from the masses. Nearly every inch of a woman's being was covered in cloth; even her face was protected from wayward stares by bonnets, veils, and fans. According to the male fashion designers, a woman's place in public view was clear—she was not to be seen.[121]

Mary's wardrobe was typical of the time, containing layers of undergarments and a variety of dresses for different occasions. Family stories include descriptions of dresses for parties, social gatherings, and day wear proving that Mary knew of, and obtained, the latest fashions. Store receipts for muslin, cambric, gimp, whalebones, and corset lace, indicate that Mary was creating undergarments for herself and Lincoln.

When working around the house or in a garden, Mary would have worn a day wrapper, a loose-fitting dress which allowed women to move more freely while doing chores. The wrapper allowed women to raise their arms to dust higher shelves, bend to clean under furniture, and stoop to pull weeds. Most wrappers were made from easy-to-clean fabrics such as a light-weight cotton or calico.

Did Mary make household linens for her home?

Store records from Irwin and Company indicate Mary bought "thirty yards of calico cotton purchased on July 3, 1844, two months after moving into their home at the corner of Eighth and Jackson streets.[122] The purchase consisted of two separate pieces of fabric, and therefore, two separate calico designs. Some historians have speculated that Mary was making curtains and other items needed for a new home. However, lengths of calico may have hung from the windows of a sod home on the prairie, but it was not suitable for the windows of an urban home. Families hung lace curtains or sheers and used a finer fabric such as silk for the summer. In the winter, a housewife changed her curtains to a heavier fabric to help keep out cold drafts. Moreen, velvet, or damask hung at the windows of urban homes.

It is not known if Mary made her household linens. However, it was customary for women to make some linens. Quilts were made from various scraps of fabric. Towels, bed sheets, curtains, and other necessities were most often made by the lady of the house. Most housewives decorated smaller linens, such as pillowcases and table runners, with elaborate embroidered designs to showcase their talents with a needle.

What type of entertainments did Mary host?

Mary often wrote notes to friends and neighbors inviting them to come to the house for dessert or to come after dinner to visit, and often invited friends to have tea with her. Isaac Arnold, a politician and attorney from Chicago, remembered an enjoyable evening meal at the Lincolns'. He wrote of Mary's genteel manner and her meal: "Her table was famed for the excellence of its rare Kentucky dishes, and in season was loaded with venison, wild turkeys, prairie chickens, quails, and other game, which in those days was abundant." It is possible that Arnold dined more than once with the Lincoln family. Mary's cousin, John Todd Stuart, complained that he was never invited to dine with the Lincolns in their home.

During this era, it was customary for women to open their doors to guests on New Year's Day. It is probable that Mary either held her own New Year's Day reception or assisted one of her sisters with theirs.[123]

Strawberry parties were held during the "berry season" continuing beyond the growing season of strawberries and into the summer months when raspberries and blackberries were at their ripest. Mary enjoyed all the berry parties. On June 26, 1859, she wrote to her friend Hannah Shearer: "For the last two weeks, we have had a continual round of strawberry parties, this last week I have spent five evenings out—and you may suppose, that this day of rest, I am happy to enjoy. . . . This last week, we gave a strawberry company of about seventy, and I need not assure you, that your absence was sadly remembered. . . . After raspberry time, we will resume, doubtless our usual quiet."[124]

Did Mary ever help another mother?

Harriet Dallman, the wife of Charles Dallman, reported that after giving birth to her son, she could not nurse the baby herself due to her own illness. Mary had recently given birth to Tad and offered to nurse the Dallman's baby. Lincoln carried little Charles Dallman, Jr. back and forth across the street for Mary to nurse and care for. Sadly, Charles Jr. did not live past early childhood. After his funeral, Lincoln took the grieving family a supper meal served on one of Mary's trays. Although history does not state that Mary prepared the meal, she could have.[125]

When Eddy died, Mary packed up his clothing and gave it to Henry Remann who later became Willie Lincoln's best friend. It was customary to pass children's clothing from one mother to another. Clothing was difficult to come by as the pieces were made by hand, and the children outgrew them so quickly. When Mary and the children were visiting family in Lexington, she wrote to her husband that she had hoped her sister Frances would send her a box containing infant clothing. Frances had decided against it thinking "it would cost more than it would come to, and it might be lost on the road."[126]

The Lincoln house was a place where the neighborhood children could be found playing with the Lincoln boys. Mary indulged them in their games. When visiting the Lincolns, Emilie Helm recalled Robert and his playmates acting out a scene from the writings of Sir Walter Scott. Mary seemed to enjoy their antics. Years later, Helm recalled a little boy in Washington who was accidentally ran over by Mary's carriage. A doctor carried the boy home with Mary following to tell the boy's mother how distressed she was over the unavoidable accident. Upon returning home, Mary sent fruit and flowers to the boy's home. As Helm noted, "Mary mothers all children."[127]

Where did the Lincolns live when they first married?

They lived in a four-dollar per week rented room at the Globe Tavern. The Globe was a popular boarding establishment for newlyweds including John Todd Stuart (Mary's cousin) and his wife Mary Virginia; William Wallace and his wife Frances (Mary's sister). The Lincolns rented the same rooms that William and Frances had previously occupied. Robert Todd Lincoln was born at the Globe.

Did Abraham and Mary ever live in a log cabin?

Although a log cabin was a common abode during the era of Mary's youth, she never lived in one. Lincoln, however, grew up living in log cabins and had never lived in a frame building until he moved to Springfield.

Where was their first home as a married couple?

In the winter of 1843–1844, they rented a three-room cottage located at 214 Fourth Street.[128] Before Christmas 1843, Mary's father, Robert Smith Todd, came to Springfield to visit his daughters and their families; most likely, it was the house on Fourth Street that he visited.

When did the Lincolns purchase/move into their own home?

In May 1844, the Lincolns gave Rev. Charles Dresser a downtown lot on Adams Street valued at $300 plus $1,200 to purchase the home on the

corner of Eighth and Jackson. At the time of purchase the home was a
modest one-and-a-half story cottage with five rooms, a loft, outbuildings,
and an eighth of an acre lot. According to Mary's niece, "The little home
was painted white and had green shutters. It was sweet and fresh, and
Mary loved it. She was exquisitely dainty, and her house was a reflection
of herself, everything in good taste, and in perfect order."[129]

Did Mary remodel their home without Lincoln's knowledge?

It would have been impossible for a married woman to make such a
business transaction alone at this time in American society. However,
there is a myth that continues to find its way into history books and
popular culture that claims Mary did exactly that. According to legend,
when Lincoln was away on business, Mary hired a contractor to make
renovations to the home. The story was first told by James Gourley, a
boot and shoemaker who lived near the Lincolns. During his interview with Herndon, Gourley claimed, "Mrs. Lincoln & myself formed
a conspiracy to take off the roff (sic) and raise the house." When Lincoln
returned, he wandered the streets, walked up to Gourley, and jokingly
said, "Stranger, do you know where Lincoln lives; he used to live here."
Mary, who stood in the doorway, greeted her husband and called him
into the home. Gourley also claimed that Lincoln scolded Mary for
running him into debt.[130] Apparently, Gourley was trying to give himself more prominence in the Lincoln story than he deserved. For if a
wife could not make such transactions, a neighbor could never order
construction on a house he did not own.

It is probable that Lincoln did joke with Gourley about where he lived,
and both men would have gotten a good laugh from the joke. Lincoln
knew where he lived, knew this to be his home, and knew the renovations
were to be made while he was away. He had hired the contractor prior to
leaving town on business. Some historians have looked at this story as an
example of Mary taking advantage of Lincoln. Another way to interpret
it is to acknowledge that Lincoln left Mary home alone to deal with
contractors, construction workers, and the dirty mess of construction
work. She surely encouraged the workers to hurry with their tasks, as
she would have wanted everything completed and the home clean when
Lincoln returned home from his business trip.[131]

When did the Lincolns remodel the home?

Abraham and Mary remodeled their home more than once; it was re-modeled six times while they lived there.

The first remodel occurred in 1846 when they added a bedroom and a pantry to the back of the house.

The second remodel was in 1849–1850. Inside the home, stoves were installed in the parlors. Outside, a brick retaining wall was added to the property and the wooden front walk was bricked over.

In 1853, the third change was the addition of a barn on the property.

The home underwent a major renovation in 1855. The front of the home was raised from 1½ to two stories. The bedroom was moved upstairs allowing a back parlor to be created from the former downstairs bedroom. This gave the Lincolns a double parlor more suited for larger entertainments. Folding doors were added to separate the front and back parlors when not in use, and the front parlor windows were permanently closed.

Just one year later, Lincoln hired Hannan and Ragsdate to enlarge the house by raising the back of the house to two full stories. A new roof was completed, and iron railings were added to the second-floor porch. The upstairs now had four bedrooms, a maid's room, and added storage. A wall was added to separate the kitchen and dining rooms, thus giving Mary and a hired girl more privacy during meal preparation.

The final additions were made in 1859 with the enhancement of the back yard. The old washing house was torn down and a woodshed was added to the barn.[132]

Did she use money from her family to pay for it?

It is impossible to know if the money came from Mary's inheritance or from Lincoln's pay as an attorney. However, she did inherit money from her father who passed away in 1849 and her grandmother who passed away in 1850. It is possible funds to renovate the house came from more than one source.

Did Mary cook on an open-hearth fireplace?

Yes, she did. When the Lincolns purchased the home, there was a cooking fireplace in the kitchen. It is possible a cooking stove was installed during the 1846 renovation. In 1860, the Lincolns purchased their second stove, a Royal Oak, No 9.[133]

Did the home have a library?

After Lincoln accepted the Republican nomination for president, journalists came to interview him in his home. Several commented on the shelves of books located in the back parlor. A writer for the *New York Evening Post* wrote, "The library, I remarked on passing particularly, that I was pleased to see long rows of books, which told of scholarly tastes and culture of the family."[134]

Did Mary like to plant a garden or flower beds?

Mary's father and at least one of her brothers raised roses. Her sister Ann's yard was filled with flowers and ornamental yard art. Mary loved flowers, but never managed to landscape her own property. The bareness of the Lincoln's yard bothered Frances Todd Wallace so much that she planted flowers around the house more than once.

One neighbor claimed that the Lincolns only planted a garden one year and never planted trees. However, Mason Brayman told a slightly different story. The Brayman family rented the Lincoln's home in 1848 while Lincoln served his term in the U.S. Congress. In February 1849, Brayman wrote to his sister: "We have an excellent house and garden—with plenty of cherries and currants, and peaches growing—with vegetables of my own raising." Brayman would have planted the garden himself, but since the trees were bearing fruit, they had to have been planted several years prior to 1848.[135]

Did the Lincolns keep many pets?

The entire Lincoln family seemed to love animals and there was always a menagerie of animals around. Some were family pets and others such as the cow and horses were animals of necessity. In May 1848, Mary wrote a letter to Lincoln in which she referred to cats as his "hobby."[136] Oral history records that the Lincoln boys (like most boys in their era) had an assortment of turtles, kittens, and perhaps even a crow as pets. The Lincoln family owned:

> Fido, a medium-sized, roughly 40-pound yellow dog of mixed
>   ancestry
> Several cats including two female cats named Susan and Jane
> Chickens were kept in the back yard and supplied the family
>   with eggs

A cow named Betsy supplied the Lincolns with milk and cream
Two horses, one named Old Buck and the other named
     Old Robin (sometimes called Old Bob) were used for
     transportation[137]

Fido is a common name for a dog. Is that because Lincoln had a dog named Fido?

Fido is the Latin word for *faithful*. It was a common name for dogs during
the Victorian era in part due to a children's book published in 1845 by
Edward Kearny Publishers in New York. The book was titled, *Fido,
Or the Faithful Friend*. The book, intended for young readers, was filled
with stories about a little boy named Charles and his dog. Charles had
found the dog in his barn one morning and tried to find its owner. Failing
to do so, his parents decided he could keep the dog, which he named
"Fido." Fido proved to be a good and faithful friend and companion who
proved much enjoyment and saved several family members from various
perils.

While it is possible some Americans have named a dog or two after
the Lincoln's dog, it is also likely that the Lincolns named their dog after
the one in the storybook.

Did Mary hire servants? Who were they? Did they live with the Lincoln family?

Victorian housewives often hired teenage girls, referred to as "hired
girls," to help with daily household chores. These girls had little or
no experience with housekeeping, and they were taught to do chores
in the manner which best suited the mistress of the house. "Servants"
were workers who lived with the family that employed them. These
employees were considered professionals in their field, such as a cook,
maid, nurse, or laborer. Their position with the family usually lasted
for several years, and in some cases, a lifetime.

Mary Lincoln employed mainly hired girls and experienced the same
problems most Victorian women experienced with them—keeping
them employed was difficult. Once a young girl married, she was often
too busy with her own household to work elsewhere. In other cases,
as the girl learned more skills (or began to speak better English if an
immigrant), she found better employment. Often, women who were

widows became hired girls to earn money to sustain their own households. Records show that the Lincolns employed help ranging in age from eight to seventy-five years of age.[138]

The Victorian feminist advisor Sarah Josepha Hale was the editor of Godey's *Lady's Book*, and author of *The Good Housekeeper*. Sarah Hale understood the problems housewives encountered by hiring young girls, and her writings included advice for both the mistress of the home and the hired help. Her writing often spoke of the Irish, and the troubles housewives could expect when hiring them. According to Sarah, "The great fault of the Irish *help* is, that they undertake to do what they have never learned. They will not acknowledge their ignorance."[139] She blamed their ignorance on the impoverished culture produced in Ireland during the potato famine when they had little to eat, and no utensils to eat what little food they were able to obtain. Their abode was described as a "hovel, with scarcely an article of furniture, save the pot 'to boil the praties.'"[140] Sarah advised against hiring them if they were newly arrived from Ireland. Only the most skilled and talented housewife should attempt to employ and train one of the "wild Irish." Mary employed several Irish girls, and apparently experienced her own troubles with them. In 1856, she wrote to her sister Emilie saying, "If some of you Kentuckians, had to deal with the "wild Irish," as we housekeepers are sometimes called upon to do . . ."[141] It is unclear which girl Mary referred to as "wild Irish," but it could have been a young girl named Mary Hogan.

In addition to Irish girls, Mary employed girls and women who were African American and those who were of Portuguese descent. Their pay averaged from one dollar to one dollar and a half per week. If they lived with the Lincolns, their boarding expenses were deducted from their salary.[142]

When the Lincolns moved to Washington in 1861, they brought two people with them whom had previously been employed in their Springfield home. In a letter to Mary Brayman, Mary mentioned Ellen and a man, William Johnson, who helped take care of the younger boys.[143]

Throughout the years, nearly twenty girls and women were hired to help Mary with her work in the home. Several men and young boys were hired to assist with heavier chores. Most likely, men were hired to chop firewood, tend to the horses, and do other jobs around the home when Abraham was out of town on business.

1. Hepsey (Epsey) Smith had been born into slavery in Kentucky, and at the age of eleven she became an indentured servant in the home of Ninian and Elizabeth Edwards. She was present at the marriage of Abraham and Mary, and afterward, Hepsey worked for the Lincolns when they lived at the Globe Tavern. Hepsey's duties included helping Mary with her new baby, Robert. It is not known how long she worked for the Lincoln family.[144]

2. Harriet Hanks was the daughter of Lincoln's stepsister Sarah Elizabeth Johnston and her husband, Dennis F. Hanks, who was Lincoln's second cousin. When Harriet came to Springfield to attend school, the Lincolns had only one child, their eldest son, Robert. It is not known if she was paid for her services, or if the Hanks family paid the Lincolns for her room and board. It is believed that she helped Mary with household chores.[145]

3. Ruth (Burns) Stanton was an African American, fourteen-year-old, live-in, hired girl who came to work for the Lincolns in 1849. For about a year, Ruth helped with the children, scrubbed floors, waited on the table, cleaned, and did dishes and laundry.[146]

4. Mary Hogan was one of the "wild Irish" who came to work for and live with the Lincolns in 1848. She stayed with the family until her marriage in January 1850.[147]

5. Catherine Gordon was an eighteen-year-old Irish immigrant whose is listed as an occupant of the Lincoln Home in the 1850 census. Catherine frequently entertained male suitors—a practice which worried Mary when Lincoln was away. Catherine worked for the Lincolns until she married in 1851.[148]

6. Margaret (Maggie) Fagan claims to have worked for the Lincoln family for two weeks when she was just eight years of age. She was taken out of school to help with domestic duties which probably included preparing food for winter. Margaret recalled seeing celery, jam, and pigs' feet while she worked in the kitchen.[149]

7. The 1860 census listed Phillip Dinkell, a fourteen-year-old boy who lived with the Lincolns and is believed to have helped with household duties. Phillip's mother was a widow from Germany with two children younger than Phillip and two elderly relatives living with her. She lived on Edwards Street between Eighth and Ninth, close enough to the Lincolns that Mary would have known of the family's misfortunes.[150]

8. The 1860 census also listed a hired girl, named M. Johnson. This was Mary Johnson, who was an Irish immigrant. In October 1859, Mary Lincoln wrote describing Mary to Hannah Shearer, "Mary, the same girl, I had last winter, is still with me, a very faithful servant, has become as submissive as possible." Most likely, Mary lost this "faithful servant" upon the girl's marriage to Wesley Knous in 1862.[151]

9. Mariah Vance was an African American woman who worked two days a week for the Lincolns from 1850 to 1860, thus making her their longest employed hired help. She reportedly was given the responsibility of cleaning, packing, and locking the Lincolns' home prior to their move to Washington. Mariah claimed to have cleaned Lincoln's law office prior to her employment for the family.[152] Known as "Aunt Maria," she worked as a cook, laundress, and maid. Beginning in 1900, Mariah told her story of working for the Lincoln family to Adah Sutton, who was then just seventeen years old. For the next four years, until Mariah's death at the age of 81, Adah listened to Mariah's stories and wrote them down in shorthand. She put them aside until the mid-1950s when she transcribed them into longhand. Decades later, the manuscript was published as a "tell-all" book with highly questionable information including stories of photographs that have never surfaced, and events that could not have taken place. Mariah claimed that Mary owned a family album which included pictures of belles from Lexington, Kentucky, and a group photo of Lincoln, Mary, and Robert as a young child. Due to Mariah's faded memory, many of the stories have elements of fiction added to a few known facts.[153]

8. Jane Pellum (or Pelham) was a mulatto woman listed in the 1855–1856 Springfield directory as someone who did washing for hire. At this time, Jane lived with her daughter Martha and her son-in-law James Blanks in the Lincolns' neighborhood. It is believed that Jane was never an enslaved person. She was called "Aunt Pellum," "Aunt Jane," or "Aunty Pellum" by her employers.[154]

9. Ellen Sheehan was a young Portuguese girl who was hired as a dressing maid and seamstress. Ellen traveled to Washington with the Lincolns but was to return to Springfield. Wanting to help the young girl find new employment as a nurse, Mary wrote to her friend Mary Brayman in 1861 stating that Ellen was, "not expert with her needle, or does not understand arranging or dressing a lady. Yet she is the most reliable, truthful, kind hearted girl about children."[155]

10. Justina Martin de Crastos was a Portuguese woman who lived with her husband and children on East Adams Street, a half mile north and east of the Lincoln Home. She was employed as a laundress during the latter part of the 1850s.[156]

11. Frances Affonsa DeFreitas was a Portuguese live-in domestic for the family from late 1859 until the Lincolns left for Washington in February 1861. Frances originally was hired to do the washing, and later she became the regular cook. Frances claimed that Lincoln gave her money for her wedding dress.[157]

12. Charlotte Rodrigues De Souza was a young immigrant from Maderia, Portugal. In May 1860, when Charlotte was twenty years old, Mary hired her as a seamstress. Until August of the same year, Charlotte arrived at the Lincolns' home at 7 a.m. and worked until 6 p.m., taking her noon meal and sometimes a late breakfast with the family. In addition to dresses, Charlotte claimed to have made shirts for Lincoln and undergarments for Mary. One dress she claimed to have made that she did not create was the dress Mary wore to Ford's Theatre the night of the assassination.[158]

13. Margaret Browne was an Irish immigrant who worked for the Lincoln family during the late 1850s, but little information has been found about her. A night cap given to Margaret by Mary is housed in the collection at the Lincoln Home National Historic Site.[159]

14. William Johnson was an African American barber in Springfield who worked for Lincoln for one year prior to Lincoln moving to Washington. Johnson accompanied the Lincoln family on the inaugural journey and served as a valet to Abraham. He also helped take care of Willie and Tad. Lincoln described Johnson as "honest, faithful, sober, industrious, and handy as a servant." With Lincoln's encouragement, Salmon Chase found a position for Johnson in the U.S. Treasury Department as a laborer and messenger. Johnson traveled with Lincoln to Gettysburg. When Lincoln became ill with smallpox, Johnson tended to the president during his illness. Catching the disease himself, he died from smallpox on January 12, 1864.[160]

15. Reverend Henry Brown was a minister with the African Methodist Episcopal Church. He was employed by Lincoln to assist with a variety of tasks. Rev. Brown had left Springfield but returned for Lincoln's funeral in 1865. He led Lincoln's horse, Bob, in the funeral procession.[161]

In addition to those whose service can be documented, there are several others who claimed to have worked for the Lincoln family. Their stories cannot be verified, but some of them have been believed for years.

1. Margaret Ryan was an Irish girl who claimed to have worked for the Lincolns for a period of two years. She was interviewed by Jesse W. Weik on October 27, 1886. In addition to the claim she made about the marital relationship of Abraham and Mary (see previous question) Margaret claimed that Mary whipped Robert "a good deal" and also struck other girls who worked in the home. Margaret is the only hired girl to give such a negative view of Mary. None of her stories can be verified.[162]

2. Eliza Early's claims to the Lincoln family are dubious. She claimed that she was born enslaved in North Carolina and was somehow owned by one of Mary's brothers. Eliza did not specify which brother, but since none of Mary's brothers lived in North Carolina, the claim is doubtful. Mary's uncle, Dr. John Todd, who lived in Springfield, did have an indentured servant named Elizabeth, but there is no evidence indicating that Eliza and Elizabeth were the same person. Eliza also claimed to have acted as a maid at the wedding of Abraham and Mary and claimed to have nursed Robert Todd Lincoln. How she traveled from North Carolina to Illinois was not revealed in her story. Eliza was declared insane in Will County, Illinois in 1912.[163]

3. Ellen Dalton Lyon Tibbs claimed to have been a family nurse who worked for the Todd family in Kentucky. Her claims include tales of attending Abraham and Mary's wedding, being a nanny and housekeeper in the Lincolns' home, moving to Washington with the family, and later accompanying Lincoln's body back to Springfield.[164]

4. Betty (Biddy) Patterson claimed to have worked for the Lincolns in February of 1861. If there is any truth to her story, she did not work for the family long. Her claim is doubtful.[165]

5. Allison Demery did live in Springfield at the time of Lincoln's presidential election. His obituary states that he worked as a servant in the Lincoln home. Having been born in 1843, it is possible that Demery worked for the Lincolns, but there is no documentation to verify the claim.[166]

6. John G. Weilein was a German immigrant who told a very doubtful story about working for the Lincoln family. Weilein claimed he was in need of money in order to return to his home. He stopped by the Lincolns' home and was offered a job for ten dollars per month with board

and washing provided. Weilein claimed he stayed with the family until the fall of 1859. Weilein also claimed to have worked for Jefferson Davis, making his story unbelievable.[167]

How did Mary afford to pay her hired help?

Mary had other income in addition to the income Lincoln provided for his family. When her father visited in 1843, Lincoln was a young lawyer building a practice. Mr. Todd knew the importance of having help; Mary had been raised in a home surrounded by enslaved servants, and Mr. Todd felt that his daughter should continue to have some assistance with the never-ending tasks involved in running a household with children. He decided to send Mary $120 per year to enable her to pay domestic help. This continued until his death in 1849. Mary's father had also given the couple eighty acres of land located three miles southwest of Springfield.

Mrs President-Elect Prepares to Move to Washington

What celebrations were held in their honor after winning the election?

One of the first was the entertainment with the Republican Presidential Nomination Notification Committee at the Lincolns' home when Mary served ice water instead of alcohol. One observer wrote of Mary, "This amiable and accomplished lady . . . she adorns a drawing room, presides over a table, does the honors on an occasion like the present, will do the honors at the White House with appropriate grace."[168]

After Lincoln won the Republican nomination and prior to the general election, a parade was held in Springfield on August 8, 1860. It is believed that 80,000 people were in attendance. The parade stopped in front of the Lincoln home, and a large crowd gathered for a photograph. Lincoln stood at the doorway to his home. He is wearing a white summer suit. Mary viewed the festivities from a window on the left side of the home.

Before leaving for Washington, the Lincolns hosted a general reception in their home on February 6, 1861.

How did the Lincolns prepare for their move to Washington?

In January 1861, Mary traveled to New York for a shopping trip. She needed a new wardrobe for herself and for Abraham. She also had several chores to do at the house, including getting it ready to rent.

What did the Lincolns do with their furniture when they moved to the White House?

They sold most of their household furniture and goods at a tag sale—like a modern yard sale. Some of the furniture was purchased by Lucian Tilton; other pieces were purchased by Samuel Melvin among others. A few pieces of furniture were stored with the Burches family who lived across the street. Jared P. Irwin was given sixty letters for a keepsake. Mary burned several items, including letters and documents, before moving. Mariah Vance claimed to have rescued a photo album before it was tossed into the burn pile.[169]

What became of the Lincoln family pets?

Fido was terrified by loud noises including fireworks and ringing church bells. Lincoln thought it best not to take the beloved dog to Washington as the noise of the train trip would be too much for Fido to endure. He was given to the John Roll family. They had two sons who were slightly younger than Willie and Tad. Fido was a house dog, and promises were made that he would receive the same loving care that he had grown accustomed to in the Lincoln home. For example, Fido was to be allowed to eat table scraps. To make the transition to his new home more comfortable, the Roll family was given the horsehair sofa that Fido used as bed. Old Bob, the Lincoln horse, was given to a drayman named John Flynn.[170]

Who rented the house, and how much did they pay?

The house was rented to Mr. and Mrs. Lucian Tilton for three hundred and fifty dollars per year. Tilton was the president of the Great Western Railroad.

Was any of the furniture returned to the home?

The Tilton family moved to Chicago in 1867 taking some former Lincoln furniture with them. Sadly, that furniture was lost during the 1871 Chicago fire.

Over the years, some pieces have been returned and are currently displayed at the Lincoln Home National Historic Site.

Before leaving for Washington, did they stay anywhere other than their home?

After renting their home, the Lincoln family spent their last weekend in Springfield at Chenery House which was located at Fourth and Washington Streets.

CHAPTER THREE

Assailed from All Sides:
The White House Years, 1860 to 1865

There is no place in the country, so safe and well guarded as
Washington.
        —Mary Lincoln to Hannah Shearer, July 11, 1861

*A*fter her husband's victorious bid for the White House, Mary was
forced into the spotlight. She was prepared to assume responsibilities as the
White House hostess and to stand by her husband's side as duty called, or so
she thought. Mary was not prepared for the public scrutiny, the outrageous
press reviews, or the wagging tongues of Washington society. No one could
have foreseen the treatment that Mary would receive. As a native of the South
and a member of a slaveholding family, many of the Northern politicians and
journalists mistrusted her. As wife of the Union president, she was taunted
as a traitor by Southern reporters—and members of her own family. As the
country engaged in civil war, Mary Lincoln and her family were thrust into
the public eye. Her half-sister Elodie described the situation best by writing,
"Surely, there is no other family in the land placed in the exact situation of
ours. And I hope [they] will never be so unfortunate as to be surrounded by
trials so numerous."[1]

Mary was beset with trials. She was criticized for redecorating the White
House, for entertaining during the war, for not entertaining while observing
mourning, for spending too much money, for wearing lavish clothing during
the nation's conflict, and for the actions of her Confederate family members
with whom she carried no influence.

Questions that arise about Mary's years in the White House years include topics such as her entertainments, fashions, spending habits, scandals,

relationships with others, and her viewpoints on abolition, the war, and its celebrities. Even questions regarding her personal relationship with her husband and children became fodder for Washington gossips and continue to plague her memory today.

By examining newspaper articles, diaries, correspondence, and family documents, one can better understand the woman who was the center of controversy and who often found her name in national headlines. In December 1860, Robert Lincoln teasingly wrote to his mother, "Ain't you beginning to get a little tired of this constant uproar?"[2] He had no idea that the din would soon become deafening.

The Inaugural Journey and Ceremony

Did Mary travel with Lincoln during the entire trip?

Among those accompanying Lincoln was his eldest son, Robert. Mary was not present. Lincoln and his party boarded the train awaiting them at the Great Western Depot on February 11, 1861. He turned to his fellow citizens and delivered what would become known as his Farewell Address. Promptly at 8 a.m. the train left the depot, and Lincoln was en route to Washington.

Due to the number of rumors of attack and possible assassination directed at the Lincoln family, the Army's General-in-Chief, Winfield Scott thought traveling separately was a safer option for the presidential party. Mary and the younger boys were scheduled to leave several days after Lincoln's departure. However, Scott changed his mind and sent a dispatch instructing Mary and her party to leave the evening of the same day.[3] In addition to Willie and Tad, Mary's travel party included her first cousin, Lockwood Todd, who served as Mary's official escort; Burnett Forbes, the assistant trip manager; and William Johnson, an African American attendant who tended to the Lincoln boys and served as a valet for the president. Mary and her entourage boarded a sleeping car and left Springfield later that evening at 6:10 p.m. They arrived in Lafayette, Indiana at 5:45 a.m., then quickly changed railroads and resumed their journey at 7:20 a.m. Scheduled to arrive in Indianapolis just moments before the Presidential Special was supposed to leave, Mary had conductors wire ahead to keep Lincoln informed as to their location and estimated time of arrival.

Reporters commented that when Mary arrived in Indianapolis, she was radiant and that "her husband did not fail to compliment her with admiring approval" as he introduced his wife to the crowd.[4]

Did Mary plan any of the receptions the Lincolns attending during their trip to Washington?

The responsibilities of hosting these events fell upon welcoming committees and often the Republican politicians' families along the journey, not the president's wife. Such events were planned in several of the larger cities along the route. It was reported in Erie, Pennsylvania that the President-elect did not indulge in liquor, but he did indulge in sweets. Lincoln requested a second piece of mince pie that had been baked by Mrs. Thomas B. Moore.[5]

On February 19, the Lincolns arrived at the Astor House in New York where the south room of Suite 37 was reserved for Mary. There she could privately greet her guests. That evening, dinner was served in a private dining room to a party of ten people. The center table held a "mound of white camellias, red roses, and violets set up in a bed of yellow pansies and green fern trimmed with tricolored satin ribbon."[6] Previously, the press following the President's Special, reported various details about the Lincoln family, but this evening was the first time they published a reception menu including every item on the menu from the Julian soup to the fruit and ice cream served for dessert.

During their visit to New York, the Lincolns attended an opera and the younger boys visited Barnum's Museum. According to Mary's cousin, Elizabeth Grimsley, about eighteen or twenty friends and family joined the Lincolns in New York. Among the group was Mary's sister Elizabeth Edwards and her husband, Ninian, their daughters Julia Baker and Elizabeth Edwards, and Mary's cousin Elizabeth Grimsley. They were to travel from New York to Washington with the inaugural party[7]

Was Mary ever in danger during the trip to Washington?

Nearly as soon as the election was over, newspapers began to report death threats from Southern citizens. Most of the threats were directed toward the new president. However, Mary must have felt somewhat threatened herself when in January she received a package from South Carolina. It was a painting of Lincoln hanging from a tree with his feet chained together and his body tarred and feathered.[8]

In Cleveland, a gun salute was fired as the presidential train entered the city. The noise and vibrations caused a window to shatter, and shards of glass landed on Mary.[9] Amid the death threats, the event would have been frightening to all on board.

How did Mary react to the assassination plot that ended when Lincoln entered Washington without her?

Two separate plots against Lincoln were discovered in Baltimore. Detective Allan Pinkerton learned of a plot to kill Lincoln at a scheduled train stop. General Winfield Scott and incoming secretary of state William Seward learned of a separate assassination plot and sent Seward's son, Frederic, to warn the president-elect. Lincoln did not want to leave his wife and children but agreed to travel into Washington on a midnight train accompanied by his personal bodyguard Ward Lamon. Of course, Mary had to be told of the plan before he left. She was horrified to learn of the assassination plot and became justifiably upset. Mary did find peace knowing that Lamon would be with her husband.

After the Presidential Special entered Baltimore, there was pandemonium. Mobs cheered for Jefferson Davis as the Lincoln family remained in their cars. The crowd "leaped upon the platforms and mounted the tops of the cars like so many monkeys, until, like a hive of bees, they swarmed upon them, shouting, hallooing, and making all manner of noises."[10] A few men were able to force themselves into the car but were forced back out by John Hay. In case additional protection was merited, Robert, Hay, and John Nicolay carried revolvers.[11]

When did Mary arrive in Washington?

She arrived on the evening of February 23, 1861.[12]

Did Mary visit the White House prior to the inauguration?

It is believed that on Friday prior to the inauguration, Harriet Lane gave Mary a tour of the White House. Neither Harriet nor her uncle, President James Buchanan were political supporters of Lincoln. When asked her opinion of Mary, Harriet said she found her to be "loud and western."[13]

Where did the family stay prior to the inauguration?

While in Philadelphia, Ward Lamon sent a note to Willard's Hotel informing the owners that the Lincoln family and party would stay at their establishment. They occupied five rooms on the second floor. The family stayed for ten days in Suite Six, which faced Pennsylvania Avenue. Lamon stated that Lincoln's family "consists of himself, Mrs. Lincoln, son grown, two children, and nurse & servant." Lamon requested adjoining rooms to Lincoln's for "his private Secretary, Judge Davis & myself." Lamon also requested that "Col. Sumner, Capt. Pope, Capt. Hazzard, Mr. Judd, Mr. Hay, and Mr. Todd should have rooms as near him as possible."[14]

Other members of Mary's family, including Elizabeth Edwards, who had temporarily relocated to Andover, Massachusetts, while her youngest son Charles attended college at Yale, had joined the traveling party during the journey. It is not known if they stayed at Willard's Hotel with the others, or if they made their own arrangements elsewhere.

Dining in their room, and treating guests to champagne and cigars, the Lincolns received a total bill of $773.75.[15]

What was Mary's role during her husband's inauguration?

Mary, her sons, her cousins Elizabeth Grimsley and Lockwood Todd, her sister Elizabeth Edwards and family, and several other Todd family members occupied seats in the diplomatic gallery during the ceremony.[16] However, they did not have specific duties in the actual ceremony.

Did Mary plan the refreshments for the inaugural festivities?

After the ceremonies at the Capitol, Lincoln and his party returned to Willard's Hotel to watch the inaugural parade and enjoy lunch. It is believed that Abraham planned the simple menu that was served that afternoon, consisting of mock turtle soup, corned beef and cabbage, parsley potatoes, blackberry pie, and coffee.[17]

Mary's cousin Elizabeth Grimsley wrote of the family's first encounter at the White House. "The Mansion was in perfect state of readiness for the incomers—A competent chef, with efficient butler and waiters, under the direction of the accomplished Miss Harriet Lane, had an elegant dinner prepared." According to Grimsley, about seventeen people sat down to dinner, then rested before preparing to attend the Inaugural Ball[18]

Was there an inaugural ball?

Yes, nearly three thousand people attended what was dubbed by the press as the "Palace of Aladdin" which had been erected in contiguity to

City Hall especially for the evening's festivities. Soldiers surrounded the parallelogram-shaped hall which was draped with red and white muslin. The Marine Band entertained the guests with lively music, and the mood of the room was light. One newspaper reported, "To judge by the youth, beauty, brilliancy, fashion, and hilarity everywhere predominate, no one would have imagined that a cloud was in our national heaven."[19]

Frank Leslie's Illustrated Newspaper mentioned several members of Mary's family who attended the ball including her sister Elizabeth and Elizabeth's two daughters, Julia Baker and Elizabeth "Lizzie" Edwards; Mary's half-sister Margaret Kellogg; and her cousin Elizabeth Grimsley.[20]

Dresses pictured in several different photos have been identified as Mary's 1861 Inaugural ball gown. What did she really wear to the ball and does the dress still exist?

The most common photo of Mary that claims to be Mary wearing her inaugural gown shows her wearing a low-cut gown, trimmed with ruffles. Her attire also included a diadem of roses and a garland of roses and blossoms as accessories. This is not Mary's inaugural gown!

Mary, who entered the ballroom escorted by Senator Stephen A. Douglas from Illinois, was superbly dressed in a low-necked, blue watered-silk gown trimmed with Alençon lace. Her hair was adorned with a blue ostrich feather and camellias. As ornaments, Mary chose to wear the six-piece seed-pearl parure consisting of a necklace, earrings, pair of bracelets, and a brooch that had been a gift from Abraham, who purchased the set for his wife from Tiffany and Company of New York City for $530—more than his weekly salary as president.

It is believed the inaugural gown no longer exists.[21]

Clothes and Fashions

Who created Mary's gowns? How did she meet the seamstresses?

Mary hired several seamstresses to create her wardrobe, but most of her clothing was designed and constructed by Elizabeth Keckly. Her book, *Behind the Scenes,* was published under the name "Keckley" and historians have used this spelling ever since. However, more recent research by Jennifer Fleischer reveals that Elizabeth signed her name using the spelling "Keckly." Fleischer observed the signature on a war pension application for Keckly's son after his death at the Battle of Wilson's Creek in 1861. Keckly signed her name using the same spelling in other documents. For clarification and respect for the subject, the spelling "Keckly" is used throughout.[22]

According to Elizabeth Keckly, she and Mary met through an introduction made by a Mrs. McClean. Elizabeth came to the White House on a Monday after President Lincoln's inauguration for an interview with Mary. Upon arrival, Elizabeth saw several other mantua makers waiting to be interviewed; Elizabeth claimed however, based on the recommendation from Mrs. McClean, and after hearing the names of her other clients, she received the position.

While it is probable that Mary and Elizabeth Keckly met through a mutual acquaintance, the identity of that acquaintance is unclear. There was not a known "Mrs. McClean" in Washington, or at least not known to Mary, though there were at least two women known as "Mrs. McLean" who Mary might have known. So, who did introduce the pair?

Margaret Foster Sumner McLean was the daughter of General Edwin Vose Sumner and the wife of Eugene McLean, who made his career as a member of the U.S. Army until the outbreak of the Civil War. He joned the Confederate Army and rose to the rank of lieutenant colonel with the responsibilities of Quartermaster. It is unknown if Mary Lincoln and Margaret McLean ever met and somewhat doubtful.

A person more likely to have arranged the meeting was Sarah McLean the wife of John McLean, Associate Justice of the U.S. Supreme Court. She did meet Mary and accompanied Mary to the White House to visit Miss Harriet Lane on March 1, 1861.[23]

Did Mary steal another woman's bonnet?

No, Mary just made another woman relinquish her bonnet's ribbons. The bonnet in question was made by Willian, a fashionable milliner on Pennsylvania Avenue in Washington, and was owned by Mary Taft, the wife of Horatio Taft who worked as an examiner in the U.S. Patent Office. Mrs. Taft had purchased a lovely straw bonnet lavishly trimmed with purple ribbon embroidered with small black figures. Mrs. Taft and her daughter Julia attended a promenade concert on the White House grounds where they encountered Mary. When Mary saw Mrs. Taft's bonnet, she requested that Mrs. Taft return the bonnet and have the milliner replace the strings. It seemed that Willian had created a bonnet for the First Lady using the same purple ribbon, but he did not have enough to also create the strings. Mary wanted her strings to match the ribbon on her bonnet, so the next day, Mrs. Taft visited Willian, who told her that if she would give up the strings, he would re-trim her bonnet with a coordinating ribbon. When the transformation was complete, Julia thought the re-trimmed bonnet more beautiful than before. Not long after the bonnet had been restrung, Julia reported to her mother that she saw Mrs. Lincoln wearing it. Mrs. Taft quickly replied, "Never let me hear you make any remark about Mrs. Lincoln's clothes, Julia. The wife of the President should be above petty gossip." Sadly, the rest of Washington society and members of the press did not share Mrs. Taft's sentiments.[24]

Did Mary purchase three hundred pairs of gloves?

According to Judge David Davis, after the president's death, he was presented with a bill from Mr. Perry, a Washington merchant, for three hundred pairs of kid gloves that Mary supposedly purchased during the first four months of 1865. Judge David Davis, administrator of Lincoln's estate, told Mr. Orville Browning that he refused to pay the bill but offered no explanation for the refusal.[25] Did he think it was a fraudulent bill from someone trying to take advantage of a grieving widow? Had Mary already paid the bill? Was there a mistake in the number of gloves purchased? Had the gloves been returned? Whatever the reason, it is only known that Mary purchased several pairs of gloves in the beginning of 1865.

To the modern shopper, the thought of three hundred pairs of gloves is outrageous. To the Victorian lady, it was a large number, but not completely outlandish. French kid gloves were made to fit the hand so tightly that the fingernails showed through. They were sold in packages by the dozen and were considered to be disposable—they were thrown away once soiled.[26] If Mary truly did buy so many pairs of gloves, the question is why would she purchase so many? Traditionally, the president and his wife, or other female relatives, held large public receptions every week during the winter months. These were described as "throwing open the Presidential mansion to everyone high or low, gentle or ungentle, washed or unwashed who chooses to go, and the net result was always a promiscuous, horrible jam, a species of social mass-meeting."[27] Crowd size often exceeded three thousand people, and they came to see the president, to meet his wife, and to shake their hands. Lincoln was known to wear several pairs of gloves at each reception: as one pair became too soiled to offer to a lady's hand, he would put on a fresh pair. Gloves were an important fashion accessory used by men and women to keep the unwashed at bay.

If Mary used ten pairs of gloves per week (which is not an outrageous number considering her social calendar), by purchasing three hundred pairs of gloves over four months, she had truly only purchased a seven-month supply. If Lincoln had not been assassinated, many more public receptions would have been held in Washington to celebrate the end of the Civil War. Mary would have used many more pairs of gloves when shaking the hands of her "soldier boys" as they returned home dusty and dirty from battle.

Perhaps historians have actually misjudged Mary for such purchases. She had actual use for the gloves, and others in similar social situations made the same types of purchases. For example, Sarah Bernhardt, the famed actress, arrived in America in 1880, her trunks included "three hundred to three hundred and fifty pairs of thirty-button gloves" needed to wear during receptions and performances.[28]

Did Mary wear mourning or half-mourning, and encourage others to follow her example, in honor of Prince Albert of England?

No, Mary did not. Prince Albert, the Prince Consort and husband of Queen Victoria, died of typhoid fever on December 14, 1861, beginning Queen Victoria's ritual of lifelong mourning. There were rumors throughout Washington that Mary Lincoln intended to wear ceremonial mourning in sympathy for Queen Victoria and planned to encourage others in Washington to do the same. If the rumors had been true, the "Republican Court" (as it was often called in the newspapers) would have glided across the polished White House floors wearing an array of purple, lavender, gray, or white at every event during the entire party season.

Ceremonial dress was common in European courts, but it was not observed in American society. With the Civil War nearing the completion of its first year, and the vast number of Union defeats, families were more concerned with the war efforts on the home front than they were with European society. Many women were already in their own various stages of mourning for deceased family members. To ask them to mourn for the Prince Consort of England for an entire social season would have been a ridiculous request.

During this period, Mary did wear at least two purple gowns. Julia Taft wrote, "one a very regal purple velvet with white cord piping and buttons. The other was a rich silk. However, she wore a fine point lace shawl with the velvet gown and white roses in her hair, which certainly was not mourning."[29]

The gown that Mary wore to her party on February 5, 1862 (the first of its kind in Washington) was described as a "lustrous white satin dress with a train a yard in length, trimmed with one deep flounce of the richest black Chantilly lace. The dress was, of course, décolleté with short sleeves, displaying the exquisitely molded shoulders of our fair 'Republican Queen.'"[30] Her floral pieces that evening were made of crêpe myrtle which represented love and marriage in Victorian society. This gown was also not an example of mourning attire.

Did Mary always wear black after her son's death?

Shortly after Willie's death, Mary's sister Elizabeth wrote that she had "persuaded her (Mary) to put on the *black* dress, that so freshly and painfully reminded of the loss, that will long shadow her pleasures. Such is her nature, that I can not realize that she will forgo them all, or even long, under existing circumstances."[31] Elizabeth was wrong, for Mary remained in mourning beyond the six-month period expected by society. It is unclear exactly how long Mary remained in mourning for Willie. She did put her mourning attire aside for special occasions. Wearing a pink silk gown, Mary hosted a wedding reception for General Tom Thumb and Lavinia Warren in February 1863. Walt Whitman reported Mary wearing "complete black with a long crape veil" in 1864. It is not known if Mary was mourning Willie or another relative. Between the deaths of her half-brothers, a brother, cousins, and a favorite uncle, Mary was in perpetual mourning.

Did Mary purchase mourning clothing in March 1865? Why would she make such an unusual purchase?

After Lincoln's death, Benjamin French wrote to a family member about Mary's odd behavior stating, "but the most unaccountable thing she ever did was to purchase about a thousand dollars' worth of mourning goods the month before Mr. Lincoln died. What do you suppose possessed her to do it! Please keep that fact in your own house."[32] In his research for "*They Have Killed Papa Dead!*" author Anthony S. Pitch was able to find only one receipt for mourning goods purchased prior to Lincoln's death: On January 16, 1865, Mary ordered 193 yards of black cambric from John Alexander. She paid $96.50 for the fabric.[33]

Was this a premonition that Mary would soon be a widow? No, it was not. Mourning customs required women to don mourning attire for all members of their family. At the time of the purchase, Mary was observing the loss of her brother Levi Todd, who had died the previous October. She was thrust further into mourning in January when two family members passed away: Harrison Grimsley, the husband of her cousin Elizabeth, died on January 5, and two days later, Elizabeth's father, Dr. John Todd, died. Dr. Todd had been a pioneer moving to Illinois in 1817 and to Springfield in 1827. A favorite uncle, Dr. Todd served as a surrogate father figure to Mary and her sisters in Springfield. Mary would have observed ritual mourning for him not just because of the family relationship, but also because of the closeness of their personal relationship.

Why did she spend so much money on clothing?

There is no easy answer to this question, and many possibilities. One reason is because as the president's wife, Mary's wardrobe was scrutinized and criticized by nearly everyone in Washington. To the Victorian, appearance was everything. French author Honoré de Balzac wrote, "Dress is a sort of symbolical language, the study of which it would be madness to neglect. To a proficient in the science, every woman walks about with a placard on which her leading qualities are advertised."[34] People expected Mary to dress well. She was setting an image not only for herself, but also for the American government. Her appearance gave credence to the stability of the nation—if she dressed richly, foreign observers would see the country as financially stable.

Another reason Mary spent large sums of money on clothing is because clothing was expensive. Fabric imported from France, lace imported from Italy, jewelry imported from European markets—the manufacturing costs of raw materials, shipping, tariffs, and the cost of a dressmaker to assemble the ensemble combine to create a hefty price for a finished garment.

There is also the possibility that Mary's purchases were not as extravagant as the press reported. Writing of their first joint shopping trip to New York, Mary's cousin, Elizabeth Grimsley wrote, "but what was our amazement upon taking up the New York papers, after our return home, to find we had been on an extensive shopping trip; that Lord & Taylor, Arnold and Constable, and A. T. Stewart had been largely patronized, that Mrs. Lincoln had bought, among other things, a three thousand dollar point lace shawl, and Mrs. Grimsley had also indulged, to the extent of one thousand, in a like purchase (and par parenthesis, this was the nearest I ever came to having one,) whereas we had not even driven by the stores."[35]

Did Mary encourage women to purchase fabric and notions from American manufactures during the war?

Yes she did, according to journalist Jane Grey Swisshelm. After Mary's death, Swisshelm wrote a "Tribute to the Dead" in honor of Mary. Swisshelm wrote of Mary, "She naturally had a full share of the general love of personal adornment: yet would have joined a society pledged to use no foreign dress goods, laces, or ornaments during the War, if Mr. Lincoln and his Secretary of the Treasury had not condemned the project, declaring that the Government needed the revenue coming from the importation of those luxuries. They thus made the wearing of rich clothing a patriotic duty; and this decision agreeing with her tastes and opportunities, she as matter of course, became noted for costly apparel; and this, in turn, made her an object of envy and reproach to those who were unable to compete with her."[36]

Redecorating and Purchasing All that Stuff

Why did Mary redecorate the White House?

The simplest answer is because redecoration was desperately needed. Harriet Lane, the niece of and official White House hostess for President James Buchanan, gave Mary a tour of the White House a few days prior to the inauguration.[37] Mary must have been shocked to find the president's home is such a state of disarray.

The day after the inauguration, Mary and others toured the building from top to bottom. William Stoddard, assistant secretary to President Lincoln, said that the basement carried "the air of an old and unsuccessful hotel."[38] Mrs. Grimsley found the "tour of observation was a disappointing one" and that the "family apartments were in a deplorably shabby condition as to furniture (which looked as if it had been brought in by the first President), although succeeding house-keepers had taken their ingenuity and patience to make it presentable." She found the best piece of furniture to be a "mahogany French bedstead, split from the top to bottom."[39]

Over the years, improvements had been made to the house. Central heating, gas lighting, and hot water had been installed by previous administrations.[40] However, the rest of the White House had become a vermin-infested, disheveled old building greatly in need of renovation. The basement reeked from rats, mildew, and other smells. Carpets were threadbare, wallpaper was peeling, a complete set of china could not be found, plaster was falling from the walls—the place was a mess. Mary felt the White House needed to be a dignified, splendidly decorated home fit for the leader of the nation and esthetically pleasing to those who visited.

How much did Mary spend on the redecoration of the Executive Mansion?

Congress gave the Lincoln administration a $20,000 appropriation to renovate and redecorate the Executive Mansion. Previous administrations had been given the same amount; several had not spent their entire appropriation and others found that they could not keep up with the cost of running the mansion. The White House was visited by thousands of people each month. Many of them were souvenir seekers who thought nothing of clipping a piece of drapery, wallpaper, or carpet to take home with them. Pieces of china and flatware often disappeared during a reception or dinner. Even buttons were secretly clipped from Mary Lincoln's clothing.[41]

Each administration had the task of trying to make the White House presentable with the allotted appropriation. Mary spent the entire appropriation and an additional $6,700. When the bills began to arrive for the expenditures, Mary sought the help of Benjamin French who was the Commissioner of Public Buildings. Among his many duties, French was the overseer for White house expenditures. Mary, knowing that Lincoln would not approve the bills that exceeded the initial amount, asked French to convince Lincoln that overruns in such an appropriation were common practice. (It still is.) Mary also requested that her request be kept in confidence and not made known to Abraham.

French approached Lincoln who was reported to have said, "It can never have my approval. I'll pay out of my own pocket first—it would stink in the nostrils of the American people to have it said that the President of the United States had approved a bill over running an appropriation of $20,000 for flub dubs for this damned old house, when the soldiers cannot have blankets." [42]

Mary believed the repairs to the president's home were government expenses, not personal expenses. French was able to have Congress pass deficiency bills, and he shifted funds from one account to another to balance the expense reports.

After all the fuss, the White House looked splendid. Everything had been washed, repaired, repapered, and repainted.

Why did Mary spend so much money on the White House and not on soldiers who needed clothes, blankets, weapons, and other items?

Not everyone agreed that the expenditures were outlandish. Years later, William Stoddard, a journalist and assistant to Lincoln's secretaries, wrote, "Speaking of that 'extravagance' there was never a more puerile humbug. Large expenditures were absolutely necessary, but all proper economy was always exercised."[43]

Additionally, the money appropriated for refurbishing the White House had nothing to do with the money appropriated for the war effort. Then, just as today, the government oversees a vast array of expenditures.

What did Mary buy when she redecorated the White House?

Since the place was filthy and caked with dirt, the windows, floors, and everything in between had to washed, painted, and repapered. Mary also ordered new books for the library, bell pulls, new carpets (one costing $2,500), new state china, stemware, a footbath, new furniture, new bed and table linens, and several other "flub dubs" for the old house.[44]

What types of books did Mary purchase and enjoy?

Mary purchased a variety of books for the White House library. She was fond of English novels and the work of American author Washington Irving. Mary enjoyed the poetry of Robert Burns, Lord Byron, Henry Longfellow, John Milton, the plays and poetry of William Shakespeare, and the works of several others. Mary was known to read literature and poetry to her sons, and to give books as gifts to friends and family.[45]

Who criticized Mary for her expenditures?

Northern and Southern journalists alike criticized Mary's purchases. One of the worst was James Gordon Bennett of the *New York Herald* who knew sensationalism appealed to readers. In 1861, he ran a daily column titled, "The Movements of Mrs. Lincoln" in which he elaborated on her shopping habits in New York and New Jersey. He did not care whether what he wrote was truth or fabrication.[46]

Did anyone praise Mary for redecorating the White House?

Leslie's Magazine was one of the publications that praised Mary's "exquisite taste" in her decorating skills and in her fashion sense.[47]

Other Scandals

Did Mary launder government money as First Lady?

There were rumors in Washington that she did. The word "launder" indicates a criminal action, and it is unclear as to whether Mary's actions were criminal or common practice. Just as in the case of redecorating the White House, government funds were shifted from one account to another.

As mistress of the White House, Mary thought it her duty to run the household. She discharged the White House steward, performed his duties, and hired a few servants to assist with household management. Lincoln's secretary reportedly told his friends that Mary collected the steward's salary herself. Former White House employees gossiped that Mary used the salary to pay her own White House expenses.[48]

Another example of questionable money management included the situation of the White House gardener and groundskeeper, John Watt. Watt padded his expense account with the purchase of more expensive plants and flowers than were ever planted at the White House. His dishonest activities were first suspected during the administration of President Franklin Pierce. It was easy for him to redirect these funds to Mary so she could pay her bills.

Despite his dishonest practices, Mary trusted Watt and he gained her confidence. She could go to the conservatory, tell Watt exactly what she wanted done and how, and the work would be done to her satisfaction. It was a mutual friendship, until he tried to blackmail the Lincolns for $20,000 with three letters that were supposedly written by Mary and incriminated her in the misuse of government funds. Watt was already under scrutiny for possible Confederate sympathies, so when the letters came into question, Watt was investigated and found guilty. He found himself unemployed in February 1862 for his role in leaking part of Lincoln's first annual message to the press.[49]

What was the "manure dinner" and is it a true story?

Dignitaries from France were entertained by the Lincolns at the White House. (Exactly which dignitaries is unclear. Some versions of the story mention the Count de Paris and the Count de Chambord. Other versions claim it was Prince Napoleon.) Since Secretary of State William Steward had urged Mrs. Lincoln to entertain them at the White House, Mary believed the government should be responsible for the expenses. However, personal entertainment expenses were the responsibility of the president and his wife. Near the time of the entertainment, manure had been delivered to the Executive Mansions' grounds for organic fertilization purposes. There were rumors that Mary sold the manure and used the proceeds to pay for the dinner. The dinner became known as the "manure dinner."[50]

Why did Mary think the Lincolns had money problems in the White House? Didn't the government pay for all their expenses?

The president and his family were responsible for all personal expenses such as laundry, personal entertainment, clothing, the salaries of personal staff, and all other expenses incurred by the family. With many expenses being the president's responsibility, Mary felt the need to economize. Upon first meeting Mrs. Keckly, Mary explained, "I cannot afford to be extravagant. We are just from the West, and are poor."[51]

Did Mary take bribes for political, or personal, favors?

There are rumors that Mary did take bribes from those seeking political appointments. Orville Browning recorded an alleged incident in his journal. He claimed that Judge Davis recalled that Simeon Draper had paid Mary a huge sum of money and in return was appointed Collector of the Port of New York. Draper also won the privilege of selling the cotton seized by General William T. Sherman in Savannah.[52] The problem with this story, and similar stories, is that it was the president who made appointments, and not the first lady. There is no other evidence that Mary had any influence in Draper's position.

It is also unlikely that a man who had championed Mary during a previous political scandal would create a new one by participation in a bribery scheme. When the White House gardener, John Watt, tried to extort the Lincolns for $20,000.00 saying he had three letters that had been written by Mary, it was Draper who resolved the matter. The Commissioner of Agriculture, Isaac Newton, asked Draper to visit Watt and make him an irrefusable offer. Draper went to the conservatory to confront Watt. With appropriate gravity, Draper informed Watt that he would be taken to Fort Lafayette—a fortification in the Narrows of New York Harbor that was being used to house Confederate prisoners of war and political criminals. Reportedly, Watt "fell on his literal marrow bones & begged, & gave up the letters & the conspiracy got demoralized, & came down, to $1,500.00." The amount was paid and settled the situation.[53]

Was Mary really a Confederate sympathizer or spy?

Accusations that Mary sympathized with the Confederacy began the day she entered the White House. Despite rumors, gossip, and journalists' accusations that Mary held the Confederate cause dear, there is no evidence to support these claims. Mrs. Eunice Tripler, a Washington socialite, was especially vicious in her attacks when she wrote that Mary sent information to her brothers who were fighting for the Confederate armies.[54] All of the accusations were fodder for gossip.

However, there is one story which may indicate that Mary was unknowingly used by someone to help the Confederacy. In 1889, James B. Swain, a correspondent of the *New York Times*, wrote to Lincoln's former secretary John Hay inquiring about a meeting between Mrs. Lincoln and Mrs. Robert E. Lee. His letter reads in part: "I was going on to ask if you yet hold in remembrance the séance which you arranged between the late Ann S. Stephens and Mrs. Lincoln, at which Mrs. Robert E. Lee, and her daughter were anticipated participants, and which was the very evening (about April 23, 1861) of Lee's flight from Arlington, and to cover which flight, evidently was the purpose of the visit of Mrs. Lee and her daughter to Mrs. Lincoln."[55]

This letter raises many questions. Did Mrs. Lee attend a White House séance? Was Mrs. Lee expected to arrive and then failed to show? Did Swain correctly remember the events? Did Mrs. Lee truly accept an invitation from Mary to cover Robert E. Lee's flight from their home in Virginia? Robert E. Lee wrote a letter from Arlington on April 20 stating "Save in the defense of my native State, I have no desire ever again to draw my sword." Three days later Lee appeared at the Virginia Convention to "accept the position your partiality has assigned me."[56]

The one verifiable aspect to the letter is that Mary did know Ann S. Stephens. She was a popular novelist during the mid-nineteenth century whose books included *The Rejected Wife* (1863), and *Esther: A Story of the Oregon Trail* (1862). Ann's first recorded visit to the White House to visit the Lincolns was April 18, 1861. She was still a welcomed guest in 1864. Since Ann was a frequent White House guest, it is probable that Mary enjoyed not only reading her stories but also her company.[57]

Did Lincoln hold a Cabinet meeting to declare that his wife was loyal to the Union?

The story, first created by E. J. Edwards in 1905, has been retold and embellished by several authors including Margaret Leech, Carl Sandburg, and anyone who has quoted them. The fable goes that a joint committee of the House and Senate (forming a Committee on the Conduct of the War) met to discuss Mary Lincoln's treasonous acts of being a spy for the Confederacy. As the committee was about to begin their discussion, Abraham Lincoln walked into the room and stood at the foot of the table. The committee members were silent as Lincoln spoke: "I, Abraham Lincoln, President of the United States appear of my own volition before this committee of the Senate to say that I, or my own knowledge, now that it is untrue that any of my family holds treasonable communication with the enemy."

It is a great story.

It is also just that, a story.

Historian Edward Steers proved that none of the parties who were supposedly members of the committee were in a position to relay this story to E. J. Edwards. The story is a fabrication created by Edwards.[58]

Who was the Rebel in the White House?

Emilie Todd Helm was Mary's half-sister and the wife of Confederate brigadier beneral Benjamin Hardin Helm. After Ben was killed in September 1862 at the Battle of Chickamauga, Emilie, who was in Georgia for her husband's funeral, began to travel north to her home in Kentucky. She was stopped at Fortress Monroe and told she must sign an oath of allegiance to travel farther. She refused. Not knowing what to do with the Confederate widow, a message was sent to Lincoln requesting instructions. He replied, "Send her to me." Emilie, who had her eldest daughter Katherine with her, was sent to Washington where they stayed with the Lincolns for nearly two weeks. The two sisters embraced one another, never spoke of the war, and mourned the deaths of Emilie's husband, Willie Lincoln, and their brother Alec Todd.[59]

What is spiritualism?

Spiritualism is a belief system, or religious practice, based on the practice of communicating with spirits, especially through a medium. The Second Great Awakening, a Protestant revival, flourished throughout the United States during the early nineteenth century, spreading mainly through the Baptist and Methodist denominations and noted for its enthusiasm and emotional connection to the supernatural. The Second Great Awakening gave birth to spiritualism in 1848 when two young girls, Maggie and Kate Fox, claimed their Hydesville, New York home was haunted. The girls claimed they could communicate with the ghosts through a series of knocks that came through the walls. Neighbors who allegedly witnessed this phenomenon helped spread the story that the girls could communicate with spirits. The basic belief of spiritualism was that death is a transition period.Once the body is shed, the spirit continues to live in another realm and is able to communicate with the living. For those could not successfully speak directly to spirits, a medium was used to help them communicate with the souls of those they had loved and lost. At its peak, spiritualism claimed over two million believers just in the United States.[60]

Was Mary a believer in spiritualism? Did she believe in ghosts?

As a child, Mary was introduced to spiritual beliefs through the ministrations of Mammy Sally. Mammy filled Mary's childhood with stories about "ole man Satan" who "bellers and shakes his head and sharpens up his horns on the ground and paws up the dust with both his front feet at once." She concluded her description by saying that Satan had painted his tail pea green. Mammy told the children that jaybirds carried messages to the devil every Friday night. According to her stories, if the children had misbehaved, Mr. Jay reported their misdoings directly to Satan, who recorded all their mischief in his "big book."[61]

Mary, as a belle in Springfield, had told her beau, Lincoln, "I always propitiate the Fates, the Furies, and the Fairies . . . my sister and I are part Scotch and we believe in fairies."[62] This was not a belief in spiritualism, but a foundation for the ability to believe in the supernatural.

For both Lincolns, an interest in spiritualism dates to Springfield in the late 1850s. Lincoln's law office library contained two books on spiritualism. While it is impossible to determine if the books belonged to Lincoln or to Herndon, it is known that most of the books belonged to Lincoln. In 1857 and 1858, at least five different mediums held lectures and demonstrations in Springfield. It is probable that both Lincolns attended these events, if only out of curiosity and for entertainment. Herndon recorded that Lincoln "did sometimes attend here, in the city, séances, I am told this by Mr. Ordway, a spiritualist."[63]

In Washington, Lincoln owned a copy of *Further Communications from the World of Spirits, on Subjects Highly Important to the Human Family*, published in 1862. The Lincolns may have purchased the book, or it could have been a gift to help the family find comfort after the loss of their son Willie.

Several séances were held at White House with a variety of mediums. Some attendees recall séances in the White House as early as 1861. Mary and her friends attended "sittings" with Lord Colchester, Nettie Colburn (later Maynard), Charles E. Shockle, Mrs. Cranston Laurie, and others, seeking communication with loved ones and advice from the spirit world. Mary was once told by Mrs. Laurie there were members of the Cabinet who were enemies of the president and would have to be dismissed. Lincoln was also given advice: Nettie Colburn encouraged Lincoln to sign the Emancipation Proclamation; Laurie's advice to him was to "go in person to the front."[64]

Whether Lincoln believed in the power of the mediums or not is questionable. Most historians consider his attendance at séances as a curiosity, entertainment, or an opportunity to discover the "tricks of the trade" such as what caused the piano to move up and down. Few consider Lincoln to be a complete believer. Mary, like so many other grieving mothers in America, was a believer. She believed, "*Death*, is only a blessed transition, to the 'pure in heart,' that a very slight veil separates us, from the loved & lost." Mary found comfort believing "that though unseen by us, they are very near." [65] When Emilie, Mary's half-sister, visited the White House, she found Mary "unnatural," "abnormal," "nervous," and "wrought up." Emilie recorded the events of an evening when Mary came to the bedroom door to tell an incredible tale of the supernatural. Mary confided, "if Willie did not come to comfort me I would still be drowned in tears." Mary continued, "He lives, Emilie!" "He comes to me every night, and stands at the foot of my bed with the same sweet, adorable smile he has always had; he does not always come alone; little Eddie [sic] is sometimes with him and twice he has come with our brother, Alec."66

A few years later, in a letter filled with Christian imagery and thoughts, Mary wrote to her friend Sally Orne, "I am not EITHER a spiritual-ist—but I sincerely believe—our loved ones, who have only, *"gone before"* are permitted to watch over those who were dearer to them than life."67 Apparently, Mrs. Orne had written to Mary about her own disbelief in mediums, and Mary felt the need to assure her friend they were in agreement.

It seems that Mary did not believe in ghostly figures that haunt or torment, but rather a spiritual being that visited loved ones to offer comfort and peace. There is a fine line between the two, but Mary made that distinction.

Life as a War Wife

Was Mary's life in danger during the war? Was there a measure to move her to safety? Why did she choose to stay in Washington?

General Winfield Scott insisted that Mary leave Washington. Mary insisted that she stay near her husband saying that she would not leave him at this juncture.

At one point, General Scott believed that the Southern troops could enter Washington at any moment, and Mary was ordered not to leave the White House without a guard. The newspapers unleashed a raft of crit-icism about spending war funds to guard the president's Southern wife who had questionable loyalties. Mary was heartbroken by the attacks.

In mid-April 1861, John Hay consulted with Major David Hunter to discuss the best measures for guarding the White House. Hunter assured Hay that whatever was requested would be granted. Troops were beginning to arrive in Washington; there were guards in place at the White House.68

Were there other times Mary was in danger?

With all the threats of assassination, warning letters received by the Lincoln family, and the general feeling of danger surrounding the White House, every unusual situation was carefully examined for evidence of foul play. Elizabeth Grimsley remembered that "One night every member of the family except the servants, was taken ill, physicians were hastily summoned, and for a time whisperings of 'Poison' were heard, but it proved to be only an over-indulgence in Potomac Shad, a new and tempting dish to western palates."[69]

Mary also had the misfortune of being involved in several carriage accidents. Some were truly accidents, while others seemed to be deliberate. One accident occurred in June 1861, Mary, Elizabeth Grimsley, and the Lincoln boys were being escorted by General Hiram Walbridge when the horses stumbled and fell. The driver was thrown off the box. Shaken, Grimsley wrote to John Todd Stuart, "I am confident that had it not been for General Walbridge . . . Taddy would have been crushed by the wheel."[70] Mary was not injured during the carriage accident. But she would not fare so well the next time.

On July 2, 1863, while the battle of Gettysburg was raging in Pennsylvania, Mary left the Soldiers' Home to return to the White House. En route, the driver's seat became detached from the carriage, throwing the driver. The startled horses ran away. Trying to save herself, Mary leaped to the ground, but she fell and struck the back of her head on a rock leaving a large, bleeding gash. She was first taken to a field hospital and then returned to the Soldiers' Home to recuperate. Her wound became infected, and Mary was terribly ill, causing Lincoln to telegram Robert and tell him to return to Washington. Mrs. Rebecca Pomroy, an army nurse, tended to Mary's health over the next three weeks. An inspection found that the screws holding the driver's seat to the carriage had been removed. It was believed someone had hoped to injure the president; Mary was not believed to be the target.[71]

The daughters of Cassius M. Clay, a Kentucky abolitionist who was a cousin to Henry Clay, visited Mary in Washington and witnessed a carriage accident during the winter of 1865. Mary B. Clay and her sister (unnamed in the article) were invited to attend Ford's Theatre. The young ladies rode in the same carriage as the president and Mary. "As we drove along, the carriage being swung very low, an iron hoop was caught under it and pierced through the seat, coming between Mr. and Mrs. Lincoln who occupied the back seat." Mary was alarmed and thought that an attack was being made on the President's life. The carriage was repaired, and the party continued their journey to the theatre without further incident.[72]

Who did Mary consider a good general for the Union Army?

Mary found several generals to be admirable. Her favorites would be those whom she knew around Washington, those who were helpful to President Lincoln and herself, and those who could win battles. Mary wrote a fond letter to General Daniel E. Sickles telling him, "In our daily circles, your name is frequently & deservedly mentioned as being among the most prominent & energetic of our brave Union defenders."[73]

Always willing to share her opinions, Mary spoke negatively of several politicians and military leaders. She referred to General George B. McClellan as a "humbug," telling Lincoln "he talks so much and does so little." Mary also informed her husband that, "McClellan & his slowness are vehemently discussed." She encouraged Lincoln to replace McClellan by stating, "Many say, they would almost worship you, if you would put a fighting General, in the place of McClellan."[74] She referred to General Ulysses S. Grant as "a butcher" who "loses two men to the enemy's one. He has no management, no regard for life."[75]

Did Mary go to Gettysburg with Lincoln?

No, Mary stayed in Washington with Tad who was ill with smallpox. The president had a slight case of smallpox as well but made the journey despite his illness.

How did Mary know how to "review the troops" Did she receive special instructions on what constitutes a troop review?

Lincoln checked several books out of the Library of Congress regarding military studies. It is possible that when the books were sitting around, Mary looked at them as well. Her participation in a review was more ceremonial than anything else. The review consisted of looking at a few rifles and uniforms—which during the early part of the war would have been difficult since most uniforms consisted of whatever clothing a soldier brought from home. During the review, the soldiers would stand in a row while Lincoln walked among them looking over a few guns. Mary would probably have remained in the carriage. Lincoln would hold up a weapon, or other aspect of the review, motion to Mary, and she would give a nod of approval.

Since there were 40,000 troops in Washington, there were many opportunities to review the troops.[76]

Did Mary visit the troops often?

Sometimes, it was Mary's idea to visit the troops at camp. After a visit to Major General Joseph Hooker at camp, the *Sacramento Union* reported, "the thoughtful wife of the President, an able and a noble woman, ought to have the credit of originating the plan of a tour through the Army by the President, as she saw what an excellent effort would be given to the troops, now in good condition and ready to march, by coming in contact with their Commander-in-Chief and his family."[77] Mary believed it was important to visit and would do so as often as her schedule and health allowed.

Duties as First Lady

Was Mary the first woman in the White House to be called "First Lady?"

President Zachary Taylor is credited with coining that phrase for the wife of a U.S. president when he eulogized Dolley Madison in 1849. However, there seems to be no documentation to verify the claim. Others say that Harriet Lane was dubbed the first lady of the land in 1860. Others believe that Mary Lincoln was the first given the title "First Lady" by the *London Times* and the *Sacramento Union*.

Prior to the Lincoln administration, there was no clear rule as to how to address the wife of a president. Martha Washington had been called "Lady Washington." Thinking the term "lady" sounded too royal, others used "Madam President," or the more formal "Madame Presidentress" by guests and journalists. Mary probably preferred the latter two. She did not appreciate some of the nicknames she was given. Behind her back, Mary was called "Queen," or "La Reine" by some regular White House visitors. As crass as these names were, the most damnatory comment came from Lincoln's secretary, John Hay, who wrote to his friend John Nicolay, "The Hell-cat is getting more Hell-cattical day by day."[78]

Did Mary have a special place to go to get away from Washington?

After the death of their son Willie, both Lincolns sought refuge from Washington. Mary often found comfort in a shopping excursion to New York or other locations. She also enjoyed a visit to Manchester, Vermont with Robert and Tad in 1864.

Together, the Lincolns found peace at a quiet cottage at the Soldiers' Home, a residence for disabled military veterans.

Did Mary travel to Richmond at the end of the war?

Mary traveled to City Point (now Hopewell), located twenty miles from Richmond, with Lincoln and others. While there, they were to review the troops led by Major General Edward O. C. Ord. Mary and Mrs. Julia Grant rode in an ambulance that kept getting stuck in the mud while the president and Mrs. Ord rode on horseback. Realizing that she would be late for the review, and that the troops might mistake Mrs. Ord for her, Mary became nervous and furious. As it became more difficult for the driver to maneuver the ambulance through the mud, it began to jolt and jerk causing the ladies to bump their heads. Mary, already distraught, was now in pain. When she arrived at the review, she was unable to control her emotions and she lashed out at Mrs. Ord and the president.

Two days later, Mary returned to Washington. Without Mary, Lincoln and Tad triumphantly entered Richmond. Mary gathered a few friends to travel back to City Point with her. When her party arrived, Mary was heart-broken to learn that her husband and son had already toured Richmond; she had wanted to be with her husband as he entered the fallen capitol of the Confederacy. Plans were made for Mary and her friends to go to Richmond where Mary was able to tour Jefferson Davis's home and other locations.[79]

Entertainments

Was Mary criticized for entertaining?

Yes. One of the most vicious criticisms was a poem titled "The Lady President's Ball" written by Eleanor G. Donnelly shortly after Mary hosted a party on February 5, 1862. While Mary's guests ate and danced, Willie Lincoln was upstairs suffering from an illness that would claim his life.

What types of entertainments were held in the White House?

Mary hosted many musical entertainments in the Red Room, including Adelina Patti, a 19-year-old opera singer, the Hutchinson Family who relayed their social messages through music, and child prodigy Teresa Carreno, a nine-year-old pianist from Venezuela. The Marine Band played in Lafayette Square every week during the summer. After Willie's death, Mary requested the concerts be canceled, but they were reinstated to help boost the morale of the troops and citizens.

Did the Lincolns serve alcohol in the White House?

Yes, alcohol was served occasionally at White House dinners and receptions. But because it was served did not necessarily mean that the Lincolns drank it themselves. William Stoddard told the story of a time when wine and champagne were served with dinner; the president had a glass of champagne at his plate and although he seemed interested in it, he did not drink it. Lincoln picked up the glass, smelled it, and did not drink. After dinner, Mrs. Lincoln told Stoddard about a gift assortment of alcohol that was in storage in the basement. She explained, "There are loads of champagne, green seal and other seal; red wines of several kinds; white wine from the Rhine; wines of Spain and Portugal and the islands; whiskey distilled from rye, and from wheat, and from potatoes; choice brandy; Jamaica rum, and Santa Cruz rum" and she suspected there was some gin mixed in as well. Mary asked Stoddard, "But what is to be done? I never use any, and Mr. Lincoln never touches any."

As a solution, Stoddard suggested the liquor be put to good use and distributed to Mary's favorite local hospitals where the "doctors will know what to do with it, if they can keep it away from the hospital nurses." Stoddard's idea was agreeable to Mary who decided to make the delivery herself. She seemed pleased that she could contribute to the hospital's medical supply.[80] (There is no documentation as to how Mary felt about Stoddard's innuendo about the hospital nurses.)

Were special entertainments held for children?

An egg roll was held on Easter Monday. It was more of a private affair than it is today. The Lincoln boys, their friends Holly and Bud Taft, and others gathered with baskets full of colored hard-boiled eggs, and raced their eggs to the bottom of the hill.[81]

The boys entertained family, friends, and staff by putting together shows and a "circus" complete with a program. For an admission fee of five cents, the audience was entertained by songs, jokes, and the boys wearing Mary's clothes as costumes, which Mary did not mind. The motto of the White house was "Let the children have a good time."[82]

Was Mary's ability to speak French a useful skill at the White House?

Elizabeth Grimsley told of an evening when an interpreter was not available, and Mary was able to hold a conversation with the Chilean ambassador and his wife. According to Grimsley, Mary "had no difficulty in speaking with ease."[83] Neither the ambassador nor his wife spoke English, but they were fluent in French. When Prince Napoleon dined at the White House on August 3, 1861, the conversation was mainly in French. The prince was delighted to speak with Mary in his native language. A month later, the newspapers reported that while Mary was in New York her plans included "the study of the French language." Either Mary was taking a quick refresher course, or the newspaper story was false. Emilie Helm claimed that Mary was an "excellent reader and her sympathy with French was perfect."[84]

What is the "Mary Lincoln Polka"?

The "Mary Lincoln Polka" (or "Mary Polka" as it is written on the musical score) was a musical tribute to Mary composed by Francis Scala, the director of the Marine Band. It was first played at a White House party held on February 5, 1862.[85]

White House Staff

Which of the White House servants had the most contact with Mary?

With rumors of Mary mistreating servants and having difficulty keeping help employed, it would be easy to believe there was a constant parade of staff entering and exiting the White House during the Lincoln administration. This is untrue; there were few changes in the staff during the war years. Several members of the White House staff had been employed prior to the Lincolns' arrival and continued their employment after Mary left Washington. Others were hired by the Lincolns for a specific task and left when the duties were completed. Stories exist claiming that Mary could be difficult; however, several servants told stories about how good Mrs. Lincoln was to the help. Rosetta Wells, a seamstress for Mary, recalled, "She had her ways, but nobody minded her, for she would never hurt a flea, and her bark was worse than her bite."[86] Mary worked closely with several members of the White House staff, especially those whose duties included housekeeping, sewing, and cooking. Servants said that Mary was "all over the kitchen" and that she knew exactly what she wanted done and how to do it. More importantly, "the steward, cook and waiters *knew* that she knew."[87]

White House staff members during the Lincoln era included:

1. Elizabeth Keckly owned her own dressmaking business; however, she also served as a dressmaker, or mantua maker, for Mary during the war. Keckly would arrive at the White House and help Mary dress for special events. She also was known to comb Lincoln's hair. It is believed that Keckly created fifteen or sixteen dresses for Mary during the spring and early part of the summer of 1861. It is impossible to know exactly which dresses were made by Keckly, or how many gowns she was hired to make during her time with Mary.

According to letters between the two women, Mary had hired Keckly to create new mourning dresses in early 1868. Later that year, the friendship ended for Mary when Keckly's tell-all book about the Lincoln family was published.[88]

2. Rebecca Pomroy was a nurse at a nearby military hospital. She went to the White House at the request of chief army nurse Dorothea Dix who was looking for a way to help the grieving Lincoln family. Tad was ill, and Mary was suffering from the loss of her son Willie. Pomroy arrived at the White House in February 1862 prior to Willie's funeral. Pomroy returned in 1863 to care for Mary after she had been severely injured in a carriage accident.

3. Charles Forbes was a footman and personal attendant throughout the Lincoln administration.

4. Mrs. Mary Ann Cuthbert was an Irish immigrant who began her White House career as a seamstress and maid and later became the chief housekeeper. She worked closely with Mary and often ran errands for her. Cuthbert also worked at the Soldiers' Home when the Lincolns were in residence, and along with Mrs. Dines, requested to return to the White House when the weather became cold.

Mary trusted Cuthbert with financial matters—a trust which later caused Mary grief. After Lincoln's death, Mary entrusted some papers to Cuthbert. Writing to Alexander Williamson in August 1865, Mary complained that Cuthbert had promised to settle the first lady's business matters but had not yet fulfilled that promise. In December of the same year, Mary feared that a hat intended for Dr. Phineas D. Gurley as a keepsake of Abraham had been given to the wrong person. Mary entrusted the delivery of the hat to Cuthbert, who possibly gave it to Edward Burke, a White House steward.[89]

In April 1866, Cuthbert accused Mary of thievery. She had a chance meeting on the steps of the Capitol Building with Orville Browning, who was then serving as Secretary of the Interior under President Andrew Johnson. According to Browning, Cuthbert requested his assistance in finding employment. Claiming she was "destitute and in distress" Cuthbert claimed that her six hundred dollars per annum salary had been "appropriated by Mrs. Lincoln."[90]

Adding to the strange relationship between the two women is that on at least fourteen occasions, Mary Lincoln signed telegrams as "Mary Cuthbert" or "Mrs. Cuthbert." These telegrams were written shortly after Lincoln's reelection in 1864. Mary had acquired large debts and historians have concluded she was using the assumed name to keep creditors at bay.[91]

This leaves the question as to whether Cuthbert's claim about not receiving her salary was true. Based on the struggles Mary had with Cuthbert in 1865, and Mary's use of Cuthbert's name (if she knew about the forged telegrams) there was reason for distrust between the two women. A disgruntled servant who has fallen on hard times may easily fabricate a story that she is owed money to procure funds from the government. An unhappy employer whose employee has not fulfilled her duties may withhold payment of salary.

5. "Aunt" Mary Dines served as a cook at the Soldiers' Home in 1862. She had been born into slavery and escaped by hiding in a hay wagon. Mary's cooking skills led her to become a favorite among the soldiers. Mary lived in a contraband camp nearby where she wrote letters for other members of the community. A gifted singer, Mary led the other residents in song. She told of one occasion when the president, Mary, and a few guests, "arrived to hear a musical performance arranged especially for them. Dines lead the singing of various Negro spirituals."

It is believed that in November, Dines relocated to the White House. Lincoln sent a telegram to his wife, who was in Boston, asking if Mrs. Cuthbert and "Aunt Mary" could move to the White House because the Soldiers Home had grown so cold.[92] No one knows why Dines left her employment at the White House in 1863.

6. Rosetta Wells was a friend of Mary Dines who did "plain sewing" for Mary at the White House. Plain sewing includes tasks such as making and repairing bed linens, mending clothing, darning socks, and creating simple garments such as undergarments.[93]

7. Cornelia Mitchell was already employed at the White House as a cook when the Lincolns arrived. Cornelia and her children lived in the servants' quarters located in the basement. Mitchell was an excellent cook known for both her simple dishes and her culinary masterpieces. It was said that the dishes she prepared "made Mrs. Lincoln's receptions the envy of Washington's official and diplomatic entertainments."[94]

8. Peter Brown served as a waiter and managed the White House dining room. His son often assisted him.

Were any of the White House servants enslaved persons?

No enslaved people served in the White House during the Lincoln administration. The federal government did not retain enslaved persons from one presidential administration to the next. Some earlier presidents were slaveholders and brought enslaved people to Washington to serve in the White House. Those servants left Washington when the president was no longer in office. The last president to bring enslaved help into the White House was Zachary Taylor.

Did the government pay the White House staff?

According to Jean Baker, Congress paid for the president's steward, doorkeepers, watchmen, gardener, and laborers. The president hired his own cooks, domestic servants, and paid for all state entertaining. Harold Holzer listed at least thirty positions held by employees who were paid through government funds.[95]

Did the staff members have problems with the Lincoln children's behavior?

Yes! In addition to tiring of Willie and Tad burying the doll among the rosebushes, Major Watt frequently became enraged at Tad. When Tad ate all the strawberries that were being forced for a state dinner, Watt fumed that he was going to let Mary know of her son's ill-mannered behavior. Julia Taft reminded him that Tad "is the Madam's son," and Mr. Watt snarled, "The Madam's wildcat."[96]

The gardeners also complained frequently of the family goats Nannie and Nanko damaging the flower beds. When Nannie goat disappeared, some thought the gardeners knew more about her disappearance than they admitted.

Social Causes

What did Mary do to help the soldiers and other war efforts?

Mary and Abraham both frequently visited the soldiers in the hospitals near Washington, often bearing gifts. According to Elizabeth Grimsley, Mary spent a great amount of time visiting the encampments and assisted in christening several of them. One of the Lincolns' favorites was "Camp Mary Lincoln."[97] Daily, bouquets were made at the conservatory and taken to the nearby hospitals, and "as often as possible, the kind-hearted lady, (Mary) took them herself."[98]

William Stoddard believed that Mary should have taken "newspaper correspondents, from two to five, of both sexes, every time she went, and she would have them take shorthand notes of what she says to the sick soldiers and of what the sick soldiers say to her." He also thought bringing the journalists back to the White House for cake and coffee afterward would benefit Mary. She could also show them the conservatory.

Julia Taft told of a note that Mr. Lincoln wrote to Hiram Barney in New York stating: "Mrs Lincoln has $1000 for the benefit of the hospitals and she will be obliged and send the pay if you will be so good as to select and send her "$200 worth of good lemons and $100 worth of good oranges" which were distributed to the different hospitals and Judiciary Square.[99]

Mary frequently brought gifts of fresh fruit and flowers to cheer the men. Sometimes, she filled her carriage with produce from the White House garden. Seed orders from this period show purchases for tomatoes, eggplants, radishes, cucumbers, cherry peppers, squash, celery, cantaloupe, pumpkins, rhubarb, and several other fruits and vegetables.

More important than bringing gifts, Mary brought joy and comfort through her visits to the soldiers. She and other women were often called "angel mothers" for their kindness. Sometimes the women would read to the soldiers; sometimes they would write letters for them. Mary wrote at least one letter from Campbell Hospital. The soldier, James Agen, was visited twice by a woman whose identity he did not know until he returned home, and his mother showed him the letter, which was published years later:

"My dear Mrs. Agen—I am sitting by the side of your soldier boy. He has been quite sick, but is getting well. He tells me to say to you that he is alright. With respects for the mother of the young soldier. Mrs. Abraham Lincoln."[100]

CHAPTER FOUR

The Darkest Night of All:
Lincoln's Assassination, April 15, 1865

Those fiends, had too long contemplated, this inhuman murder, to
have allowed *him*, to escape.
—Mary Lincoln to Francis Bicknell Carpenter, November 15, 1865

Shouts of celebration had filled the air throughout Washington in the
days leading up to April 14. Just three nights earlier, with Mary visible to
the crowd through one window, Lincoln stood at another and addressed the
crowd that had gathered on the White House lawn.[1] General Robert E. Lee
had surrendered his troops to General Ulysses S. Grant, virtually ensuring
the war that had divided the nation and its families for four years would end
soon. Robert, who had served on General Grant's staff and was with him when
Lee surrendered, was coming home. The Lincoln family would be reunited.
Mary felt that peace had come to the country and her family was now safe.
Plans were made for relaxation, and the president, who always enjoyed the
theatre, was determined to see *Our American Cousin* featuring Laura Keene.

It was a happy day for the Lincolns when they awoke on the morning of
April 14. Plans had been made to attend Ford's Theatre that evening. Mary
and Abraham enjoyed their lunch in a private parlor. They then went for a
carriage ride and stopped at the Navy Yard to view three monitors (small
warships with revolving turrets) that had been damaged during an engagement
in Fort Fisher, North Carolina. Upon returning to the White House between
6 and 7 p.m., they were greeted by friends from Illinois, including Governor
Richard J. Oglesby. The play was already in progress when the presidential
party entered Ford's Theatre around 8:30 p.m. As the Lincolns entered the
special viewing box, Laura Keene turned to face the audience and ad-libbed,

"Well, anybody can see *that!*" as she gestured toward the presidential party.[2] Thunderous applause swept throughout the theater while people waved their hats and handkerchiefs. The orchestra played "Hail to the Chief" followed by "The Conquering Hero Comes." The house lights were raised so everyone could see the man who had saved the Union. Before taking their seats, Lincoln bowed to the audience twice and Mary beamed while she curtsied repeatedly. For the next hour and forty-five minutes, the Lincolns relaxed, laughed, and enjoyed the comedy that was being presented on stage. Then, suddenly, John Wilkes Booth stepped into the box with the Lincolns and their guests and committed one of the most heinous murders in America's history.

For Mary, what had begun as a joyous, peaceful day, suddenly turned into the darkest night of her life.[3]

Did Mary have premonitions that Lincoln would be killed?

There were threats against Lincoln's life from the day he announced his candidacy until the day he died. For Mary, it was a fact of life that there was danger in Washington and the entire family could become victims. (One of the reasons she did not want Robert to enlist in the army was a fear that he would be captured.) Mary did not have dreams or premonitions that Lincoln would die, but he had them. On at least two occasions, Lincoln dreamed that he died during his second term of office. Even though Mary did not have the dream herself, she was frightened by the vividness of Abraham's dream.

Who attended the theatre with the Lincolns?

Although the Lincolns had invited several people to attend the performance, including General Grant and his wife, and Robert Todd Lincoln, invitations were declined for a variety of reasons. It was Major Henry Rathbone and his fiancée Clara Harris who sat in the president's theatre box that evening.

Where was Mary when John Wilkes Booth entered the theatre box to murder the president?

She was seated to Lincoln's right, touching his right arm, and resting her head upon his shoulder. She had just said to her husband, "What will Miss Harris think of my holding on to you so?" Lincoln replied, "She won't think anything about it."[4]

Did Mary immediately realize that the president had been shot?

She realized that a gun had been fired. Major Rathbone leaped to his feet and tried to stop Booth from escaping, but Booth wielded a large knife and sliced a deep wound in Rathbone's arm. At first, many in the theatre did not realize something was wrong. Some did not hear the gunshot, and many believed it was part of the play. It was Mary's screams and Booth jumping onto the stage that made everyone realize something was amiss. Many stood, frozen and stunned, in silence. Then someone yelled, "Stop that man!" as Booth made his way out the back of the theatre. Suddenly, chaos erupted, and the sound of Mary's shrieks filled the air. Some claimed that her words were incoherent. Others said she screamed, "My husband is shot!"[5]

Who was the first person to enter the presidential box? What did Mary say to him?

Dr. Charles Leale was the first person to enter the box. He had to be lifted from the stage because Booth had locked the door to the presidential box. Leale had graduated from medical school only six weeks earlier. He reported that Mary said, "Oh doctor, is he dead? Can he recover?" She then wept as she held Lincoln upright in his chair and said, "Will you take charge of him? Do what you can for him. Oh, my dear husband!"[6] Two other physicians, Dr. Charles Taft and Dr. Albert King, also quickly entered the box.[7]

Where were Robert and Tad at the time of the assassination?

Tad, who was attended by a chaperone, was at Grover's Theatre watching a production of *Aladdin and His Magic Lamp*. Some sources identify his tutor Alexander Williamson as the chaperone.

Earlier in the day, Robert returned to Washington from witnessing General Robert E. Lee's surrender to General Grant. He arrived in time to have breakfast with his family at 8 a.m. and have a long visit with his father. Shortly before the Lincolns left the White House, Robert spoke briefly with his father again. Lincoln invited Robert to come along, but being tired, Robert declined the invitation. He and John Hay were at the White House catching up when they learned the president had been shot.[8]

Who took Mary to the Peterson House?

Using a shutter as a stretcher, four soldiers carried Lincoln across the street. A young lieutenant walked in front of them clearing a path and across the street to the Peterson House. Following the soldiers, Laura Keene helped support Mary. They were escorted by Major Rathbone and another man. After arriving and placing Lincoln on the bed, Dr. Leale requested that Mary leave the room so he could examine Lincoln thoroughly. She went to the front parlor, sat on a sofa, sobbed, and waited.[9]

Was Robert with Mary at the Peterson House?

Robert and John Hay left the White House and hurried to the Peterson House. Some accounts place Senator Charles Sumner with them. After being told by Dr. Robert Stone that there was no hope for Lincoln's recovery, Robert freely gave vent to his emotions. Throughout the night he tended to his mother and kept vigil at his father's bedside.[10]

Who else stayed with Mary at the Peterson House?

As Mary waited for word from the doctors, Miss Clara Harris tried to offer comfort. Robert sent for Mary's friend Elizabeth Dixon, the wife of Senator James Dixon of Connecticut. Mary asked that Tad be allowed to come in the hope that Lincoln would respond to their son. Tad never arrived. It is possible that Robert and others thought the scene would have been too much for a child to witness. Mary asked Benjamin French to bring Mrs. Mary Jane Welles and Mrs. Emma Gurley to the parlor. He took a carriage to the Welles' home where he was told Mrs. Welles was too ill to come. However, once she heard the circumstances, she went to the Peterson House to sit with Mary and try to offer her comfort and support. Others waiting through the night with Mary included Mrs. Mary Kinney (a sister to Elizabeth Dixon) and her daughter Constance. The next morning when Mr. French arrived at the White House, he found Mrs. Welles sitting with Mary in her room.[11]

Where was her friend, Mrs. Keckly?

According to Elizabeth Keckly, she was awakened at 11 p.m. and told that the president had been shot and the entire Cabinet assassinated. She hurried to the streets seeking information and tried to get to the White House. Soldiers denied Elizabeth—and everyone else—entry to the executive mansion. A bystander told her that Lincoln was dying. The next morning, around 11 a.m., a carriage arrived to take Elizabeth to Mary at the White House. Upon arrival, she found Mrs. Welles and Mary in a darkened bedroom. Mary explained that she had sent for Elizabeth and wondered why she did not come. Apparently, three carriages had been sent to bring Elizabeth to the Peterson House, but all three went to the wrong address and no one could find Elizabeth.[12]

Why did so many government officials come to the Peterson House during the night?

Many came as soon as they heard that Lincoln had been shot because they wanted to see for themselves if the rumors were true. Most were there as a form of security. Secretary of State William Seward, recovering from a carriage accident, was attacked in his bed, and there were rumors that other government officials were targeted. Secretary of War William Stanton oversaw the night's events and tried to maintain order throughout a night of chaos.

Did Mary say anything memorable at the Peterson House?

The last time Mary saw Lincoln, she said, "Love, live but for one moment to speak to me once, to speak to our children." Shortly after saying this, the president's breathing became raspy. Mary cried out, sobbed with grief, and fainted.[13]

Who said, "Now he belongs to the ages?"

When Lincoln died, Dr. Phineas Gurley asked for everyone to pray. At the end of the prayer, William Stanton wept openly and buried his head in the blankets. When he had somewhat recovered he uttered the phrase. However, some witnesses claimed that Stanton's actual words were, "Now he belongs to the angels." Either phrase demonstrates the great admiration and respect that Stanton felt for Lincoln.

Was Mary able to see her husband before he died?

Yes. About once an hour, clean napkins were placed by the president's head to cover the blood-stained pillows. Mary would then come and sit by the bed until her emotions overwhelmed her. She would then return to the parlor.

What time did Lincoln die? Was Mary with him?

Dr. Charles S. Taft wrote that Lincoln stopped breathing "at 7:21 and 55 seconds in the morning of April 15, and 7:22 and 10 seconds his pulse ceased to beat."[14] Mary was in the front parlor. After praying at the president's bedside, Rev. Gurley comforted Mary and Robert and led them in prayer. Mary reportedly said, "Oh my God, and have I given my husband to die."[15]

Lincoln's Funeral

Did Mary attend Lincoln's funeral? Did Tad or Robert attend?

It was not customary for women of the upper classes to attend the funeral of a loved one. Some women attended the church service but did not go to the graveside burial service. The belief was that women should not demonstrate great emotions in public, and few women could contain their grief at the loss of a loved one.

Mary may have found the noise of the funeral preparations and thousands of mourners entering the White House to pay their respects to the slain president overwhelming. She never entered the East Room while the president laid in state. When Elizabeth Keckly entered Mary's bedroom, she found Mary in a "new paroxysm of grief." The room was filled with "the wails of a broken heart, the unearthly shrieks, the terrible convulsion, the wild, tempestuous outbursts of grief from the soul." Tad, who was consumed with his own grief, would throw his arms around his mother and sob, "Don't cry so Mamma! Don't cry, or you will make me cry, too! You will break my heart."[16]

Just as when Willie had died, Mary could not control her grief and remained in her room upstairs during the funeral.

Journalists who were present at the funeral differ in their accounts as to whether Lincoln's sons attended. George Alfred Townsend reported "Tad, his face red and heated cried as if his heart would break." Noah Brooks reported Robert was the only immediate family member who attended the president's funeral: Accompanied by John Hay and John Nicolay, Robert stoically sat at the foot of his father's casket.[17]

Who planned the president's funeral?

According to Benjamin Brown French, he "gave all the directions I could as to the preparations for the funeral." He also gave directions for the

Capitol to be draped in mourning.[18] French may have taken more credit than he deserved. Lincoln's memorial service followed the customs for state funerals which had been established with the deaths of presidents William Harrison and Zachary Taylor. The responsibility of managing the details fell to George R. Harrington, the Assistant Secretary of the Treasury. Harrington most likely consulted with Robert Todd Lincoln regarding details such as who to invite, who not to invite, which minister to preside over the service—personal, family matters. Other details such as how many chairs to set up, where the press would sit, traffic control, and all other details fell to Harrington. Benjamin French visited with Harrington to "aid in making the programme (*sic*) of arrangements" for the funeral. Getting twenty-five thousand mourners in and out of the White House took skillful planning.

Luckily for future historians, Harrington arranged a press section containing fifteen chairs allowing reporters to publish firsthand accounts of the funeral.[19]

Did the Lincoln family pay for the president's funeral?
No, the U.S. government paid the $30,000 in funeral expenses. After Lincoln was buried in Springfield, creditors began to hound Benjamin French, who oversaw White House expenditures, to receive their pay. Congress was so slow in approving the funds to pay the expenses that French went to President Johnson and suggested a public auction of the mourning materials to help defray the costs.[20]

Aftermath

What happened to the various items the Lincolns wore to Ford's Theatre?
Mary gave her seamstress Elizabeth Keckly the president's cloak. Elizabeth also received the bonnet Mary wore that evening. The bonnet is currently owned by the Chicago History Museum as is the cloak worn by Mary. Pieces of Mary's dress are currently owned by a variety of historical archives.

Did Mary believe any of the conspiracy theories surrounding her husband's death?
Yes, she believed that then vice president Andrew Johnson was connected to the assassination plot. Johnson did not own a home in Washington,

but roomed at the Kirkwood House, a hotel located on Pennsylvania Avenue. Earlier in the day of the assassination, Booth stopped by the Kirkwood House to leave his calling card with the scrawled message, "Don't wish to disturb you. Are you at home? J. Wilkes Booth."[21] The desk clerk placed the card in Johnson's mailbox. Unknown to Mary, Johnson was on the list of government dignitaries to be assassinated that evening. By leaving his calling card, Booth may have been trying to determine Johnson's location for a possible attack.

In 1866, Mary wrote of concerns about a connection between Booth and Johnson to her friend, Sally Orne. Mary questioned why the card was for Johnson. She felt there was a connection between the two men. Mary despised her husband's vice president and described him as "that miserable inebriated Johnson." Her accusations were harsh; she wrote, *he* had an understanding with the conspirators & *they* knew *their man*. Did not Booth, say, 'There is one thing, he would not tell.' There is said, to be honor, among thieves."[22]

It is not known if Mary ever changed her opinion of Johnson and his connection to the assassination, but based on her reputation for holding a grudge, it is doubtful.

Did Mary ever speak or write about the events of that night?

On November 15, 1865, Mary wrote a long, chatty letter to Francis Bicknell Carpenter, who stayed at the White House for six months while he worked on his famous painting, *First Reading of the Emancipation Proclamation of President Lincoln,* which currently hangs in the United States Capitol. Mary chatted about photographs, complained about the cost of living, discussed her sons, and then turned to the fatal night. She wrote to Carpenter:

> How I wish you could have seen my dear husband, the last three weeks of his life! Having a realizing sense, that the unnatural rebellion, was near its close, & being most of the time, away from W[ashington], where he had endured such conflicts of mind, within the last four years, feeling *so encouraged,* he freely gave vent to his cheerfulness. Down the Potomac, he was almost boyish, in his mirth & reminded me, of his original nature, what I had always remembered of him, in our own home—free from care, surrounded by those he loved so well & *by whom,* he was so

idolized. *The Friday*, I never saw him so supremely cheerful—his manner was even playful. At three o'clock, in the afternoon, he drove out with me in the open carriage, in starting, I asked him, if anyone, should accompany us, he immediately replied—"No—I prefer to ride by ourselves to day." During the drive he was so gay, that I said to him, laughingly, "Dear Husband, you almost startle me by your great cheerfulness," he replied, "and well, I may feel so, Mary, I consider *this day*, the war, has come to a close—and then added, "We must *both*, be more cheerful in the future—between the war & the loss of our darling Willie—we have both, been very miserable." Every word, then uttered, is deeply engraven, on my poor broken heart. In the evening, his mind, was fixed upon having some relaxation & bent on the theater. Yet I firmly believe, that if he had remained, at the W. H. on that night of darkness, when the fiends prevailed, he would have been horribly *cut to pieces*—Those fiends, had too long contemplated, this inhuman murder, to have allowed, *him*, to escape.[23]

Slightly over a decade later, Mary wrote to her great-nephew, a brief statement about the death of loved ones and a Heavenly reunion with them. She was living in France and spent many hours remembering those she had loved and lost. She wrote of her husband, "My bereavements, have been *so* intense, the most loving and devoted of husbands, torn from my side, my hand within his own at the time."[24]

There is no other evidence that Mary spoke of the evening or wrote of it to others. Many of her letters mention her desire to die and be reunited with her husband. For Mary, this evening was not about the political changes, or the historical changes that resulted from a heinous murder. For Mary, it was about the changes in her family—the destruction of her life. She lost her comforter, her lover, her husband, her all.

Ninian Edwards and his wife, Elizabeth—Mary's oldest sister—
lived at this house in Springfield, Illinois. *Author's collection.*

C. M. Smith and his wife, Ann—Mary's younger sister—lived at this house
in Springfield. *Courtesy of The Abraham Lincoln Presidential Library Collection.*

Mary Lincoln in 1846, daguerreotype taken by Nicholas H. Shepherd.
Courtesy Library of Congress, Prints & Photographs Division, LC-USZC4-6189.

Abraham Lincoln in 1846, daguerreotype taken by Nicholas H. Shepherd.
Courtesy Library of Congress, Prints & Photographs Division, LC-DIG-npcc-19616.

Mary with her sons, Willie and Tad, in 1860. *Edward Anthony/Wikimedia Commons/Public Domain.*

Mary, Abraham, and their sons lived at the corner of Eight and Jackson Streets in Springfield, Illinois, from 1844 until they moved to Washington, D.C., in 1861. *Author's collection.*

The White House as the Lincolns knew it. *Courtesy Bauer Family Lincoln Collection.*

Mary Lincoln in 1861, wearing a striped dress she later gave to her cousin, Elizabeth Todd Grimsley. *Author's collection.*

Mary Lincoln in 1861, wearing a gown often mistaken as her inaugural ball gown. An early photograph of this image states this image was taken in 1861 by M. B. Brady at his Washington D.C. studio. *Author's collection.*

Mary Lincoln in 1861, wearing a black silk day dress
embroidered with strawberries and leaves. *From the
Lincoln Financial Foundation Collection, (LN-1083).*

It is believed Mary wore this gown in 1861 or early 1862. The engraving was published in *Harper's Weekly* in November 1862. *Author's collection.*

Frank Leslie's Illustrated Newspaper (February 22, 1862) published this engraving of the gown Mary wore to a party held on February 5 at the White House. Willie Lincoln was terribly ill, and the Lincolns took turns visiting him in his bedroom. *Author's collection.*

Just three miles from the White House, the Soldier's Home served as a summer retreat from the city, offering the Lincoln family a safer environment and relief from the heat. *From the Lincoln Financial Foundation Collection,* (71.2009.081.1703).

The Lincoln family was never photographed together. This composite image depicts the family in 1864, with Robert standing behind his parents and Tad on Abraham's left. Willie's photograph hangs on the wall. *National Portrait Gallery, Smithsonian Institution; gift of Dr. James S. Brust. https://npg.si.edu /object/npg_S_NPG.2003.37*

The white flowers in her bonnet, white undersleeves, and white collar indicate that Mary was mourning Willie when this photo was taken, circa 1863. *Courtesy Bauer Family Lincoln Collection.*

CHAPTER FIVE

Widowhood and Exile, 1865 to 1882

In this distant land . . . It is such a pleasure to be remembered, when
we are separated from those we truly love.
—Mary Lincoln to Eliza Slataper, December 13, 1868

*M*ary outlived her husband by seventeen years. Those years were filled
with unhappiness, grief, isolation, humiliation, and health issues. She became a
nomad, living in a variety of hotels, boarding houses, and the homes of relatives.
Her letters are filled with sadness, a longing to join her husband and children
in Heaven, and concerns about her financial affairs. Mary's grief consumed
her, and she gradually isolated herself from others, even those who tried to
help her. Her behavior, bitterness, and grief often caused her loved ones and
friends to avoid her.

Mary could find neither physical nor emotional rest; therefore, she traveled
throughout the United States and Europe seeking medical treatment and
solitude.

Mary's letters are filled with information about her struggles, her health,
and her travels. The Civil War diaries and memories of Mary's family and
friends provide information about her last days in the White House. Newspapers provide details about her travels, her death, and her funeral.

Questions asked about Mary concerning the last years of her life include
questions about her health, her travels, and her debts. Mary's life ended dras-
tically differently from how it began: The little, vivacious girl of the Bluegrass
had become the sad, bitter, widow.

After Lincoln's Death and the Fight to Bury the President
Who stayed/visited with Mary after the assassination?

Mrs. Keckly claimed that she was Mary's "only companion, except her children in the days of her great sorrow." Mary's sister Elizabeth sent word "as a sister and mother" offering Mary a place to stay if she wished to come to Springfield for Lincoln's funeral services. Mary requested that her cousin Elizabeth Todd Grimsley, who had recently become a widow, come to Washington, but she was unable to do so. Mary allowed few visitors. She accepted comfort from her children, and her friends Keckly, Elizabeth Dixon, and Mary Jane Welles. Others identified as visiting with Mary included Sally Orne, Elizabeth Blair Lee, and Dr. Anson G. Henry[1]

One person who did not visit Mary during this time was the new president, Andrew Johnson. Mary explained to Sally Orne that "No one ever heard, of Johnson, regretting my sainted husband's death, he never wrote me a line of condolence, and behaved in the most brutal way."[2] There is no evidence that Johnson, or his wife, ever called upon Mary to comfort her in her grief. Even if the president can be excused for not visiting due to the chaos caused by Lincoln's assassination, Victorian etiquette required that he—or someone in his administration—send a perfunctory message of condolence.

Why did Mary remain in the White House for so long after Lincoln's death?

Mary never explained why she remained in the White House for nearly 40 days after her husband's death. Most believe that she was too grief-stricken and emotionally distraught to summon the strength to go through the process of packing and moving. Mrs. Keckly remembered that upon entering Mary's room, she "found her in a new paroxysm of grief."[3] Mary had suffered loss in her life before, but to lose her husband seemed unbearable to her. Friends came to offer their sympathy, but nothing could stop Mary's tears. William H. Crook, Lincoln's body-guard, stated that, "No one could get near enough to her grief to comfort her."[4] Perhaps Mary was simply too distraught to deal with the everyday tasks of preparing to leave the White House.

Mrs. Keckly offered another explanation—there was just too much to do. Before Mary could leave Washington, there were decisions to be made and incomplete tasks to finish. Someone had to sort through the family's possessions, deciding what to give away, what to leave, and what to pack. As Mrs. Keckly explained, "Mrs. Lincoln had a passion for hoarding old things." The boxes were packed very loosely, many only holding a few items, and in Mrs. Keckly's opinion, much of their contents were "articles not worth carrying away."[5] Mary did not take all their belongings. She distributed some of the president's personal items and clothing to friends and political supporters.

Another possible reason for Mary's extended stay may give insight into her mental stability. William Crook wrote that a few days after Lincoln's death, "women spiritualists in some way gained access to her." Pretending to receive messages from Lincoln for Mary, these women filled her head with false messages from her husband. Distraught and weakened with grief, Mary clung to their messages not realizing these women were lying, and possibly did not want to leave the White House for fear the message would stop. Crook believed the women "nearly crazed her."[6] This may explain why Benjamin French believed that "the sudden and awful death of the President somewhat unhinged her mind, for at times she has exhibited all the symptoms of madness."[7]

While it is impossible to know for certain, others believe Mary remained nearly forty days for religious symbolic reasons. (If she had left six hours later, it would have been exactly forty days after Lincoln's death.) Is it worth considering Mary sought spiritual meaning and solace by spending an additional forty days in the home she shared with her husband? Or might she have been too distraught to even notice how many days had passed? Judeo-Christian scriptures use the time frame of forty days to indicate important time periods. In the Old Testament, the flood lasted for forty days. In the New Testament, Jesus was tempted in the desert for forty days, and Christ's ascension occurred forty days after his death. Would Mary have paid such close attention to a symbolic detail in her time of grief? Perhaps.

Since Lincoln was assassinated on Good Friday, ministers across the nation underscored the parallel to Jesus in their Easter morning sermons, many claiming that Lincoln's murder was the "atonement for the sins of the nation and a promise of its redemption." One such minister was Rev. Henry W. Bellows of New York, who told his congregation, "Heaven rejoices this Easter morning in the resurrection of our lost leader. Dying on the anniversary of our Lord's great sacrifice, a mighty sacrifice himself for the sins of a whole people."[8] These sermons were printed in major city newspapers, and Mary would have relished reading them and comparing her husband to Jesus. It was a comparison she continued throughout many of her letters. In 1866, she wrote of Lincoln, "the crown of immortality was his—he was rejoicing in the presence of his Savior, and was in the midst of *the* Heavenly Jerusalem, where his troubles were ended, and his life, had been sacrificed, for his love to his Country."[9]

Perhaps Mary's departure was dependent upon having a diversion occurring in Washington so the press could not turn it into a public event. On May 23 and 24, veteran troops gathered on East Capitol Street and paraded for their final review before going home to their loved ones. Benjamin French estimated "more than 50,000" participated on the first day.[10] Perhaps Mary longed to leave the city before this military display. President Johnson and General Grant would have been present and leaving gave Mary an excellent excuse to avoid them.

Or, perhaps her reason for overstaying her welcome was much simpler. William Crook recorded that Mary had been weakened by the events of her husband's death, and that her physician, Doctor Stone, refused to allow Mary to be removed from the White House until she was somewhat restored.[11]

Whatever the reason for the timing of her departure, it was time for Mary to leave Washington.

What "loose ends" did Mary need to settle before leaving the White House?

In addition to packing, Mary wrote letters of recommendation for those Abraham had planned to help find new positions She had to settle some debts. She and Robert came to an agreement for a final resting place in Oak Ridge Cemetery for Lincoln. When Mary read in the newspapers that her wishes were not going to be followed, but instead those of the newly formed National Lincoln Monument Association which had formed in Springfield, Mary was about to have a fight on her hands against family and friends.[12]

Did Mary make the arrangements for Lincoln's burial in Springfield?

Shortly after Lincoln's death, a group of Illinois citizens formed the National Lincoln Monument Association. The group, consisting entirely of men—powerful men, such as Governor Richard Oglesby, Mary's cousin John Todd Stuart, local and state politicians, and men who had been long trusted friends to Mary and Abraham. As committees often do, this one began to flex its muscle. Their intent was to build a burial vault on the highest point of ground within city limits, visible from the Chicago and Alton Railroad, and suitable as a place to attract future tourists to downtown Springfield. Located in an area known as Vinegar Hill, the Mather Block was, indeed, an honorable place of burial for the martyred president. It sat in the southwest area of town, along Second Street, between Jackson and Monroe. It was the perfect location. The problem was that no one consulted Mary, or her children, about their desires. And Mary refused to be forced to stare at her husband's gravesite every time she visited her sister Elizabeth, whose home also was located on South Second Street.

According to Isaac Arnold, when the Lincolns were visiting Virginia, they had gone for a drive through the countryside and stopped by a peaceful graveyard. Lincoln said to his wife, "Mary, you are younger than I. You will survive me. When I am gone, lay my remains in some quiet place like this."[13] Those words were embedded in Mary's memory, and she was determined her husband's wishes would be fulfilled. She wanted a place where the entire family could be buried together, and she was determined Lincoln would be buried in Oak Ridge Cemetery with "the written promise that no other bodies, save the President, his Wife, his Sons & Sons families, shall ever be deposited within the enclosure."[14]

Oak Ridge Cemetery, located on Monument Avenue, north of North Grand Avenue, now lies within in the city limits of Springfield. However, it 1865, it was three miles north of the city. Mary was determined to win this battle.

The Mather Block eventually became the location of the new Illinois State Capitol Building.

How did Mary finally convince the Lincoln Monument Association?

Mary showered Governor Oglesby with letters of protest. In a letter dated June 10, 1865, Mary wrote, "If I had anticipated, so much trouble, in having my wishes carried out, I should have readily yielded to the request of the *many* & had *his* precious remains, in the *first instance* placed in the vault of the National Capitol."[15] The following day, she again wrote to Oglesby, "It is very painful to me, to be treated in this manner, by some of those I considered my friends."[16] Still, the committee ignored her. Mary enlisted the assistance of two relatives, her son Robert and her cousin John Blair Smith (JBS) Todd, and two friends, Secretary of War Edwin Stanton, and Dr. Anson G. Henry. A series of telegrams went back and forth between Springfield and Washington. Those in Washington argued that the family's wishes must be considered, and the group in Springfield argued that plans in Springfield had progressed too far to be changed.

The tone of the telegrams between Robert, John Todd Stuart, and JBS Todd provide glimpses into family personalities and hierarchies. John Todd Stuart seems to have thought of himself as a family patriarch. Robert's telegrams are polite and request that his mother's wishes be followed. The reply dismissed Robert's request. Robert insisted, and was told that plans had already been made, and the committee's plans were best for the community. The conversation went back and forth for a few days. The telegrams from JBS Todd were more forceful. His messages included comments such as "the remains of the President shall be deposited in Oak Ridge Cemetery and nowhere else. See that it is done." By the end of April, the Springfield group was still fighting Mary's wishes. JBS Todd once again sent a telegram to Stuart stating: "Have your dispatch of 29th. The remains of the President must be placed in the vault of Oak Ridge Cemetery—and nowhere else. This is Mrs. Lincoln's fixed determination. My letters of the 28th and 29th explain her news fully. Your arrangements for using the Mather Vault must be changed."[17]

The final letters written to the committee threatened to bury Lincoln in Chicago. The committee agreed to a monument in Oak Ridge Cemetery, and by the time Robert arrived in Springfield to bury his father, all was settled. Robert wrote to Stuart saying that he had shown Mary a map of the cemetery and she was "well pleased with the selection of a lot." Stuart and the other members of the association had finally agreed to bury Lincoln in Oak Ridge Cemetery—a place Mary found suitable for a funeral monument. Mary and Robert were pleased with the selection. Robert wrote to Stuart, "I suppose there will be no trouble on this point."[18]

When did Mary finally leave the White House?

After the battle over her husband's burial location, Mary was able to finish packing her things and leave the White House for the final time on May 22, 1865, slightly after 6:00 p.m. in an unceremonious fashion.[19] Mr. French came to bid her farewell. Mary was accompanied by her two sons, her friends Dr. Anson Henry and Elizabeth Keckly, and two guards, Thomas Cross and William Crook. Mrs. Keckly noted that "there was scarcely a friend to tell her good-by." In a painful silence, the widow and her party "passed down the public stairway, entered her carriage, and quietly drove to the depot."[20]

How many trunks full of stuff did Mary take from the White House when she left?

Keckly recorded that Mary had "fifty or sixty boxes, not to count her score of trunks."[21]

What was in Mary's trunks when she left the White House?

Personal items such as her clothing and the clothing of her children were packed. Voluminous ball gowns, dresses, hoops, underpinnings, and bonnets required numerous boxes and trunks. She certainly would have taken Tad's and Robert's personal belongs such as books and toys. Other items in her trunks included accessories, personal china, silver sets, her personal letters from Abraham, and other small items. Lincoln's two secretaries, Hay and Nicolay, along with Robert Lincoln, packed Lincoln's presidential papers and shipped them to David Davis; he stored them in a bank vault for several years.

After Mary left Washington, rumors flew concerning the disappearance of White House furnishings. Some suggested Mary stole them while others claimed she sold them. During the days leading up to Lincoln's funeral, thousands of visitors filed past his coffin to get a glimpse of the slain president and, perhaps, to take a souvenir or two. Due to a lack of supervision, it was believed that several of the servants had carried away pieces of furniture.[22]

Months after President Johnson and his family moved in, a Committee on Appropriations of the House investigated the lack of housekeeping items found in the White House. According to Benjamin French, the bedding, table linens, and all necessary housekeeping utensils were gone, but he had no knowledge as to how they had disappeared. The committee did not find any evidence that Mary had taken, or sold, anything that did not belong to her.[23]

In Mourning and Creating Financial Mayhem

Was Mary truly poor? Was she in debt when she left the White House?

Poor—no; in debt—yes. The exact amount of Mary's debt is unknown.

According to Elizabeth Keckly, Mary confided that she was deeply in debt. Much of the debt was owed to stores for clothing expenses worn to official receptions and events held in preparation for the inauguration and its festivities. Mary also claimed that sometimes Benjamin French was too slow to pay bills for governmental expenses, and she had to personally pay for ordered items that actually belonged to the White House. According to Keckly, Mary believed if politicians learned the particulars of her debts, the information could be used against Lincoln during his reelection campaign in 1864. Keckly claimed prior to the election, Mary's debts amounted to twenty-seven thousand dollars.[24]

The exact amount of Mary's bills is unknown. In 1868, Keckly estimated them to be seventy thousand dollars. Historian Jean Baker estimated the amount to be closer to ten thousand dollars. Other historians have reported the estimates range from six to seventy thousand dollars.[25]

How did Mary get out of debt?

To lower her debt, Mary sought ways to raise funds with the help of her friends. A letter to Sally Orne contained a request to purchase, or help find someone who would purchase, "a *very* elegant lace dress . . . lace flounce . . . double lace shawl" that were valued at $3,500. Mary was willing to part with these articles for $2,500. Mary also offered white moire silk for eleven dollars per yard, and another silk dress for $125. None of Mary's friends accepted her offer.[26] She engaged the assistance of Alexander Williamson to run errands, return items, haggle with creditors to lower bills, find buyers for items such as Lincoln's carriage, and solicit funds from political allies.[27] To further raise funds, Mary enlisted the help of Noah Brooks to sell three certificates for wildcat stock in a silver mine she identified as the "Nevada Claims." Not wanting to be listed as a stockholder while Lincoln was president, Mary had purchased the certificates under the name Frances T. Lincoln. The certificates were never sold, and Mary never received anything from her investment.[28]

Within weeks of the president's death, the *New York Tribune* released an article requesting the American people to collect $100,000 to help Lincoln's widow and his children. Several fund-raising campaigns were organized, including one by James Y. Smith, the governor of Rhode Island.[29]

Williamson was successful in raising some funds for Mary. She wrote specific instructions encouraging him to call upon various politicians, friends, businessmen—men of wealth—whom she believed would be sympathetic to her cause. She instructed Williamson to sign the letters "Charles Forsyth" and promised to give a portion of the money collected to him.[30]

Mary was never able to raise the amount of money she had hoped for. She cut her expenses by choosing to live in a cheaper boarding room in Chicago. She lived a frugal lifestyle—at least for someone of her social station. As a result of her efforts, Mary was able to clear her debts, but she continued to economize for the remainder of her life.

Did she inherit money from Lincoln's estate?

Yes—eventually. Although Lincoln had practiced law for years, he did not legally prepare for his own death. He never wrote a personal will. By noon of April 15, 1865, Robert Lincoln sent a telegram to family friend Judge David Davis asking him to come to Washington to oversee the estate. It would not be an easy task, but Davis assumed the responsibility.[31] Newspaper reports estimated the estate value to be $75,000, but it was closer to $85,000. The estate would be divided equally three ways, among Mary and her two living sons. Mary's annual income from the estate was between $1,500 and $1,800 depending upon interest rates. Tad's portion was placed in a trust until he was twenty-one years of age. Mary described her annual income as "A clerk's salary." When the estate was finally settled in 1867, Davis took no pay for his years of service to the family. As the widow, Mary could have received an additional cash allowance, but she refused it. The Lincoln family was grateful for Davis's shrewd management of the estate. By the time it was settled, the estate was worth $110,296.80 to be divided equally among the three heirs. Mary's portion was $36,991.54.[32]

Did she receive a pension?

Mary petitioned Congress to award her the one hundred-thousand-dollar salary Lincoln would have made as president over the four years of his second term. They granted her twenty-five thousand dollars, or one year's salary, tax free. The fight for more money quickly followed.

On January 14, 1869, Oliver P. Morton of Indiana introduced a bill in the Senate for financial relief for Mary. He stated that "upon the same principles and for the like reasons with any other officer who fell in the war" Mary should receive a pension. Morton did not suggest an amount for the pension, so Charles Sumner made the request for an annual pension of five thousand dollars. In March, the issue came to vote, and failed. Sumner tried to have the bill voted upon again, and it was thrown back to committee. On May 2, 1870, the House of Representatives passed a bill awarding Mary a pension of three thousand dollars per year. However, the next day when it was read before the Senate, it was revealed that the Pensions Committee still had the original Senate bill. Their decision was to table the matter indefinitely.

Mary's reputation again became fodder for the press. Most reporters believed Mary did not need a pension because between the money Congress had allotted her, and her share of Lincoln's estate, she was a wealthy woman with a personal wealth of over fifty-eight thousand dollars. Mary was accused of living "royally" and above her means. It was insinuated she had pilfered public funds for private use. Richard Yates of Illinois even went as far as to stand in the Senate and attack Mary's loyalties during the war. He claimed that Mary was sympathetic to her Confederate relations and, therefore, had been disloyal and unfaithful to her husband.[33]

Finally, enough was enough. The lady's reputation had been tarnished and trashed. On July 14, 1870, Simon Cameron of Pennsylvania recalled good memories and spoke of when the Lincolns first came to Washington. He spoke about how the gossips of the town did everything they could to destroy the reputation of the Lincolns. They could not destroy Lincoln, but they could tarnish Mary. He called for a vote, and the bill passed. It was signed by President Grant on the same day.

The fight was over, and Mary Lincoln became the first presidential widow to receive a pension.

Why did Mary choose to live in Chicago?

It was a major city and a short train ride to Springfield, but far enough away from Springfield that she did not have to face family and friends. When Rev. Gurley traveled to Springfield for Lincoln's funeral, he was surprised to hear the residents speak harshly about Mary. He later wrote,

"Hard things are said of her by all classes of people, and when I got to know how she was regarded by her old neighbors and even by her relatives in S I did not wonder that she had decided to make her future home in Chicago."[34]

Where did Mary live?

Mary moved frequently during her time in Chicago. Upon first arriving, the Lincoln family moved into an apartment at the Tremont House. It was a large and popular hotel, but it proved to be too expensive for the family. Robert moved the family to Hyde Park just seven miles south of the downtown area. Mary then purchased a home on West Washington Street. Within a year, she rented her home and moved into the Clifton House located at Wabash Avenue and Madison Street. A few months later, Mary returned to her old neighborhood. Not satisfied, she again returned to the Clifton House.

When Mary and Tad returned from Europe, they stayed with Robert and his family on South Wabash but they did not stay long. On June 8, Mary wrote to her friend, Rhoda White, to address future letters to room 21 at Clifton House, then located at the corner of Washington and Halsted streets.[35] The two were living at the Clifton House when Tad died. After the loss of her son, Mary returned to Robert's home. She was there during the Great Chicago Fire on October 9, 1871.

By 1874, Mary rented a room at the Grand Central Hotel on LaSalle Street.[36] By April 1875, she was lodging at the Grand Central Hotel in Chicago.[37]

Did Mary ever purchase a home?

In June 1866, Mary was able to purchase and furnish a modest stone-front home located at 375 West Washington Street in Chicago. Her stay there was short-lived. By September of the following year, Mary was writing to friends about her need to economize and complained, "I find it will be absolutely impossible to continue housekeeping on my present means."[38] Her plans were to move out of the house and rent it, sell her furniture, and look for a cheaper place to live. She also devised a way to generate funds from pieces of her old wardrobe. By trying to sell her clothes and jewels, she could create funds to maintain her lifestyle. Instead, she created more scandal.

What was the "Old Clothes Scandal?"

According to Elizabeth Keckly, when packing to leave the White House, Mary turned and said, "Lizzie, I may see the day when I shall be obliged to sell a portion of my wardrobe. If Congress does not do something for me, then my dresses some day may have to go to bring food into my mouth, and the mouths of my children."[39] On September 16, 1867, Mary's foreboding became reality. Planning to wear mourning attire for the rest of her life, Mary had no future use for her fashionable wardrobe. Her gowns were made of the finest materials and if sold, Mary could invest the money and earn a modest income from the interest. Under the assumed name of "Mrs. Clark" from Chicago, Mary tried to sell her elaborate wardrobe through the establishment of Brady & Company, located at 609 Broadway in New York. Mary wished to remain incognito, thinking that if her name were attached to the sale, serious buyers would be hindered from attending and the crowds would be mostly curiosity seekers. William Brady and his partner Samuel Keyes convinced her that if her identity and financial needs were made known to the public, a larger sum could be raised. Soon, the garments were displayed at Brady's store, but the results were the opposite of what the interested parties had expected. Not only did the plan back-fire, it failed miserably.

Articles began to appear in newspapers across the country with titles such as "Disgraceful," "Something to Wear," and "Disrespectfully Dedicated to Mrs. Abraham Lincoln."[40] The press printed former accusations about Mary's loyalty to the government during the war. She was accused of stealing furniture and other bits of government property from the White House. One newspaper accused Mary of pretending to be pregnant so she could stay in the White House longer to pack up more valuables. Another newspaper claimed Mary was about to marry again. Mary felt betrayed by Mr. Brady. Private letters she had written to him found their way to the printed pages of The New York World. The sale was not only a flop; it was a nightmare that was a personal and financial blow to Mary.

There were not accurate records kept as to what was taken to Brady's, what was sold, and what was returned to Mary. The newspapers mentioned a few specific gowns including Mary's attire for her husband's second inauguration. One source reported this set included a dress, handkerchief, flounces, white point lace shawl, and a parasol cover. Originally valued at nearly forty-five hundred dollars, these items were considered a bargain at the asking price of two thousand dollars. This was an obscene amount of money. Just two years before, *Peterson's Magazine* had advertised a three-story suburban residence complete with modern water closets for slightly over four thousand dollars.[41]

Travels Abroad and Domestic

Why did Mary and Tad move to Europe?

The American press had been relentless in their criticism about Mary's financial status and questioned her mental state openly after the Old Clothes Scandal. She felt that wherever she went, people stared at her out of curiosity and pity. She had no peace. The thought that she could live more cheaply in Europe was appealing. Plus, Tad needed to attend school where his daily routines would not be published in the newspapers because he was the fallen president's son. He also needed discipline—something German schools excelled in instilling, Mary could achieve a quieter, more peaceful life, for her and her son in Europe.

Where did Mary travel in Europe?

Mary and Tad boarded the steamer the *City of Baltimore* on October 1, 1868. Their passage was paid for by a stranger, a man named Joseph Seligman who lived in New York. He had read about Mary's financial status in the *New York World* and wanted to help her. For the next several years, Joseph and his brothers sent money to Mary and looked after her.[42]

Mary and Tad left Baltimore and docked in Bremen, Germany. Immediately, they moved to Frankfurt-am-Main where they occupied one room at the Hotel d'Angleterre, the city's most expensive grand hotel. It proved to be too pricey, and shortly afterward they moved to the Hotel de Holland on Goethplatz 5. Tad attended school at Dr. Johann Heinrich Hohagen's Educational Institute and Business School. It was in the upscale West end located at Kettenhofweg 15.[43]

For a short time, Mary was happy in Frankfurt. She wrote to her friend Eliza Slataper, "I like Frankfort exceedingly, the true secret is, I suppose I am enjoying peace." Mary wrote of her upcoming plans to travel to Italy and how she had visited a "building 1,000 years old to see portraits of about fifty German Emperors."[44]

Her peace did not last, for everyone in town seemed to know who she was. Being the widow of an American president, local merchants and hotel managers thought Mary was a woman of wealth. They charged her top prices for goods and services, and her ideas of living cheaply were crushed.[45]

Due to the expense, her trip to Italy was postponed. When the weather became too cold in Frankfurt, Mary traveled to Nice, France.

Mary's most enjoyable European journey was in the summer of 1869 when she and Tad spent seven weeks sightseeing. They began the trip by traveling through Paris to London, spending five days in each city. The two then traveled to Scotland where they visited Edinburgh, Glasgow, Alloway (the birthplace of Robert Burns), numerous castles, and many other places of interest. They visited with their former pastor, Rev. James Smith who had been the pastor of the First Presbyterian Church in Springfield and was now the U.S. Consul to Dundee. Mary remembered her trip in a letter, "I cannot begin to enumerate, all the places of interest we visited. I *am convinced,* that I shall never again be able to arouse myself to take *such another* interest in any other country, I may chance to visit."[46] Mary and Tad returned to Frankfurt via Brussels and went to the battlefield of Waterloo.

After returning to Germany, Mary traveled within the country; she went first to Cronberg to visit a castle. After Tad finished his education at Hohagen's Institute, he spent two months attending school in Oberursel, just outside of Frankfurt. While living in Frankfurt, Mary wrote several letters to friends complaining of her health and her lack of funds.[47]

In June of 1870, mother and son were again in Frankfurt, but they would not remain there long. Tad was to attend school in Brixton, just outside of London. Mary's travels took her to Innsbruck, in Tyrol in western Austria; back to Frankfurt; York, England; Leamington Spa, Warwickshire, England; and then to London where she rented rooms in Woburn Place, off Russell Square. A month later, Mary escaped the cold weather of London by traveling through Tyrol, Milan, Lake Como, Genoa, Florence, and Venice. On April 29, 1871, Mary and Tad boarded the *Russia* in Liverpool and were on their way home to America.[48]

Did Mary meet Queen Victoria?

In a letter to Rhoda White (dated August 30, 1869) Mary wrote that she "visited Balmoral —when the Queen was absent."[49] Therefore, most historians have concluded that the two women did not meet. However, according to family legend, Mary did meet Queen Victoria—or at least she attended the queen's court. If the legend is true, the meeting probably occurred in 1871 when Mary was living in London.

According to descendants of Mary's niece, Louisa Todd Keys, Mary was presented at court at St. James's Palace. Because Queen Victoria wore perpetual mourning for her husband, Prince Albert, it would have been inappropriate for those attending court to wear mourning attire. No one should "out mourn" the queen in her own home. Thus, Mary had a gown of white silk fashioned for the event. A few years later, Mary gave the gown to her niece, Louisa. When Louisa was a young child, her mother died, and her father (Mary's brother Levi) sent her to Springfield to live with his and Mary's sister, Ann Smith. Family members recalled Louisa had the dress's skirt altered into a "dancing skirt" when she wore it at her October 10, 1876 wedding to Edward Keys.[50]

Even though some family members insist the story about the dress is true, others disagree. Shortly after Mary embarked on her second journey to Europe, Elizabeth Edwards wrote to Robert about his mother's travel plans. She mentioned that before Mary left, she pulled the dress from one of her trunks to give to Louisa. According to Elizabeth, the white silk had yellowed with age, and Mary had never worn the gown.[51]

Where did Mary travel in the United States?

During the White House years, Mary had managed several vacations from Washington. She made shopping trips to Philadelphia, Boston, and New York. She visited the seashore. With the president, she visited a few battle fields and City Point at the close of the war. Her most enjoyable vacation was one made with Tad to the White Mountains in New Hampshire during the summer of 1863. Robert joined his mother and brother during the trip, and the three of them had a pleasant trip away from the summer heat of Washington.[52]

Once Mary moved to Chicago after Abraham's death, she did not travel much until 1867. She went to Racine, Wisconsin looking for a proper school for Tad. (She chose to enroll him in Chicago Academy instead.) Then she traveled to New York to sell her wardrobe. She made a few trips to Springfield. Mary and Tad then left to spend time in the Alleghenies at a health resort in Cresson Springs, Pennsylvania, and then went to Baltimore before Robert's wedding to Mary Harlan in Washington. After the wedding she made a brief stop again in Baltimore before leaving for Europe.[53]

When Mary and Tad returned to the United States, she once again made her home at the Clifton House in Chicago. Tad's death on July 15, 1871 put Mary into a tailspin. As her own health failed her, Mary traveled looking for medical treatment, rest, and peace. She traveled to Waukesha, Wisconsin to a health resort. In 1873, Mary traveled to Canada. In December, Mary wrote to her cousin, John Todd Stuart, "whilst in Canada for months" and nothing more was mentioned about her trip.[54] She traveled frequently, and in 1875 made a long trip south to Florida, where she spent three months in Green Cove, Florida. The closest city to Green Cove which was used for communication and transportation was Jacksonville. During this trip, she became frantic about Robert's health and sent a telegram to his law partner expressing her concerns for her son. She then sent a telegram to be delivered to Robert stating, "My dearly beloved Son Robert T. Lincoln rouse yourself—and live for my sake." She returned to Chicago to find Robert, his wife, and the children well. Mary was frantic, and the battle over her mental state and her freedom began.[55]

After Mary's second insanity trial and after her belongings were restored to her by court order in 1876, she made one more long journey in America. While Mary stayed with her sister Elizabeth, she developed a close relationship with her sister's grandson, Edward Lewis Baker, Jr. He had been living with his grandparents while his parents were in Argentina on a diplomatic mission. "Lewis" reminded Mary of her beloved Tad, and she was able to dote on him as she longed to do for her own son. Lewis was able to help calm his great-aunt Mary, making her feel safe and protected. When Mary decided to relocate to France, she asked Lewis to escort her to New York. In 1876, the two took the scenic route and traveled to Kentucky on their way to New York. In Lexington Mary was able to "enjoy herself for a day or two in visiting scenes of her childhood." It is unclear if they visited with anyone while in Lexington. They did manage a trip to Mammoth Cave, the longest cave system in the world.[56]

Other than family members, did Mary have traveling companions?
Mary often wrote of seeing friends during her travels, but none of them traveled with her. Robert hired at least one nurse to accompany his

mother during her illnesses and during some of her travels. He reportedly hired Mary Fitzgerald, a widow from Chicago and the mother of famous actor and vaudeville star, Eddie Foy Sr. Mrs. Fitzgerald was hired as a "nurse, guard, and companion" beginning in February of 1872. She mostly stayed with Mary in Springfield, but she did make one or two trips with her.[57]

Sometimes after a death, the mourner idealizes the deceased. Did Mrs. Lincoln idealize her marriage to Lincoln after his death?

She idealized and idolized Lincoln in her letters. Mary often referred to Abraham as her *beloved* or *idolized* husband. She also referenced him as "the best man that ever lived." Shortly after Lincoln's death, Mary dubbed him the "immortal Savior & Martyr for Freedom." It seems that her mission was to immortalize her husband throughout the world by using emotional language.[58]

Did Mary's high emotions help found these images she maintained about her marriage?

Probably. Just as she manipulated words to describe Lincoln, Mary used impassioned verbiage to convey her own status as a widow. By using expressions such as "bowed down & heart broken, in my terrible bereavement," by describing herself as "blind with weeping," and having "passed through such a baptism of sorrow," Mary was able to elevate her image as a widow. She was not just a widow; she was *the widow* of the greatest man and martyr of the country, perhaps even the world.[59]

Did Mary live, or stay, in a convent in Racine, Wisconsin?

She did not. This story began with a Lincoln collector who learned that a damaged portrait of an unknown woman had been found in a barn. The subject of the portrait "resembled" Mary Lincoln; therefore, the collector purchased the painting and had it restored. The portrait's subject wears a headdress like one worn by Spanish Catholics during the mid-nineteenth century. The unknown lady's jewelry clearly depicts her Catholic faith. She sits next to a window overlooking what appears to be a church or monastery. According to the collector, the portrait looked like Mary; he paid a large sum of money to have it restored; he hung it in a museum; therefore, without a doubt, the subject of the portrait had to be Mary Lincoln when she stayed in a convent in Racine, Wisconsin.

The theory is flawed because the subject of the portrait is not Mary Lincoln. The clothing and jewelry of the portrait's subject clearly indicates the lady was Catholic. Mary was not. Even if there was a remote possibility that Mary donned this style of attire to hide her identity, she never stayed in a convent in Racine, Wisconsin—for one has never existed.

What did Mary do in Pau?

When Mary first arrived in France, she took a room at the Hotel de la Paix, Place Royale in Pau where she stayed "in the strictest secrecy."[60] She roomed there for about three weeks before moving to the Grand Hotel on Montpensier Street. Still trying to live as frugally as possible, Mary finally settled in the less expensive Henri IV which overlooked a noisy marketplace. She did travel to various parts of France and Italy, but always returned to Pau. Many Americans came to Pau, and the English language was almost as common as French. Her health prevented her from traveling far. Mary did travel to Paris, and she was able to go to Rome. She visited mineral baths, sought out medical facilities, and wrote many letters to Jacob Bunn of Springfield who was handling her financial matters. Mary wrote letters to some family members, including her nephew, Lewis Baker. She sent a few gifts to her granddaughter, Mary "Mamie," but if she wrote to her son, Robert, the letters have never been found.

What was the last photo of Mary?

The last known photo of Mary was the "ghost" photo taken about 1872. Mary always had a strong belief in spiritualism which helped satisfy her desires to reach those lost to her by death. When Mary attended a séance in Boston, she believed she felt Abraham's hand rest on her shoulders.

Spirit photographer William H. Mumler reinforced Mary's belief when he presented her with a photograph as "proof" that Lincoln's spirit did indeed visit and comfort her. According to Mumler, a lady wearing the deepest of mourning attire and a heavy veil came to him using the name "Mrs. Lindall." After her photo was taken, Mumler's wife, who was a medium, had to encourage the heavily veiled woman to identify the ghost image in the photo. Mary thought she could keep her identity unknown.

The photograph is not flattering to Mary. The evidence of her grief and weeping are evident in the photo. She appears older than her years with a sagging face and clouded eyes. In the image, the ghost of Lincoln stands behind his widow, his hands resting on her shoulder, and his eyes looking downward at her.

Mary may have been convinced, but Robert was not. In addition to the absurd notion that someone could conjure spirits for photographs, he also found the cost of the photo extravagant. Mumler "charged ten dollars per photograph at a time, when an average portrait costs merely pennies."[61] For Robert, it was one more piece of evidence that led him to doubt his mother's ability to reason and make rational choices.

Final Return to Springfield and Final Days

When did Mary return to the United States? Where did she live?

Mary left Europe on October 16, 1880 aboard the *L'Amerique*. During the voyage, Mary was standing at the top of a stairway when the ship jerked due to rough waters. She nearly tumbled down the stairs, but another woman grabbed Mary's skirt to prevent what may have been a fatal accident. The lady who grabbed Mary's skirts was the famous actress, Sarah Bernhardt. Upon learning that she had saved the life of the widow of President Lincoln, Sarah felt: "I had just done this unhappy woman the only service that I ought not to have done her—I had saved her from death."[62]

The boat was scheduled to dock in New York, and Mary asked her grand-nephew Lewis Baker to meet her there. Mary was returning to Springfield to live with her sister Elizabeth. To help cover her expenses, Mary paid $125 per month to rent a room in the home where she had married her beloved Mr. Lincoln so many years ago.

Did Mary ever reconcile with Robert?

In May 1881, Robert stopped in Springfield en route to Fort Leavenworth, Kansas. While in town, he stayed at the Leland Hotel. His cousin, Fannie Wallace, had died unexpectedly and Robert planned to visit his Aunt Frances Todd Wallace and her family. Robert spent an entire day with his mother and the Edwards family. The visit had been arranged by Elizabeth Edwards. Until this visit, Mary had not been willing to see her son. It was through Elizabeth's coaxing that the mother and son were reunited. According to historian Jason Emerson, Elizabeth was "probably the only person who *could* have brought them together." She understood her sister's moods and tantrums and was able to help Mary work through the past hurts to reestablish a relationship with Robert and his family.

Robert later brought his daughter Mamie to see her grandmother. During the remaining few months of Mary's life, Robert and his family visited a few times.[63]

Was Mary pleased when Robert was appointed Secretary of War?

A journalist visiting Mary in 1881 did not think so. He commented, "She has not smiled over congratulations on Robert's honorable account." It was with a heart broken by her husband's assassination, and the concerned heart of a mother, that Mary would sit and repeat, "Secretary of War? Secretary of War? Then he'll be shot for sure! That's always the way in war."[64]

What did Mary do in Springfield during her final years?

According to family members she mostly stayed in her room, mended her dresses, and packed and unpacked her trunks over and over. Elizabeth was overheard to express her amazement that Mary, who was ill and mostly bedridden, "was able to be up all day bending over her trunks." Robert was happy that Mary was no longer buying items, although she did manage to purchase a "silk cloak lined with white ermine and a lace shawl totaling $700."[65] Elizabeth's granddaughter, Mary Brown, recalled that one of the upstairs floors sagged from the weight of sixty-four trunks and crates packed with her aunt's clothes and personal belongings. According to Brown, one of Elizabeth's maids left because she was afraid to be in the room that stored Mary's trunks for fear of the floor giving way. Mary enjoyed spending her time looking at her treasures and remembering happier times. She was preoccupied by a deep desire to die and was convinced she would do so soon.[66]

Did Mary know of the attempts to steal her husband's body?

There is no evidence that she knew about the attempt, but it seems likely she did. The attempt to steal Lincoln's body occurred on November 7, 1876, at which time Mary was living in Pau, France. Few of her letters from this time exist, and those that do were written to her banker, Jacob Bunn. The letters are mostly about her finances, but there are a few personal tidbits of information. On December 12, Mary wrote that she had received a letter from Elizabeth Edwards concerning the health of Mr. Jesse Dubois. In the same letter, Mary wrote that she read the "Daily Galignani of Paris, which receives constant news, from America." Mary had access to American newspapers including the New York Times, New York Tribune, and the Herald. One would think that trying to steal the martyred president's body would have been considered newsworthy by at least one newspaper.[67]

How many times did Mary visit Abraham's grave?

In December 1865, Mary, Robert, and Tad traveled to Springfield for the removal of Lincoln's body from the receiving vault to the temporary tomb. Mary later wrote to her friend, Sally Orne saying, "I was not present, at the removal, but passed the morning of the same day, there, accompanied, by my dear son Robert & Cousin John T. Stuart."[68] To Mary Jane Welles, she wrote of her trip to Springfield and the cemetery and described how Stuart had showed her the "niche" beside Lincoln's resting place that was reserved for her.[69]

In September 1866, President Johnson and a party of friends traveled through Illinois. Mary wished to be out of town when they came to Chicago, and chose that time to visit her husband's grave. By the time the Johnson party arrived in Springfield, Mary was en route back to Chicago, thus avoiding the president in both cities.[70]

While these are documented trips to Lincoln's grave site, there were probably more. During her final years, when Mary lived with her sister, there would have been many opportunities to take a carriage ride to Oak Ridge. Such visits would have been private and not recorded.

What illness and ailments did Mary have when she died?

While living in Pau, Mary wrote that she had drunk Vichy water, a mineral water which was used to treat a variety of ailments including diabetes, disorders of the kidneys, gout, rheumatism, stomach disorders, and several other conditions.[71] Mary wrote explaining the waters were not helpful, "However, I was not very much in need of them save for the continual running waters, so disagreeable and inconvenient."[72] The evidence of urinary incontinence and her rapid weight loss are both symptoms of diabetes. She had written to her nephew in 1879, "My great bloat has left me & I have returned to my natural size." She later wrote to him, "I have now run down to 100-pounds, EXACTLY."[73] Mary's obituary published in the *Chicago Tribune* listed her ailments, including the boils that ravaged her body. She had pain in her left side and back, and she was lame and ailing. The slightest light hurt her eyes, and she mostly stayed in a darkened room. The obituary stated that Mary "underwent treatment for a disease of the eyes and for diabetes".[74]

Was Robert with Mary when she died? Who was with her?

Mary died at her sister Elizabeth's home. Robert was not there as he was serving as Secretary of War and living in Washington, D.C. Mary was surrounded by her sisters Elizabeth Edwards and Ann Smith, her physician Dr. T. W. Dresser, and various other family members.[75]

When did Mary die?

On the afternoon of July 15, 1882, Mary collapsed. She slipped into a peaceful sleep (which is thought to have been a diabetic coma or a stroke) and received her "beloved sleep" the next evening, July 16, 1882 at 8:15 p.m.[76]

What was Mary's cause of death?

Dr. Thomas W. Dresser listed "paralysis" as the cause of death on Mary's death certificate. In his letter to Jesse Weik, Dr. Dresser stated Mary's cause of death "a slight apoplexy, producing paralysis." He concluded that he believed Mary suffered from a cerebral disease. More modern historians agree that Mary died from a stroke which may have been caused from untreated diabetes.[77]

What were Mary's last words?

"I am dying."[78]

Was there an autopsy performed on Mary? Was a brain tumor found in the autopsy?

There is a rumor that there was an autopsy. However, there was no autopsy, making it impossible to know whether Mary had a brain tumor. To say she had one is pure speculation.

In his 1927 book, *The Women Lincoln Loved*, William E. Barton wrote that Mary's attending physician "issued a statement that for years she had been the victim of a cerebral disease."[79] Years later, author Patricia Bell wrote, "But Mary Lincoln probably cannot be held responsible for her most maddening traits, because they were either directly attributable to or heightened by a mental illness not understood in her own day. An autopsy performed at her death revealed that Mrs. Lincoln had been suffering from a brain tumor; all her life she had been subject to severe headaches."[80] Since then, several writers of both fiction and nonfiction have helped perpetuate the rumor that Mary suffered from a brain tumor.

Did Mary have a large funeral?

Mary had given specific instruction about her wishes for funeral arrangements. She had wanted to be buried in a white silk dress, but that particular dress could not be found. White was considered the deepest mourning color, and many Victorian women were given a "white funeral." Shortly after Mary's death, Elizabeth and Ninian sent a telegram to Chicago for white silk thus ensuring that Mary would be buried in a white dress even if not the one she had planned."[81]

Mary's body lay in the north double parlor of the Edward's home, the same parlor in which she had married Abraham some forty years before. The newspaper reporters remarked that her "hands were visible in the casket and they noticed her wedding ring."[82]

The funeral service was held at the First Presbyterian Church on July 19. All Springfield businesses closed in honor of Mary, and the church was filled with mourners. Honorary pallbearers Governor Shelby M. Cullom, Judge Samuel H. Treat (judge of the United States District Court) and Colonel John Williams (a Springfield merchant and banker) entered the church in front of Mary's casket. Carrying the casket were Esq. James C. Conkling (friend to Abraham and Mary since before their marriage), Milton Hay (Springfield lawyer and family friend), General John A. McClernand, Ozies M. Hatch (former Illinois Secretary of State), Captain John S. Bradford, and Jacob Bunn (both Springfield merchants).[83]

The church was decorated with several large floral displays including a three-foot-tall floral representation of "Pearly Gates Ajar" which stood behind Mary's casket. Under the symbolic arch was a bust of Abraham Lincoln. Three ministers spoke at the funeral. Reverend R. O. Post of the First Congregational Church read scripture and led a prayer. Reverend James A. Reed from First Presbyterian Church gave the sermon, in which he compared Abraham and Mary's lives to two large pine trees which had grown so closely together that their roots were intertwined. One tree was killed during a storm. Years later, the other tree wasted away and died as well—so it was with Abraham and Mary. The funeral ended with a prayer led by Reverend T. A. Parker of First Methodist Church.[84]

The mourners followed the carriage hearse to Oak Ridge Cemetery. There, Mary's body was placed in a crypt beside her husband.

Mary had once explained her thoughts about death to her friend Senator Charles Sumner:

> My belief, is so assured that Death, is only a blessed transition to the "pure
>> In heart," that a very slight veil separates us, from the "loved & lost" and to me,
>> There is comfort, in the thought, that though unseen by us, they are very near.[85]

Mary had been granted her greatest desire. The veil had been lifted, and at long last she was reunited with her "loved & lost."

CHAPTER SIX

The Issue of Sanity

I have worshipped my son and no unpleasant word *ever* passed between us, yet I cannot understand why I should have been brought out here.

—Mary Lincoln to Myra Bradwell, August 3, 1875

*F*rom Mary's perspective, to be branded a "lunatic" was the ultimate humiliation and betrayal. She saw no issues with her behavior. She saw no problem with traveling from place to place and not making a home. She believed she could manage her own affairs—especially her financial affairs. For her son to think otherwise was unforgiveable, even dishonorable. In Mary's eyes, Robert had committed high treason against his mother, and against God. For if a child is to "honor his father and mother" (Fifth Commandment), then surely Robert had committed a great sin by having his mother declared insane and placed in an institution. At least, that was Mary's opinion, and the opinion of some of her friends. Mary let Robert know that she had been discussing the matter with friends who thought "it advisable to offer up prayers for you in church, on account of your wickedness against me and High Heaven."[1]

Robert viewed things differently. His mother was behaving erratically. Her paranoia had become heightened. She surrounded herself with those whom Robert deemed "shady." What concerned Robert the most was Mary's uncontrollable spending and her concerns over money. Mary's income was enough to generously pay her expenses and give her an affluent lifestyle. Yet Mary professed poverty, while at the same time she made purchases for items that her family members found to be frivolous and needless. Robert took the steps he felt necessary to protect his mother.

When Robert Lincoln died, he left behind a folder marked "MTL Insanity File." Found in a file room off his study at Hildene, the file was tied with a ribbon like a gift to future historians. It contained documents, court papers, and letters which Robert had collected. Perhaps he thought he needed evidence in case the subject of his mother's insanity arose again. Perhaps he gathered them to ease his own guilt over the pain he caused his mother. Robert's choice to preserve these documents instead of burning them as he did so many family papers, led his grandson, Robert Todd Lincoln Beckwith, to believe the contents should be made public.[2] Historians Mark E. Neely, Jr., and R. Gerald McMurtry published them in 1986 under the title, *The Insanity File: The Case of Mary Todd Lincoln.*

Questions regarding the trial include those about those of Mary's actions which led her son to take legal measures against his mother. Questions about the legal proceedings, the aftermath, and Mary's struggle to regain her freedom are often asked.

Readers who are interested in further reading about the insanity trial and Mary's mental health are encouraged to read the writings of Neely and McMurtry, and of Jason Emerson. These works give intimate details that can only be covered by full-length manuscripts.

Well, was Mary insane?

Insanity is a legal term and not a medical term. Therefore, from a purely historical viewpoint, the answer is yes, Mary Lincoln was declared insane by a jury in a Chicago courtroom on May 19, 1875. However, when most people ask this question, what they really want to know is whether Mary suffered from mental illness. This is more difficult to answer: "maybe," "probably," "historians will never agree" seem to be the more politically correct answers in contemporary opinion. Theories abound with speculation that Mary suffered from Post-Traumatic Stress Disorder; depression; menopause; diabetes; a nervous breakdown; Bipolar Disorder; Manic-Depressive Illness; Pernicious Anema; or even syphilis, and that it is one or more of these illnesses which caused her erratic behavior. Others believe that her thoughts were controlled by prescription drugs, and she was a victim of overmedication. It is impossible to diagnose without a body. It is impossible to determine a modern diagnosis using nineteenth-century records. At times, Mary did exhibit strange behavior—some of it can be explained, some cannot. Whatever the causes of her behavior, Mary always believed herself to be of sound mind, and considered her son Robert guilty of "wicked conduct," "robbery," and "wickedness against (her) and High Heaven."[3]

What did Mary do that was considered "odd behavior?"

She suffered from fears and phobias ranging from a fear of fire and a fear of storms, to a fear of being left penniless. Mary was in Chicago during the Great Fire of 1871. From that time on, the sight of chimney smoke could throw her into a panic that the city was about to be engulfed in flames. At various times throughout her life, she experienced hallucinations, depression, sleep deprivation, mood swings, and many physical ailments. These conditions may have contributed to her eccentric behaviors. When Mary displayed her emotions, it was obvious she felt them deeply. She did not mourn her dead according to social customs—she mourned them for years. (To the modern reader, the idea of having time restrictions for emotions such as grief is ridiculous. However, to the Victorians, it was customary. To waver from the norm was often considered odd, even insane, behavior.)

One thing which seemed to give Mary a sense of euphoria was shopping. Mary not only enjoyed shopping, "for her it was almost an art form."[4]

Why was there a trial for insanity?

Having a trial was a positive part of the legal system. Women had few property rights and no right to vote in nineteenth-century America. In many states, even if she could obtain a divorce, a mother could lose custody of her children. Women had little, if any, control over money they earned from their trade. The laws in some states were so lacking in protection for women that if the closest male relative wanted a woman out of his life (often to pursue another woman), he could have her declared "insane" upon request. Having a trial helped deter such action. To protect the innocent, Illinois had a state lunacy law which stated, "a person could be involuntarily committed to medical care only after a jury trial."[5]

Robert was concerned about his mother's erratic behavior and her spending habits. He consulted trusted family and friends including Mary's first cousins, John Todd Stuart and Elizabeth (Todd) Grimsley

Brown, and attorneys Judge David Davis and Leonard Swett. All agreed some sort of intervention was needed for Mary's protection.

On May 16, 1875, a meeting was held to discuss the state of Mary's mental health. Present were Robert Lincoln; his attorney, B. F. Ayer; attorney and family friend Leonard Swett; and Drs. Hosmer Allen Johnson and Charles Gilman Smith, who had both cared for Tad during his final illness. These physicians had observed Mary during Tad's illness, but it is unknown whether they treated her. Also present was Dr. Nathan Smith Davis, an expert on the nervous system; Dr. Ralph N. Isham, who was not only Robert's personal physician but had treated Mary in the past; Dr. Robert J. Patterson, the proprietor of Bellevue Place Sanitarium in Batavia, Illinois; and Dr. James Stewart Jewell, the chairman of Nervous and Mental Diseases at Chicago Medical College. After the meeting, Robert was certain immediate action needed to be taken to ensure his mother's safety.[6]

Was Mary arrested? Why?

On May 19, three days after meeting with his team of experts, Robert, following the current laws, filed a petition for Mary to be arrested, charged with insanity, and brought to trial in the Cook County Courthouse. Instead of having the sheriff show up unannounced and drag Mary away in handcuffs, Leonard Swett offered to go to the hotel, retrieve Mary, and bring her to the courthouse in his private carriage. He arrived at Mary's hotel at 1:00 p.m. The trial began one hour later.[7]

Did Mary say anything to her son at the insanity trial?

During a court break, Robert approached his mother and tried to offer her comfort. She was overheard to exclaim, "Robert, to think that my son would ever have done this."[8]

Who testified against Mary?

At least sixteen witnesses (gathered by Robert) testified that Mary was deranged.[9] Witnesses included four physicians, five staff members of the Grand Pacific Hotel, five local merchants or jewelers, an agent for the United States Express Company, and her only surviving son. Dr. Willis Danforth testified that Mary heard voices and believed Abraham's spirit protected her. Robert testified that his mother "has been of unsound mind since the death of father; had been irresponsible for the past ten years."[10]

Did anyone testify on Mary's behalf?

No. Not even Mary spoke in her defense.

Was there a transcript of Mary's trial?

No, there was not. However, there were some newspaper reporters in the courtroom who printed excerpts of the testimony.

Who was Mary's defense attorney?

Isaac Arnold, a friend, and later biographer, of Abraham Lincoln.

How long was the trial?

Mary's trial lasted three hours. After the last witness left the stand, the jury adjourned. Then minutes later, they returned with a verdict: "Mary Lincoln is insane and is a fit person to be sent to a State Hospital for the Insane."[11] Because she was declared "insane," her son Robert was appointed conservator by the court, to manage Mary's financial accounts and personal property.

What was Mary's reaction to the trial?

Mary felt betrayed by her son, her husband's friends, and several members of her family. She had been publicly humiliated by the trial, and now she was to be robbed of her possessions and her freedom.

Unsure that life mattered any longer, she tried to commit suicide by obtaining a mixture of poisons from a local druggist. Mary visited Squire & Company at the Grand Pacific Hotel to make the purchase of laudanum and camphor. The pharmacist first told Mary there would be a delay in filling the order. Mary then went to Rogers and Smith where she was told they were out of stock. At William Dale's drug store, Mary was told they did not sell laudanum retail. Frustrated, Mary returned to Squire & Company where she was given a placebo. As she reached the sidewalk, Mary swallowed the mixture. She went back inside and was given a second, harmless dose. The pharmacist had recognized Mary and notified other local pharmacist not to give Mary any medications. He also sent for Robert.[12]

Where was Mary committed?

Instead of placing Mary in a state facility, Robert planned for her to be cared for at Bellevue Place Sanitarium in Batavia, Illinois. It was a sixteen-acre estate, with landscaped grounds. She was taken there the next day.[13]

Who was Mary's doctor?

Mary was under the care of Dr. Robert J. Patterson.

What would Mary's experience in the asylum have been like?

Late nineteenth-century psychiatric treatment was less than helpful to patients. Many physicians thought that insanity was caused by a disease that could be weakened by bleeding the patient. Other methods of treatment included a hysterectomy or brain surgery. Hydrotherapy was intended to "shock" patients back to their senses by dousing them with frigid water. If sent to a state facility, Mary could have encountered any of these methods of treatment.

Dr. Patterson did not follow any of these practices. He believed the best treatment was rest, relaxation, and quiet time. He encouraged walks around the property, lots of fresh air, and carriage rides. Mary could leave her room during the day and had a carriage at her disposal, although she rarely rode. Her room was on the second floor, but she took her meals with the Patterson family on the first floor. Mary could read, walk through the conservatory, and correspond with loved ones as she wished. Mary had a private nurse or assistant while at Bellevue. Overall, she had a pleasant stay at Bellevue, until darkness fell. At night, the door to Mary's room was locked from the outside and she felt imprisoned. She could leave her room only with the assistance and permission of her attendant.

Was Mary allowed visitors?

Yes, Mary was allowed visitors, but few came. Robert visited his mother at least seven times and twice brought his eldest daughter, "Mamie." Mary was visited by two newspaper reporters, Mrs. Rayne of the *Chicago Evening Post & Mail*, and Mr. Franc B. Wilkie, an editorial writer for the *Chicago Times*. Other visitors were General Farnsworth, and Judge and Mrs. James B. Bradwell who helped orchestrate a publicity campaign which eventually led to Mary's release from Bellevue.[14]

Did Mary die in an insane asylum? How long was she there?

Mary did not die in an insane asylum. She was admitted to Bellevue on May 20, 1875. One hundred and thirteen days later, on September 10, 1875, Mary left Bellevue to travel to Springfield, Illinois where she stayed with her sister Elizabeth Edwards and her family.

How and why was Mary released from Bellevue Place?

The plan to escape from Bellevue began when Mary went to the post office to mail letters to her sister Elizabeth. In addition to those, she smuggled letters to General John Franklin Farnsworth as well as Judge Bradwell and his wife, Myra. Mary chose Farnsworth because he had been a loyal friend to Abraham and was present at his deathbed. The Bradwells were legal experts who supported the reform of laws governing persons who had been declared insane. During her charity work throughout the Civil War, Myra encountered both social and legal obstacles due to her gender, which inspired her to turn her efforts to feminist causes. Mary Lincoln had chosen a powerful team to help her achieve her goal of release.[15]

Farnsworth and the Blackwells visited Mary on the same day. Farnsworth informed Dr. Patterson that Mary had requested his help to gain her freedom. It was Myra who suggested that Mary have an extended visit with Elizabeth Edwards and her family. The thought of returning to Springfield excited Mary. She agreed that seeing her sister would be beneficial.[16]

Myra wrote to Elizabeth and suggested the visit. While letters were going back and forth between Elizabeth and Robert, Myra and Elizabeth, and Robert and Dr. Patterson, the Judge and Myra invited two newspaper reporters to visit Mary at Bellevue. Soon newspapers published articles stating that Mary was "entirely sane" and that she was being "deprived of her liberty."[17]

Eventually tiring of the bad press his institution was receiving, and Mary's agitated state from the visitors and reports, Patterson wrote to Robert, "Now that so much is said about Mrs. Lincoln's removal to Springfield, I think it would be well if she could go at once."[18] On September 10, 1875, Robert met his mother at the Chicago train station. After a one-night stay in the city, Robert reluctantly took Mary to Springfield to stay at the Edwards's home. He honestly believed that once there, she would not visit with her family members and would stay in her room. Just a few days later, Elizabeth sent Robert a letter stating that Mary was enjoying visiting with her friends and family. She had even accompanied one of Elizabeth's daughters to visit the wife of one of Abraham's old friends. Just a few weeks later, in early November, Elizabeth informed Robert that she had "no hesitation, in pronouncing her sane, and far more reasonable, and gentle, than in former years."[19]

Did Mary ever return to Belleview Place, or any asylum?

No, she did not.

A second trial to determine Mary's mental state was held on June 15, 1876. Her brother-in-law, Ninian Edwards testified that Mary was able to conduct her own affairs and no longer needed a conservator. After a few minutes of deliberation, the jury returned and announced, "Mary Lincoln is restored to reason and is capable to manage and control her estate."[20] Mary continued to stay with the Edwards until later that year when she left for Europe.

Did Robert ever feel remorseful about having Mary declared insane?

At the time, Robert believed his actions were in his mother's best interest. In August 1875, Robert wrote to his aunt, Elizabeth Edwards, "Rightly or wrongly I consider that I alone must assume the entire and absolute charge of her unfortunate situation and I must deal with it as my condition allows me to do, I am alone held responsible and I cannot help it .... I have done my duty as I best know and Providence must take care of the rest." In the spring of 1879, after Mary's self-imposed exile to France, Robert wrote to Elizabeth expressing a change of opinion. "If I could have foreseen my own experience in the matter, no consideration would have induced me to go through it—at the ordinary troubles and distresses of life are enough without such as that."[21] It would be five years before the mother and son saw one another again.

Will historians ever agree as to whether Mary was insane?

Probably not.

CHAPTER SEVEN

Family Relationships

I propose to act in a more civilized *manner in the future, which conclusion will greatly please your* very dear *Grandma.*
  —Mary Lincoln to Edward Lewis Baker, Jr, October 17, 1876

For some, the word "family" may conjure visions of large family gatherings
filled with the joyous clatter of children and the loving support of parents,
aunts, and uncles. For others, "family" dredges up memories of feeling lonely,
quarrels, and perhaps even the feeling of being the "bad seed." For Mary Lincoln, both were true in her family relations.

As a child, Mary had many wonderful moments of fun and frolic when
visiting with cousins and playing with her siblings. She was a proud member
of the Todd clan and relished the advantages the family gave her. Various
members of Mary's family had settled new lands, fought wars, developed cities, established institutions of higher learning, created laws, and preached
God's word. They were religious, educated, well-manned, and wealthy—they
were the aristocracy. Sisters and cousins comforted Mary when her mother
passed away, and at an early age, Mary learned to rely on the support of her
Todd family.

When Mary moved to Springfield, she was warmly greeted by several
family members: Two sisters (Elizabeth and Frances), a beloved cousin (John
Todd Stuart) and his family, another cousin (lawyer Stephen Trigg Logan),
and a doting uncle (Dr. John Todd) had already made Springfield their home.
Her uncle John Todd had moved to Springfield in 1827; he practiced medicine
there for many years. Dr. Todd filled the role of surrogate father to Mary.
When bitter words flew between Mary and her sister Elizabeth over Mary's

upcoming wedding to Abraham, Mary implored her Uncle John to "go and tell my sister that Mr. Lincoln and I are to be married this evening." Dr. Todd was a favorite among his nieces living in Springfield. Katherine Helm reported that he served as a "suave and diplomatic advocate for Mary's cause and soon had them all in smiling good-humor."[1]

Mary's close relationship with her Uncle John also extended to his children. Dr. Todd's daughter Elizabeth was a bridesmaid for Mary, a friend, and companion. Elizabeth joined Mary and the boys on the inaugural trip to Washington and stayed for an extended six-month visit. Uncle John's son Lockwood also had a close relationship with Mary. He traveled to Washington with the Lincoln family and was with the inaugural party at Willard's Hotel.[2] Another of Dr. Todd's children, John Blair Smith Todd, joined his siblings for an extended visit to the White House while he campaigned for President Lincoln to grant governmental jobs to various friends and relatives.[3]

During Mary's years in the White House, various members of the Todd clan surrounded the Lincolns with semi-scandals—much to the delight of political opponents who were able to use the stories against Lincoln, his family, and his administration. Like many families throughout the country, the Todd family was torn apart by war, and united by tragedy. Mary found her family drama used as political fodder for the front page of gossip newspapers. Her name was often in headlines as she became the target of slanderous accusations in both Northern and Southern newspapers.

Most days the only emotions Mary felt for the members of her family who supported the Confederacy were betrayal and anger. She felt they—even those whom she had loved deeply—had become her enemies. As the Todd siblings were choosing sides in the war, it was soon evident that most of the children of Elizabeth Humphreys Todd—Mary's half-siblings—would support the Southern cause. While they distrusted Mary politically, they recognized that she held a certain prestige and even power. The sisters were mindful of Mary's position, and on occasion tried to use it to their advantage.[4]

Once the Lincolns settled in Washington, the name "Todd" soon appeared in the newspapers and in letters back home. The chatter was not limited to the Southern relations. Those who supported the Union also created havoc and caused embarrassment to Mary. They descended on Washington and the Lincolns seeking jobs, requesting favors, and causing scandals. In a letter to her cousin, Elizabeth Todd Grimsley explained, "The papers announce the presence of 100 Todds and all wanting office."[5] There were many present, but not as many as reported.

Visits by the Todd family continued throughout the Lincoln administration both giving Mary comfort and causing her grief. After Willie died, Lincoln sent word to Springfield for Elizabeth Edwards to come to Washington. He wanted her by Mary's side to offer comfort and consolation. Elizabeth wrote home describing Mary as "distressed and subdued," and "nervous, and dependent upon the companionship of some one (sic)." Elizabeth also requested that other family members come help take care of Mary. Elizabeth thought it was a good opportunity for younger members of the family to visit the city and enjoy its cultural offerings.[6] Another sister who came to the White House was Emilie Todd Helm, nicknamed by Lincoln, "Little Sister." Emilie's visit lasted close to two weeks. According to Emilie, the two sisters comforted one another in their grief over the loss of both the Lincolns' son Willie and their relatives killed in service to the Confederate Army—especially Emilie's husband Benjamin Hardin Helm, who had been a favorite of both Lincolns, and the sisters' brother Alec. Emilie recalled how the two sisters wept together and how both Lincolns were considerate to her feelings and did not mention the war—even when General Daniel Sickles demanded of Lincoln, "You should not have that rebel in your house."[7]

Emilie may have believed Mary's grief for Alec and Ben ran deep, but Elizabeth Keckly told a different story. When Mrs. Keckly heard of Alec's death, she hesitated to say anything to Mary. However, Mary approached the topic with "apparent unconcern" and explained, "He made his choice long ago . . . I see no special reason why I should bitterly mourn his death."[8] Mary's emotions regarding her family relationships were always complex.

Just as during the war, Mary's relationships with her siblings, cousins, and other family members afterward became more strained. Yet at times, she depended on them more than ever. As Mary's relationship with Robert disintegrated, Mary relied more upon her sister Elizabeth (see chapter 5). Mary argued with her sisters, looked for relationships with her nieces and nephews which would have been filled by her own sons had they lived, and turned to her cousins for support and sympathy. Overall, Mary was both supported and annoyed by most of her relatives and vice versa.

The family relationships that gave Mary the most joy were those of wife, mother, and eventually, grandmother. These were also the relationships that brought Mary the deepest sorrows.

This chapter includes questions about Mary's deepest relationships with her family members. Source materials for these questions include diaries, letters, family documents, and newspapers.

The Todds

Was Mary related to Dolly Todd Madison?

No, the two women were not related. Dolly's maiden name was Payne. Her first husband was a Todd; however, he was not related to Mary Lincoln either. The confusion began with Katherine Helm's book, in which she quoted heavily from her mother's wartime diary. While at the White House, Emilie was given a tour of the various rooms, including the Red room, which contained "the portrait of Washington which Dolly Madison cut out of the frame to save from the British." Helm concluded by noting, "Dolly Madison's first husband was a Todd."[9] Emilie did not say that there was a family connection, but her allusion to it has caused confusion for the past century.

Was Mary related to Jane Todd Crawford from Kentucky?

The Todd family related to Mary Lincoln is large, but there is no documentation connecting Jane Todd Crawford to it. Jane holds her own place in women's history, and medical history, as being the first survivor of an experimental ovarian surgery.

In 1809, when Jane was 46 years old, she thought she was expecting a child. When the pregnancy lasted longer than a normal gestation period, Jane sought medical treatment from Dr. Ephraim McDowell of Danville, Kentucky, who determined that Jane needed surgery. She traveled sixty miles to the doctor's home, where the surgery was performed on Christmas Day while most people were at church. Jane was given opium for the pain—anesthesia had not yet been invented. During the twenty-five-minute procedure, Jane sang hymns while she was held down. Dr. McDowell removed a twenty-two-pound cyst from her ovary. Jane recovered at the McDowells' home, and returned to Greensburg, Kentucky in January 1810.

Did Mary have strained relationships with her sisters in Springfield?

At one time or another throughout her life, Mary had strained relationships with her three sisters who lived in Springfield. Some of it was due to political alliances, some due to family squabbles, and some just because all the Todd women were emotional and quick-tempered.

Many scholars have assumed that Mary's relationship with Ann was always strained and remained so until Mary's death. One reason for this assumption is that Ann is the only one of Mary's sisters from Springfield who did not attend Lincoln's inauguration.

Mary wrote to her cousin, Elizabeth Todd Grimsley: "Tell Ann for me, to quote her own expression, *She* is becoming still further removed from "Queen Victoria's Court."[10] Mary may have been hurt that Ann was ignoring the opportunity to enjoy Washington society, but Ann had her own problems. During the years 1860—1863, Ann buried three young sons. Two were named after their father, Clark Moulton Smith, and one was named Lincoln. In 1861, after the death of their mother, two of Levi Todd's daughters came to live with Ann and Clark. Ann was adjusting to life both as a grieving mother and as a guardian to her nieces. Attending social events in Washington was not a priority (see appendix 1).

Mary's relationship with her oldest sister, Elizabeth, is complex. At times, Elizabeth appeared to mother Mary. It was Elizabeth who gave Mary a place to stay upon her arrival in Springfield. Mary would return to Elizabeth's care after being released from Bellevue, and again after her travels in Europe. Elizabeth rushed to Washington and offered comfort after Willie's death. Yet the two sisters bickered over political and personal matters. Mary was appalled and unforgiving when the Edwards gave their political support to Stephen Douglas in the 1860 presidential election. Elizabeth, who was then staying in Geneseo, New York, wrote to her son-in-law that the "democrats about here, express a strong faith in some combination, that will make Douglas the next President."[11] When Ninian caused a political scandal by abusing his authority as Springfield's commissary commissioner—a position Lincoln had granted to Ninian—relationships became strained. Mary, who was often quick to criticize her family members, must have been furious with her brother-in-law.

Mary and Elizabeth also squabbled over personal and family matters. Immediately after Lincoln won the November election, reporters began to speculate about Mary and her family's activities and relationships with one another. Within weeks, newspapers stated that Mrs. Edwards of Springfield, and a "good looking niece about eighteen years old" would travel to Washington with Mary.[12] Apparently, a newspaper printed comments about Mary's family relationships. Elizabeth felt the

comments were unflattering and without knowing if Mary made negative
comments, or if they were the creation of a zealous reporter, Elizabeth
became angry. Her temper was further inflamed after she and several
other family members were invited to the inaugural festivities. Wanting
Elizabeth to be dressed as well as any member of Washington society,
Mary offered to purchase a new gown for her sister, but rather than
appreciating the offer Elizabeth was furious. Feeling that Mary's offer
was a condemnation of her wardrobe, Elizabeth wrote to her daughter
Julia, "I cannot express my surprise, at your Aunt Mary's, most singu-
lar, and undignified conduct. It is really mortifying, to see, that she is
making herself so ridiculous, in the eyes of the public . . . if the remarks,
attributed to her are true, she deserves, severe condemnation . . . I have
been very much in choice society, and never could cultivate the feeling,
that fine; and elaborate dress, was indispensably necessary."[13] Mary was
also unhappy with Elizabeth's daughter Julia's behavior during her visit
to Washington, and this also caused a strain between the two women.

When Mary turned to Elizabeth for help over Robert's actions that
lead to Mary's confinement to an institution for insanity, the sisters
had been at odds for a decade. After Mary retuned from Europe, they
argued over whether Mary should forgive her sisters who had sided with
the Confederacy. Throughout her adulthood, Mary's life choices were
criticized by Elizabeth. But despite the arguments, Mary knew that if
she needed Elizabeth's support, Elizabeth would help her. The two tried
to maintain a sisterly relationship until Mary's death (see Appendix 1).

**What type of relationship did Mary have with her stepmother,
Elizabeth (Betsy) Humphreys Todd? Did it change after Robert
Smith Todd's death?**

The relationships between Betsy and all the children born to Eliza
Parker Todd seem to have been strained and Mary's was no exception.
More than once, Mary thought Betsy was unfair and demanding.

In 1848 while Lincoln was in Washington City, Mary stayed with
the family of her father's second marriage. Perhaps because she was a
mother herself, or perhaps because she had more sympathy for a woman
who took on the task of raising six stepchildren, Mary had softened
somewhat toward Betsy. Mary wrote to Abraham, "she is very obliging
& accommodating, but if she thought any of us, were on her hands again,
I believe she would be *worse* than ever."[14]

No letters of Mary's exist that may have discussed Betsy after the death of Robert Smith Todd. According to Katherine Helm as told in *The True Story of Mary: Wife of Lincoln*, Mary's visits to Kentucky to settle the estate of her father and grandmother were pleasant, although as a child, Mary may have been influenced by her Grandmother Parker who resented the "new" Mrs. Todd. Mary often clashed with her stepmother, but according to Helm, "in later years they became very good friends as they had many tastes in common."[15] However, Helm's goal in writing her book was to improve Mary's image and her positive comments regarding the relationship between Mary and her stepmother are often open to question.

Since Mary did not get along well with her stepmother, did she find other women who may have served as a mother figure?

There were many women in Mary's life who fulfilled the role of "mother." Even though she was enslaved, Sally likely offered Mary comfort throughout Mary's childhood. Since Mary did not leave written commentary about her relationship with any of the Todds' enslaved persons, it is impossible to know the extent of the relationships they shared. It is possible Mary turned to them for motherly comfort. It is also possible that she did not.

Robert Smith Todd's sister, Maria Logan Todd was unmarried when Mary's mother, Eliza, died. Maria came to both help with the children in the Todd home and help manage the household.[16] Mary also looked to her sister Elizabeth and her Grandmother Parker as mother figures. After moving to Springfield, Mary was close to her Uncle John Todd and his wife Elizabeth. They became role models and surrogate parents to Mary, her sisters, and other relatives who came to the Midwest.

What did her family think of Lincoln? Did they ever respect him?

Elizabeth Edwards thought that Mary was better suited to Stephen A. Douglas—or any man other than Lincoln! Stephen Logan, a distant cousin, called Lincoln "the rough diamond" and considered him too rugged to be a suitable husband for Mary.[17] Other family members found him to be "ignorant of social forms and customs" with a desultory education and a nebulous future.[18] Mary's sister Frances Wallace, who had gone out with Lincoln once or twice, found him to be "not much for society."[19]

Years after Lincoln's death, Frances told a reporter that Lincoln "was the most tender hearted man I ever knew."[20]After years of marriage, after Lincoln was elected President, after he gave so many political appointments to members of the Todd family, and after he was hailed a martyr after his death, most members of the Todd family said only kind and loving things about him. The major exceptions were Mary's brother George Rogers Clark Todd and her half-brother David Humphreys Todd, who both supported the Confederacy and both despised Lincoln.

How did the relationship between Robert Smith Todd and Lincoln differ from that of the other sons-in-law?

According to Mary Edwards Brown (Mary's grandniece and one-time caretaker of the Lincoln Home) prior to the Lincoln's marriage, Robert Smith Todd had referred to Lincoln as "poor white trash" and was opposed to the wedding. He changed his mind about Lincoln after a visit to Springfield in 1843. Robert came to Springfield on business and to visit his family members there including his new grandson and namesake, Robert Todd Lincoln. During the trip, he gave Mary a $25 gold piece, and arranged to give her a yearly sum of $120 per year. Before his death, it had amounted to $1,157.50. Todd deeded eighty acres of land to his daughter and new son-in-law. He turned over some business and instructed Lincoln to keep whatever he collected from unpaid debts.[21] By 1846, Todd spoke favorably of all his sons-in-law, including Lincoln. Todd wrote, "I feel more than gratified that my daughters have all married gentlemen whom I respect and esteem and should be pleased. . . . I will be satisfied if they discharge all their duties and make as good wives, as I think they have good husbands."[22]

Who did the Lincolns call "Little Sister"?

Mary's half-sister, Emilie Perret Todd was eighteen years younger than Mary. Lincoln dubbed Emilie "little sister" in 1847 when he brought Mary and the children to Lexington en route to Washington. Emilie recalled that she was "always after that called by him 'little sister.'"[23]

Emilie traveled to Springfield in 1856 and spent six months visiting with her four older sisters. The sisters had hoped to find Emilie a suitable husband in Springfield, but she returned to Kentucky and married Benjamin Hardin Helm, the son of John LaRue Helm, who had served as the lieutenant governor and governor for the Commonwealth of Kentucky.[24]

As a Wife

Did Mary have a relationship with members of Lincoln's family?

By the time of his marriage to Mary, Lincoln had few remaining relatives. Both of his siblings were deceased. His mother had died while the family lived in Indiana. Lincoln's father and stepmother lived in Coles County, Illinois along with Lincoln's stepsiblings and his cousin, Dennis Hanks. Dennis's daughter, Harriet, lived with the Lincolns in Springfield while she attended school.

Lincoln would visit his family while traveling the judicial circuit. He often gave them money to help with expenses. While some believe that the relationship between Lincoln and his father was strained, there must have been affection, as Tad was named "Thomas" after his paternal grandfather.

In December 1867, Mary contacted Sarah Lincoln, sending her "these few trifles" along with ten dollars to have a dress made. This is the only surviving letter, though there may have been others.[25]

Did Mary meet her in-laws or attend their funerals?

There is no evidence that Mary ever met Thomas Lincoln or his wife Sarah. Shortly before his father's death on January 17, 1851, Lincoln received a letter from his stepbrother, John D. Johnston, stating that Thomas was ill. Lincoln could not come to visit his dying father or attend his funeral in part because Mary had recently given birth to Willie and was still recuperating. Sarah passed away in April 1869 when Mary was living in Germany with Tad.

As a Mother

Where did the boys attend school while in Washington? Did Mary teach the boys or hire a tutor?

Robert was a student at Harvard College. Willie and Tad had a tutor at the White House. Mary had a desk and blackboard set up in the state dining room so the boys could have a classroom. She requested that their friends Bud and Holly Taft also be allowed to attend the tutoring sessions.[26]

Were there conflicts between Mary and Robert other than money?

Robert once commented that his mother was sane concerning all issues except money. Other than the insanity issues, Robert and Mary appear to have had a normal relationship. He was a loving son, and she was a doting mother.

During the election of 1861 and during the presidency, there was one major personality difference between the two. Whether the press was favorable or cruel, Robert wanted to live a life out of the public eye. If the press was favorable, Mary enjoyed the attention.

Did she reconcile with Robert after he had her committed?

Elizabeth arranged for Robert to visit Mary during her final illness. Robert was en route to Fort Leavenworth, Kansas and stopped in Springfield to see her. It was the first time the estranged mother and son had seen one another in five years. Robert found his mother in poor health and learned that she had not left her room in six months. It is believed that during this visit, Mary forgave her son and the two settled their disagreements. According to historian Jason Emerson, after that first visit, Robert "and his family visited her every few weeks for the rest of her life."[27]

Family Relations during the War

During the Civil War, did Todd family members have plantations with vast number of enslaved persons?

Three of Mary's sisters lived in Springfield, Illinois, and owned no enslaved people. Most of the Todds who lived in states where slavery was legal lived in cities and held a few enslaved persons as household servants. During the course of the Civil War, many family members lost all their property, including their enslaved people; several members of the Todd family were left destitute.

Lincoln intervened, on more than one occasion, to help a member of the Todd family regarding the loss of property. One case was the situation with Mary's cousin Susan and her husband, John Anderson Craig.[28] The Craigs owned a cotton plantation and enslaved persons in Arkansas along the Mississippi River. As the Union forces occupied the state, the Craigs fled, leaving their plantation. When they wished to return to their home, Lincoln wrote a letter of protection allowing the couple to safely move past the Union troops and reoccupy their plantation. The letter directed that they were not to be molested or harmed as long as they "demean themselves as peaceful, loyal citizens of the United States." However, they would not be allowed to return to their home and continue to maintain enslaved people.[29] This was one example of the many times Lincoln assisted members of the Todd family during the war.

How many of Mary's brothers fought for the Confederacy?

Mary's youngest full brother, George Rogers Clark Todd, served in the Confederate Army as a surgeon. Her half-brothers David, Samuel, and Alexander enlisted in the Confederate Army. Three of her brothers-in-law (Benjamin Hardin Helm, Clement B. White, and Nathaniel H. R. Dawson) and one future brother-in-law (William W. Herr) supported the Confederate forces.

Did Mary's Confederate relatives ask for favors during the war?

Mary's half-sister Elodie must not have felt that her relationship with Mary was close. Whenever she needed a favor, she would enlist Katherine (known as "Kitty" among the siblings), the youngest of the Todd siblings, to write to Mary. Early in the war, Elodie's beau, Nathanial H. R. Dawson, who was in Virginia commanding a company in the 4th Alabama Infantry Regiment, wrote to Elodie, "Can't you use your influence, or get your sister Kate to use hers? I hope her influence with Mr. Lincoln will save me the trouble of being hanged should I fall under his power." Elodie assured him that she hoped if he were captured that he would be "presented with a passport to leave King Abe's Kingdom and returned to me with care."[30]

Other members of the Todd family requested passes to travel between "enemy" lines throughout the war.

Did any of Mary's siblings support the Union?

Her brother Levi Owen Todd was too old to enlist, but he was a Union man and supported Lincoln's reelection in 1864. Her sisters Elizabeth, Frances, and Ann supported the Union. Mary's half-sister Margaret Kellogg supposedly supported the Union, and she and her husbanded attended Lincoln's first inauguration. However, they had strong ties to the Confederacy and supported it when convenient.[31]

Did any of Mary's family members die during the war years?

Two of Mary's half-brothers, Samuel and Alexander (Alec), were killed during battle while fighting for the Confederacy. Her brother-in-law

Confederate Brigadier General Benjamin Hardin Helm was killed at the battle of Chickamauga.

Her brother Levi died in 1864, and her uncle John Todd died before the war's end in 1865. While each of these deaths was difficult for Mary, the worst was the death of her son Willie in 1862.

Family Relations after the War

Who was "Dear Lewis" in Mary's letters?

"Dear Lewis" was Edward Lewis Baker Jr., Mary's great-nephew, and the grandson of Elizabeth Edwards. His mother was Elizabeth's daughter, Julia. Lewis frequently served as Mary's traveling companion. They corresponded when Mary was in Europe, and when she came home in 1881, it was Lewis who met her in New York at the harbor.[32]

Did Mary ever talk to her Confederate family members after the war?

No. Mary considered them traitors to herself, her husband, and her country. When her brother Alec had been killed in friendly fire, Mrs. Keckly hesitated to mention his death to Mary. Keckly was surprised when Mary responded, "He made his choice long ago. He decided against my husband, and through him against me. He has been fighting against us; and since he chose to be our deadly enemy, I see no special reason why I should bitterly mourn his death." Mary continued, "They would hang my husband to-morrow if it was in their powers, and perhaps gibbet me with him. How then can I sympathize with a people at war with me and mine?"[33] They had made their choices and would never be part of Mary's life again. Mary felt betrayed. But most painful betrayal came from Emilie, the half-sister whom Lincoln and Mary both had loved as a daughter.

What happened between Mary and Emilie and did they reconcile?

Both Elizabeth Edwards and Ann Smith tried to reconcile the sisters, but their attempts were unsuccessful.

As Union troops moved through the South, Emilie realized that she needed to sell her six hundred bales of cotton in the North. To leave it where it was would mean certain destruction by the soldiers. She was a widow with three young children, and the funds generated from the sale would help support her family. Desperate to protect her investment, Emilie traveled to Washington with the hopes of obtaining a pass from her brother-in-law to travel south and move the cotton. When Lincoln did not oblige the request, Emilie demanded that he do so. Again, Lincoln refused. Emilie may have been Mary's sister, but she was also the widow of a Confederate officer, and she continually refused to take the oath of allegiance to the United States. Lincoln was constantly scrutinized for issuing passes to persons of questionable loyalty. Emilie's loyalty was not questionable; it lay with the Confederacy. For Lincoln to have granted Emilie's request would have created a public and political scandal.

Emilie did not understand Lincoln's logic. When she returned to Kentucky, she wrote a seething letter to Lincoln saying that she had "used up all her money to go on her long, tedious, unproductive, and sorrowful visit" to the White House. She continued by blaming Lincoln for the death of her husband, her brothers in the Confederacy, and the death of her brother, Levi, from "utter want and destitution—another sad victim of more favored relatives." This statement was to remind Lincoln that Levi had requested a government position but received none. (Emilie failed to mention Levi's trouble with alcoholism.) She again demanded that Lincoln grant her a pass to travel south to retrieve her cotton. Then in late October 1864, Emilie penned the words that Mary could never forgive, "I have been a quiet citizen and request only the right which humanity and justice always gives to widows and orphans. I would also remind you that your *minnie bullets* (*sic*) have made us what we are & I feel I have that additional claim upon you."[34]

Several months later, Lincoln ordered General Grant to allow Emilie to move her cotton north. Lincoln was able to forgive; Mary was not. She never spoke to, saw, or wrote to Emilie again. Letters written to Mary by Emilie were returned unopened.[35]

The betrayal of one so loved was too much for Mary to forget. Mary had opened her heart and home to her grieving "Little Sister" after the death of her husband, General Helm. By doing so, she endured criticism and gossip from friends and political and military personnel who questioned her own loyalties. From Mary's perspective, Emilie had gone too far.

As a Grandmother

How many grandchildren did Mary and Abraham have?

Robert and his wife Mary had three children: Mary, Abraham II (Jack), and Jessie.

Did Mary ever meet her grandchildren?

She met Mary (Mamie) and spent time with her after Tad's death. There is no documentation about how much time she spent with any of the grandchildren. Since Jack was born in 1873, two years prior to the insanity trial, Mary must have met him and spent time with him at Robert's home prior to her exile to Europe. Jessie was born after the insanity trail, so it is possible that Mary never met her. However, it is also possible Robert could have brought Jessie with him as he visited with his mother during the last few months of her life.

Mary Lincoln, circa 1863. It appears this photograph (possibly taken by William H. Mumler of Boston) was taken the same day as the previous photo. With the acceptation of the bonnet, Mary's attire is the same. The lace netting at the back of her hair would have been worn to keep her hair in place under a bonnet. *Author's collection.*

While Southern newspapers had no love for Mary, Northern newspapers criticized her, too, as shown on the cover of *Vanity Fair*, August 24, 1861. The New York newspaper called her "The Republican Queen." *Courtesy Bauer Family Lincoln Collection.*

Left, Captain David Humphreys Todd (1832–1871) (Mary's half-brother) served in the CSA, 21st Louisiana Infantry Regiment. Known for his cruel treatment of Union soldiers, David caused embarrassment to the Lincolns. He survived the war and died in 1871. *Courtesy Bauer Family Lincoln Collection.*

Right, Samuel Brown Todd (1830–1862) (Mary's half-brother) had moved to New Orleans before the Civil War. He joined the 24th Louisiana Regiment and was killed at the Battle of Shiloh in April 1862. *Courtesy Bauer Family Lincoln Collection.*

Left, Alexander "Aleck" Todd (1839–1862) (Mary's half-brother) served in the Confederate Kentucky "Orphan Brigade" as an aide-de-camp to his brother-in-law, Brigadier General Benjamin H. Helm. Aleck was killed in friendly fire at the battle of Baton Rouge in April 1862. *Courtesy Bauer Family Lincoln Collection.*

Elizabeth Todd Grimsley was Mary Lincoln's cousin and friend.
She attended Lincoln's inauguration in 1861 and stayed at the White
House for a six-month extended visit. Elizabeth accompanied Mary
on her travels during that time and helped Mary with White house
duties. *From the Lincoln Financial Foundation Collection, LFA-0431.*

Mary Lincoln wearing what appears to be mourning attire for
her brother Levi Todd and her uncle Dr. John Todd, circa 1864.
From the Lincoln Financial Foundation Collection. (LN-0068).

During her 1868 trip to Frankfurt, Germany, Mary stayed first at the Hotel d' Angleterre, shown here circa 1850. *Courtesy of the Institut für Stadtgeschichte, Frankfurt am Main, Germany. (S7A1998/9343).*

Finding the Hotel d'Angleterre too expensive, Mary soon relocated to the Hotel de Holland, shown here circa 1840. *Courtesy of the Institut für Stadtgeschichte, Frankfurt am Main, Germany. (S7Võ/1098).*

From February 1869 to September 1870, Tad attended
classes at Dr. Johann Heinrich Hogagen's private school,
shown here in 1967. *Courtesy of the Institut für Stadtgeschichte,
Frankfurt am Main, Germany. (S7C1998/20702).*

Stereo view of the west side of the courthouse square in Springfield
as it looked in 1870. *Courtesy Bauer Family Lincoln Collection.*

In 1872, spirit photographer William H. Mumler reinforced Mary's belief that Lincoln's spirit visited her by offering this composite photograph as "proof." *From the Lincoln Financial Foundation Collection. (OC-0275).*

The Lincoln Tomb, circa 1874, as it looked the following year when Mary returned to live in Springfield. *Courtesy Bauer Family Lincoln Collection.*

Engraving of Mary Lincoln's funeral by an unknown artist. *Author's Collection.*

Is it possible this is a previously unknown photograph of
Mary Lincoln? *Courtesy Bauer Family Lincoln Collection.*

CHAPTER EIGHT

Mary, the Issue of Slavery,
and African Americans

Tell Mr. Douglass, and every one, how deeply my feelings were enlisted in the cause of freedom.
        —Mary Lincoln to Elizabeth Keckly, October 29, 1867

*M*any questions have been asked about Mary's feelings regarding the
"peculiar institution" of slavery. Not just because she grew up in a slaveholding
family, but also because she became the wife, and later the widow, of the Great
Emancipator. Mary's thoughts about slavery changed and developed throughout her life, just as Lincoln's had done. As a child, Mary was dependent upon
enslaved people to prepare her food; create, mend, and launder her clothing;
clean her home; drive her around town; calm her when frightened; and tend to
her every need. As the mistress of the Springfield home, and the White House,
Mary depended upon freed African Americans to do many of the same tasks
the Todd enslaved people had performed during her youth. The difference
was that her thoughts about slavery changed from the innocent, childhood
acceptance of the way things were, to the mature realization of how things
could be. Catherine Clinton explained Mary's thoughts by writing, "Mrs.
Lincoln held views typical for her class, race, and region: asserting repeatedly
in her writing that African Americans were a 'far inferior' race. Yet as First
Lady, she exhibited atypical behavior upon occasion."[1] As a child, Mary saw the
worst aspects of slavery. The Cheapside Slave Auction Block, one of the largest
slave markets in the United States, was in Lexington. Near Mary's childhood
home, on Short Street, stood the slave pens where Lewis C. Robards managed
a market specializing in the sale of "fancy girls," young mulatto women sold
as concubines mainly to traders, gamblers, and saloon keepers.[2]

This chapter looks at Mary's relationship with her family's enslaved people as well as with former enslaved persons, African American servants, and abolitionists. Mary's seamstress, the formerly enslaved Elizabeth Keckly, is given special attention.

Family letters, court documents, tax records, and memories reveal Mary's progression of thought regarding the African Americans in her life.

Mary and the Todd Family Enslaved Persons

Was the Todd family a slaveholding family? How many enslaved people did they own?

Yes, the Todd family had several enslaved persons, the number of which fluctuated. Robert Smith Todd bought, owned, inherited, and hired enslaved workers from other slaveholders. Census records, tax records, and slave schedules give some insight into the number of enslaved people the Todd family claimed. However, the documents are often difficult to decipher because enslaved people might be loaned, borrowed, emancipated, and sometimes hired, thus making accurate numbers difficult to obtain. The records show:

1807: Robert Smith Todd inherited a young, enslaved woman named Hannah from his father's estate.

1815: Robert Smith Todd, John H. Morton, and Thomas Bodley purchased household property, horses, wagons, and three enslaved girls from David Todd (Robert's older brother), allowing him (David) to pay $3,810 worth of outstanding bank notes. It is unclear how the property, including the enslaved people, was divided. Did all three of the enslaved girls go to one person? Did each man receive one enslaved servant? Did the three men share ownership, and the three women worked for a given amount of time at each household? The names of the women and their appraised value are known: Henney was valued at four hundred dollars; Evelina was valued at three hundred and fifty dollars; and Gatty (or Getty) was valued at three hundred and fifty dollars.[3]

1820: Census records indicate three enslaved women lived in Robert Smith Todd's home. We cannot assume these are the same women purchased in 1815 from David Todd. The names of the enslaved people recalled by members of the Todd family do not match the names of those who were purchased from David Todd. It is most likely they were different women, for by this time, Robert and his wife Eliza were raising their family and had additional enslaved persons living in their home.

1830: Census records indicate ten enslaved men living in the Todd home. Names are not listed.

1839: Tax records indicate five enslaved people in the Todd household.

1840: The 1840 Census indicates there were two enslaved men, three enslaved women, and one formerly enslaved woman in the Todd home. Who was the emancipated woman? Did Robert Smith Todd or another family member grant her her freedom? Did she purchase her freedom? The records do not provide specifics, and sadly, the information is lost.

1842: The tax record shows five enslaved people at the Todd home in Lexington.

1848: The tax schedule states a total of eight enslaved people claimed by Robert S. Todd. Two of them were over 16 years of age.

1849: At the time of Robert Smith Todd's death, the tax schedule reports that he owned twelve enslaved persons.

1850: Records indicate there were four enslaved men and two enslaved women living in the Todd home in Lexington. However, the tax schedule for 1850 states that Robert S. Todd's widow held no enslaved people. Her daughter, who was ten years old, held seven enslaved people. This was just one year after Robert Smith Todd had died. The 1850 Slave Schedule indicates that Oldham, Todd & Company, owned in part by Robert Smith Todd, possessed three enslaved men. It is unclear where these three men lived.

The following enslaved persons were known to Mary either in her childhood or when she returned to Lexington to visit her family. Their names are either listed in documents or recalled in family oral histories, the accuracy of which depends on the quality of the person's memory. In October 1852, lawsuits regarding inheritances were filed and disagreements over the appraised value of the enslaved people who were scheduled to be sold erupted between the heirs. Mary's brother George believed they were appraised too low. Elizabeth (Betsy) Humphreys Todd, Mary's stepmother, thought they were too high. The disputed amounts, and the names of the enslaved people, were recorded in the affidavits of the lawsuits.[4] Those born after the settlement of Mary's father's estate are not included:

1. Hannah: The inventory of General Levi Todd's estate lists Hannah as a "girl" valued at $300. This would indicate she was of childbearing age. It is not known if Robert S. Todd kept or sold Hannah.

2. Sally: "a jewel of a black mammy." Elizabeth Humphreys Norris remembered Sally telling the Todd children that, "jay birds went to hell every Friday night and told the devil all of our shortcomings of the previous week."[5]

3. Nelson: Nelson became lame, but "did tolerably well in the dining room. He was a good financier—he did the marketing and managed to save enough out of the market money to buy himself a horse."[6]

4. Chaney Dickerson: Described as a "delightful cook, but very cross and ill-tempered,"[7] it is thought perhaps she is the cook mentioned as the creator of a pecan cake which Abraham Lincoln claimed was one of the best cakes he ever ate.[8] Years later, Chaney was living in Western Kentucky with Alexander Todd, the youngest son, who was managing farmland owned by his father. Chaney and two of her children were sold together as a family unit after Robert Smith Todd's death to David Humphreys, Elizabeth Humphreys Todd's brother. The infant boy, the little girl Mary Ann, and their mother, Chaney, were appraised at nine hundred and fifty dollars.[9]

5. Mary Ann: Chaney's daughter.

6. Chaney's infant son: This child's name is unknown. At the time of the appraisal, he was just six weeks old.

7. Jane (Wales) Sanders: Jane, described as "a treasure," married Lewis Sanders at the Todd home in August 1835. Kentucky law did not recognize slave marriage, so Jane and her husband lived apart for the first twenty years of their marriage. Jane lived with the Todd family, loaned to them by Mary Humphreys, the mother of Elizabeth Humphreys Todd. Grandmother Humphreys granted Jane her freedom through her will, but there were stipulations. The will was recorded in April 1836, and Jane received her freedom on December 25, 1844. The will also said that Jane's children (should she have any) were not to be given their freedom until they reached a certain age: boys were freed at the age of 28; girls were freed at the age of 21. Gradual emancipation, based on age, was a common practice, used by individuals as well as territories and states as they phased out slavery.[10]

8. Judy: Judy was a young assistant nurse who lived in the Todd home but was not owned by the Todd family; like Jane, Judy was enslaved

by Grandmother Mary Humphreys. Judy was described as "good, and reliable, and versatile." She was granted her freedom on December 25, 1839, via Mrs. Humphreys' will. The stipulation applied to Jane's children applied to Judy's children as well.[11]

9. Dick: Elizabeth Humphreys Norris told a story of when little Dick was seven or eight. The Todd family was at their country home, Buena Vista, located outside Frankfort. All the children, both enslaved and slaveholder, were busy playing when Dick was asked to fetch a pitcher of fresh water. He did so but muttered loudly enough for everyone to hear him, "The white folks just works me to death."[12]

10. Harvey: Harvey was one of the enslaved persons sold after Robert Smith Todd's death. Appraised at seven hundred dollars, Harvey was purchased by David Humphreys. Elizabeth Humphreys Todd claimed this amount was excessive because "the face of Harvey was badly scarred."[13]

11. Pendleton: Pendleton's appraised value was five hundred and fifty dollars. He was a boy described by Betsy as being "delicate and subject to a bleeding at the nose." Although Pendleton had lived with Levi Todd, he was sold during the settlement of Robert Smith Todd's estate and purchased by David Humphreys. Pendleton was Chaney's son.[14]

12. William: William was sold because he frequently ran away.

13. Mary Jane: Mary Jane was mentioned in Katherine Helm's book as a "young slave girl belonging to Mrs. Todd" who accompanied Elizabeth Humphreys Norris to retrieve Mary from Madame Mentelle's school. According to Elizabeth's story, Mary Jane "shied off from Mary like a skittish colt" when she heard Mary speaking French.[15]

14. Celia: Celia was a mulatto enslaved girl from New Orleans who was owned by the Brands family (unidentified). Betsy Todd hired her (her wages were paid to the Brands family) to be a nurse for Alexander "Alec" Humphreys Todd, Mary's youngest half-sibling, for a period of one year.[16]

15. John Sanders: John was the older son of Jane and Lewis Sanders.

16. Jim Sanders: Jim was the younger son of Jane and Lewis Sanders.

How did the Todd family treat the enslaved people they owned?

When it comes to slave relations, the views of the slaveholder and the views of the enslaved person are extraordinarily different. Elizabeth Humphreys Norris recalled that Sally "alternately spoiled and scolded

the children, but they loved her and never rebelled against her authority."
She also wrote, "I think the slaves rather managed us, and we heard of
no cruelty to the slaves of our friends who seemed to love and trust their
servants as we did ours . . . Mary and I wondered if Mammy wanted to
be free; we concluded she did not. How could we do without Mammy,
and how could she exist without us?"[17] These seem to be the thoughts
of children who cannot imagine life being any different from their reality. Helm indicates she thought the enslaved people living in the Todd
household were mostly happy. She mentions enslaved children playing with white children. She wrote that their enslaved people were "a
very important, loved, and venerated part, of our family."[18] It is highly
doubtful that any of those enslaved by the Todd family felt "happy" in
servitude. William obviously longed for freedom, for he ran away on
several occasions. During the court proceedings over the settlement of
Robert Smith Todd's estate, Elizabeth Humphreys Todd testified that
her stepson, Levi, had whipped Pendleton, a young, enslaved man who
lived with him.[19] The testimonies show those who were enslaved had a
vastly different opinion of slavery than the white children.

Was Mary aware of the negative impact slavery had on those held in bondage?

As a child, Mary seemed unaware that the institution of slavery was
morally wrong. She only understood it as she saw it—an accepted part
of life. However, Mary was horrified by stories of abuse, cruelty, and
torture. Mary's friend Elizabeth Humphreys Norris wrote of an incident
from New Orleans that was reported in the newspapers. "The house of
Mr. and Mrs. Lalaurie being discovered in flames; the doors were broken
open and several unfortunate slaves were discovered chained in the attic!
They were removed to a place of safety where they would be protected
from the cruelty of their owners." A riot of protest broke out among the
citizens, and the Lalauries left New Orleans, never to return.[20]

When Elizabeth wrote these words to Katherine Helm, perhaps her
advanced age had softened her memories. In their youth, Mary and her
step-cousin were surrounded by images and symbols of cruelty the institution of slavery contained. When the public whipping post decayed
so badly that it could no longer be used, the county court held a special
session and "ordered that the three-pronged poplar tree in the Court-
House yard" be established as the new public whipping post.[21] The

local newspapers were often filled with notices of freedom seekers, slave auctions, and criminal activities toward those who were enslaved and by enslaved people themselves. As the daughter of a Lexington politician, Mary would have been aware of these incidents.

Did any such incidents happen to the Todd family?

The presence of Celia, an enslaved girl hired from the Brands family in New Orleans to care for Alec, caused the child to cry. For an unknown reason, Alec would shrink and hold back whenever Celia tried to touch him. Though Alec was examined from time to time, no one ever found a mark on him, and the family was mystified by his behavior. The other servants, who were afraid of Celia, waited until she returned to New Orleans before telling Elizabeth Humphreys Todd that Celia had a habit of holding Alec upside down by his feet until his face would turn blue.[22]

Was Mary aware of incidents when enslaved servants mistreated their owners?

When the Lincolns stopped in Lexington to visit the Todd family in 1847, much of the male population was away due to the Mexican War. Several slaveholders felt that with the men away, those who were enslaved had few restraints. Lawlessness became prominent throughout the city, and several attempts were made upon the lives of slaveholders. John and Martha Hamilton were served pounded glass mixed in with their gravy by an enslaved girl named Cassilly. Another enslaved girl served Hector P. Lewis a cup of coffee containing a deadly poison. In addition, it was believed that Mrs. Elizabeth Warren was murdered at the hands of enslaved individuals.[23]

Did any of the men in Mary's family father enslaved children? Did Mary know about them?

Yes, and according to historian William H. Townsend, all of Lexington knew as well. Mary's father's first cousin, Mary Owen Todd, married Colonel James Russell. They had one son, John Todd Russell. In 1816, while John was attending Princeton, he returned to Kentucky for a summer visit with his maternal grandmother, Jane Hawkins Todd Irvine. There he met a young, enslaved girl named Amelie "Milly" Crawford, who was of mixed race and considered to be seven-eighths European descent. The two became involved in what historian William Townsend described as "a secret but ardent attachment."[24] However, some believe it was rape. The result was the birth of Alfred Francis Russell in 1817. In 1822, when John became ill, and was near death, he acknowledged that Alfred was his son. Alfred was five years old when his father died.

Jane Hawkins Todd Irvine, who owned Milly and Alfred, also died in 1822. Mary Owen Todd Russell, who was Jane's daughter and John's mother, purchased Milly and Alfred, her grandson, for twelve hundred dollars. The little boy, although still enslaved, was treated as the heir of his grandmother's estate, which consisted of two thousand acres of land near Lexington. When Mary Owen Todd Russell married Robert Wickliffe in 1826, she learned that Kentucky law mandated that all her enslaved persons, included her grandson and his mother, were now the property of her husband. He refused to grant them emancipation unless she conveyed to him her entire estate, which was valued at a quarter of a million dollars. Mrs. Wickliffe agreed to her husband's terms, and in 1833, she emancipated Alfred, Milly, Milly's cousin Lucretia, and Lucretia's four children. She sent them to Liberia where they would be safe from Kentucky slave laws. Alfred grew up to become a planter and politician. In 1881, he became vice president of Liberia.

Townsend found the story of Milly and Alfred fascinating enough to devote an entire chapter to their tale in his book, *Lincoln and the Bluegrass: Slavery and Civil War in Kentucky.*[25]

Did Mary's father/other family members try to keep enslaved families together?

It is difficult to know for certain whether he did or not. There is an entry in a deed book indicating Robert Smith Todd purchased a enslaved person for a use other than his household staff. In 1842, Robert Todd, William Barr, and William Rodes jointly purchased an eight-year-old enslaved boy named Henry at a sale by Samuel Briggs Todd. (Samuel was Robert's younger brother.) Robert then conveyed Henry to Edmund Barr for $1.00 and other considerations. Barr was the trustee for Caroline Barr, who was Samuel's wife.[26] What is unclear is why Henry was for sale. If he were truly bought at Samuel's sale and returned to Caroline, it is possible Samuel was selling property to pay debts. It is also possible the child was purchased to reunite him with a biological family. There are many possibilities, and no clear answers.

During the estate auction of Robert Smith Todd, Chaney, her young daughter, and her infant son were purchased together by David Humphreys, and it is possible he returned Chaney and her children to his sister, the widowed Elizabeth Todd.[27]

Who called Mary "the arm/limb of Satan?"

The "limb of Satan" story was first recorded by Katherine Helm. Katherine wrote that when the children misbehaved, Sally called them "a limb of Satan loping down the broad road leading to destruction." She must have used the phrase often, becauser it became a bit of a joke among the children, and they would use it when teasing one another. Years later, a historian mistakenly attributed the phrase as one used by Mary's stepmother Betsy (Elizabeth Humphreys Todd) instead of Sally, and people have been misquoting the story ever since.[28]

Did Robert Smith Todd have anything to do with the Main Street Baptist Church (African American) that is next door to the Todd Home?

No, but his children did. According to the church's website, John De-Garris (unidentified) purchased the property from the heirs of Eliza Parker Todd in 1853 for Pastor Frederick Braxton to open the Independent Baptist Church (later the Main Street Baptist Church). The land had originally belonged to Mary's maternal grandfather, Robert Parker. He had passed away in 1800, and his wife, Elizabeth Porter Parker died in 1851. At the time the property was purchased by the church, it would have been part of Elizabeth Parker's estate. As the grandchildren of Robert and Elizabeth Porter, and the children of their daughter Eliza, the property would have been purchased from them.[29]

Was the Todd Home part of the Underground Railroad?

No, but there is a mysterious story that originated in the letters of Elizabeth Humphreys Norris which caused speculation. Katherine Helm published the story in her book, leading a few historians to try to find a connection between the home and the Underground Railroad.

According to Elizabeth, she and Mary heard knocking at the back door one night. Mary was supposed to have said, "Mammy, what is that knocking? It disturbs me so I can't read." Sally explained that it *might* be a freedom seeker. She told the girls that she herself had placed a mark on the fence so that if a person escaping slavery was hungry, he would see the mark and know he could stop to pick up cornbread and bacon. Mary, knowing it was illegal to help a freedom seeker, became fearful for Sally's safety. According to Kentucky law, if an enslaved person was caught helping an escapee, that person could be sold immediately to the deepest part of the South, such as Alabama or Louisiana, where the exploitation of slave labor had a crueler reputation than that of the Border States. Reportedly, in the Deep South enslaved persons were sometimes worked till they dropped dead in their tracks. Even if the person helping was emancipated, he or she could be sold into slavery. Others who helped freedom seekers would be placed in jail, or worse. In a town near Lexington, posters announced that antislavery speeches were illegal and punishable by death.[30] Not wanting her beloved nurse to be punished, Mary jumped up and said she would take the food down herself: No one would dare put a young white girl in jail. Elizabeth Humphreys Norris said that Sally had to restrain Mary from going to the door, and that she explained if a white hand reached out in the night, the escapee would hide "like a scared rabbit." The girls kept Sally's secret, and as hard as they listened, they never heard the knocking again.[31]

While it is almost certainly true that the girls heard knocking at the back door; and Sally gave an explanation as to why there was knocking, the question is: Was Sally telling the truth? Since Mary was stopped from seeing who was at the door, and since the girls never heard the knocking again, no one knows. Perhaps it truly was a freedom seeker. Perhaps it was a messenger. Perhaps Sally had a late-night boyfriend coming to call. To say the Todd home was part of the Underground Railroad is pure speculation and probably not true. Whether or not there was a mark on the fence post is a mystery, but it is doubtful. If anyone had found the mark, the enslaved people could have been sold. Mary's father would have been arrested and his political career would have been destroyed. It is likely the risk was too high for anyone in the Todd household to have helped escapees.

What were the Todds' feelings about emancipation?

Members of the Todd family (i.e., Robert Smith Todd, his siblings, cousins, and their ancestors) seem to have sat on both sides of the fence concerning slavery. Newspaper articles and court documents show that members of the Todd family bought and sold enslaved people, inherited them, witnessed business transactions involving them, and offered rewards for freedom seekers. The family supported and depended upon slave labor.

Several members of the Todd family believed in gradual emancipation and thought slavery would eventually die out on its own. Several of them left provisions in their wills for enslaved persons to be given their freedom. Mary's grandmother Elizabeth Rittenhouse Porter Parker gave two of her enslaved women their freedom, a pension, and burial plots. Mary's father had former enslaved servants working in his home. Emancipation was not foreign to the Todds of Kentucky, but it was not practiced by all of them either.

In 1849, Robert Smith Todd was nominated for a second term in the Kentucky Senate by the Whig party. His opponent, Colonel Oliver Anderson, was a proslavery advocate. During the campaign, he charged Todd as being an emancipationist, resulting in Todd being labeled as the Emancipation Candidate. Even though Todd issued a statement denying he favored emancipation or that he would "interfere with slavery as a vested right in any manner whatever," he also admitted he had always been "ever in favor of the Act of 1833, prohibiting the importation of slaves into the Commonwealth."[32] Politically and personally, Todd was a contradiction. He did not consider himself to be an abolitionist, but he deplored the institution of slavery. He took pride in having neither sold or bought an enslaved person for several years, but he was dependent upon the people he owned and had no plans to grant their freedom.

What happened to the Todd family enslaved persons after Robert Smith Todd died?

According to the settlement of Robert's estate, some of them were bequeathed to his son Levi O. Todd. Some were sold. Some remained with his widow, Elizabeth.[33]

Did Mary ever own, or inherit, enslaved persons from her family?

As an adult, Mary lived in Illinois—a free state. Mary was never a slaveholder either at her home, or while living in Washington.

The question of inheritance is debatable. If a person wanted to "split hairs" over the technicality of the law, it could be said that Mary was part owner of her father's estate while it was being settled. His estate included enslaved persons. However, she was not a slaveholder in the sense of having control over enslaved people or being in possession of them. Mary did not reside in the same state as her father. Although Abraham and Mary were never slaveholders themselves, they did financially benefit from the sale of enslaved persons who were sold at auction during the settlement of Robert Smith Todd's estate.

Were the Todd family members in Illinois slaveholders?

Yes, and both Abraham and Mary had contact with the enslaved servants on a regular basis.

Hepsey Arnsby Smith claimed to have been a gift to Illinois governor Ninian Edwards (father-in-law to Elizabeth Todd Edwards). Her claim to have been an enslaved person owned by the governor may be debatable; however, there is no doubt she was an indentured servant in the household of Ninian and Elizabeth Edwards. On October 29, 1845, at the age of eleven, Hepsey and the twenty-six-year-old Ninian Edwards entered in a contract which ensured Hepsey would "learn the art and mystery of domestic housewifery." She was to serve the Edwards family until she turned eighteen. In return, Hepsey would receive, "meat, drink, washing, lodging, apparel suitable and proper for such an apprentice, and needful medical attention." Edwards was to "cause her to read." She would receive no monetary pay for her services, and when the contract was filled, she would receive "a new Bible, and two suits of clothes suitable and proper for summer and winter wear."

Hepsey served the family for seven years and was present at the wedding of Abraham and Mary. She later claimed that one of her duties was to open the door when Lincoln came to court Mary. Hepsey also claimed that she assisted Mary in the Lincoln's home and was a nurse to Robert Todd Lincoln. Her claims to have worked in the Lincoln household and nursed Robert are not documented.[34]

Another member of the Todd family who was a slaveholder, or at least had indentured servants in his home, was Mary's uncle, Dr. John Todd. Phoebe was a young woman about twenty-two years of age when Dr. Todd sold the services of her and her three young children to Maria L. Todd (Dr. Todd's sister, and Mary Lincoln's aunt) in Madison County, Kentucky. It is not known how many years Phoebe served Maria. Her daughter did so until her eighteenth birthday; the two sons served until they reached the age of twenty-one years.[35]

Mary and the African American Citizen

Did Mary hire African Americans as servants or hired help in her Springfield home?

Yes, Mary hired several African American girls and women to assist with household duties. The Lincolns also hired at least four African American men to assist with labor (see chapter 2 for more information).

Did Mary prefer hiring African American servants because they reminded her of her family's slaves?

Katherine Helm wrote that Chaney, the enslaved cook, voiced her concern that the "po' white trash Irish didn't even know how to make good co'n bread." Helm also wrote that Sally was "insufferably arrogant for days after Miss Mary wished she had a good old black nurse for little Willie."[36] Katherine may have believed Mary did prefer enslaved help, or she may have wanted to create a softer, kinder image of the relationship between the Todd family and their enslaved servants. Since Helm's father, Confederate Brigadier General Benjamin H. Helm, had died in battle at Chickamauga, and her mother was one of the women who became known as the "mother" of the Orphan Brigade, Katherine's writings regarding the relationships between the enslaved and slaveholder probably depict more of her own feelings than those of Mary Lincoln.

Mary was a frugal Victorian housewife in a frontier town. She employed domestic help of several national origins. Her choice of employees had more to do with wages, capability, and availability than ethnicity.

Did Mary feel superior to her hired help, or did she see them as equals in society?

Having been raised in an aristocratic family, Mary recognized that her lifestyle was on a different social plane than that of most Americans. As the wife, and later widow, of an American president, her social plane rose even more. As a dotng grandmother, Mary wanted to ensure that her daughter-in-law and granddaughter wore clothing that depicted the family's social position. While in Europe, one of Mary's favorite pastimes was to find beautiful garments for the women in the family. In 1872, when questioned about the purchases, Mary responded that it, "is not too much, for people in *our station* of life—The very *middle classes* in Europe, dress their children quite as much & as I do not consider ourselves in that category, I would not care what the MEAN & ENVIOUS, would say."[37]

Mary viewed herself as part of the aristocracy, but that does not mean she did not treat everyone equally or that she believed she was "better" than others. While they are difficult to prove, stories such as the child-hood story of King Solomon and her treatment of the White House staff indicate that she was hospitable to everyone. Colonel William H. Crook stated that Mary was "kind to all the employees of the White House" and that she was generally well liked.[38]

Mary and the Free African American Community in Washington

Did Mary entertain African Americans at the White House?

At least twice, the White House lawn was the location for events held by African American churches. On July 4, 1864, the St. Matthews Colored Sunday School held a gathering on the lawn between the Executive Mansion and the War Department. Local newspapers advertised the event as a festival to help raise funds to build a schoolhouse. Entertain-ment would consist of "speaking, singing, and a fine band."[39] Francis Carpenter wrote of the event, "no celebration of the day presented a greater appearance of enjoyment and success."[40]

In late July, Mr. J. R. Pierre, the superintendent of the Third Colored Baptist Sabbath School, wrote a letter requesting use of the same lawn to hold a demonstration of appreciation. This was a religious service featuring several ministers from local African American churches. At the Jubilee, attendees were treated to refreshments that included fresh fruits, cakes, and lemonades. Swings were hung from the trees for chil-dren and adults to pass the time. This event also was an opportunity to sell refreshments to those passing by. The funds raised were used to purchase a banner for the school. "The Banner of Freedom" was to contain "a life size picture of President Lincoln, together with a design representing the freeing of slaves from bondage to freedom."[41] There is no documentation that Mary attended either of these events.

In April 1864, an African American woman named Caroline Johnson came to the White House to present the president with a gift of appreci-ation. Born into slavery, she had made her way to Philadelphia and was an active nurse in the hospitals during the war. She created a "superb collection of wax-fruits, together with a stem-table" and traveled with her minister, Mr. Hamilton, to Washington to present the gift to the president. The two arrived on a reception day. Lincoln sent word that he would receive Caroline at one o'clock; Mary was present.[42]

Did Mary support emancipation?

As with many women of the nineteenth century, Mary's opinions regarding slavery and emancipation were complicated, sometimes contradictory, and evolved over time. As a child, Mary could not imagine that those enslaved people she saw everyday wanted to be anywhere other than with her family. Her home was their home; their children were her servants and her playmates. Young Mary's feelings most likely mimicked those of her parents; Henry Clay; and her step-grandmother, Mary Humphreys, all of whom owned enslaved persons and depended upon them for labor but also supported emancipation in some form. Mary's desire to emulate Grandmother Humphreys was reflected in her declaration that, "If I can only be, when I am grown up, just like Grandmother Humphreys, I will be perfectly satisfied with myself."[43] Mary Humphreys was described as an emancipationist who had great influence on forming Mary's views about slavery. In Humphreys' twenty-four paragraph will, eight of them discuss the future and emancipation of her enslaved people.[44]

The Clay and Todd families held similar political views regarding slavery. Neither wanted it to spread throughout the country. And neither could maintain their lifestyle without their slave labor.

As an adult in Springfield, Mary held political views, but she rarely wrote about them. At this time, neither Mary nor Lincoln considered social equality between the races to be possible. Mary shared her husband's views that slavery needed to be left alone where it was, but not be allowed to spread into new territories. She had to find a middle ground between her slaveholding family and her husband's antislavery political views. When Lincoln joined the Republican Party, Mary, feeling the need to explain to her family that her husband was not an extremist, wrote to her sister Emilie, "Altho' Mr. L. is, or was a *Fremont* man, you must not include him with so many of those, who belong to *that party*, an *Abolitionist*."[45] Mary also complained to her sister about the lack of decent domestic help in Springfield stating, "If some of you Kentuckians, had to deal with the 'wild Irish,' as we housekeepers are sometimes called upon to do . . ."[46] While Mary did not say it, the indication is that she wished she could find help in Springfield that was as well trained as the enslaved workers she remembered from her childhood. The immigrant servants she hired were not as particular about their work.

In Washington, Mary grew to loathe the idea of slavery. This may have been in part because of her deteriorating relationships with her Confederate relations. They had turned their backs on the country, her husband, and her. She disassociated herself with them, their lifestyle, and their culture. Mary specified that her Confederate brothers were "*half*-brothers . . . whom she had not known since they were infants," and that she, herself, had "left Kentucky at an early age" and held sympathies that were entirely Republican.[47]

Mary surrounded herself with those who supported emancipation, such as Massachusetts senator Charles Sumner. As the war progressed, Mary took more of an active role in promoting the antislavery movement. African American guests such as Frederick Douglass and Sojourner Truth were welcomed guests, not just outside, but also inside, the White House—a rare occurrence for the times. Mary did not limit the White House guest list to prominent African Americans who worked toward emancipation. She also invited African Americans who had other occupations and endeavors. Once, she invited an African American teacher to the White House for tea. The doorman had the honored guest arrive through the servant's entrance. Mary became angry upon hearing of the doorman's mistake but expressed nothing but kindness to the teacher. When it was time to depart, Mary reached for the teacher's hand and warmly shook it.[48] It was a small gesture that expressed the changing views about emancipation held by the First Lady.

Did Mary support any charities, or take an active role in organizations, that focused on the welfare of the freed African American community in Washington?

Mary's seamstress, Elizabeth Keckly, created the Contraband Relief Association during the summer of 1862 for "the benefit of the suffering blacks." Contraband camps were often established near Union forces by escaped enslaved refugees. Since the refugees were considered Confederate property, the Union forces considered them "contrabands of war." Populated primarily with women, children, and older men, the camps became a way station between slavery and freedom. Keckly wrote that

when she presented the idea of supporting these camps to the congregation of her church, the members found the idea popular. According to
Keckly, when she told the First Lady of the efforts, Mary "immediately
headed my list with a subscription of $200."[49] Mary wrote a letter to her
husband requesting that the donation be taken from a fund containing
one thousand dollars. She explained that the freedmen living in Washington were in dire need of bed coverings for they had nothing to cover
themselves.[50] Keckly noted in her memoirs that "Mrs. Lincoln made
frequent contributions, as also did the President." One of the highest
priorities within the camps was education for both adults and children.
Mary was reported to have purchased books to send to the camps.[51]

What was Mary's relationship with Mrs. Elizabeth Keckly? Were they close? Why did she become so close to a formerly enslaved person?

Elizabeth Keckly was hired as a mantua maker to create a wardrobe for
Mary that was worthy for someone of social prominence. Her client list
included the wives and daughters of senators and military leaders, as
well as the wife of Jefferson Davis. Upon hearing the names of Keckly's clientele, Mary hired her to create a special dress—a rose-colored
moiré-antique gown—for a levee. Keckly arrived at the White House,
dressed Mary, and arranged her hair. Lincoln voiced his approval of
Mary's appearance, "I declare, you look charming in that dress." Mrs.
Keckly's success at creating a stunning gown ensured her position as
Mary's regular modiste. Over the next several months, she created fifteen or sixteen dresses for the First Lady.[52]

Keckly became more than a dress maker to Mary. She became somewhat of a friend and confidante. Keckly would often come to the White
House and help Mary dress for events, and the two women would con-
fide in one another while Mary dressed. They discussed the war, politics,
and money. They bonded over the loss of children. Keckly comforted
Mary when Willie died, and she sat with Mary after Abraham's death.
The two women shared things that only women understand. For Mary,
it was easy to become close to the woman who was lacing her corset.

At the same time, it must be remembered that the relationship was
also a business relationship. Mary paid Keckly to create the gowns and
serve as a dresser. While the two women shared confidential information, Keckly was on the payroll. Keckly was not invited to the White

House parties. She did not sit down to dinner in the White House dining room.

Theirs was a complicated friendship that could not always escape the social rules of race, rank, and society. It was an important relationship to Mary, and one that she depended upon during some of her most devasting days. Unfortunately, the relationship did not last.

What caused the friendship to end? Did Mary reconcile with Elizabeth Keckly?

After Lincoln's death, Mary gave Keckly several items that had belonged to the president: the cloak and bonnet Mary wore to Ford's Theatre the night of the assassination, Lincoln's brush and comb, a glove worn at the first reception after the second inaugural, and Lincoln's overshoes. These were items Mary expected to be cherished mementoes. Instead, Keckly donated them to Wilberforce College (now University) to help the school raise funds after a devastating fire. Her late son had attended the school, and Keckly wished to support it in his memory. Mary was furious the gifts had been given away. The two continued to communicate, but the relationship became strained.[53]

Two years later, Keckly wanted to help Mary's public image and thought writing a tell-all book would depict Mary in a kinder light and explain why she had tried to sell her old wardrobe. Keckly enlisted the help of James Redpath to write *Behind the Scenes or Thirty Years a Slave, and Four Years in the White House.* The book was in part an enslaved person's narrative. But it was the tell-all, behind-the-White-House-doors chapters that were scandalous. Keckly had loaned private letters Mary had written her to Redpath, who included them in the text. Conversations between Mary and her husband were disclosed. Keckly included topics which were discussed in confidence.

The book was published in 1868. Mary felt betrayed, that Keckly had violated her privacy and betrayed her confidence. The Victorian codes of social behavior and the lines between employer and employee were shattered. Keckly's attempt to benefit Mary, and make a profit for herself, failed miserably. The friendship between the two women was broken and they never reconciled.

CHAPTER NINE

Personality and Personal Habits

I have thought seriously over the whole business, and know what I am about.
> —Mary Lincoln to Elizabeth Keckly, November 24, 1867

*L*earning aspects of a person's personality and their personal habits allows one to understand, and somewhat know, another individual. Friendships and romantic relations are built on gleaning information and finding common interest between two people. In getting to know Mary Lincoln, one would find that she enjoyed a good joke, beautiful music, many kinds of literature, and fine horses. Her sister Elizabeth described Mary as "quick, lively, gay, and frivolous." She found Mary to be a social woman who loved "glitter, show, and pomp, and power."[1] Through her voluminous collections of chatty letters to her friends, Mary does appear to have been an extremely friendly and social person. Elizabeth may have thought that Mary loved "pomp and power," and she did, but she did not like everything associated with it. Because of the power held by her husband, the press often followed Mary everywhere she went. Mary struggled to keep many aspects of her life private.

In the present day it often seems that anyone can find information about everyone simply by searching the World Wide Web. The thirst for personal knowledge about celebrities, politicians, and even our friends, continues to consume society. Victorians would have been mortified to have such tidbits of personal information divulged; Mary and members of her family were classical Victorians and found no reason for such information to be shared. Still, through letters, interviews, and memoires, a few clues about Mary's personality and her personal habits can be found.

Personal Traits

Did Mary have musical knowledge? Did she like to sing? Did she play the piano or any other musical instrument?

Yes, yes, and yes. The study of music was part of the curriculum at Madame Mentelle's school; therefore, Mary understood music and may have received piano lessons as part of her studies. Singing was a common form of entertainment for many people during the Victorian era; stories of the Coterie members singing together and caroling during the Christmas season have been passed through the generations. Even Abraham Lincoln was known to break into song.

It is known that the Lincoln children studied music. James M. Davidson traveled throughout Illinois teaching music and piano and in his later years, he claimed that both Mrs. Abraham Lincoln and her son Robert had been among his pupils.[2] Willie and Tad Lincoln both studied piano under the guidance of Hester Reeves, who was the daughter of Springfield's confectioner, W. Watson. In a letter dated May 5, 1862, Mary wrote a condolence letter to Charles Reeves (Hester's husband) upon Hester's death, mentioning that Hester had been Willie's first piano teacher.[3] Family lore claim that both Willie and Mary would practice the piano at the Edwards' home as the Lincolns did not own a piano.

There was a piano in the White House. According to the reminiscences of Alexander Williamson, Robert Lincoln was heard playing "a selection from the opera *Maritane* on the piano in the White house library."[4] Julia Taft Bayne remembered practicing her piano pieces as Mary stood beside her and turned the pages. To have done this, Mary had to know music well enough to follow the score and turn at the appropriate moment, a task which requires counting the beats, and being able to read multiple lines of music simultaneously; this ability requires a deep understanding of composition and music theory. Such skills would have given Mary the ability, at the very least, to know how to play the simplest of compositions on the instrument. Mary also encouraged Julia Taft to learn several pieces of music including "Colonel Ellsworth's Funeral March" which she insisted was Julia's duty to learn: Mary would have encouraged Julia to learn the piece because Ellsworth was a close friend to the Lincoln family and the first commissioned officer to die during the Civil War. Julia wrote, "with some help from my teacher, my mother and Mrs. Lincoln, I finally mastered the composition and Mrs. Lincoln had me play it for the President, who was good enough to compliment me in his kindly way on its rendition."[5]

Did Mary collect anything particular?

When Mary was a young girl, her father bought pieces of Meissen porcelain; she continued collecting as an adult.

Meissen was the first hard-paste porcelain created in Germany. It is identified by its trademark crossed swords. Collected by wealthy families throughout Europe and America, several collections have become the property of museums. There are pieces of Mary's collection currently in museums.

Visitors to the Lincoln Home in Springfield often notice a display of seashells. A bowl of shells was a common decoration in many Victorian homes.

J. S. Bliss told William Herndon that when visiting the Lincolns, he saw "a whatnot in the corner of the room was laden with various kinds of shells." Bliss thought one of the shells may have been a "trowsby." Either Herndon misheard the name of the shell or his handwritten notes were misread for there is no shell called a "trowsby."

In 1869, Mary wrote to her daughter-in-law, "if you like shells—you will find plenty of them—in a large red bowl—they were gathered together, in my own happy S. home . . . "[6]

Did Mary sew, knit, or do other fiber arts?

All the Todd daughters, including Mary, learned to sew, embroider, and knit. After finishing her school lessons, one of Mary's nightly chores was to knit "ten rounds of sock."[7]

In an early letter written while visiting her cousin Ann in Missouri, Mary wrote to her friend Mercy Levering, "I have scarce a leisure moment to call my own, for several weeks this fall a formidable supply of *sewing*, necessary to winter comfort, engaged our constant attention."[8] It was a daunting task for every married woman to provide her family with clothing, bed coverings, curtains, table clothes, napkins, and all other linens.

Several friends and family members have referenced Mary's ability as a seamstress. Her sister Frances stated that Mary was "one of the best seamstresses I ever knew. She made all of her clothes and her children's clothes; and they were better made than most anyone else's."[9] When Lincoln was in Congress, and Mary and the boys were visiting family in Lexington, Mary wrote to him about a box of children's clothing she had hoped Frances would send to her. Children, especially toddlers, require many changes of clothing, and Mary hoped that the clothing "might save me a few stitches."[10]

In addition to her own clothing and the children's clothing, Mary most likely made Abraham's shirts and undergarments. Whether Mary owned a sewing machine in Springfield is unknown; most of her sewing was probably done by hand. Family history includes stories that Mary and other ladies gathered at the home of a neighbor woman to take advantage of the sewing machine she owned. Sadly, the name of the neighbor and any corroborating evidence has been lost.[11] With many relatives and friends in Springfield, Mary probably had access to a machine even if she did not personally own one.

Did Mary make Jack the Doll for Tad and Willie?

No, she did not. Jack was sent to Tad by the Sanitary Commission fair in New York. The Lincoln boys regularly court-martialed the doll, which was dressed in a Zouave uniform,[12] found him guilty of desertion, or being a spy, then ordered him to be "shot at sunrise." The doll was given a proper military funeral and buried among the roses. This happened on a regular basis, until finally the White House gardener, Major Watt, suggested the doll be pardoned so the roses could grow in peace. The boys presented their case to President Lincoln who granted the pardon and told the boys, "It's a good law that no man shall twice be put in jeopardy of his life for the same offence." Tad vowed never to bury Jack again, but within a week, Jack was found hung from a tree.[13]

Did Mary ever keep a diary?

No, she did not. However, some readers of *Loving Mr. Lincoln* by Kay Dupont are convinced she did. This book is the fictitious story of someone finding Mary's diary in an old desk and publishing its contents.

What type of books did the Lincolns read? Did Mary continue to read French books after moving to Springfield? Washington?

There are 152 books located in the Abraham Lincoln Presidential Library which are associated with the Lincoln family. Mary loved the works of

Shakespeare, Robert Burns, Lord Byron, and many others. She learned to speak and read French as a young girl and continued to do so as an adult. Henry B. Rankin, a young lawyer in Springfield, relayed a story about Mary's mastery of the French language: Knowing her fondness for the French poet and novelist Victor Hugo, Rankin brought Mary an issue of *Southern Literary Messenger* which contained a translation of one of Hugo's speeches. Mary had issues with the translation and asked Rankin if he could find a copy of the original. Two months later, Rankin brought her the desired copy. He recalled how Mary read it, "stopping often to compare the translation with the original. She read with such clearness and dramatic fervor, and translated with such sympathy that . . . I could only sit entranced." According to Rankin, Mary read both the newest writings and best classic French literature in the original.[14]

Why was Mary so jealous of other ladies closely affiliated with Mr. Lincoln, such as Mrs. Ord and Mrs. Grant?

Jealousy may not have been the feelings Mary truly had regarding these women. Mary followed the rules of etiquette for Victorian women and had no tolerance for women who overstepped their place in society. Mary felt both women did just that—especially Mrs. Ord who placed herself next to the President during a review of the troops.

Was Mary a kind woman or a shrew?

In his 1860 *Life of Abraham Lincoln*, author John L. Scripps described Mary as a "lady of charming presence, of superior intelligence, of accomplished manners, and in every respect well fitted to adorn the position for which the election of her husband to the presidency will place her."[15] Like many, he found Mary to be a dignified woman possessing southern charm and genteel kindness.

Others found Mary to be moody, prone to temper, and lacking self-control—or as Shakespeare termed it, a "shrew." Lincoln's law partner William Herndon called her "a she wolf." Herndon also wrote to a friend that Mary was "a very curious—Excentric (*sic*)– *wicked* woman."[16] Some historians dismiss Herndon's comments, stating that the two despised one another. Herndon disliked Mary because her place in society was on a different social plane than his; Mary disliked Herndon because he was a drunkard. But others found Mary's behavior shrewlike. Lincoln's secretaries referred to Mary as "hell-cat" and "her Satanic majesty."[17]

Some who knew her, such as Benjamin French, saw two sides to Mary's personality. By the end of 1861, he wrote that he liked "Mrs. L. better and better the more I see of her and think she is an admirable woman. She bears herself, in every particular, like a lady, and say what they may about her, I will defend her." However, when Mary left the White House in May 1865, French wrote that he believed she "exhibited all the symptoms of madness" and that it was "well for the nation that she is no longer in the White House." Even if one is inclined to dismiss French's later comments because Mary was a grieving widow at the time, note that he also wrote this: "It is not proper that I should write down, *even here*, all I know!"[18]

Like any person, Mary cannot be defined by a single adjective. Her personality comprised many moods, temperaments, thoughts, and emotions that could change depending on her surroundings and the events affecting her life. Was she kind? Yes, at times she was a generous, gracious woman who showed love and kindness. Was she a shrew? Yes, at times her temper overcame her, and she lashed out, scolding those around her. She could express a wide range of emotions.

The Favorites

What was Mary's favorite color?

Mary never recorded a favorite color; however, she did like to wear blue and purple.

What was Mary's favorite food?

Mary made very few comments about food, but it can be assumed she enjoyed a good biscuit and cornbread. When the Lincolns visited the Todd family in 1851, Mary tried to take directions of a "pinch of this, a little of that, and sweeten to taste" from Chaney, the family's enslaved cook, who was distressed because Mary had no one to make beaten biscuits and cornbread for her.[19] Years later, Mary wrote to her great-nephew, Lewis Edwards, about other missed foods from her youth: "How I long to see you all—to have a taste of your dear Grandma's good food—waffles, batter cakes, egg corn bread—are all unknown here—as to biscuits, light rolls && they have never been dreamed of—not to speak of buckwheat cakes."[20]

Mary's Appearance

How tall was Mary?

She was approximately five feet, two inches tall.

Was Mary fat?

At one point in her life, Mary considered herself to be overweight. In 1879, she wrote that she had been recently weighed and she weighed the same as she had in 1861. She continued, "since then, as a matter of course many pounds of flesh have departed . . . Therefore, I may conclude, my great bloat has left me & I have returned to my natural size." Three months later, Mary wrote, "I have now run down to 100- pounds, EXACTLY." So, even if she had once considered herself "fat" by the last years of her life and at her death, she was a very small woman.[21]

Was Mary considered a pretty woman?

Beauty is in the eye of the beholder. William Crook, a White House bodyguard, described Mary as, "a pretty woman, small and plump, with a round baby face and black eyes." (Family members claimed Mary's eyes were blue.)[22] A plausible occurrence at a White House reception indicates Lincoln agreed with Crook. Reportedly, Lincoln told a bystander at a White House reception, "My wife was as handsome as when she was a girl, and I, poor nobody then, fell in love with her, and what is more, have never fallen out." Since the story was not recorded until 1872, it may not contain Lincoln's exact words, or it may never have happened.[23] Whether or not Lincoln uttered the words, it is hoped he felt the sentiment. It is believed that Lincoln considered his wife to be attractive.

Health and Well Being

Did Mary take laudanum for migraines?

It is not known exactly what medication Mary took for headaches. Laudanum was a combination of ten percent powdered opium and one percent morphine. The other main ingredient was alcohol. Laudanum was prescribed for a variety of ailments, but its primary use was as a cough suppressant. It was also given to patients to relieve pain, induce sleep, ease diarrhea, relieve the discomforts of menstrual cramps, and many other physical ailments. It is probable that Mary took laudanum for something at some time during her life.

What did Mary's migraines signify, if anything, about her overall health?

When Lincoln served in the House of Representatives, he wrote to Mary commenting that she was free from headaches and that it was the first spring she had not suffered from them since he had known her. Therefore, since at least 1840, Mary suffered from migraine headaches every spring. These disabling headaches continued to plague Mary until at least 1867, and maybe longer. In his biography of Mary, Dr. W.A. Evans seemed to think the headaches were caused by a womanly nature and were related to the sex organs or possibly her sex life. He concluded that as women experience menopause, the headaches recur less often until they completely stop.

In November 1862 while visiting New York, Mary wrote to Lincoln, "I had one of my severe attacks, if it had not been for Lizzie Keckly, I do not know what I should have *done*—Some of *these periods*, will launch me away."[24] Mary was probably referring to periods of illness, not her menstrual cycle.

Since Mary's headaches were worse in the spring and fall, it is possible they were connected to pollen, blooming spring flowers, ragweed, or other plant allergens.[25]

Whatever the cause of the attacks, Mary defined them as "severe" indicating that she was in great pain.

Did other members of Mary's family suffer from migraines?

There are no records indicating that any other family member suffered from migraines.

What sort of physical ailments and conditions contributed to Mary's mental condition and behavior?

It is impossible to say that any of Mary's physical ailments contributed to her mental condition, other than to say that she often complained of "pain," which can cause stress. Mary also complained of a persistent cough and "weak lungs." During her trip to Florida in 1875, she was confined to bed for three weeks and needed a nurse. Being bedridden can cause stress but is not a factor in a patient's mental condition and behavior.[26]

Was Mary diabetic?

It is generally accepted that Mary suffered from the onset of Type II diabetes beginning around 1876. Mary complained of boils and her weight dropped to slightly over 100 pounds; these are both symptoms of diabetes. While living in France, Mary drank Vichy water, but she claimed that it did not help her. (Drinking the water is supposed to help soothe the digestive system, cure gout, rheumatism, ulcers, and other related illnesses.)

Personal Beliefs

Did Mary support the women's suffrage movement?

There is no evidence that indicates Mary supported the women's suffrage movement. She did write letters to loved ones about the happiness she experienced from being a wife and mother. When someone told Mary's daughter-in-law that "housekeeping and babies were an uncomfortable state of existence," Mary countered with, "a nice home—loving husband and precious child are the happiest stages of life." Mary clearly favored her son's wife being at home tending to her family.[27]

Did Mary attend church on a regular basis?

Emilie Helm described Mary as a "dyed-in-the-wool Presbyterian."[28] Most members of the Todd family were members of Presbyterian churches, and several of the men were ordained ministers in the faith. In Lexington, the Todd family attended what became Second Presbyterian Church, where as a child, Mary learned to recite the Shorter Catechism.[29] Mary and the boys attended church services even when Abraham did not. The Lincolns paid rent for a pew in the First Presbyterian Church of Springfield. They attended the New York Avenue Presbyterian Church in Washington, D.C. It is not clear if Mary attended church on a regular basis after Lincoln's death. She frequently mentioned her belief in God and her religious beliefs in her letters. Her funeral was held in the First Presbyterian Church in Springfield.

CHAPTER TEN

Beyond the Grave

> My belief, is so assured, that *Death*, is only a blessed transition, to the "pure in heart," that a very slight veil separates us, from the "loved & lost" and to me, there is comfort, in the thought, that though unseen by us, they are very near.
>
> —Mary Lincoln to Charles Sumner, July 4, 1865

After the death of her husband and three of her sons, Mary was consumed with the thought of death. She was preoccupied with a deep desire to die and was convinced she would do so soon. Mary wrote about death, prayed for it, and longed for it to take her to another realm. Her view of death was that it was a transition into another life where she would be reunited with her loved and lost. In Heaven, she would find her family waiting for her.

Mary seemed to have little interest in what would happen to her possessions or what her legacy would be after death. She did care about the legacy of her husband but thought hers would be only a slight mention in a history book. Mrs. Abraham Lincoln believed she would be remembered as a footnote.

She was wrong.

Mary Lincoln remains one of the most talked about, written about, and argued about First Ladies in American history. She is more than a footnote; she is an enigma. Interest in Mary's life has launched the writing careers of several historians. She has been a focal character in film and visual arts. Her images, fashions, and jewelry have inspired lines of collectables that admirers have sought to find and possess. Mary Lincoln's memory has become a business. If Mary Lincoln were to visit any Lincoln museum gift shop today, she would be flabbergasted at the quantity of merchandise embossed with her image that is available for purchase.

She would be astonished to learn that two centuries after her birth, people remember her and ask questions about her life.

The questions in this chapter are those that Mary would never have been able to answer in her life. They include questions about her estate and the division of her possessions. There are questions about the Lincoln Tomb and the museums across the country which represent Mary's life. There is an interest in collectible items and where they can be purchased. This interest would surprise Mary. However, what would be most compelling to her are the honors, tributes, and memorials which have been established in her memory. Mary expected the world to remember the name "Abraham Lincoln" as one of political greatness, and it does. However, with Mary standing beside him, Abraham is also remembered as a loving father and husband. Her memory evokes the kinder, gentler aspect of Lincoln's personality. It is impossible to separate the two. They are forever intertwined in the same manner as "the roots of two large pine trees which had grown so closely together." [1]

Did Mary leave a will?

Yes, she did; however, until recently when historian Jason Emerson found two pages of the surviving document, historians have believed Mary died intestate. It was a logical conclusion as at the time of Mary's death, Robert had to petition the Sangamon County Court to receive the estate.

Mary's will was dated and signed July 23, 1873; Judge James Bradwell and his wife Myra witnessed it. The will divided her estate between her son Robert and his children. The home in Chicago was bequeathed to Robert; the remainder was bequeathed by trust to Robert's children. Instructions in the will established Judge David Davis and John Todd Stuart (Mary's first cousin) as trustees of the estate. In 1874, Mary added a codicil setting aside a $1,000 U.S. Savings Bond to be paid to her grandson, Abraham "Jack" Lincoln II upon his twenty-first birthday. She had intended for the interest earned by the bond to be paid to Jack semiannually for "pocket money."

The will was never probated. According to the Bradwell family, at the time of Mary's death, Judge James Bradwell did not wish to make the document public for "it would have brought on another clash with Robert Lincoln . . . and reopened the old, unpleasant controversy." [2]

Mary's will is located in the Library of Congress.

Did Mary leave a large estate?

The sum of her estate was $84,035.00.

How many times has the Lincoln Tomb been remodeled?

Remodeled, or rebuilt? It has been rebuilt twice.

In 1899, it was learned that the six-foot-deep foundation was not strong enough to support the structure. The Lincoln family members' bodies were moved to a secure location. The entire structure had to be demolished and each stone numbered and stored for reuse. A new, twenty-three-feet deep foundation was laid, and the obelisk was rebuilt. After two years of demolition and reconstruction, a new, sturdier, improved Lincoln Tomb was ready for public viewing. It was similar in style to the original tomb, but 22 feet taller. It was a monument fit to honor the man who "belongs to the ages."

Sadly, it did not last. By 1928, the number of tourists and a leaky building caused such deterioration that the tomb had to be reconstructed again. Lincoln's body had been encased in cement in 1901; it therefore remained in his grave. The remains of the other family members were moved to a temporary vault. The statues were removed; granite stones again were removed and labeled. The terrace floor was replaced with concrete. The newly renovated Lincoln Tomb was reopened in 1931.[3]

What did they do with the bodies during construction?

At the time of the first reconstruction in 1899, the Lincoln Tomb was the final resting place for Mary; her sons, Willie, Eddy, Tad; and her grandson, Abraham "Jack" Lincoln. During the reconstruction, their bodies were cleverly camouflaged and secretly buried just a few feet from the tomb.

Construction began in 1928 for the second overhaul of the Lincoln Tomb. This time, the bodies of Mary, her boys, and her grandson were taken to the Oak Ridge Mausoleum and secretly marked so that only a few officials knew the exact locations. When it was time to move the family back to the Lincoln Tomb, Jack was not with them: In 1929, his mother requested that Jack be removed from Oak Ridge Cemetery and reinterred beside his father in Arlington National Cemetery. Jack was buried in Arlington in May 1930.[4]

There are those who believe that Mary was buried alongside her husband and not in the wall of the tomb. They point out that the grave was big enough for two caskets. Any idea how this got started and whether it could be true?

Mary is not buried alongside her husband in the Lincoln Tomb. After the failed attempt in 1876 to steal the body of the president, Robert Todd Lincoln was concerned another attempt would be made. Under Robert's direction in 1901, the Culver Construction Company opened the tile floor and dug a 10-foot hole. A steel cage was placed around the coffin, and it was lowered into the new grave. To ensure it could never be dug up again, two tons of concrete was poured on top of the coffin, and the grave was sealed.[5] Lincoln's body will never be moved again.

The idea that Mary is buried alongside her husband is a myth that continues today because in our culture married couples are usually buried side by side. It is sometimes difficult to believe that Abraham and Mary are forever separated by tons of cement.

Why is Robert not buried in the Lincoln Tomb with the rest of the family? Is it because of his difficult relationship with his mother?

Several historians have thought that Robert chose to be buried elsewhere because he did not want to forever be interred with his mother. Others have speculated the decision was made by his widow, Mary Harlan Lincoln. Robert had a deep emotional connection to his family and had every intention of being buried in the Lincoln Tomb. In September 1890, Robert wrote to O. M. Hatch, a member of the Lincoln Monument Association: "the desire came upon me that if it is met the views of every member of the Monument Association arrangement might be made for the burial in the monument of my son and thereafter of myself, and my wife, and of my two daughters unless they should marry."[6]

Robert died in his sleep during the night of July 25–26, 1926, from a cerebral hemorrhage induced by arteriosclerosis. When notifying the family of her husband's death, Mary Harlan Lincoln sent a telegram to Robert's cousin, Benjamin Hardin Helm saying: "Services here on Wednesday. Deferring Interrment (*sic*) at Springfield until Autumn." Clearly, at the time of Robert's death, the plan was for burial in the Lincoln Tomb. However, Robert's widow Mary quickly changed her mind. In August 1926, she wrote a letter to Katherine Helm—Robert's cousin with whom she held a close friendship.

Dearest Twin,

You will, I know be surprised at what I am going to tell you—
A thought came to me, by inspiration, [underlined twice] on the
night of the 11th of Aug, and it was this. That the beloved one
should be intered (sic) in the Arlington National Cemetery at
Washing, (sic) instead of within a crypt at Springfield.—After
prayerful thought over this, for many weeks I knew I was right, so
I began to set the wheels in motion—When we leave Manchester
we will go directly to Washington, where he will have a temporary
resting place, until I have had a suitable tomb built for him, final
interment to take place next Spring, probably— . . .

You know our darling was a personage, made his own history,
independently [underlined five times] of his great father, and
should have his own place 'in the sun'!

With her mind resolved, Mary Harlan Lincoln began making plans
for Robert's interment in Arlington. She chose a "beautiful wooded
knoll" located near Robert's good friend President William Howard
Taft. Robert's gravesite was in a direct line between the Lincoln Memorial and the home of Robert E. Lee. This seemed a fitting place to
Mary H. Lincoln as during his public life, Robert had fought to ease the
harsh policies of Reconstruction—something he felt his father would
have wanted. Robert's monument was made from "the finest and rarest
pink granite" from Branford, Connecticut. It bears his name, and the
years 1843–1926. Robert was interred on March 14, 1928.[7]

**Why do some historians refer to her as "Mary Todd Lincoln" while
others refer to her as "Mary Lincoln?" Which name did Mary use?**
Mary signed her name thirteen different ways, but she never signed
"Mary Todd Lincoln." The letters written to her friend Mercy were
signed "Mary." After her marriage, Mary signed letters to friends and
family with "Mary L," "ML," or "M. Lincoln." Letters written to friendly
politicians and businessmen were signed "Mrs. A. Lincoln." When Mary
ordered a new bonnet, asked for a political favor, or conducted financial business, she usually signed the letters "Mrs. Lincoln," or "Mrs. A.
Lincoln," "Mrs. President Lincoln," or "Mrs. A.L." The surviving letter
written home to a soldier's mother was signed "Mrs. Abraham Lincoln."
When writing to Robert's wife, Mary H. Lincoln, Mary usually signed

her own name "Mary Lincoln." After Abraham's death, Mary reached out more to her family members and often included her relationship in her signature, "Your Aunt Mary Lincoln" and "Your Sister, Mary Lincoln." One noticeable distinction is the letter dated June 19, 1876, written to Robert Lincoln shortly after Mary's release from Bellevue. This one was signed "Mrs. A. Lincoln."[8] One odd signature was "Mary Ann Cuthbert"; Cuthbert was a housekeeper at the White House. Letters dated from January 19, 1865 through May 19, 1865, indicate Mary used the maid's name to hide some of her own bills. Mary may have used this pseudonym as early as the fall of 1864.

Oddly, when printing Mary's obituary, a couple of Illinois newspaper referred to her as "Mary Todd Lincoln." It is generally thought that the newspapers used "Todd" to distinguish Mary from her daughter-in-law. At the time of Mary's death, her son Robert was the Secretary of War and a prominent member of Chicago society. Confusion could have easily occurred with an obituary simply stating "Mrs. Lincoln" or "Mary Lincoln." Many newspaper obituaries referenced Mary as "the Widow of President Lincoln."

Biographies written about Mary are split as to whether to use the name "Todd." W. A. Evans' published work, *Mrs. Abraham Lincoln: A Study of Her Personality and Her Influence on Lincoln* (1932) made clear use of Mary's name. "Mary Todd" was used when Evans wrote about Mary as a young woman prior to her marriage. "Mrs. Lincoln" was used when writing about her as a wife or widow. In *The Women Lincoln Loved* (1927), William Barton referred to the president's wife as "Mary Todd Lincoln." Honoré Willsie Morrow wrote *Mary Todd Lincoln, An Appreciation* (1928) following the example of other authors. It has been predominately male scholars who have inserted "Todd" into her name when writing her biographies, but it was an article written by her sister, Emilie Todd Helm which made it popular. In 1898, Emilie wrote an article for *McClure's Magazine* titled "Mary Todd Lincoln: Reminiscences and Letters of the Wife of President Lincoln." Emilie used "Todd" in her own signature, and she inserted it into her sister's name as well. The first part of the article focuses on the historical contributions the Todd family made to American history. Emilie's focus was clearly "Todd."

When the president of Sayre School in Lexington, Kentucky wanted to create a memorial to honor Mary, he established the Mary Todd

Lincoln Memorial Committee to raise funds for the project. By writing to wealthy businessmen and politicians and advertising his committee, he helped change Mary's name. Even though the name change began in Kentucky, it soon spread.

By the 1920s, Mary Lincoln had become "Mary Todd Lincoln." The addition of her maiden name did help distinguish her from her daughter-in-law, Mary (Harlan) Lincoln. It also helped identify her as Robert's mother since he always signed letters and other documents as "Robert Todd Lincoln" or "Robert T. Lincoln."

Mary would probably find the conflict over her name a bit amusing. She clearly chose her name to be "Mary Lincoln."

Are there any statues of Mary?

There are two. Sculptor Frederick Hibbard created the first statue dedicated to the memory of a U.S. president and his wife. Dedicated on July 4, 1943, it became the first statue of Mary. The seven-ton memorial was funded through the estate of Lena Rosewall who left $20,.000 for a monument depicting Abraham and Mary Lincoln. Its location, East Park in Racine, Wisconsin, was chosen because it was in this area that Mary Lincoln often "relaxed during her daily strolls around the downtown area when she visited Racine for several weeks in 1867."[9]

The couple is mounted on a five-foot base of pink granite from nearby Minnesota. "Abraham and Mary" were created from Georgia's Elberton gray granite. Mary stands seven feet high beside Abraham, who is seated. Hibbard made "an attempt to portray Mr. and Mrs. Lincoln at the time they entered the White House."[10] Mary wears a ball gown with a plain skirt and bodice. Around her shoulders is what appears to be a granite version of her famous white lace bertha. The artist carefully sculpted the Tiffany seed pearl necklace, bracelets, and earrings which had been a gift from Abraham. Her ensemble is completed with a floral corsage and a floral diadem made of roses. She holds her gloves.

Vandals have attacked these statues several times over the years. Their noses were damaged twice in the 1960s, one in the late 1990s and again in 2009.[11]

Unveiled on June 5, 2004, the second statue of Mary is part of a family scene. Created by Larry Anderson as part of the "Here I Have Lived" for the Looking for Lincoln Heritage program, four bronze sculptures depict the Lincolns as a family unit. The statues are located in front of the Lincoln/Herndon Law Office and across from the Old State Capitol Building in Springfield. The statues depict a scene "set on October 4, 1854 as Lincoln is walking towards the Old State Capitol to give a speech. The sculptures are grouped in two couplets. Willie stands with Abraham and Mary while Robert is across the way as he leaves for school. Mary is adjusting her husband's lapels, symbolizing her influence on his political and social life."[12] Mary is depicting wearing attire suitable for walking in the brisk fall air. A shawl covers the bodice of her dress. The stitches on her gloves indicate they are leather, and her bonnet is trimmed with roses.

What about life-sized figures of Mary? Are there any of those?

Yes, there are several. In most, Mary wears period attire, but not necessarily a dress that is copied from known articles of her clothing. Some used fashions believed to have been worn by Mary but others left it to the imagination of a seamstress to determine fabric selection and color. One such example is located at the Plymouth Historical Museum in Plymouth, Michigan. Mary and Abraham stand ready to greet their guests at a White House reception. Mary is shown wearing a white ball gown with black lace and lavender trim.

When a museum in Springfield, Illinois closed, the wax figures of Lincoln were purchased and placed in the Lincoln Museum in Hodgenville, Kentucky. The collection did not include a figure of Mary, so one was purchased from Dorfman Museum Services to complete the tableau of the Lincolns at Ford's Theatre.[13] A black dress, black gloves, and a black headdress were the chosen attire for this figure.

The American Civil War Wax Museum in Gettysburg features Mary wearing a tan dress and seated beside Lincoln at Ford's Theatre. Also, in Gettysburg, the Hall of Presidents and First Ladies portrays Mary wearing her purple velvet dress and carrying a purple parasol.

The Tussaud's London Wax Museum in St. Petersburg Beach, Florida displays an unusual depiction of Abraham and Mary. Lincoln is lying diagonally across his death bed, while Mary sits in a chair at his bedside with her hands gently folded in her lap. She is wearing a dress similar to one of her 1861 reception gowns: a white ball gown with ruffles across the bodice and the bottom edge of the skirt. She wears a floral diadem on her head, and a floral garland crosses her bosom and cascades down the front of her dress.

The Abraham Lincoln Presidential Museum in Springfield, Illinois features more life-sized figures of Mary than any other historical venue. The museum offers visitors six dioramas featuring Mary. The welcoming rotunda displays a family group that includes Abraham and the boys. The courting scene depicts Abraham and Mary as they sat on the horse-hair sofa in the parlor at the home of Elizabeth Edwards. In the diorama of the Blue Room, Mary is shown dressing for a levee with the assistance of her seamstress, Elizabeth Keckly. Willie's bedroom scene explores the pain of a mother and father who look on helplessly while their son lay in bed during his final illness. The mourning corner scene depicts the depth of Mary's grief after the death of her child, Willie. The final scene features Mary in the viewing box at Ford's Theatre resting her head on her husband's shoulder just seconds prior to his assassination.

The Smithsonian has a white figure which displays the purple velvet gown Mary wore at a White House reception during the first year of the Lincoln administration. The figure has no defining facial features, but the shape of the hair, and Mary's original dress, fan, and parasol give a lovely interpretation of the lady.

Past museums featuring wax figures included the former Mammoth Cave Museum in Kentucky and the American History of Wax located in Gatlinburg, Tennessee. Mary's image crossed the nation's borders when the former Musee de Cire Ville Marie Wax Museum opened its doors in Montreal, Quebec. Mary was depicted wearing a white dress and seated next to the president while John Wilkes Booth lurked in the corner.

Lots of places are named after Abraham, are there places or businesses named after Mary?

Probably the most famous business to use Mary's name was the Mary Lincoln Candy Company which started in 1916. A few years later, the company was sold to the L.R. Steel Company which reorganized and renamed the confectionary Mary Lincoln Candies, Inc. The factory operated at 168–170 Easton Street, Buffalo, New York. With the motto, "Old Fashioned Goodness in Every Piece." The business soon expanded again when in 1922, eighty shops were opened under the name "Mary Lincoln Candy and Coffee Shop" in cities such as Cleveland, Pittsburgh, and Chicago. The chain store used the same color scheme of white, black, and buff and had the same decorations, and the same white Vitrolite-topped tables in each store. Customers could purchase candy, coffee, and treats at the soda fountain, a light lunch, and the store's signature Mary Lincoln Buttermilk Chocolate. Within another year, 500 shops and 50 factories were opened nationwide.[14]

The L.R. Steel Company declared bankruptcy in 1923, but Mary Lincoln Candies, Inc. brand of candy continued until the early 1950s.

Are there commemorative collectors' coins of Mary?

There have been a few, but not nearly as many coins have been made to honor Mary as have been made of Abraham. Sometimes, Mary's image is included on a Lincoln coin.

The Life of Lincoln Coins included a coin featuring the marriage of Abraham and Mary.

In 1976 to commemorate the U.S. Bicentennial, a series of President and First Lady Coins was released. The front image was the left profiles of Abraham and Mary Lincoln.

The Franklin Mint Company produced a President and First Ladies Series of silver coins in 1977. A First Lady of the United States series featured a head and shoulder image of Mary engraved on an ounce of silver.

Most recently, the U.S. Mint released a series of First Spouse coins. A commemorative coin featuring a head-and-shoulders image of Mary on the front was released in 2010. The reverse side of the coin depicted Mary giving flowers and books to wounded soldiers. This coin was issued as a bronze coin and as a gold coin.

What other types of commemorative items have been produced?

Over the years, manufactures have released Mary's image on anything they think will sell. Items have included such things as paperweights, advertising plates, Christmas ornaments, playing cards, and various works of art. Her image has been molded into salt and pepper shakers, bells, and bobble-head Pot Belly knickknacks.

Special mention should be made of "Mary Lincoln" dolls. These are a favorite among doll collectors and souvenir seekers. In the 1860s, Conte and Bohme created an 18-inch doll named "Mary Lincoln." The head, arms, and legs were made of glazed porcelain. The face featured painted blue eyes and rosy cheeks. The hair was painted brown with a gold snood. A few years later, another china doll named "Mary Lincoln" was manufactured. This one had gold bows on the side of its head and a rounder face. Both dolls were very popular with young girls in the

nineteenth century. Since then, doll designers and manufactures have
continued to create dolls to honor Mary. Some try to create a doll that
resembles Mary while others issue a doll series that has no resemblance
to but uses the names of historical characters. Manufacturers often
create clothing based on Mary's known gowns; others create a doll dress
based purely on a designer's creativity.

The variety of dolls continues to grow. Some of the more famous
ones have included:

1929: Ruth Moser created a wooden doll, 20 inches in height. It was
made with a wooden socket head and a wooden ball-jointed body. The
face included painted blue eyes. This doll was created exclusively for the
Wisconsin Historical Society and remains in their collection.

Circa 1930s or 1940s: A paper-mache doll wearing a rendition of Mary's
purple velvet dress was made by Madelon Lyle of Pittsburg, Pennsylvania. The 10-inch doll had blonde hair and included a parasol.

1957: Magge Head Kane created a doll consisting of a bisque head,
legs, and arms, and a soft cloth body. This one has a lovely face and
resembles Mary.

Circa 1950 or 1960: The Plastic Molded Arts Company issued a doll
series titled "Album of Americana." Their plastic doll featured brown
hair and wore a maroon dress. Each doll came in a box which opened like
a story book. A biography of Mary Lincoln was printed on the inside flap.

Circa 1960: By saving labels from Blue Bonnet Margarine and mail-
ing them to the company, a person could receive a 7½-inch American
Heritage Series promotion doll. There were many dolls in the series.
The doll representing Mary Lincoln wore a red and white striped dress
accessorized with a black lace shawl and hat.

1970s: Madame Alexander created a doll to honor Mary for their
President's Wives Series. The doll has the same face as many of their
dolls but wore a purple velvet dress based on Mary's dress, which is
housed at the Smithsonian Museum.

1974: Faith Wick created a 22-inch doll. The head, hands, and boots
were wax over porcelain, and the body, arms, and legs were made of
cloth. The doll wore a pink dress and bonnet.

1976: Madame Alexander sold a Mary Lincoln doll wearing an ivory
ball gown with ruffles.

1983: American Heritage Dolls created a plastic doll which came stored
in a plastic dome display case. The doll had no physical resemblance to

Mary. The doll's dress was a taffeta red and white stripe, patriotic in style and appropriate for a Fourth of July costume. This appears to be the same dress worn by the Blue Bonnet Margarine promotional doll in the 1960s, the only difference being the addition of the plastic dome storage case.

1980s: Yield House produced Mary Lincoln doll kits which when made, created an 18-inch doll. Each kit contained a bisque head, legs, and arms. A pattern was included to create a soft cloth body and a dress.

1984: The doll which most resembled Mary was created and sold by the United States Historical Society—a 10-inch porcelain doll wearing a white gown with a ruffled skirt, a floral garland, and beautiful jewelry.

1984: A 20-inch, doll by Lady Anne, titled "Mary Todd Lincoln" was created by the Williamsburg Doll Factory. The doll wore a wine brocade dress trimmed with embroidered lace and small flowers made from ribbons. The ensemble was completed with a lace bag.

1985: Suzanne Gibson was commissioned by the Smithsonian to design dolls for the Reeves International Company's First Lady Series of dolls. Each one is a 12½-inch plastic doll with jointed head, arms and legs. Each wears a dress based on a gown in the First Ladies Collection at the Smithsonian. The doll depicting Mary wears a purple gown.

2013: A 4½ inch folk art creation by UneeKDoll Designs had a sage green dress trimmed with peach and yellow ribbon roses. The doll was made from wood, wire, clay, and paint.

2013: For the Cissette dinner at the Madame Alexander Doll Convention in Louisville, Kentucky the company created a limited-edition souvenir doll named "Mary of the Kentucky Todds." She stood 10 inches tall and had dark brown hair worn in ringlets. Her gown was a lavender dress with white lace trim on the neckline, sleeves, and hemline.

Other companies such as Nortel, Carlson, and Brinn's, have sold "First Lady" dolls. In addition, cloth dolls and puppets have been mass produced and are still sold in souvenir and gift shops. Folk art dolls of Mary are currently sold at various festivals, festivals, and, on occasion, one appears on an online auction site such as eBay or Etsy.

Paper dolls have been popular toys for decades, and for the avid paper doll collector, presidents and their wives make excellent paper dolls. In the early 1980s, *Abe & Mary Todd Lincoln Paper Dolls* was released by artist Charles Ventura. His designs included clothing based on images of other women of the Civil War era including Mary's half-sister Emilie

Todd Helm, Julia Grant, and Kate Chase. *Abraham Lincoln and His Family Paper Dolls* was designed by Tom Tierney in 1989. These are still sold in gift shops today.

There is a Lincoln Rose; is there a flower that honors Mary?

Yes, the Mary Todd daylily was first registered in 1967. Since then, it has won several awards including the 1978 Stout Silver Medal given by the American Hemerocallis Society. The Mary Todd daylily has 6-inch yellow blooms with wide petals. It is a hardy plant and grows in most conditions.

Is there any type of memorial for Mary?

The Lincoln Home National Historic Site in Springfield, Illinois is a tribute to the Lincoln family, but many consider it to be the ultimate memorial to Mary. Victorian culture deemed the home part of the women's sphere, and it was up to the woman of the home to determine its décor, maintenance, and the general atmosphere. The home was considered a reflection of the Victorian woman. As her home appeared, so she appeared to society. Today the home is decorated as it was in 1860 when the Lincoln family left for Washington. If the Lincolns returned to the home today, they would find things just as they left them.[15]

In 1860, journalists who visited Abraham made several observations about the home. One wrote, "I found Mr. Lincoln living in a handsome but not pretentious, double two-story house ... Everything about it had a look of comfort and independence." The *New York Herald* stated, "The internal appointments of his house are plain but tasteful, and clearly show the impress of Mrs. Lincoln's hand, who is really an amiable and accomplished lady."[16] Mary must have beamed with pride when reading this tribute. She had accomplished what every Victorian wife desired. The *New York Semi-Weekly* summed it up: "The hand of the domestic artist was everywhere visible. The thought that involuntarily blossomed into speech was, 'What a pleasant home Abe Lincoln has.'"[17] Mary would be pleased to know that people who visit today share the same sentiment.

Another memorial to Mary is located at 578 West Main Street in Lexington, Kentucky. Built between 1803 and 1806, the building was originally the Sign of the Green Tree Tavern. Robert Smith Todd purchased the home on May 7, 1832, and converted it into a home suitable for his growing family. After his death in 1849, the home was sold by the family and served as a residence, boarding house, brothel, grocery store, and plumbing supply warehouse. Over the years, the building fell into despair and showed nothing of its former grandeur. In the mid-1970s, Mrs. Beula C. Nunn, the First Lady of Kentucky, organized a campaign to save the structure, restore it, and open it as a tribute to Mary Lincoln. The home was renovated to reflect the Todds' residency and opened for tours in 1977. Today, the Mary Todd Lincoln House remains the first and only home dedicated to the memory of a First Lady. It is owned and operated by Kentucky Mansion Preservation Foundation, which is dedicated to historic preservation and educational opportunities.

When did the State of Illinois receive the Lincoln Home?

Upon Lincoln's death, the home was still rented to Lucian Tilton. After he moved from the home, a variety of renters came and went, sometimes leaving the home in need of repairs, as often happens with an absentee landlord. In 1879, Robert Lincoln contacted the Lincoln Monument Association stating that neither he nor the family wished to keep the property, "but were willing to convey it to the Association in trust." The home would be opened to tourists.[18] The Association declined the offer due to the home's poor condition. C. L. Conkling, who worked as an agent for Robert, made some repairs to the house and helped Robert find a tenant. The last renter was O. H. Oldroyd and his family. Oldroyd displayed his growing collection of Lincoln memorabilia in the home's front and back parlors and charged visitors 25 cents to take a look. Suffering from financial problems, Oldroyd wanted the home to be established as a memorial operated by the state, and he wished for himself the position of paid custodian. In 1883, Oldroyd managed to convince State Representative James M. Gregg to submit a resolution in the Illinois House of Representatives establishing such a memorial. Robert Lincoln quickly let the governor know that the home was not currently for sale.

In April 1887, Robert was again surprised to learn that a special committee of the House of Representatives had met with Conkling. Robert responded by saying, "If the State will offer to preserve the house as an object of public interest, all question will be avoided and you may say to the chairman that upon such an offer being made I will convey the property to the State without compensation." An agreement was reached, and Governor Richard J. Oglesby signed the law on June 16, 1887, and the Lincoln Homestead Trustees was created.[19]

Robert and his wife signed the deed over to the board of trustees with the stipulation that the home should always be kept in good repair, and "free of access to the public."[20] Oldroyd had accomplished his goal: He was hired as the first custodian of the home.

Did any of Mary's relatives ever live in the Lincoln Home after her death?

Yes. The third custodian of the home was Mary's nephew, Albert Stevenson Edwards, the son of Ninian and Elizabeth Edwards. Albert and his family moved into the home on July 1, 1897. After his death, his wife, Josephine, managed the home with the assistance of two daughters. Upon Josephine's death, the position was given to Mary Edwards Brown, one of Albert and Josephine's daughters. The younger sister Georgie never married and remained in the home to help Mary with running the home.

The next custodian for the home was another relative, Virginia Stuart Brown, the great-granddaughter of John Todd Stuart, a favorite first cousin to Mary Lincoln.

Other than the Todd Home, is there a memorial in Kentucky dedicated only to Mary?

No, but there almost was one. In the early twentieth century, J. M. Spencer, the President of Sayre College in Lexington, Kentucky, wanted to build a memorial to Mary. He formed the Mary Todd Lincoln Memorial Committee for the purpose of raising funds for this endeavor. The committee included men who had known Mary as well as several politically prominent men such as Major-General Daniel E. Sickles (committee president); General Frederick D. Grant; Commodore A. V. Wadhams, U.S.N. (committee vice-president); Governor John A. Dix of New York; and William O. Stoddard.

The proposed memorial was a three-story building with an accessible basement. The stairs led up to a portico including four white columns joined by a railing. A bronze plaque featuring Abraham and Mary seated at a table heavily laden with books was to be placed inside the building.[21] Such a plaque focused on Mary's education and Abraham's love of reading.

Spencer's plans for fundraising included the manufacturing of a Mary Todd Lincoln doll. However, only the prototype was completed. In a letter to Robert Lincoln, Spencer outlined his other plan to "write in connection with this movement the true history" of Mary's life. He had already gathered essays and information from her friends who were still living. He began traveling throughout the East giving lectures about Mary which were hailed as "the finest contribution of the century to the Lincolnian literature."[22]

Two years later, the attacks originally written by William Herndon had been republished in the *Boston Herald*. Henry Watterson encouraged Dr. Spencer to write a defense of Mary Lincoln to counter the attacks.[23] Spencer's article was submitted to *Century Magazine* for consideration. The editor, Robert Yard, sent the manuscript to Robert Todd Lincoln for approval. He wrote to Robert, "in the hope that you will read this material and will express to me exactly what you feel about the publication of any part of it. It is needless to say that I shall be entirely guided by your desires."[24] Robert Todd Lincoln returned the manuscript to Yard with the instructions that he would not stop its publication, but he would not be happy if it was published. It was never published, and Spencer's plan to write a biography of Mary ended. Without revenue from the book, and other failed attempts to raise funds, the Mary Todd Lincoln Memorial could not be built.

What was the first biography written about Mary?

Technically, *Behind the Scenes or Thirty Years a Slave, and Four Years in The White House*, is a biography about Elizabeth Keckly; however, there is so much information about Mary's White House years and early widowhood that the title was included in Jason Emerson's annotated bibliography of Mary.[25] The book was written in 1868, and details events in the White House, shares conversations between the Lincolns, and discusses Mary's finances after the war and through the "Old Clothes Scandal." Keckly's intent was to defend Mary and present a positive image of the former first lady, but the results were far from positive. Mary was horrified that her personal comments and letters were published. Robert Lincoln was embarrassed that such a "tell-all" book was written about his parents. Many readers felt the book made Mary appear pathetic. Despite the outrage at its publication, and the criticism bestowed upon Keckly for writing the book, it remains to this day one of the better sources for Mary's time in the White House and the first couple of years of her widowhood.

The first true biography written about Mary was the one authored by her niece, Katherine Helm (see next question for complete discussion).

Was there an "authorized" biography about Mary?

The True Story of Mary, Wife of Lincoln, written by Katherine Helm, remains the only biography of Mary Lincoln that was authorized by family members.

Robert's wife Mary felt that current biographers were treating her mother-in-law unfairly in their works. She was especially angered by the writings of William Barton. In a letter to Katherine, Mrs. Robert Lincoln explained:

> I believe that we shall soon see that evil has no real power and that all of these infamous lies will be blotted from consciousness. Truth must prevail! That devil Barton and his lies will be forgotten!!! When some dastardly things about the character of George Washington were going the rounds of the newspapers lately, Coolidge, in his dry manner remarked, 'Well, I see the Washington Monument still stands!'—so will the Lincoln Memorial stand—the people who are now writing these wicked lies are channels for the devil to talk through.[26]

Then Robert and Mary Lincoln proposed a plan to combat the sudden onslaught of negative articles and manuscripts. They wanted to oversee the writing of an authorized biography that would be sympathetic to Mary and the entire Lincoln and Todd families. After convincing Katherine to write the book, the Lincolns assisted her by providing photographs, letters, and personal stories. Katherine also had access to her mother's Civil War diary, family documents, and correspondence. She also remembered her own visit to the White House in 1862 after her father had been killed at the battle of Chickamauga. No other author had such a treasure trove of primary source material about Mary Lincoln's childhood and the Todd family.

This was the story Robert Lincoln and his wife wanted told, and they felt strongly enough about the endeavor to finance it. In an undated letter, Mary H. Lincoln reminded Katherine, "Must not forget that it will be my pleasure to finance your book. I am enclosing this [a check] to apply where needed."[27] After the first draft of the manuscript was finished and ready to submit to a publisher for consideration, Katherine traveled to Washington, D.C. to visit with Robert and Mary Lincoln. They were to read the pages, make corrections, and give their approval. Katherine wrote to her mother and siblings that a few changes would be made before having the manuscript typed for submission. Of course, "Cousin Mary" was going to pay for the book to be typed and copyrighted.[28]

In 1928, *McCall's* magazine offered Katherine $10,000 for the serial rights to *Mary, Wife of Lincoln*.[29] Later that same year, Harper Brothers Publishing Company released a special edition, limited to 150 copies. It was published with a special watermarked paper and bound with a piece of the red damask draperies which had hung in the Todd home, inlaid in the book's cover. A hardback trade issue with a maroon cover was released the same year.

What is the best/worst biography about Mary?

The answer depends on what part of Mary's life a person wishes to study. For primary source material about Mary's youth in Kentucky, Katherine Helm's book, *Mary, Wife of Lincoln* is the best. The author was the daughter of Mary's half-sister Emilie and Confederate General Benjamin Hardin Helm. Katherine used her mother's documents and local history to create a vivid, but sentimental, account of Mary's childhood. However, the author also created several misconceptions about incidents, added dialogue that no one could possibly know, and elevated some Todd family members' position in history. One of the best biographies for scholarly overview and interpretation is *Mrs. Abraham Lincoln* by W. A. Evans. For those interested in learning about the insanity trial, recommended books include The *Insanity File* by Mark Neely and *The Madness of Mary Lincoln* by Jason Emerson. To understand Mary's voice, and for general facts about her life, *Mary Todd Lincoln: Her Life and Letters* by Justin G. Turner and Linda Levitt Turner is a must read.

One of the most obscure and absurd biographies about Mary was written by Charles J. Bauer. The *Lincoln Douglas Triangle with Naughty Mary Seduced by the Latest Paris Fashions* (1980) remains one of the most dreadful books ever written about the Lincolns.

Who painted the portrait of Mary that hangs in the White House?

Katherine Helm, the author of *Mary, the Wife of Lincoln*, painted Mary's portrait, and just as in the case of writing the book, the portrait was financed by Mr. and Mrs. Robert Todd Lincoln. On May 18, 1924, Mary

H. Lincoln wrote to Robert's aunt Emilie suggesting, "do you not think, that we "Todds" ought to put our heads together and see to having a fine portrait of Robert's mother placed in the White House, by the side of her husband? This is a project I have had near my heart for some time. And I want cousin Kate to paint it."[30] Cousin Kate had studied art in New York. Prior to painting Mary's portrait, Kate had established a reputation as a fine artist and had painted portraits of several political and military figures.

Mary Harlan Lincoln encouraged Katherine to come to Washington, visit the family, and paint the portrait. Katherine chose, instead, to paint in her home studio in Lexington, Kentucky. For inspiration, she used articles and engravings which had been previously published in *Harper's Illustrated*. She received letters from women who had known Mary during the Civil War. By the time the task was finished, Katherine had painted six portraits of her Aunt Mary. Mary Harlan Lincoln's influence in the project continued to be felt after the portraits were completed. It was Mary Harlan Lincoln who secured the space in the White House for the portrait to hang. It was Mary Harlan Lincoln who made the final arrangements for the unveiling ceremony. As the special day drew near, Mary Harlan Lincoln wrote to Katherine:

> When you read the enclosed articles about the re-arrangement of portraits of 'First Ladies' at the White House, you will agree with me that it is quite important that we should be on hand early, with our dear Aunt Mary portrait, so that our First Lady will be properly cared for. We must see to it that the portrait has the prominent position it deserves, both on account of the illustrious Lady and the artist.[31]

Today, the portrait hangs in the Lincoln Bedroom of the White House.

Do any of Mary's gowns still exist?

Yes, but sadly, not very many. There are two at the Smithsonian. One is a beautiful, unaltered purple velvet gown with two bodices. The other began its life as a beautiful, vertically striped, silk ball gown, but it was altered by removing one or more panels from the skirt and making a new day bodice. The "strawberry dress," a black silk with embroidered berries and leaves, was donated to the Abraham Lincoln Presidential Library by the family of Alvin Keys (Mary's niece Louisa married Alvin Keys).

Dresses that are assumed to have belonged to Mary are located at the Chicago History Museum and at the First Ladies' Library in Canton, Ohio.

Other items of clothing exist, such as bonnets, shawls, gloves, skirts, and a cloak, but these are the only known complete dresses.

What happened to the rest of Mary's elaborate wardrobe?

When Mary Lincoln died, the task of sorting through the trunks and dividing their contents fell upon Robert and his wife. Some items remained in Springfield and were given to members of the Todd family. Robert arranged to have sixty-five trunks and their contents sent to Mount Pleasant, Iowa, the childhood home of Mary Harlan Lincoln, and the family's summer residence. There, Robert's two daughters, Mary and Jessie, enjoyed playing with their grandmother's old dresses. They admired the richness of the fabric and lace and cut several of Mary's gowns apart and used the fabric to make reticules (small purses) for their friends. To them, the dresses were not important historical artifacts; they were nothing more than "grandmother's old clothes."

The embarrassment Robert had suffered from the Old Clothes Scandal probably left him with the belief that old clothing would never have historical significance. Thus, he most likely would not have refused his daughters in their quest of giving gifts to their friends made from his mother's old clothing.

It is not known if the Lincoln granddaughters altered any of Mary's gowns to wear themselves; however, Mary H. Lincoln wrote to a friend that the dresses would "one day make splendid gifts for her daughters." Photographs of the girls indicate that, like their grandmother, they were fashionable women: They had inherited their grandmother's sense of fashion and love of fine clothing.[32]

Did Mary donate any of Lincoln's letters or items to historical archives? What happened to the items in her trunks? What became of her letters?

At the time of Mary's death, there were few historical museums; Mary chose not to donate items to them. She did give several items of clothing, jewelry, and other remembrances to friends and family. Robert and his family also gave items to friends and family; they also gave items and papers of historical value to museums and archives.

Even though there are many Lincoln family documents and letters in archives and personal collections, a large number were destroyed.

Which museum has the largest collection of Mary's artifacts?
The Abraham Lincoln Presidential Library in Springfield has more items belonging to Mary than any other museum.

Robert and the Children

Who and when did Robert marry?
He married Mary Eunice Harlan on September 24, 1868. She was the daughter of Senator James Harlan and Ann Eliza Peck.

Did Robert burn his mother's letters?
Yes. As the only surviving child, Robert had the responsibility of helping shape the memory of his parents. Robert burned letters and documents which he deemed extremely personal, or of no historical value. According to family members, Robert wrote to other relatives requesting they do the same. Many of the family, confidential, or business letters pertaining to the Lincolns were destroyed by family and friends.[33]

What is the best thing Robert did to secure his mother's legacy?
There were many things that Robert did to procure the historical image of his parents. He donated his father's papers (which contained some items related to Mary) to the Library of Congress. He turned over ownership of the Lincoln's home to the state of Illinois. One of the greatest things he did was to help his mother secure a final resting place for the Lincoln family.

Did Robert live in the Lincoln Home after his mother's death?
No. At the time of his mother's death, Robert made his home in Chicago and in Washington, DC.

In 1903, Robert purchased 400 acres near Manchester, Vermont as a location to build what he would later call his ancestral home. He named it Hildene, combining the old English words "hil" and "dene" meaning "hill" and "valley with a stream." The twenty-four-room, Georgian Revival style mansion was completed in 1905. The property also contained a formal garden, smaller gardens, and a carriage house. Robert had a lifelong interest in astronomy and built an observatory just northeast of the house.

Peggy Beckwith (Mary Lincoln's great-granddaughter) bequeathed Hildene to the Christian Science Church. The Friends of Hildene purchased the property from the church to open as a historic site. Hildene is currently open to the public for tours all year.

Why did Robert choose Manchester?

Robert, his mother, and youngest brother Tad had visited Vermont in 1864. Robert apparently was taken by the beauty of the landscape. He also liked to play golf, and Manchester is near one of the oldest golf courses in Vermont. Also, his law partner, Edward Isham, owned a home nearby, enabling them to maintain a friendship.

What did Robert do for a living?

During the last months of the Civil War, Robert served as a captain in the U.S. Army on the staff of General Ulysses S. Grant. Robert did not participate in any major battles, but he was present at Appomattox Court House when General Robert E. Lee surrendered his troops After the war, having to take care of his mother and younger brother, Robert moved to Chicago with them. After studying law and passing the bar exam, Robert read law with J. Young Scammon. He then opened his own law firm with Scammon's son, Charles, but the partnership dissolved quickly. In 1872, Robert became a partner in the law firm Isham, Lincoln, and Beale.

Politics beckoned Robert even though he often refused nominations and appointments. He served as Secretary of War under presidents Garfield and Arthur. President Benjamin Harrison appointed Robert as Minister to London. Robert later resumed his law career and was council to the Pullman Car Company. After the death of George Pullman, Robert became the new president of the company.

Were there Lincoln grandchildren? What did they do for a living? Where are they buried?

Robert had three children.

Mary "Mamie" Lincoln (October 15, 1869–November 21, 1938) married Charles Isham. He was a distant cousin to Robert's law partner and was appointed Robert's personal secretary prior to the marriage. Charles traveled to London with the Lincolns, where he and Mamie were married on September 2, 1891.[34] They had one son, Lincoln Isham. In her mother's will, Mamie inherited both Hildene and the home in Washington, DC. She is buried alongside her husband, Charles, in Woodlawn Cemetery, Bronx New York.

Abraham "Jack" Lincoln II (August 14, 1873–March 5, 1890) was Robert's only son. In the summer of 1889, Jack felt a carbuncle under his arm. It continued to grow and was removed in early November. The wound did not heal properly, however, and Jack developed blood poisoning. Despite the efforts of London's best physicians, Jack died after months of suffering. Jack was originally buried in the Lincoln Tomb, but he now rests alongside his parents in Arlington Cemetery.

Jessie Harlan Lincoln (November 6, 1875–January 4, 1948) was the "problem child" of the family. While attending Iowa Wesleyan College, Jessie met and fell in love with the school's star quarterback, Warren Wallace Beckwith, who bore the nickname "Lady-Killer." Robert and Mary strongly disapproved of the relationship between Warren and Jessie.

The young couple applied for a marriage license in Mt. Pleasant and planned to marry secretly. When Robert learned of this scandalous behavior, he yanked Jessie out of school and brought her back to Chicago. On November 10, 1897, under the pretext of a shopping trip, Jessie met up with Warren and traveled to Milwaukee where they were married. When the couple returned to Chicago to tell the Lincolns their news, Jessie went to her family's home alone while Warren took a room at Chicago's Clifton House. Robert was furious. For days, Robert Lincoln would not allow Jessie to leave the house or see her groom.[35] Warren returned to Mount Pleasant alone.

Jessie's mother intervened; she wanted her daughter to be happy. On November 14, Jessie and Warren reunited in Aurora, Illinois and traveled together to Mount Pleasant. A few days later, Jessie was seen in the stands watching her husband play football for Iowa Wesleyan College.[36]

Jessie's marriage created a scandal that made headlines in both the Chicago and Mount Pleasant newspapers. Reporters speculated whether Beckwith would be given employment by Robert Lincoln in the Pullman Car Company. Beckwith had hoped to work with his own father, Captain Warren Beckwith, Sr., who was a retired railroad administer and founder of the Western Wheel Scraper Company. A position did not appear from either side.

By the time Jessie was expecting their first child, Beckwith still needed to find a job. He found a job working for the Chicago Gas Light and Coke Company, but the job did not last. Not wanting to completely give up his days as a star athlete, Warren signed a contract to play professional baseball in Iowa; two weeks later he was dismissed. Robert agreed to give Beckwith a job if he would forgo the urge to play professional sports and settle down to support the family. Instead, Beckwith enlisted as a private in the Iowa National Guard.[37]

Jessie and Warren had two children, a daughter Mary Todd Lincoln Beckwith (called Peggy), and a son, Robert Todd Lincoln Beckwith. A stillborn child was born December 28, 1901 and is buried in Forest Home Cemetery, Mt. Pleasant, Iowa.[38] The marriage was never a good match. Warren worked various jobs and was often gone from home for months at a time. Jessie and Warren Beckwith divorced in 1907 and Beckwith never saw his children again.[39] With no alimony or child support, Jessie returned to Hildene to live with her parents.

In 1915, Jessie married artist and archeologist Frank E. "Ned" Johnson. Jessie created another family scandal when Johnson wrote to Robert Lincoln saying that he had returned home to find Jessie in bed with Robert Randolph.[40] A divorce request was quickly filed and granted. Jessie's third and final husband was the man found in her bed, Robert John Randolph. They married December 26, 1926, just five months after the death of Robert Todd Lincoln. Family members were shocked at news of the union. Robert Lincoln's cousin, Katherine Helm, wrote to the family saying that she was surprised to hear of the wedding, and "I hope it may turn out better than we expect and that she may at least be contented and happy." Kate continued to express her concern that the marriage would not turn out well; however, her greatest fear was for "the unhappiness of the children."[41] The couple lived off of the money Jessie received as her share of the income from the Lincoln's estate. Jessie did purchase her own home, but in her later years, she left her husband and returned to Hildene to live with her daughter "Peggy." Jessie is buried in Dellwood Cemetery near Hildene.

What did the Lincoln great-grandchildren do for a living?

Lincoln Isham (June 8, 1892–September 1, 1971), the son of Mary "Mamie" Lincoln and Charles Isham, married Leahalma Correa on August 30, 1919. She was a widow with a young daughter. The couple never had children of their own. Isham left an estate of 1.5 million dollars to be divided between his stepdaughter, long-time employees, and various charities, including the American Red Cross and the Salvation Army. Linc (as he was called) is buried in Dellwood Cemetery in Manchester, Vermont.[42]

Mary "Peggy" Lincoln Beckwith (August 22, 1898–July 10, 1975), the daughter of Jessie Lincoln and Warren Beckwith, became the keeper of Hildene. According to Mary Harlan Lincoln's will, her daughter Mamie would inherit Hildene. Upon Mamie's death, the estate would become Peggy's.[43] Peggy seemed to enjoy working on and managing the farm. In the early days of aviation, Peggy received a pilot's license and often flew over her property. In addition to flying, Peggy enjoyed outdoor sports including hunting and fishing. Many of her neighbors considered Peggy to be a "little bit nuts" as she loved animals so much, she allowed them the run of the house. Pet raccoons lived in a second-story bedroom while mice occupied the crannies of the pipe organ. Keeping with the tradition of having personal documents destroyed, Peggy requested that her personal papers be burned. She willed her Lincoln artifacts to her brother. Peggy was cremated and her ashes were spread along the formal garden at Hildene.[44]

Robert Todd Lincoln "Bud" Beckwith (July 19, 1904December 24, 1985) once listed his occupation as "Gentleman Farmer of independent means." In an interview he said that he "enjoyed sailing . . . raising Black Angus cattle . . . and car racing," and concluded by saying "I'm a spoiled brat."[45] A playboy, Robert married three times: first to Hazel Holland Wilson, second to Annemarie Hoffman, and finally to Margaret Fristoe. Robert lived on Woodstock Farms in Virginia and spent the last year of his life in a nursing home in Saluda, Virginia. His ashes were poured into the James River alongside Woodstock Farms.[46]

Did the Lincoln family start any charitable foundations or organizations as the Kennedy family has done?

No. However, Robert Lincoln's widow, Mary, left money to the Christian Science Church, the American Red Cross, and Iowa Wesleyan College. The Lincoln estate was worth three million dollars.

When did Robert and his wife die? Where are they buried? Why is Robert not buried in the Lincoln Tomb?

Robert died on July 26, 1926; Mary died March 31, 1937. Since Mary outlived her husband, Robert's burial arrangements were left to her discretion.

Are there any Lincoln descendants living today?

No—unless one believes the claims of Annemarie Hoffman. At the age of 63, Robert Beckwith married the 27-year-old Annemarie Hoffman. The following year, she gave birth to a son, named him Timothy Lincoln Beckwith, and listed Robert as the boy's father. However, Robert claimed he could not be the boy's father since he had a vasectomy with a prostatectomy six years earlier. During the divorce proceedings, Annemarie refused to allow the seven-year-old Timothy to undergo blood testing, making it impossible to prove or disprove her claims. The judge ruled the child must have resulted from an "adulterous relationship."

When Robert Beckwith passed away, the three charities that were to inherit the Lincoln fortune wanted to ensure that Timothy did not have a claim on any of the money—especially since Robert Beckwith's name appeared on Timothy's birth certificate. They offered Timothy a settlement (about $1 million) to agree that he had no future claims to the estate. Timothy accepted—thus ending the Lincoln line of descendants both biologically and legally.

Are there Todd descendants today? My husband's grandmother [insert whatever the relationship] was a Todd from Kentucky. How is she related to Mary?

The Todds were a large family. Mary's father was one of twelve children, most of whom had descendants. However, proving a connection to Mary Lincoln is often difficult. While Mary had fifteen siblings, many of them did not have children. Her two brothers, and two of her half-brothers, had children. The children of her sisters had different surnames. Only one of Mary's uncles remained in Kentucky. Many of the family members moved to Illinois, Missouri, and further west.

The Other Questions

Who has portrayed Mary in a film?

Many actresses have portrayed Mary in movies. Some of the more re-membered performances were given by Ruth Gordon, Julie Harris, Mary Tyler Moore, and most recently, Sally Field.

I often see Lincoln presenters. Are there Mary presenters as well?

Yes. The Association of Lincoln Presenters lists several women who bring Mary to life through various programs and theatrical endeavors.

Are there organizations which support Mary's legacy?

In addition to the Association of Lincoln Presenters, Mary Lincoln's Coterie is dedicated to the study and enhancement of the memory of Mary Lincoln and the women who were her friends and family.

Are there special events held to honor Mary's legacy?

Each year on the anniversary of Mary's death (July 16) members of Mary Lincoln's Coterie host a memorial program and wreath-laying ceremony at the Lincoln Tomb in Springfield, Illinois. This event is open to the public. They also hold monthly book discussions and programs via Zoom.

Are there any new mysteries or unanswered questions about Mary?

Occasionally, a photograph will emerge in someone's collection and the owner will question if the image is Mary Lincoln. Most often, the pho-tograph is easily and quickly proven not to be. However, a few years ago, a new photograph of a woman who resembles Mary surfaced, and it is has not yet been proven to be, or not to be, Mrs. Lincoln.

The photo was taken in New Haven, Connecticut at the studio of J. Horace Wells and David C. Collins. The woman in the photograph wears a simple travel ensemble, complete with bonnet, umbrella, and cape. While it is not the usual attire Mary wore for photographs, she was photographed wearing a similar style with her sons shortly before leaving Springfield for Washington. The question then becomes, was Mary ever in New Haven, Connecticut? It was possible.

In July 1862, shortly after Willie's death, Mary traveled to New York City with Tad. They were joined by Robert. During this trip, Robert visited his friend, Clinton L. Conkling who was a student at Yale University in New Haven.[47] Clinton was also the son of Mary's dear friend, Mercy Levering Conkling. It is not known if Mary was with Robert during his visit or not. But even if she were not, the following summer, an opportunity to be in New Haven arose again.

From July through September 1863, Mary traveled to New York City and into the White Mountains in Vermont. Her eldest son Robert accompanied her on the trip. It is not known if the mother and son team stopped by to see a familiar and friendly face from home, but it is possible. Mary traveled frequently after Willie's death. Her day-to-day activities were not always recorded. Whether she traveled to New Haven is unknown.

Until more information is discovered, it is not outside of the realm of possibility that Mary did, indeed, travel to New Haven and stop in at the photographers to have a portrait taken.

ACKNOWLEDGMENTS

APPENDIXES

NOTES

BIBLIOGRAPHY

INDEX

ACKNOWLEDGMENTS

*O*ne of the inspirational messages that popped onto my computer screen from Pinterest read:

> A person's most useful asset is not a head full of knowledge, but a heart full of love, an ear ready to listen and a hand willing to help others. (Author Unknown)

Over the years, while researching Mary Lincoln and her family, I have been fortunate to have met people who owned all these qualities, including a head full of knowledge. To each of them I owe my thanks and gratitude.

I wish to express my thanks and appreciation to the archivists, curators, docents, and historians at the many historical sites and museums during my quest for information about Mary. The first person who offered to help me dig deeper into the history of the Todd family and Lexington was Lou Holden, the former curator at the Mary Todd Lincoln House in Lexington, Kentucky. Lou, and her successor, Kathy Taab, introduced me to a member of the MTL House's board of directors who not only had known Emilie Todd Helm, but lived in her home. The late Mrs. Mary G. Townsend Murphy allowed me to sort through her stacks of files, letters, family documents, and photos which had belonged to the Todd family. These three women sparked on interest in Mary and her life that has driven me to always search for the smallest details.

The staff members of several other institutions have led me to find answers to questions to which I did not know whether an answer could be found. Many thanks to several staff members, both past and present, at the Abraham Lincoln Presidential Library for access to their files and photographs. These include Ian Hunt, Jane Ehrenhart, Kathryn Harris, Roberta Fairburn, Mary Ann Pohl, Jan Perone, Gwenith Podeschi, Dennis Suttles, and others. A special acknowledgement is deserved by Dr. James Cornelius (formerly of the ALPL) who shared his wealth of information about the Lincolns, offered advice about inclusive information, and served as mentor and encourager during the process of writing the book. I will also be thankful to Eva Elisabeth who put me in contact with Jessica Kotschi at the Institut für Stadtgeschihte in Frank-fürt, Germany and the unique photographs they offered. Other photographs were found with the help of Jacob M. Sheff at the Indiana State Museum and Historic Sites, and Emily Rapoza with the Lincoln Financial Collection, Allen Count Public Library.

My deepest gratitude is owed to the team of historians who offered advice, shared their files and their own research, and encouraged me to see this project through to completion. I owe many thanks to Dr. Michael Burlingame, Jason Emerson, Kim Bauer, Max and Donna Daniels, Darin Jolliffee-Hass, Elizabeth Taylor, and Roger Norton. For reading the manuscript in its many phases, checking the facts, and helping keep the answers non-biased, I am indebted to Valerie Gugula and Joan Howard. A very special thank you to Gerald Swick for reading the manuscript and sharing his vast research on the Todd family and his knowledge of military history.

I would like to acknowledge the work of the editors and staff at Southern Illinois University Press who have guided me through the process of manu-script development and offered encouragement when needed. My editor, Sylvia Frank Rodriguez, has been exceptional during this process.

And, thank you to Dr. Gerald J. Prokopowicz who has been a beacon of inspiration since he served as the director of the former Lincoln Museum in Fort Wayne, Indiana. Dr. Prokopowicz's book, *Did Lincoln Own Slaves? And Other Frequently Asked Questions about Abraham Lincoln* (Pantheon Books, 2008) served as the inspiration for this manuscript.

Finally, and most important, my deepest gratitude goes to the thousands of people who asked the questions. Whether the question was asked in per-son after a performance or lecture, sent electronically through social media, or received through an old-fashioned phone call, each question asked helped shape the content of this manuscript. For those questions asked, and for the people who asked them, I will be forever grateful.

APPENDIX I: HER FAMILY

Our cheerful little family circle
—Mary Lincoln to Mary Jane Wells, December 6, 1865

Grandparents:

General Levi Todd (paternal grandfather)
(October 4, 1756–September 6, 1807) and
Jane *Briggs* Todd (paternal grandmother)
(June 3, 1761–July 22, 1800) married February 25, 1779.

General Levi Todd was born in Montgomery County, Pennsylvania, the fourth child of David and Hannah *Owen* Todd. He received a classical education in Virginia under the direction of his uncle, Reverend John Todd, and studied law under Andrew Lewis. In the summer of 1775, Levi and a group of men arrived in Kentucky to establish a new settlement. Paying tribute to the recently fought first battle of the American Revolutionary War in Massachusetts, they named their settlement Lexington. Levi was appointed as the first county clerk in 1777. Due to the war, it took several years for the area to be developed into a frontier city. When the city plans were adopted on December 26, 1781, Levi Todd's name was listed as one of the first purchasers and land holders.[1]

During the Revolutionary War, Levi served as a lieutenant under the command of General George Rogers Clark. He was a member of the troops fighting in the western theater of the Illinois campaign. For his service, Levi was awarded over two thousand acres of land in Clark's Grant, located in what is now Clark and Floyd counties in Indiana.[2]

Levi encouraged other pioneers to settle in the area around Lexington. He was one of the defenders of the fort at Harrodsburg and later at Logan's Fort at St. Asaphs. It was there Levi married Jane Briggs in 1779. She was the daughter of Captain Samuel and Sarah *Logan* Briggs. A Todd family tradition claims that Jane wove her wedding dress from a weed known as wild cotton. Later that year, the couple moved to Todd's Station just outside of Lexington. In addition to being one of the first lot owners in Lexington, Levi served as clerk of the District Court of Kentucky. He became clerk of the Circuit Court of Fayette County in 1780 and held the office until the time of his death nearly twenty-seven years later. Over the years, he accumulated vast amounts of property. By the end of his life, Levi owned 7,000 acres of land. His lived on a large estate outside of Lexington on what is now the Richmond Road. His house, which he dubbed "Ellerslie," was the first brick home in Fayette County and the second in the state of Kentucky. The home was expanded until it contained twenty rooms. The property also contained several outbuildings, one of which was a round stone house where court documents were stored in Levi's personal office. After a court decision threatened the property rights of squatters and tenant farmers, a mob planned to destroy the documents. On January 31, 1803, the round stone house was set ablaze destroying many early records including land claims. Some believed that Ellerslie was in jeopardy as well. The estate was spared and the records that were partially burnt were copied. [3]

Levi rose to the rank of General in the Fayette County Militia. He was one of the first trustees at Transylvania University.

General Todd and his wife Jane *Briggs* had eleven children. After her death, Levi married Jane *Holmes* Tatum with whom he had one son. Levi and both wives are buried in Lexington Cemetery.

Robert Porter Parker (maternal grandfather)
(October 12, 1760–March 4, 1800) and
Elizabeth Rittenhouse *Porter* Parker (maternal grandmother)
(September 27, 1769–January22, 1850) married March 16, 1789.[4]

Robert Porter Parker was born in Montgomery County, Pennsylvania, and was the son of James and Mary *Todd* Parker. After serving as a major during the Revolutionary War, Robert and Elizabeth married in Pennsylvania. As newlyweds, they set out on horseback for Lexington, Kentucky.

A land grant gave Robert, his brother James, and five other men 710 acres to "establish a town by the name of Lexington." According to the first street map of the new town, Lexington was divided into three streets with a total of 87 lots. On the north side of town lay the fourth avenue, a smaller street called Short Street with four large lots identified by letters instead of numbers. These lots were double and sometimes triple the size of the other city lots. It was on this street that Robert Parker and his wife raised their six children.[5] While the home of Levi Todd was the first brick home in the Fayette County, the Parker home was the first brick home within the city limits.[6]

Robert Parker was a man of distinction who served as the first surveyor of Fayette County and was elected clerk of the first board of trustees of Lexington. He died in the prime of his life.

Elizabeth Rittenhouse *Porter* was the eldest daughter of General Andrew Porter and his first wife, Elizabeth *McDowell* Porter. When her husband died, Elizabeth became a young widow raising two daughters and four sons and was often referred to as "Widow Parker." She was a comfort and source of support for her granddaughter, Mary.

According to her will, upon her death Elizabeth's three household slaves, Prudence Jones, Ann Bell, and Cyrus were granted their freedom. Prudence was granted a "12 a month for life," and both women were provided burial spots in the Parker family plot of Lexington Cemetery.[7]

Parents

Robert Smith Todd (father) (February 25, 1791–July 16, 1849)
married to Eliza Ann *Parker* on November 12, 1812;
married to Elizabeth Humphreys on November 1, 1826.[8]

Robert was the seventh child of his parents. He lived his entire life in Lexington, Kentucky. At the age of fourteen, he enrolled in Transylvania University, and graduated four years later. He apprenticed at the law with Thomas Bodley and later with George Bliss. Robert was admitted to the Kentucky Bar at the age of twenty. He first chose a military career, and served in the 5th Regiment, Kentucky Volunteers during the War of 1812. As a businessman, Robert was a successful cotton merchant and a planter, and was named president of the Lexington branch of the Bank of Kentucky in 1836. His political career included both local and state offices. In Lexington, he was a member of both the Fayette (Fiscal) Court and the City Council. In 1821, Robert was unanimously elected to serve as Clerk of the Kentucky House of Representatives, a position he held for twenty years. He then was elected as a member of the House of Representatives representing Fayette County. In 1845, he was elected to the Kentucky State Senate, and was a candidate for reelection at the time of his death.[9]

In the summer of 1849, a cholera epidemic swept through Lexington. Robert, then married to his second wife, sent the family to their summer home,

Buena Vista, located outside of Frankfort, Kentucky. He remained in Lexington to tend to political business. Soon, he contracted cholera. Apparently, Robert was able to reunite with the family at Buena Vista, for according to a family Bible entry, Robert "died July 17th, 1849. at 1 o'clock am at night at his farm in Franklin County KY in his 59th year."[10]

At the time of his death, Robert's estate consisted of the house and lot in Lexington, thirty-eight acres of land in Franklin County, household furniture, livestock, slaves, and a one-third interest in the cotton manufacturing plan of Oldham, Todd, & Company. This was valued at approximately $23,392.57.[11]

Eliza Ann *Parker* Todd (mother) (1795–July 5, 1825)
married November 12, 1812.[12]

Eliza was the daughter of Robert and Elizabeth *Rittenhouse* Parker. At the age of seventeen, she married Robert Smith Todd. Eliza and Robert were related, but not as closely as some have suspected; the newlyweds were half-second cousins.[13] The couple lived in a home on the corner lot belonging to the bride's mother (Elizabeth Parker) on Short Street. Eliza bore seven children, four daughters and three sons; six of the children lived to adulthood.

Eliza died from childbed fever shortly after giving birth to her son George. She is buried in the Lexington Cemetery with her son Robert Parker Todd who preceded her in death at the age of eighteen months.

Elizabeth L. *Humphreys* Todd (stepmother)
(January 1, 1800–February 14, 1874)[14]

Elizabeth L. Humphreys (Betsy) was the daughter of Dr. Alexander and Mary *Brown* Humphreys. She was born in Staunton, Virginia and raised in Frankfort, Kentucky.[15] Betsy's marriage to Robert Smith Todd in 1826 made her the matriarch of a family consisting of six small children. She may have found controlling the children difficult due to interference from family members. When Robert and Betsy were first wed, they lived next door to Elizabeth Parker, the children's maternal grandmother. Grandma Parker believed the marriage had happened too quickly after the death of her daughter, and her home became a refuge for her daughter's children whenever they felt the need to escape their stepmother's domain. Over the next fifteen years, Betsy gave birth to nine of her own children; the firstborn, a son, died in infancy. Due to the growing family, in 1832, the family moved into a larger home located on Main Street—still close to Grandma Parker, but not directly under her watchful eye.

During the Civil War, three of Betsy's sons and three of her sons-in-law were Confederate soldiers. By July 1866, Betsy had moved to Madison, Indiana with her daughter Emilie and Emilie's three young children. Betsy died in Madison in 1874. Her body was returned to Kentucky to be buried in the Lexington Cemetery.[16]

The children of Robert Smith Todd and Eliza Parker Todd)

Elizabeth Porter *Todd* Edwards (sister) (November 18, 1813, in Lexington, Kentucky–February 22, 1888 in Springfield, Illinois) married Ninian Wirt Edwards on February 16, 1832.[17]

At the age of nineteen, Elizabeth married Ninian while he was still a law student at Transylvania. The couple lived with the Todd family until Ninian completed his studies. In 1833, they moved to Illinois. Katherine Helm (daughter of Emilie Todd Helm) mistakenly wrote that Elizabeth "went to Springfield, Illinois, to preside over the governor's mansion, her father-in-law, Governor Ninian Edwards, being a widower."[18] The senior Ninian Edwards had a successful political career having served as the only governor of Illinois Territory (1809–1818), as U. S. Senator (1818–1824), and as the governor of the state of Illinois (1826–1830). He died of cholera on July 20, 1833 in Belleville, Illinois. At the time of his death, Governor Edwards was neither a presiding governor nor a widower. His widow, Elvira *Lane* Edwards outlived her husband by nearly six years. She died in Belleville on June 7, 1839.[19]

When Ninian and Elizabeth moved to Illinois, they first went to Belleville to settle the estate and to help Elvira with the household. In 1834, Governor John Reynolds appointed Ninian as Attorney General of Illinois. The law required the Attorney General to reside in the state capital which at the time was in Vandalia; Ninian did not like Vandalia, so he resigned his position and moved to Springfield in 1835.[20]

Together, Elizabeth and Ninian had six children; four of whom lived to adulthood.

Mary lived with the Edwards family when she first came to Springfield, and again when she was a widow and chose not to live by herself. Mary was married in her sister's home and died in her sister's home. The Edwards were part of the inaugural party, and Ninian, although a staunch Democrat was awarded a government position as Army Paymaster during the Civil War. Abraham had to rescind Ninian's commission amid charges of misuse of government funds. This was a source of embarrassment to Lincoln and created a rift between the two families.

While a loving hand was always extended to Mary, the same cannot be said about the relationship between the Edwards family and Abraham Lincoln. Their relationship was either kind and loving or cool and aloof depending on the social and political climate of the day. In the beginning of the Lincoln marriage, social standing influenced the Edwards' opinions of Lincoln. During Lincoln's campaign for the presidency, politics separated the families. However, no matter what the personal issues were, Elizabeth was there for Mary during every crisis of her life. She cared for Mary at the death of their mother. She came to Mary's side when Eddy and Willie died. Elizabeth gave Mary a place to stay when she was released from Bellevue, and again after her return from European travels.

Frances Jane *Todd* Wallace (sister)
(March 7, 1815 in Lexington, Kentucky–August 14, 1899
in Springfield, Illinois) married
William Smith Wallace on May 21, 1839.[21]

Frances moved to Springfield to live with her sister Elizabeth and to find a suitable husband. She had a brief courtship of one or two dates with Abraham Lincoln; however, she found her suitable husband in William Smith Wallace, and together they had six children. They lived in the Lincolns' neighborhood, diagonally across the street from the current location of the First Presbyterian Church. William was a physician and owned the pharmacy located below Abraham's law office. He often treated the illnesses of the Lincolns and their children. The families visited one another often, and oral history claims that at least once Frances planted flowers in the Lincolns' garden when Mary was not feeling well.[22]

Both Frances and William were part of the inaugural party. During the war, Lincoln appointed William as a U.S. Army Paymaster. His position required that he spend part of his time at the front on the lower Mississippi River. His exposure to the southern climate left him exhausted and debilitated. He never fully regained his health after the war and died in 1867.

A controversy surrounds Frances's birth date. Her death record and tomb-stone record her birth date as March 7, 1817. This is incorrect as her younger brother Levi was born in June 1817.[23] No one knows why there is a discrepancy in Frances' birth date. Perhaps as a young belle, she wanted to appear younger to her beau. Once she had bent the truth of her birthdate and became his bride, she had to maintain the ruse the rest of her life.

Levi Owen Todd (brother)
(June 25, 1817 in Lexington, Kentucky–October 27, 1864
in Lexington, Kentucky)
married Louisa Searles on January 17, 1843.[24]

Levi held the position of assistant manager and bookkeeper for Oldham, Todd & Company. Later he worked as a commission and forwarding merchant—a person who arranged for merchandise arriving at a train station or port to be forwarded to its destination.[25] Levi married Louisa Searles, and together they had six children. Two of the children died before reaching the age of ten. The couple had a turbulent marriage caused by Levi's drinking, financial despair, and by the death of their young children. She filed for divorce in 1859; her petition asked that he be restrained "from disturbing or in any wise interfering with the plaintiff or any of the children until the further order of the Fayette Circuit Court." The case was unresolved when Louisa died in June 1861.[26] After Louisa's death, the remaining children were separated. Two remained in Lexington while the two eldest girls were sent to Springfield to live with their aunt, Ann Smith. Although Levi did not serve in the military during the Civil War, he was a staunch Union supporter and was one of the few men in the Todd family, and in Lexington, who supported Abraham Lincoln as a presidential candidate. This was despite two lawsuits in the 1850s the brothers-in-law had brought against one another.

Levi lived his entire life in Lexington, at one time returning to the home on Short Street where he and his siblings lived as small children. An unsigned note written to Emilie Helm states that Levi "died from a short illness at the Broadway Hotel, and was buried from his father's house on Main Street." He was 50 years old at the time of his death.[27] Levi was buried in an unmarked grave in the Todd family plot of the Lexington Cemetery.[28]

Mary Ann *Todd* Lincoln (December 13, 1818 in Lexington, Kentucky–July 16, 1882 in Springfield, Illinois) married Abraham Lincoln on November 4, 1842.

Robert Parker Todd (brother) (May 1821 in Lexington, Kentucky–July 1822 in Lexington, Kentucky)[29]

Robert died at the age of fourteen months. His funeral was held on July 22, 1822, at his parents' home on Short Street.[30] He was originally buried in a cemetery on Main Street and was later reinterred in the same grave as his mother when the larger Lexington Cemetery was completed.

Ann Marie *Todd* Smith (sister) (1824 in Lexington, Kentucky–March 21, 1891 in San Francisco, California) married Clark Moulton Smith on October 25, 1846.[31]

Like her older sister Frances, Ann maintained a mystery about her date of birth. She was born sometime before September 1824. Most likely she came to Springfield after Mary's marriage to be with her sisters and to find a suitable husband. As a belle, Ann was said to have courted every gentleman she knew. During a summer vacation, Ann met and had a whirlwind relationship with Clark Smith, a store owner living in Carrolton, Illinois.[32] The couple married quickly, and moved to Carrolton and lived there until 1852 when they moved to Springfield. Clark opened a dry goods store with his brother Stephen and his former employer, William Yates. This store became a favorite of the Lincolns.

Ann frequently entertained and soon became one of the city's most famous hostesses. Her entertainments were often worthy of mention in the newspaper's society pages. Ann was also remembered for her quick temper.

The relationship between Ann and Mary has often been debated. Ann did attend the farewell reception held for the Lincolns before they left Springfield. However, she was not present at Lincoln's inauguration. Her absence may have been an indication of a rift with her sister. Or, Ann's absence may have been an indication that she was overwhelmed with personal tragedies. Ann buried her first-born son, Clark Moulton Smith, Jr., in June 1860 and was still in mourning. She was either pregnant at the time of his death, or became pregnant shortly afterward. When the next child, a boy, was born, he was given the same name as his deceased brother. Sadly, before the end of

1863, Ann would bury her new baby and another son, named Lincoln. Ann was likely too grief stricken to travel to Washington, and with the arrival of her two nieces to raise, she was too busy.[33]

Despite Ann's grief, there was a rift between the two sisters that was known throughout the family and mentioned in letters between Mary and her cousin Elizabeth Grimsley. However, there was also closeness between them, for when Mary lay dying, it was Ann who sat at her bedside throughout the night.

Abraham and Clark shared a relationship that was perhaps much closer than the two sisters. Oral history tells of the two brothers-in-law walking to and from work together. When president-elect Lincoln needed a quiet place to write his inaugural address, Clark offered a private room in his store. [34]

Ann and Clark had eight children; they named the son born in 1855 Lincoln. After Clark's death, Ann sold their home on South Fifth Street. She had grown tired of keeping house and began traveling with her daughters, Clara and Minnie. Ann enjoyed the west and made her base in San Francisco.[35]

George Rogers Clark Todd (brother)
(July 4, 1825 in Lexington, Kentucky– April 27, 1900
in Camden, South Carolina) married Ann H. Curry
in 1851. The couple later divorced. George married
Martha Belton Lyles sometime after April 1865. [36]

George studied medicine at Transylvania University in Lexington and completed his medical thesis in 1848. He was the only sibling of Mary's to attend the university that had been affiliated with the Todd family in the previous generation. After his father's death in 1849, George and his brother Levi brought a lawsuit against their stepmother, Betsy, over the estate. She decided to sell the Todd family home and its contents, including several family slaves, at public auction. Even though it is possible that George and Levi may have been justified in their accusations, Lincoln represented the sisters who lived in Springfield in the settlement of their father's estate and felt that George and Levi should leave the widow alone. George, therefore, despised Lincoln and everything he represented. During the war, George served as a surgeon for the Confederate forces and oversaw First South Carolina Hospital, Rickersville, located about four miles from Charleston.[37]

George and his wife Ann *Curry* Todd had one daughter. They were not a happy family, for just a few years after their marriage, Ann had divorced her husband on the grounds of abandonment and cruelty. It is not known if the cruelty charge was based on physical abuse, George's drinking, or mental and emotional abuse from being abandoned. It is known that while George was serving at a wayside hospital in Camden, South Carolina during the war, he met Martha "Mattie" Belton Lyles; she was a nurse at the hospital. Mattie was known for her "rare beauty and charm."[38] Shortly after the war's end, the couple married and they lived in Camden where George founded the Confederate Wayside Hospital. The couple later moved to George, and finally settled in Barnwell, South Carolina where they lived out their last years. He and Martha had two children.[39]

Half-Siblings (the children of Robert Smith Todd and Elizabeth "Betsy" Humphreys)

Robert Humphreys Todd (half-brother)
(1827 in Lexington, Kentucky–1827 in Lexington, Kentucky)[40]

The second son to be named after his father, Robert died a few days after his birth.

Margaret *Todd* Kellogg (half-sister) (December 14, 1828
in Lexington, Kentucky–March 13, 1904 in Daytona, Florida)
married Charles Henry Kellogg on October 28, 1847.[41]

As newlyweds, Margaret and Charles resided in New Orleans. Later they moved to Covington, Kentucky. Although the couple attended Lincoln's inauguration and stayed with the Lincolns for several days visiting, both had strong ties to the Confederacy. Whether the truth or merely a rumor, it was reported that, during the war Margaret went to Camp Chase in Columbus, Ohio with her mother to take medical supplies to the Confederate soldiers who were held there as prisoners of war.

After the war, Margaret and Charles made their home in Cincinnati, Ohio where Charles worked as a merchant. They had seven children.

In December 1903, experiencing failing health, Margaret was taken to Daytona, Florida—most likely for the warmer climate. Margaret died at the Troy Hotel after a prolonged illness which had left her bedridden.[42]

Samuel Brown Todd (half-brother) (March 20, 1830,
in Lexington, Kentucky–April 8, 1862 en route to Corinth,
Mississippi) married Clelie Cecile Royer in 1856.[43]

Sam attended Center College. After his father's death, Sam went to Rose-
land Plantation in St. Charles Parish, Louisiana to live with the widow of his
deceased maternal uncle John Humphreys. The property belonged to the
Kenner family, into which Sam's uncle had married. Sam met and married
Clelie, the daughter of Charles Royer, in the New Orleans area. The couple
had four children. In March 1862, Sam joined the newly formed Crescent
Regiment of New Orleans as a private. This unit was often referred to as
the "Kid Glove Regiment" because so many of its members were the sons of
landowners with large estates. On the second day of fighting at the battle of
Shiloh in 1862, Sam was mortally wounded when a Minié ball went through
his abdomen. He died en route to the hospital at Corinth. His commanding
officer wrote, "He demonstrated himself in every respect at [sic] becomes a
first-class soldier."[44] Because he was a brother to the Union's First Lady, Sam's
obituary was printed in both Southern and Northern newspapers. Never had
the death of a private received so many headlines.[45]

David Humphreys Todd (half-brother) (March 30, 1832 in
Lexington, Kentucky–July 30, 1871 in Huntsville, Alabama)
married Susan Turner Williamson in April 4, 1865.[46]

David left home at the age of 14 to join a regiment and fight during the Mexican
War. A few years later, he was in California looking for gold and silver, and
according to a letter from his younger brother Alec's girlfriend, David was
successful.[47] During the Civil War, David obtained the rank of captain in
Company A 21st Louisiana Infantry CSA. He served as a guard, or a jailer, in
the prison system and served at Libby Prison. Some prisoners reported that
David was often intoxicated and took every opportunity to torture Union
prisoners; others dispute the charges. David was wounded near Vicksburg.
The family maintained that he was shot through the lungs.

When David married Susan, she was a widow with a small daughter. Susan's family lived in Huntsville, and David joined her family's business as a
merchant. They had one daughter together.

Martha K. *Todd* White (half-sister) (June 9, 1833 in
Lexington, Kentucky–July 9, 1868 in Anna, Illinois)
married Clement Billingslea White in 1852.[48]

Martha and her husband lived in Selma, Alabama where Clement was part
owner of the Central Warehouse Company. He served as a major in the CSA;
Martha pledged her loyalties to the Confederacy and attended the inauguration of Jefferson Davis. In 1864, Martha scandalized the Lincoln White
House when a rumor emerged that she had visited Washington and filled
her pockets with quinine for the Confederate troops. While the rumor was
believed to be untrue, newspapers printed the story, causing the Lincolns great
embarrassment. After the war, Martha and Clement moved to Anna, Illinois.

When Emilie Helm created the Todd family genealogy, she reported that
Clement and Martha had no children. However, it is unclear whether they
had a child who had died prior to Emilie's work. The 1860 census lists a young
boy named William King White living with Clement and Martha in Selma,
Alabama. It is unclear if the child was theirs or a relative. He does not appear
in other census records.[49]

Emilie Parret *Todd* Helm[50] (half-sister) (November 11, 1836
in Lexington, Kentucky–February 20, 1930 at Helm Place in
Lexington, Kentucky) married Benjamin Hardin Helm on
March 20, 1856 at Buena Vista near Frankfort, Kentucky.[51]

Emilie traveled to Springfield in 1855 to spend six months visiting with her
three sisters and their families. Years earlier, Lincoln had dubbed Emilie "Little
Sister," and always treated her more like a daughter than a sister-in-law.

Emilie's husband, Ben Helm, was a West Point graduate who rose to the
rank of brigadier general in the Confederate Army. Emilie was never far from
Ben during the war—when he was killed at the Battle of Chickamauga on
September 20, 1863, Emilie was able to attend his funeral in Georgia. While
trying to make her way back to Kentucky, Emilie was stopped at Fortress
Monroe. She was asked to take the oath of allegiance to the United States and
refused, feeling that to have taken such an oath would be considered disloyal
to her husband. Word was sent to President Lincoln, who telegraphed, "Send
her to me." Emilie arrived at the White House and stayed for eight days. Her
presence caused a stir among Washington society.[52]

In mid-December, Emilie returned to Kentucky where she lived for the
next two years. She never remarried and raised her three children with the

help of her mother. In 1866, Emilie, the children, and Betsy moved to Madison, Indiana. The children attended school, and Emilie provided for the family by teaching piano lessons and playing the organ at the Christ Episcopal Church. After her mother's death, Emilie returned to Kentucky.[53] Later, with the assistance of her nephew Robert Todd Lincoln, Emilie was appointed to the position of postmaster in Elizabethtown, Kentucky.

Later, Emilie and her three adult children moved to a stately home and farm on the outskirts of Lexington. They dubbed it Helm Place and there lived their remaining years.

Alexander Humphreys Todd (half-brother) (February 16, 1839 in Lexington, Kentucky–August 5, 1862 in Louisiana)[54]

Alec (or Alex, or Aleck) served in the 1st Kentucky CSA Cavalry, first as an assistant quartermaster and later as an aide-de-camp on the staff of his brother-in-law, Brigadier General Benjamin Hardin Helm. Alec rose to the rank of first lieutenant.

Exactly what happened the night of Alec's death is unclear. He was part of a group of soldiers making its way into Baton Rouge, where, just outside of the city, General Helm had called for the men to wait until dawn before attacking. Suddenly, horses were heard charging down the dark road and confusion followed. After a rapid volley of "friendly fire" it was soon discovered that General Helm had been wounded, and Alec killed. He was buried in the plum orchard at the Pratt family farm. Years later, Emilie Helm arranged to have his body moved to the cemetery in Lexington with other family members.[55]

Elodie "Dee Dee" Breck *Todd* Dawson (half-sister) (April 1, 1840 in Lexington, Kentucky–November 14, 1877 in Selma, Alabama) married Nathaniel Henry Rhodes Dawson in May 1862.[56]

Elodie was nicknamed "Dee Dee" but was sometimes called "Jane" by family members. Elodie was visiting her sister Martha White at the outbreak of the war. She attended the inauguration of Jefferson Davis and met her future husband at the festivities. Nathaniel served as Captain of the Selma Cadets which later became the 4th Alabama Infantry Regiment CSA. During the war, Elodie spent most of her time sewing items for Confederate soldiers. Elodie and Nathaniel had four children.[57]

Catherine "Kitty" Bodley *Todd* Herr (half-sister)
(October 7, 1841 in Lexington, Kentucky–April 17, 1875
in Louisville, Kentucky) married
William Wallace Herr on January 11, 1866.[58]

Catherine was called "Kitty" by her family. Kitty traveled to Springfield to visit the Lincolns after the presidential election in 1860. It is believed she may have been the "Miss Todd" listed as a member of the inaugural party.

As the war progressed, Kitty more staunchly supported the Confederacy. After the war, she married William Wallace Herr who had served in the CSA under the command of his future brother-in-law, General Benjamin Helm. William was one of the soldiers who removed the wounded general from the battlefield at Chickamauga.

Kitty and William had six children, most of whom died young. Kitty died ten days after giving birth to her last child, a son named William who died three months later.

The Children

Robert Todd Lincoln (August 1, 1843–July 26, 1926)
married Mary Eunice Harlan on September 24, 1868.

Robert was named after Mary Lincoln's father, Robert Smith Todd and as a child was called "Bobby." Soon after completing his studies at Harvard University, Robert was appointed the rank of captain in the Union Army and served on General Ulysses S. Grant's staff. After the war, Robert practiced law in Chicago. He was appointed Secretary of War in 1881 and held the position until 1885 having served during the administrations of presidents James A. Garfield and Chester A. Arthur. From 1889 until 1893, Robert served as the Minister to the United Kingdom under the presidential administration of Benjamin Harrison. Upon returning to the United States, Robert put his political career aside and returned to his law practice. One of his clients was the Pullman Palace Car Company. Robert became the company's president in 1897, and later served as its chairman of the board.

Robert and his wife Mary had three children. The eldest, Mary "Mamie" Todd Lincoln (1869–1938) married Charles Isham. They had a son, Lincoln Isham, who married but never had children. A son named Abraham "Jack" Lincoln II (1873–1890) died of blood poisoning while the family lived in London. The youngest child, daughter Jessie Harlan Lincoln (1875–1948) first married Warren Beckwith with whom she had two children. The marriage ended in divorce, and Jessie married twice more. Her children, Mary Lincoln Beckwith (1898–1975) and Robert Todd Lincoln Beckwith (1904–1985) had no descendants.

Robert Todd Lincoln had intended to be buried in the Lincoln Tomb in Springfield. After his death, his wife Mary decided to have him interred in Arlington National Cemetery in Virginia. She also arranged for their son to be removed from the Lincoln Tomb in Springfield and reinterred in Arlington. Mary is buried beside her husband.[59]

Edward Baker Lincoln (March 10, 1846–February 1, 1850)

Edward was named after his father's good friend, Edward Dickinson Baker. The nickname "Eddy" was used by both parents in their 1848 letters to one another. Eddy was less than two years of age when his father was elected to the US House of Representatives.[60]

When the family left Springfield for Washington in October 1847, Eddy made the journey with them. He fell ill in December 1849, and for 52 days, Mary watched over her baby, who died from what was probably tuberculosis. Eddy was laid to rest in Hutchinson Cemetery, but in 1857, the city of Springfield passed an ordinance forbidding any burials within the city limits. Approximately 600 bodies were removed from Hutchinson and reburied in Oak Ridge Cemetery. In December 1865, Eddy was reinterred in the new tomb that had been built for his father and brother.[61]

William Wallace Lincoln
(December 21, 1850–February 20, 1862)

Named after Mary's brother-in-law, Dr. William Wallace, the third son born to Abraham and Mary became known as "Willie." He was the child most like his father in temperament: Julia Taft, who visited the Lincolns often in the White House, described Willie as, "the most lovable boy I ever knew, bright, sensible, sweet tempered and gentle manner."[62]

In February 1862, both younger Lincoln boys became ill with what was probably typhoid fever. Tad's condition was not as severe as Willie's. For two weeks, Willie lay in bed while Mary tended to him constantly. He succumbed to his illness leaving both parents devasted. Willie's funeral was held in the East Room of the White House. He was first buried in Oak Hill Cemetery in Georgetown. When Lincoln was assassinated, Willie's body was placed on the train alongside his father's and returned to Springfield where he was later interred in the Lincoln Tomb.[63]

Thomas Lincoln (April 3, 1853–July 15, 1871)

Thomas was nicknamed "Tad" by his father, who thought he resembled a tadpole when he was born. The boy, named after his grandfather, Thomas Lincoln, was a rambunctious child who cared for neither books nor school. He enjoyed riding horses and loved animals in general. Julia Taft described Tad as "very affectionate when he chose, but implacable in his dislikes." Elizabeth Grimsley said Tad "was "the life, as also the worry of the household."

Tad traveled to Europe with Mary and attended school in Germany. After returning to America and residing in Chicago, Tad became ill and died from what was either tuberculosis or pneumonia. His funeral was held in Robert's home, and it was Robert who accompanied Tad's body to Springfield for burial in the Lincoln Tomb—Mary was too distraught to make the journey.[64]

Other Relatives Significant in Mary's Life

Edward Lewis Baker (great-nephew, son of Julia Edwards Baker, daughter of Elizabeth Edwards) (October 27, 1858–1923)[65] married Elizabeth Rebecca Cook.

Edward, whom Mary called "Lewis", was a favorite of hers. After Tad's death, Mary began to dote on Edward. He traveled to New York with Mary when she left for Europe and was waiting for her when she returned in 1881. Later, Edward served as the Assistant Clerk of the Supreme Court of Nebraska.[66]

Elizabeth J. *Todd* Grimsley Brown (cousin, daughter of Dr. John Todd) (January 29, 1825–September 23, 1895) married first Harrison J. Grimsley on July 21, 1846; after his death married Rev. John Howe Brown on January 29, 1867).[67]

Elizabeth and Mary were cousins and the best of friends. Elizabeth was a bridesmaid at the Lincolns' wedding, and the two women remained close. Elizabeth attended Lincoln's inauguration and stayed for a six-month visit at the White House. She traveled to New York and Philadelphia with Mary, helping her choose the best fabrics and furnishings to redecorate the Executive

Mansion. When Elizabeth returned to Springfield in September 1861, Mary gave her a couple of dresses and a beautiful shawl as parting gifts.[68]

Elizabeth and Harrison had two children. After his death, Elizabeth married Rev. John Howe Brown who was the pastor of the First Presbyterian Church in Springfield.

Ann Eliza *Todd* Campbell (cousin, daughter of Judge David Todd) (1820–1876) married Thomas M. Campbell on June 6, 1842.[69]

Ann and Mary became very close when Mary visited the family of her uncle, Judge David Todd, during the summer of 1840. The two Todd cousins were popular belles in Columbia, Missouri society and each was courted by several young men. In 1859, Ann and her husband Tom were one of the couples who traveled with the Lincolns and others to assess the property of the Illinois Central Railroad.

Eliza *Todd* Carr–(aunt, sister to Robert S. Todd) (1782–October 1865 in Fayette County, Kentucky) married Charles M. Carr.[70]

Eliza was one of the relatives who helped take care of Mary and her siblings after the death of their mother. According to historian W. A. Evans, after Robert S. Todd married Betsy, Mrs. Carr "was rather sympathetic with the antagonism of the first family to the stepmother." Descendants of the Carr family gave statements to Mr. Evans that the Todd children lived with the Carr family "more than half the time." Since it is impossible to verify this claim, it can only be said that the members of the two households maintained a close relationship.[71]

Anna Marie *Parker* Dickson–(cousin, daughter of Dr. John Todd Parker and Jane Logan Allen) (October 18, 1826 in Versailles, Kentucky–March 6, 1885 in Avondale, Ohio) married Judge William Martin Dickson (b. September 19, 1827 in Lexington, Indiana–d. October 15, 1889 in Cincinnati, Ohio) of Lexington, Kentucky on October 19, 1852.[72]

Lincoln spent a week with the Dickson family while he worked on a case in 1855. William traveled to Washington during the Civil War to visit the Lincolns. Anna and William had six children.[73]

Louisa Howard "Lu Lu" *Todd* Keys (niece, daughter of Levi Owen Todd) (January 27, 1856–May 30, 1943) married Edward Keys on October 10, 1876.[74]

Louisa was the daughter of Levi Owen and Louisa *Searles* Todd. In 1860 when Louisa was just five years of age, she and her older sister Ellen moved to Springfield to live with her aunt, Ann Smith. Louisa became a favorite of Mary's and was given many gifts of jewelry and clothing. For Louisa's wedding, Mary gave her a white silk dress which was reported to have been worn by Mary when she was presented at St. James's Court (although there is no documentation that Mary was ever there). Louisa had the dress converted into a dancing dress for her wedding. Louisa and Edward had three children.[75]

Stephen Trigg Logan (cousin) (February 24, 1800–July 17, 1880) married America T. Bush on June 25, 1823.[76]

Stephen was a distant cousin to Mary; their kinship is not as close as many historians have assumed. Mary's great-great grandfather, David Logan was Stephen's great-grandfather, making Stephen her second cousin once removed. The more important connection was between Stephen and Lincoln—Stephen was a senior law partner to Abraham Lincoln from 1841 to 1843, and the two men remained friends until Lincoln's death. Stephen and America had eight children, two of whom lived to adulthood.

Hannah *Todd* Stuart (aunt, sister to Robert Smith Todd) (February 28, 1781–March 21, 1834) married Rev. Robert Stuart in 1802.[77]

Family lore claims that Hannah was the first white child born in Kentucky. In her youth, Hannah was described as a "beauty," and in later years as a woman of "uncommon force of character."[78]

Her husband Rev. Stuart was the pastor at the Walnut Hill Presbyterian Church from 1803 to 1842. This church was built on land donated by Hannah's father, General Levi Todd and was located six miles outside of Lexington on Richmond Pike Road. In addition to his ministry work, the Stuart family worked a 184-acre farm which had also been deeded to them by General Todd. Hannah and her family always maintained a close relationship with Mary's father, and with Mary.

John Todd Stuart (cousin, son of Rev. Robert and
Hannah *Todd* Stuart) (November 10, 1807–November 28,
1885) married Mary Virginia Nash on October 25, 1837.[79]

John Todd Stuart moved to Springfield on October 25, 1828. He served as a
major during the Black Hawk War, in the same battalion as Abraham Lincoln. The two men became lifelong friends and for nearly four years were law
partners. However, Stuart's true interest was politics. He was a state legislator
for two terms; a state senator for one term; and a member of the US House
of Representatives for three terms.

The two families visited one another often and mostly had a loving relationship. The relationship between Mary and her cousin became strained when
Stuart headed the Lincoln Monument Association and proposed burying the
martyred president in a tomb in the middle of town. Mary disapproved and
wanted her husband buried outside of the city limits. Another issue arose
between the two when Stuart supported Robert's plan to have his mother tried
and committed for insanity. John Todd Stuart and his wife had seven children.

Eliza Ann *Stuart* Steele (cousin, daughter of
Rev. Robert and Hannah *Todd* Stuart)
(November 17, 1805–August 11, 1884) married
Rev. Samuel Steele on November 16, 1843.[80]

Eliza was her husband's second wife. The couple had no children together,
but she raised his two children from his previous marriage. Samuel had been
called to be the pastor of the Presbyterian Church in Hillsboro, Ohio on June
2, 1834, where he served for 35 years until his death in 1869[81] Mary wrote to
Eliza in 1871 requesting her cousin come to Chicago for a visit. It is not known
if Eliza made the journey.

Judge David Todd (uncle, brother to
Robert Smith Todd) (March 29, 1786–June 9, 1859)
married Elizabeth "Eliza" Barr on April 7, 1812.[82]

David moved his family from Kentucky to Franklin, Missouri in 1817. From
1818 to 1819, he was one of five trustees who were responsible for selling and
developing lots in what would become the city of Columbia, Missouri. In
1819, President James Monroe appointed David as the territorial circuit judge.

Judge Todd was a favorite of Mary's, and she came to visit him and his family in the summer of 1840.

Dr. John Todd (uncle, brother to
Robert Smith Todd) (April 27, 1787–January 9, 1865)
married Elizabeth Fisher Blair Smith on July 1, 1813.[83]

John was one of the first graduates of Transylvania University in Lexington, Kentucky. He later attended and graduated from the medical department of University of Pennsylvania. During the War of 1812, he served as a surgeon in the 5th Kentucky Regiment and was appointed Surgeon General of the Kentucky Troops. After the war, he first practiced medicine in Bardstown, Kentucky, then moved to Edwardsville, Illinois in 1817. In 1827, President John Quincy Adams appointed John to the position of Register of the United States Land Office in Springfield, Illinois and his family soon moved again. John practiced medicine in Springfield and was elected president of the first Medical Society of Illinois. A devoted member of the Presbyterian Church, John helped establish a Presbyterian Church in Springfield and served as an elder.

John was a surrogate father to Mary and her sisters living in Springfield and often served as their physician. John and his wife Elizabeth had six children.

Lockwood M. Todd (cousin, son of
Dr. John Todd) (June 17, 1826–January 9, 1894)
married Emilie Husbands on April 18, 1866.[84]

Lockwood traveled to Washington with the Lincolns during the inaugural journey. During the war, he served as a commissary and was with General Sherman during his March to the Sea. Lockwood is best known for having been photographed with Willie and Tad Lincoln.

Dr. Lyman Beecher Todd (half-cousin, son of
James Clarke Todd and Maria Blair. James and
Robert Smith Todd were half-brothers) (April 16,
1832–May 15, 1902) married Sarah Frances Swift.[85]

Lyman Beecher Todd was appointed Postmaster of Lexington, Kentucky by President Lincoln. He was in Washington at the time of Lincoln's assassination and was at the President's bedside when he died. Lyman assisted Mary with the burial arrangements for her husband. During the dispute over where in Springfield Lincoln should be buried, Lyman championed Mary: He sent several telegrams to family members, including John Todd Stuart, expressing Mary's wish that her husband be buried in Oak Ridge Cemetery and not in a downtown lot.

Lyman and Sarah had at least six children.

Margaret *Stuart* Woodrow (cousin, daughter of Rev. Robert and Hannah *Todd* Stuart) (September 20, 1817–March 23, 1916)[86]

Just five years younger than Mary, Margaret had vivid memories of her childhood at the Stuart family home, Walnut Hill, when the Todd family came to visit. As a young belle, Margaret traveled to Springfield to visit her brother and other relatives. She stated that "she saw much of Mrs. Lincoln, but little of her husband, who was then making his canvass for Congress. She knew Mr. Lincoln, but not well." Margaret married Joshua Woodrow of Hillsboro, Ohio. They had one child, Robert S. Woodrow, who had served in Company C, Ohio 2nd Cavalry Battalion during the Civil War.[87]

APPENDIX 2: HER FRIENDS

By way of impressing upon your mind, that friends must not be *entirely* forgotten . . .

—Mary Lincoln to Ozias M. Hatch, October 3, 1859

Girlhood Friends in Lexington

Elizabeth Bodley was the daughter of Thomas Bodley and Katherine Harris Shiell. Thomas was an officer during the War of 1812, presidential elector, grandmaster of the Masonic Grand Lodge of Kentucky, and an attorney. Their home was "Bodley House," where the children had a French governess and an English head nurse. The Bodleys were distant cousins to Mary. Elizabeth married Erasmus Boyle Owsley, who was the son of William Owsley, the sixteenth governor of Kentucky. She later lived in Louisville, Kentucky.[1]

Elizabeth Humphreys was the daughter of Samuel P. Humphreys, an older brother of Elizabeth *Humphreys* Todd. The young girl was orphaned when her father died in 1824; she then went to live with her aunt Elizabeth Todd while attending school in Lexington.[2] Elizabeth and Mary shared a bedroom and became good friends. Elizabeth married Mr. Norris and moved to Garden City, Kansas. During the mid-1890s, Elizabeth wrote several letters to Emilie Helm depicting a number of incidents which had occurred during her childhood friendship with Mary. Katherine Helm used the letters as documentation when she wrote her biography, *The True Story of Mary, Wife of Lincoln.*[3]

Mary M. Redwood and Mary's relationship is unclear. A recently discovered, previously unknown note indicates they were friends:

> November 4, 1861
> Mrs. Redwood, the lady who writes the within, was at school with
> Mrs. L. & would be glad if she could be given some employment,
> such as she indicates, or any other which is suitable.
>
> A. Lincoln[4]

Mary Jane Stuart and Margaret Stuart were the daughters of Rev. Robert Stuart and Hannah Todd, and Mary's first cousins. Although Mary Stuart was several years older than Mary, the two remained in contact at least until the Civil War. The Stuart family lived on a 184-acre farm that had been given to them by Hannah's father, Levi Todd. In the winter months, the Todd children often spent weekends with their aunt and uncle.[5] (See Appendix 1 for more information)

Catherine Cordelia Trotter was the daughter of General George Trotter Jr., a prominent merchant and one of the heroes of the Battle of the Thames. He was a colonel of the old 42nd Regiment of Kentucky Militia in which Robert S. Todd has been a captain. The Trotter family lived at "Woodlands."[6]

Mary Jane Warfield and Julia Warfield were the daughters of Dr. Elisa Warfield and his wife Marie Barr. Dr. Warfield was a noted surgeon and professor of surgery and obstetrics at Transylvania. The family lived at "The Meadows" where Dr. Warfield bred fine racehorses.

The Warfield sisters attended Shelby Female Academy with Mary.[7]

Mary Jane later married Cassius Marcellus Clay; after forty-five years of marriage the couple divorced in 1874, with Clay claiming that Mary Jane had abandoned him. Actually she would no longer tolerate his marital infidelities.

Mary Wickliffe and Margaret Wickliffe were daughters of state senator Robert "Old Duke" and Margaret Wickliffe. Their father was one of the largest and wealthiest slave owners in Kentucky. The family had a mansion, "Glendower" on Second Street in Lexington. The girls attended Shelby Female Academy and were classmates of Mary's.[8]

Mary Wickliffe married Colonel John Preston; Margaret married William Preston.

During the war, Margaret contacted President Lincoln requesting a pass to travel through Union lines to visit her husband, a general in the Confederate Army. Mary asked that her friend's request be granted. Lincoln sent a telegram to Margaret explaining that he would like to oblige the request but could not.[9]

The family of Henry Clay was close to the family of Robert Smith Todd. Henry and Robert were political allies and good friends, and their wives were good friends. The two families often visited one another, and the children were playmates.[10]

Springfield Friends and Neighbors

Elizabeth *Dale* **Black** married William Black, and the couple moved to Springfield in late 1851. They did not stay long; by January 1852, he had established a business in St. Louis. Elizabeth remained in Springfield until the couple was prepared to completely move to St. Louis by summer's end in 1852. While in Springfield, Elizabeth kept a diary listing her social visits and activity; in one entry Elizabeth wrote of spending one evening at the Baptist Church and laughing "all the way home at Mrs. L. and Mrs. Reman(n)."

Elizabeth and Mary both joined the First Presbyterian Church on April 13, 1852. In addition to seeing Mary at church functions, Elizabeth frequently visited her at home.[11] After Elizabeth moved to St. Louis, the woment stayed in touch. Mary wrote to her requesting assistance in finding a white fur hat for her son Tad, who was then six months of age.[12]

Mary *Lamb* **Bouman** was the wife of Joseph G. Bouman and a close friend to Mary prior to her marriage to Abraham. One week before Mary Lamb's wedding, Mary Lincoln wrote to Mercy Levering stating that her friend was "about perpetrating the *crime of matrimony*."[13]

Mary Brayman married Mason Brayman. The Brayman and Lincoln families first became acquainted when the Braymans rented the Lincoln's home during Lincoln's term in the 30th Congress. Shortly afterward, the Braymans purchased property at the corner of Edwards and Eight Streets. As neighbors, the Braymans were frequent guests in the Lincoln Home. The two women maintained a close friendship after the Lincolns moved to Washington.[14]

Mercy Ann *Levering* **Conkling** was a dear friend to Mary during their "belle" years in Springfield. Mercy later married James C. Conkling. Mercy and Mary corresponded with one another throughout the Lincolns' stay in Washington.[15]

Harriet Dallman married Charles Dallman. They lived a few doors west of the Lincolns on Jackson Street. In 1853, Harriet gave birth to a son named Charles, Jr. Too sick and weak to nurse her child, Harriet turned to her friend, Mary for help. Mary offered to be a wet nurse for the newborn, and Lincoln carried the child back and forth. Sadly, little Charles died when he was just 15 months of age. Once again, Mary offered her assistance to the Dallman family by providing meals during their grieving.[16]

Adelia Dubois was the second wife of Jesse Dubois, who served as the state auditor. The Dubois family lived on South Eight Street. Dubois and Lincoln were political allies as well as good friends; Adelia and Mary were also close friends. The DuBois' named their firstborn child after their dear friend, Lincoln. The two women maintained their friendship after the president's death.[17]

Helen *Dodge* Edwards was born in 1819 in Kasdasdia, Illinois. After her father's death in 1825, her family returned to their native New York where Helen was raised. In 1838, Helen met Benjamin Edwards who was studying law at Yale University, and they married the following year. When they first arrived in Springfield, the couple stayed with Ninian Edwards (Ben's brother) and his wife Elizabeth. Mary was already living with Ninian and Elizabeth and met Helen the night Helen arrived. The two women became friends, and according to Helen, they remained friends until Mary's death. Helen and her husband were invited guests at the Lincoln wedding. Her home on Fourth Street was a center of entertainment, and the Edwards' guest list often included the Lincolns. Years later, Helen wrote of Mary, "I was attracted towards her at once. The sunshine in her heart was reflected in her face."[18]

Eliza Henry was the wife of Dr. Anson G. Henry. When Mary and Abraham broke their engagement, it was Dr. Henry who helped the couple toward reconciliation. After Lincoln's death, Dr. Henry was one of the few friends Mary turned to for support. He sat with her for hours offering comfort and assuring her that although death separated loved ones, they were always nearby. After Dr. Henry's death, Mary wrote to Noah Brooks requesting assistance in selling a few stocks. She planned to give some of the proceeds to her dear friend Eliza, who needed financial assistance.[19]

Susan H. *Cranmer* Lamb was the wife of James L. Lamb who ran a firm for merchandising and pork packing. Mary mentioned visiting Susan in a letter dated 1841, and in an 1880 letter mentioned the location of Susan's home. While the depth of the friendship is unknown, it seems it lasted four decades. [20]

Charlotte *Dawson* Marsh was the wife of William Marsh, a Springfield photographer who photographed President-elect Lincoln. Charlotte was a piano teacher. Willie and Tad Lincoln were two of her pupils.[21]

Sarah Melvin was the wife of Dr. Samuel Melvin. The Melvin family lived a few houses away from the Lincolns on Eighth Street. Their boys often played together, and the mothers were friends. Sarah gave birth to a daughter in 1861 who was named "Mary" in honor of Mary Lincoln. Mary sent her "sweet little namesake" a bonnet cap from Washington.[22]

Mary *Black* Remann was the widow of Henry Remann and the sister of William Black. Mary Remann became one of Mary's dearest friends. The Remann family lived in the neighborhood on Market Street, just a block north and around the corner from the Lincolns' home. Willie Lincoln and Henry

Remann were friends and playmates. When Willie was in Chicago with his father, he wrote a sweet letter to his friend Henry.[23]

Jane *Huntington* Ridgely was the second wife of Nicholas Henry Ridgely, who came to Springfield as a banker. He organized Clark's Exchange Bank and was elected its first president. In 1859, his son joined the banking team, and the bank's name was changed to N. H. Ridgely & Co. Ridgely's business interests were not limited to banking. He purchased an old railroad that ran between Springfield and Naples, rebuilt it, and renamed it the Sangamon & Morgan Railroad. He was active in the Whig political party until its demise. Mary and Jane were friends prior to their marriages.[24]

Anna Rodney was the grandniece of Caesar Rodney, who signed the Declaration of Independence. Mary mentioned Anna in a letter to Mercy Levering written in 1841. Apparently, both Anna and Mary had been invited to accompany an acquaintance on a bridal tour. Mary declined the invitation, but Anna accepted. Anna also accepted Mary's request to be a bridesmaid when Mary and Abraham were wed.[25]

Hannah *Rathbun* Shearer was the wife of Dr. John Henry Shearer. Upon moving to Springfield, Hannah, a widow with two sons, lived with her brother, the Reverend Noyes W. Miner and his family. Eventually, her sons required medical attention, and they were treated by Dr. Shearer. John not only tended to the boys, he also took a romantic interested in Hannah.

The Shearers became friends with the Lincolns, a friendship Mary and Hanna continued after the Shearers moved to Pennsylvania. They wrote chatty letters to one another, and Hannah named her third son William after Willie Lincoln.[26]

Julia Ann Sprigg, the widow of John C. Sprigg, purchased a home one block south of the Lincoln family where she lived with her seven children. Her daughter, also named Julia, frequently helped Mary with her boys.[27]

Rev. James Smith served as the minister of First Presbyterian Church in Springfield. Rev. Smith conducted Eddy Lincoln's funeral and offered pastoral care to the Lincoln family during their time of grief. Rev. Smith was the author of *The Christian's Defense,* a book designed to challenge religious skeptics. Lincoln read the book and enjoyed theological conversations with its author. In 1863, Lincoln appointed Rev. Smith as the American consul to Dundee, Scotland, allowing the minister to return to his native country.[28]

Mary continued her relationship with Rev. Smith after his return to Scotland. The two exchanged letters, and in July 1869, Mary was able to travel to Scotland where Rev. Smith acted as her tour guide.

Matilda *Edwards* Strong, who was from Alton, Illinois, was a cousin to Ninian Edwards. Matilda, four years younger than Mary, was born in Lexington, Kentucky. Arriving in Springfield for a family visit in 1840, Matilda stayed with Ninian and Elizabeth. Mercy Levering had left Springfield before Matilda arrived, and Mary wrote to her describing Matilda as "a most interesting young lady" and saying, "a lovelier girl I never saw."[29] There has been speculation that perhaps Matilda was one of the causes for the broken engagement between Lincoln and Mary, but the validity of the claim is unknown.

Matilda married an attorney, Newton Deming Strong, and the couple lived in Reading, Pennsylvania. Matilda died at the age of twenty-nine.

Julia *Jayne* Trumbull married Lyman Trumbull, who later became a Senator for Illinois. Julia and Mary were members of the Coterie during their belle years in Springfield. Julia is believed to have been a co-author of the "Rebecca Letters" which resulted in the almost-duel between Abraham Lincoln and James Shields.

Mary and Julia dissolved their friendship in 1855 due to a political maneuver made by Lincoln to ensure that James Shields would not be elected senator. Lincoln had more votes, but not enough to win. Shields was second on the ballot, and Trumbull trailed the race with only five votes. Lincoln cast his support and votes to Trumbull thus assuring him the Senate seat. Mary was furious, for she thought it would have been more appropriate for Trumbull to have withdrawn instead of Lincoln.

Throughout the years, friends tried to reunite the Mary and Julia, especially during the Civil War. During a visit to Washington, Dr. A. G. Henry wrote to his wife, "Mary and Julia have both made me their confidant telling me their grievances and both think the other *all* to blame. I am trying to make peace between them."[30]

But peace would not come for them. After Lincoln's death, Julia deepened the wounds by not visiting Mary. By July 1865, Mary referred to Julia as "a whited Sepulchre" and the friendship was never mended.[31]

Beaux

Stephen A. Douglas was a political and social opponent to Lincoln. According to Harriet Chapman, Douglas and Mary were engaged. However, Mary had strong political opinions and it is doubtful she would have considered yoking herself to a Democrat. Whether or not they were engaged, they were at least flirtatious with one another. After Douglas had been appointed a judge of the Illinois State Supreme Court, Mary wrote to Mercy, "I feel disposed . . . to lay in my *claims*, as he is talented & agreeable & sometimes *countenances* me." Stephen Logan teased Mary about Douglas being a Yankee on her string, and continued saying, "I fear I am in grave danger of having to welcome a Yankee cousin."[32]

James Shields was a politician and Lincoln's opponent in what was nearly a duel. Shields was born in Ireland. Upon coming to America, he quickly aligned himself with the Democratic Party. He was the state auditor when the Illinois State Bank collapsed in 1842. According to Stephen Logan, Shields was another beau on Mary's string."[33]

James Winston was the grandson of Patrick Henry, the famous American Revolutionary. When Mary visited her Uncle David's family in Missouri, she wrote a letter to Mercy Levering telling of social and romantic updates. She wrote, "*one* being here, who cannot brook the mention of my return, an agreeable lawyer & grandson of *Patrick Henry—what an honor!* Shall never survive it—I wish you could see him, the most perfect original I had ever met, my beaux have *always* been *hard bargains* at any rate."[34]

Winston was a grandson through Dorothea Spotswood Henry and her husband George Dabney Winston. James never married. He ran for public office, but his campaigns were unsuccessful.

Edwin B. Webb was a charming widower and admirer of Mary's. Mary mentioned Webb in letters written to Mercy Levering. She referred to him as "a widower with two children," "a widower of modest merit," and "our principal lion." Despite his wearing of a mourning pin in honor of his deceased wife, members of Springfield society paired Webb and Mary together, and by June 1841, he was the "winning widower." Although others may have thought the two would wed, Mary was reluctant. She mentioned the "slight difference of some eighteen or twenty summers" in their ages and his two "sweet little objections."[35]

Washington Friends

Clara Harris was a socialite and the daughter of New York Senator Ira Harris and his first wife Louisa . A few years after Louisa's death, her husband married Pauline Rathbone, the mother of Clara's future husband Henry Rathbone. Rathbone joined the Union Army during the Civil War and rose to the rank of Major. The young engaged couple, who married in 1867, were at Ford's Theatre the night of Lincoln's assassination.

Their story ended tragically as Henry became mentally unstable. On December 23, 1883, Rathbone shot his wife in the head, killing her, and tried to attack their children. When a groundskeeper stopped him, Rathbone stabbed himself in an attempted suicide. At his trial, he was found to be insane and was placed in an asylum where he died in 1911.[36]

Elizabeth *Hobbs* Keckly was born a slave in Dinwiddie, Virginia. At the age of 18, Elizabeth was given to a family friend, Alexander Kirkland, who raped her repeatedly over a four year period. She bore a son through the relationship. Elizabeth proved to be an excellent seamstress and was able to help support the family through her sewing. In 1852, with the help of patrons, Elizabeth raised $1,200 to secure freedom for herself and her son, George. She soon moved to Washington City where she established her own business and created gowns for some of the city's most influential women. It was through a client, Mrs. Margaret McLean, that Elizabeth was introduced to Mary Lincoln. As Mary's personal modiste (dressmaker), Elizabeth and Mary developed a bond of friendship. Mary trusted Elizabeth and shared many personal moments with her.

After Lincoln's death, Elizabeth was able to offer Mary comfort, and later was one of the traveling companions who accompanied Mary and her sons to Chicago. The two women remained close until Elizabeth wrote a tell-all book revealing intimate conversations, personal letters, and private moments with the former First Lady. Mary was appalled, deeply wounded, and furious. The friendship quickly dissolved.

There has been a difference of opinion regarding how to spell Elizabeth's last name. For over one hundred years, historians have used "Keckley" as that was the spelling used for her book's publication. However, through the research and writings of Jennifer Fleischer, "Keckly" has become the more accepted spelling.[37]

Elizabeth *Blair* Lee was the wife of Samuel Phillips Lee, a Union naval officer during the Civil War. Elizabeth was one of the few women whom Mary leaned on for comfort after her husband's assassination. When the remaining Lincoln family members left Washington, the Lee children were given Tad's pet goats.[38]

Sally B. Orne was the wife of James H. Orne, a wealthy contributor to the Republican Party and to the war effort. The couple was from Philadelphia. Sally and Mary developed a loyal friendship; Sally was one of the few women who visited Mary in the White House after Lincoln's assassination. When

Mary was committed to Bellevue Place, Sally corresponded with Robert Lincoln regarding his mother's care.[39]

Eliza Jane *Lee* Slataper was the wife of Felician Slataper, a civil engineer from Pittsburgh, Pennsylvania. Mary and Eliza met in 1868 at a resort in Cresson Springs, Pennsylvania. Eliza's oldest son, Daniel, was a friend to Tad Lincoln. Whether the boys met through their mothers, or the mothers met through their sons is unclear. The two women became friends, and while it is believed they never saw one another again, they continued their friendship through correspondence.[40]

Jane Grey *Cannon* Swisshelm was an antislavery journalist and feminist from Minnesota and Pittsburgh, Pennsylvania. The level of the friendship between Jane and Mary is unknown. Jane was critical of both Lincolns until she met them at a White House reception in 1863. Her opinions changed dramatically; afterward, she spoke kindly of them. Jane worked in Washington as a clerk in the quartermaster general's office. During her free time, she worked as an army nurse in and around Washington, including Campbell Hospital where Mary Lincoln often carried flowers, food and gifts to the wounded soldiers.[41]

Mary Jane *Hale* Welles was the wife of Secretary of the Navy Gideon Welles. She was a devoted friend to Mary and often accompanied her to the military hospitals. Having lost six children of her own, Mary Welles understood the first lady's pain when Willie passed away. Mary Welles was such a loving friend, that even though she was suffering from a cold the night Lincoln was killed, she went to the Peterson House to sit with Mary and stayed until the next morning.[42]

Rhoda White was the wife of James W. White, a justice of the New York City Superior Court. Rhoda and Mary saw one another occasionally during the war years. Afterward, they continued to correspond with one another. When Mary returned from Europe in 1871, she stayed in New York for a few days, during which time she visited with Rhoda.[43]

The Male Champions

Noah Brooks, a journalist and editor, came to Washington in 1862. Brooks proved to be a loyal and loving friend to both Lincoln and Mary.[44] If Lincoln had been able to finish his term of office, Brooks would have taken John Hay's position as Lincoln's personal secretary. In 1895, Brooks released his biography of Abraham, *Washington in Lincoln's Time*.

Benjamin Brown French was originally from New Hampshire and came to Washington in 1833. During his career, he held several government positions. Lincoln appointed French Commissioner of Public Buildings. He had a variety of duties including introducing Mary at receptions held in the Blue Room. In addition, French oversaw the expenditures for redecorating the White House. At first, Mary considered French a supporter and a friend. Over the years, their feelings toward one another changed, and they became adversaries.

Senator Charles Sumner was from Massachusetts. He served in the U.S. Senate from 1851 to 1874. During the Civil War, Sumner was the leader of the Radical Republicans, a devoted abolitionist, and the Chairman of the Senate Foreign Relations Committee. He supported Lincoln during his presidential campaign and encouraged him to move more swiftly toward emancipation. As a friend to both Lincolns, Sumner was a frequent guest at the White House, where he was often found among a circle of friends with Mary. He was her favorite visitor, and he seemed to dote on her. Sumner often accompanied Mary to the opera or to other outings. During Mary's battle to secure a government pension, Sumner sponsored legislation supporting her cause. He remained her champion until his death in 1874.[45]

Widowhood Comforters

Elizabeth *Emerson* Atwater was a noted naturalist and the wife of Samuel T. Atwater. Mary met Elizabeth when they were both boarding at the Clifton House in Chicago. The few remaining letters of Mary's to Atwater depict gossipy news about Tad and Mary's journey to Racine, Wisconsin. Atwater was an educated woman who collected plants, shells, and other items. She was connected to the Chicago Academy of Science and upon her death willed them thirty boxes of natural specimens. Her husband was an insurance agent.[46]

Myra *Colby* Bradwell was a publisher, political activist, feminist, lawyer, and the wife of James Bradwell. Myra and her husband were able to visit Mary when she was confined to Bellevue Place. Myra published Mary's story in order to gain public support for Mary's attempt to be released from Bellevue and to regain control of her own affairs.

Alice *Davidson* Shipman was the wife of Paul Roberts Shipman who was an associate editor of the *Louisville Journal* during the Civil War. Alice was the daughter of William Henry Davidson and Letitia Hamilton *King* whom Katherine Helm identified as "one of Mrs. Lincoln's intimate girlhood friends."

It is doubtful that Mary and Letitia knew one another as young girls—Letitia married Davidson in Washington City, in 1828, when Mary was only ten years old.

The Davidsons made their home in Carmi, White County, Illinois. Davidson was an attorney and politician; for twelve years he spent much of his time in Springfield as a member of the state legislature. Two of those years he served as Lieutenant Governor. It is probable that the two women became acquainted during one of Davidson's visits to Springfield and then became friends. Davidson and Lincoln were both members of the Whig party and were friendly with one another.

Alice came to visit Mary in Chicago in the late 1860s. She had heard that Mary was not receiving visitors, but Mary greeted her warmly. Alice lived in Louisville, Kentucky and knew Joshua and Fanny Speed. The connection to such a dear friend of Abraham's may have given Mary comfort. Mary and Alice became friends and wrote to one another while Mary was traveling in Europe.[47]

APPENDIX 3: TIMELINE

Since I last wrote you, I have again been wandering.
—Mary Lincoln to Hannah Shearer, October 2, 1859

Mary Grows Up in the Bluegrass (The Lexington Years)

1818

December 13: Mary Lincoln was the fourth child born to Robert Smith Todd and his wife Eliza Parker. The family lived in a brick home on Short Street located on the corner lot of property belonging to Mary's maternal grandmother Elizabeth Parker.

1825

July 5: Eliza *Parker* Todd died after having given birth to her seventh child, a son named George Rogers Clark Todd.

1826

Mary began school at Dr. John Ward's Shelby Female Academy.
November 1: Robert Smith Todd married Elizabeth (Betsy) Humphreys in Frankfort, Kentucky.

1832

February 16: Elizabeth Todd (sister) married Ninian W. Edwards in Lexington, Kentucky and they moved into the Todd home.
The Todd family moved into a fourteen-room, brick home on Main Street.
Mary finished her studies at Dr. Ward's and entered Madame Mentelle's Boarding School.
September 29: President Andrew Jackson, campaigning for reelection, came to Lexington causing a verbal disagreement between Mary and a friend.

1833

Elizabeth became the first of the Todd sisters to leave Lexington when she and her husband, Ninian, moved to Belleville, Illinois.

1835

Summer: Mary and Frances travel to Springfield to visit their sister Elizabeth.[1]

Wife, Mother, and Friend: The Springfield Years

1837

Spring: Mary completed her studies at Madame Mentelle's.

May: Mary traveled to Springfield, Illinois for a three-month visit.

Fall: Mary returned to Lexington and once again returned to school. While it is not known what course of study Mary pursued, it is believed that for the next two years she studied under the tutorship of Dr. John Ward.[2]

1839

Mary finished her studies with Dr. John Ward.

October: Mary moved to Springfield to live with her sister Elizabeth Edwards. Soon afterward, she met Abraham Lincoln who at the time was her cousin John Todd Stuart's junior law partner.

1840

January 4: Mary met Benjamin and Helen Edwards when they came to Springfield. Mary and Helen developed a deep friendship.[3]

June: Mary traveled to Columbia, Missouri with her uncle Judge David Todd to visit him and his family. She stayed until mid-September. Some believe Lincoln visited Mary while she was in Missouri attending the Whigs of Central Missouri political meeting in Rocheport.[4]

July 22: Mary, Ann Todd, and others returned from a week-long excursion to Boonville, Missouri.

September 21: By this date, Mary had returned to Springfield.[5]

It is speculated that sometime within the year, Abraham and Mary became engaged.

1841

January: Early in the month, Abraham and Mary ended their engagement.

1842

September 22: Lincoln and James Shields engaged in a duel over the Rebecca letters which had been published in the *Sangamon Journal* earlier in the month. The letters were written as political satire, and Shields felt they were a personal attack on his character.

Fall: Abraham and Mary renewed their relationship and became secretly engaged.

November 4: Abraham and Mary were married in the home of Ninian and Elizabeth Edwards. The newlyweds move into the Globe Tavern which was located at 315 East Adams Street and was operated by Mrs. Beck.

1843

August 1: Robert (Bobby) Todd Lincoln was born.

August: Robert Smith Todd came to visit Mary, his grandson and name-sake, and his other family members living in Springfield.

1844

The Lincolns moved to a rented home on Monroe Street. By the end of the year, they were living in their own home at the corner of Eight and Jackson.

1846

March 10: Edward (Eddy) Baker Lincoln was born.

1847

October 25: Abraham, Mary, Robert, and Eddy boarded a stagecoach bound for Saint Louis. Once in Saint Louis, they boarded a steamboat. Lincoln had been elected to the U.S. House of Representatives, and the family was on its way to Washington.

October 27: The Lincolns visit with Joshua F. Speed at Scott's Hotel on the corner of Third and Market Streets in Saint Louis. It is not recorded if Speed's wife Fanny was present.[6]

November 2 (about): The Lincolns arrived in Lexington, Kentucky to visit Mary's family for the next three weeks.

December: Abraham, Mary, and the boys boarded at Mrs. Ann Sprigg's boardinghouse on Capitol Hill in Washington. Lincoln took his seat in Congress on December 6.

1848

By April, Mary and the boys, Robert and Eddy, had returned to Lexington while Abraham remained in Washington to finish his congressional term. Sometime before September, Mary and the children had reunited with Lincoln in Washington.

September 9: Lincoln and his family left Washington for a speaking tour in New England. They traveled to Massachusetts, New York, and Niagara Falls.[7]

September 28: The Lincoln family boarded the *Globe* to travel to Chicago.

October 4: The *Globe* stopped in Milwaukee.[8]

October 5: Abraham and Mary registered at the Sherman House Hotel in Chicago.

October 10: The Lincoln family returned to Springfield.[9]

1849

July 16: Mary's father, Robert Smith Todd, died of cholera.

October 18–November 14: Abraham, Mary, and the children traveled to Lexington to handle litigation involving the estate of Robert Smith Todd.[10]

1850

January 22: Mary's grandmother, Elizabeth *Porter* Parker died in Lexington, Kentucky.

February 1: Edward (Eddy) Baker Lincoln died at home in Springfield, Illinois.

Spring: Abraham and Mary returned to Lexington, Kentucky.

December 21: William (Willie) Wallace Lincoln was born.

1851

January 17: Abraham's father, Thomas Lincoln, died in Coles County, Illinois. Since Mary was recovering from the birth of Willie, Lincoln did not attend the funeral.

1853

April 4: Thomas (Tad) Lincoln was born. He was named after his paternal grandfather.

1854

Robert Smith Todd's estate was settled. The case of *Oldham, Todd, and Company v. Abraham Lincoln* was dismissed.

December: Emilie Todd came to Springfield for an extended stay with her sisters. Virginia Stuart (wife of John Todd Stuart) wrote that Emilie was "considered the belle of the season."[11]

1855

December: The Lincolns held a party. A check was written to W.W. Watson Confections to pay for refreshments, but no notice was made of what items were purchased.

1856

February: The Lincolns held a large party.

1857

February 5: The Lincolns held a large party where they had invited 500 people but "owing to an *unlucky* rain, 300 only" attended.[12]

July: Abraham and Mary traveled to "Niagara Falls, Canada, New York, and other points of interest." On July 24, they registered at the Cataract House in Niagara Falls.[13]

September 5–30: A second story was added to the Lincoln home.

1858

October 15: Mary traveled to Alton, Illinois to hear her husband debate Stephen Douglas. It was the only Lincoln/Douglas debate that Mary attended. Lincoln and Mary stayed at the Franklin House.

1859

June 26: Mary accompanied Abraham to Chicago.[14]

Fall: Mary traveled to St. Louis and stayed with her cousin, Judge John C. Richardson.[15]

December 21: Mary hosted Willie's ninth birthday party with fifty to sixty children in attendance.[16]

1860

May 24: Abraham and Mary attend the dedication of Oak Ridge Cemetery in Springfield, Illinois.

November 21: Mary traveled to Chicago with Lincoln as he met with politicians about cabinet positions. On either November 21 or 22, Abraham and Mary visited with Joshua and Fanny Speed at Tremont House. Abraham offered Speed a cabinet position.[17]

Assailed from Both Sides (The War Years)

1861

INAUGURAL JOURNEY

January 10: Mary, along with her brother-in-law C. M. Smith, left Springfield bound for New York City for a shopping trip. Smith was married to Mary's younger sister Ann.

January 12: The travelers arrived in New York.

January 24: Mary returned to Springfield.

February 6: A reception held at the Lincoln's home allowed well-wishers to bid them farewell.

February 8: The Lincoln family moved out of their home. They lodged at the Chenery House, located at Fourth and Washington Streets, until it was time to leave for Washington City.

February 11: Abraham and Robert left the Chenery House around 7:30 a.m. and headed to the Great Western Railroad Station. There, they boarded the train, and Lincoln gave his Farewell Address. He spent that evening in Indianapolis. Mary and the younger boys left Springfield on a 6:10 p.m. train to begin their journey to Washington City. She was accompanied by her cousin Lockwood Todd.

February 12: The Lincoln family was reunited in Indianapolis, Indiana to continue the inaugural journey. Other Indiana short stops included Shelbyville, Greensburg, and Lawrenceburg. They arrived in Cincinnati, Ohio where a levee was held in their honor at the Burnett House Hotel.

February 13: In Columbus, Ohio, an evening reception was held at the governor's residence for the Lincolns.

February 14: Mary and the younger boys had to run for the Presidential Special as it pulled out before its scheduled 8 am departure time. That evening, the family checked into the Monongahela House in Pittsburgh.[18]

February 15: During a dinner, as the Canton Zouaves stood guard, a salute was fired so close to the building that windows shattered including one close to Mary who was sprinkled with flying glass.[19]

February 17: Abraham and Mary were guests of Millard Fillmore at his residence on Niagara Square in Buffalo, New York. A reception was held at the American Hotel on Main Street.[20]

February 18: Former President Fillmore and Lincoln attended the Unitarian Church.[21]

February 19: At 3 p.m., the party of the president-elect arrived in New York. A parade was held in honor of Abraham. Mary and the children were taken directly to the Astor House where suite number 37 was reserved.

February 20: Tad and Willie, accompanied by a nurse, attended the play *The Seven Sisters* at Laura Keene's Theatre. That evening, vice-president-elect Hamlin and his wife joined the Lincolns at the Astor House. The politicians held a reception in one parlor while the ladies held another in a different suite. Approximately 500 guests were in attendance.[22]

February 21: The party had traveled to Trenton, New Jersey where the family was guests at the home of Attorney General William Dayton and his wife, Margaret. The presidential party left Trenton and traveled to Philadelphia.

February 22: At 9 a.m. the Lincolns departed Philadelphia. At a stop in Leaman Place, the crowd called for Mrs. Lincoln to appear. When she stepped onto the rear of the platform, Lincoln told the audience they had "the long and short of it."[23]

February 23: Due to assassination threats, Lincoln would take an earlier train to Washington. Accompanied by W. H. Lamon, and Allan Pinkerton, Lincoln left Philadelphia and arrived in Washington at 6 a.m. He sent Mary a telegram letting her know that he had arrived safely. At 9 a.m., Mary and the boys left Harrisburg. Mary, accompanied by Senator Seward and Illinois Congressman Elihu Washburne, entered Willard's Hotel in Washington at 4 p.m. The family stayed in an apartment (Suite Six) consisting of five rooms on the second floor Their final hotel bill was $773.75.[24]

1861
WASHINGTON CITY

March 4: Abraham Lincoln was inaugurated as the sixteenth President of the United States.

March 5: Mary met Elizabeth (Lizzie) Keckly who would become her modiste and confidant.

March 8: Mary held her first White House reception.

May 9: Mary and her family attended a matinee given at the navy yard barracks by the 71st New York Regiment, Dodworth's Band. An elegant dinner party, hosted by Secretary Seward, followed.[25]

May 10–21: Mary, William S. Woods, Colonel Robert Anderson, Elizabeth *Todd* Grimsley, and a niece (probably Elizabeth Edwards' daughter Elizabeth) left Washington to visit New York City by way of Annapolis and Philadelphia. They arrived at the Metropolitan Hotel in New York on the evening of May 11. There, Mary attended Rev. Henry Ward Beecher's Plymouth Church, visited several merchants including Stewart's, Lord & Taylor's, and E. V. Haughwout & Company. Mary attended Laura Keene's Theatre and visited several sites including the Brooklyn Navy Yard. She visited Robert at Harvard and then returned to New York for more shopping.[26]

May 24: Abraham and Mary drove to the Navy Yard to view the body of their young friend, Col. Elmer E. Ellsworth. A few days later, his body would lie in state at the White House.

June 19: Abraham and Mary visited the Navy Yard.[27]

June 21: Mary, Elizabeth Grimsley, and General Walbridge visited military camps. On the way to Arlington, there was a carriage accident. A pole broke, the horses bolted, and soldiers rescued the party.[28]

July 2 or 4: Mary invited American opera singer Meda Blanchard to sing for a small gathering at the White House. Lincoln was so moved by her singing that he requested an encore.

July 6: Abraham and Mary attend Meda Blanchard's concert at Willard's Hotel.[29]

August 3: At noon, Prince Napoleon Joseph Charles Paul Bonaparte of France met with President Lincoln. That evening, Mary hosted a dinner party in his honor.

August 13: Mary, Willie, Tad, and Elizabeth Grimsley left Washington traveling first to Philadelphia where Mrs. Hannah Shearer joined them.

August 14: The party stayed at the Metropolitan Hotel in New York, and ended their journey at Long Branch, New Jersey.[30]

August 15: In a New York hotel, Mary visited Princess Clothilde, the wife of Prince Napoleon.

August 22: Former Governor William Newell of New Jersey accompanied Mary to a demonstration of life-saving equipment and later hosted a "grand hop" at the Mansion Home in her honor.[31]

August (after 22nd): Robert joined his mother and younger brothers in New York. They traveled to Auburn, New York to visit the Sewards.

August 28: Mary arrived in Lockport, New York for a shopping trip. While in town, she stayed at the International Hotel. Her purchases included mats, cushions, and a worked tablecloth.[32]

September 1: Mary and her traveling companions visited Niagara Falls.

September (first week): Mary and her companions returned to Washington. Mrs. Grimsley returned to Springfield.

October 8: Mary accompanied her husband to General McClellan's review of artillery and cavalry on plain east of the Capitol.[33]

October 21: Colonel Edward D. Baker, a longtime friend of the Lincolns, was killed at the Battle of Balls Bluff. Baker had left his seat in the U.S. Senate to serve his country. He was the only senator killed during the war. Baker's body was taken to the residence of Major J.W. Webb as per Baker's request.

October 24: Mary shocked Washington society by wearing a lilac ensemble complete with matching gloves and hat to the funeral of Senator (Colonel) Edward D. Baker.

November 4: The *National Republican* newspaper in Washington published Willie Lincoln's poem eulogizing Colonel Edward Baker.[34]

November: Mary returned to the White House from another trip.

1862

January 1: Mary hosted her first White House New Year's Day reception.

February 5: Mary hosted a White House ball. The White House renovations were completed, and it was time to celebrate. Sadly, during the festivities, Willie Lincoln was upstairs and very ill. His parents took turns visiting his sick bed throughout the night.

February 20: William "Willie" Lincoln died.

April 6–7: Battle of Shiloh. Mary's half-brother Samuel Brown Todd (CSA) was killed.

May 28: Abraham and Mary went to Ford's Theatre for the first time. They saw an opera, Donizetta's *LaFiglia del Reggimento*.[35]

Summer: The Lincolns spent most of the summer at Anderson cottage, Soldiers' Home.

June 20: The *Chicago Daily Tribune* reported that nearly every day, Mary could be found comforting wounded soldiers in the nearby hospitals.[36]

July 9–17: Mary and Tad registered at the Metropolitan Hotel in New York. Robert joined them the following day. They visited Flushing Bay. They were joined by others, including Mary's cousin Ann *Todd* Campbell for a tour of New York Harbor. Mary also visited the New England Soldiers' Relief Association. Mary, Robert, and Tad left New York and returned to the Soldiers' Home in Washington.[37]

August 5: Half-brother Alexander H. Todd (CSA) was killed in friendly fire near Baton Rouge, Louisiana.

October 20–November 27: Mary left the Soldiers' Home and arrived at the Metropolitan Hotel in New York. There she engaged in shopping excursions and a visit to the harbor.

November 7–27: Mary and Tad visited Robert. She returned to the Metropolitan Hotel on November 13 and stayed for several days. Mary and Tad left New York on November 27 in a special railroad car via Philadelphia and Baltimore.[38]

November 29: Mary returned to Washington after visiting New England.

December 21: Mary was at the Continental Hotel in Philadelphia.

1863

January 1: Mary held the annual White House New Year's Day Reception. It was the first public reception held since Willie's death. President Lincoln signed the Emancipation Proclamation on this day.

February 13: Mary hosted a small reception for about 50 guests in honor of Charles Sherwood Stratton (General Tom Thumb) and his new bride Lavinia Warren.

April 4: The presidential party of seven (including Mary and Tad) boarded the steamer *Carrie Martin* at the Washington Naval Yard.[39]

April 5–10: The presidential party arrived at Aquia Creek, Virginia where they were greeted by Major General Daniel Butterfield. They traveled three miles to General Hooker's headquarters in Falmouth, Virginia, arriving around noon. They stayed on the King farm in makeshift accommodations consisting of three walled tents, each with a wooden floor, stoves, camp bedsteads and real sheets. Later in the day, they reviewed the cavalry.

April 7: Mary visited the camp and hospital of the V Corps.

April 10: Abraham and Mary traveled to Stafford County Court House to review the XI and XII Corps. The party boarded the *Carrie Martin* in the afternoon for the return trip to Washington. Around midnight, they were back in the White House.[40]

July 2: While returning to Washington from the Soldiers' Home, Mary was thrown from her carriage along Rock Creek Road near Mount Pleasant Hospital. According to news reports, her coachman's seat had become detached, and he had fallen to the ground leaving Mary alone in the carriage. The horses ran away tossing Mary from the carriage. She fell to the ground, hitting her head on a stone causing a bloody wound on the back of her head. Mary was taken to the nearby Mount Pleasant Hospital and the wound was quickly stitched together. Her wound was so serious that she had to remain under a nurse's care for three weeks. At one point, the wound became infected and had to be reopened. By July 11, the severity of her situation could no longer be ignored, and Lincoln sent Robert a telegram saying, "Come to Washington."[41]

July 4: During the battle of Vicksburg, Mary's half-brother David H. Todd (CSA) was badly wounded.

July 20: Mary and Tad left Washington for New York and Vermont.[42]

August 6: Mary and Tad were at the Tip Top Hotel in the White Mountains of New Hampshire.

August 20: Mary was in New York and visited the French frigate *La Guerriere* in the North River. She then traveled to a larger ship for a cruise.[43]

August 24: Mary and Tad left New York and traveled to the Equinox House in Manchester, Vermont.[44]

September 15: Mary had returned to New York where she was registered at the Fifth Avenue Hotel. She visited the Russian ship, *Osliaba*. Mrs. Nathaniel

P. Banks, General John A. Dix, and Russian Consul-General Baron d'Osten-sacker were also in attendance.

September 20: Mary's brother-in-law, General Benjamin Hardin Helm (CSA) was killed at the battle of Chickamauga.[45]

September 24: Mary visited West Point with General John A. Dix. She returned to New York and dined with General Scott.

September 28: In the evening, Mary returned to Washington.[46]

November 19: Lincoln was in Gettysburg for the dedication of the National Cemetery. Mary remained in Washington with Tad who suffered from a case of smallpox.

November: Creditors begin to demand Mary's unpaid bills be paid, or they would sue her.

December 3–7: Mary was in New York at the First Avenue Hotel.

December 7–14: Emilie *Todd* Helm, recently widowed after her husband was killed fighting for the CSA, visited the Lincolns at the White House.

1864

January 1: The New Year's Day reception was held.

April 27: Mary sent a telegram to the manager of the Metropolitan Hotel in New York letting him know that she and Tad were leaving Washington and would arrive early the next morning.

May 3: Mary was at the Soldiers' Home.

May 29: Mary and Abraham visited Campbell Hospital in Washington and gave flowers to soldiers recovering from surgery.

June 16: Mary was reported to be in Philadelphia.

June 24: Mary was in Boston.

July 31: Abraham, Mary, and a few friends traveled to Fortress Monroe.

August 10: Mary wrote a letter to the mother of a wounded soldier named Col. James Herman Agen who was a patient at Campbell Hospital.[47]

August 24: Mary, Robert, Tad, and a servant registered at the Equinox Hotel in Manchester, Vermont.

September 23: Mary was again at the Soldiers' Home.

October: By the end of the month, Mary was mourning the death of her brother Levi Todd.

November 8: Lincoln was elected to a second term.

December: Robert T. Lincoln enlisted in the army and joined the staff of General Grant as a captain.

1865

January 2: The New Year's Day reception was held having been postponed one day.

January 7: Mary's uncle, Dr. John Todd passed away. She had thought of him as a surrogate father figure. The deaths of John Todd and Levi Todd caused Mary to purchase huge amounts of mourning attire and goods.

March 4: Lincoln was inaugurated for his second presidential term. A reception for six thousand people was held that evening; however, the ball was postponed until March 6.[48]

March 18: Abraham, Mary, and Charles Sumner attended the opera.

March 21: Abraham and Mary attended the opera *La Dame Blanche* featuring the celebrated tenor, Theodore Habelmann. It was the last opera either of them saw.[49]

March 23: Abraham, Mary, and Tad left on the steamer River Queen to visit City Point, Virginia.

March 24: The presidential party visited Fortress Monroe. Mary sent a telegram to Mrs. Mary Ann Cuthbert, the White House housekeeper. The Lincolns arrived at City Point later that evening.

March 25: While riding in a field ambulance with Mrs. Grant and Adam Badeau, Mary became furious when she believed the young wife of General Charles Griffin had visited Abraham alone to request permission to remain at the front.

March 26: Mary and Julia Grant traveled to a review of the troops in a slow ambulance. She arrived late and the review was already in progress. Mrs. Ord was horrified when Mary lashed out at her for riding alongside the president during the review of the troops.

April 1–2: Mary left City Point after the president dreamt the White House had burned.

April 2: Mary arrived in Washington and sent a telegram to Lincoln that everything was all right at the White House.

April 3: The Confederate capital of Richmond was captured.

April 4: Abraham and Mary visited Richmond.

April 6: Mary returned to Fortress Monroe en route to City Point.

April 8–9: The Lincolns left City Point with Charles Sumner, and Senator and Mrs. Harlan aboard the River Queen. They arrived in Washington the following evening.[50]

April 9: Confederate General Robert E. Lee surrendered his troops to Union General Ulysses S. Grant at the home of Wilmer McLean of Appomattox Court House, Virginia. Captain Robert Lincoln was present.

April 14: In the afternoon, Mary and Abraham enjoyed what would be their last carriage ride together. That evening, the couple attended a production of *Our American Cousin* at Ford's Theatre. While Mary rested her head on her husband's shoulder, he was assassinated. The wounded president was carried across the street to the home of William Peterson.

April 15: At 7:22 a.m., Lincoln died.

Widowhood and Exile

1865

April 28: Mary's feud regarding Lincoln's final burial location began with the Lincoln Monument Association.

May 4: Lincoln was buried in a receiving vault in Oak Ridge Cemetery, Springfield, Illinois.

May 22: Mary, Robert and Tad quietly left the White House.

May 24: Mary, her two sons, Dr. Anson Henry, Mrs. Elizabeth Keckly, and two White House guards arrived in Chicago where the Lincolns registered at Tremont House.

May 31: Mary and the boys moved to the Hyde Park Hotel on the southern fringe of Chicago.[51]

December (mid-month): Mary traveled to Springfield to visit the resting place of her beloved husband. She was accompanied by her cousin, John Todd Stuart.[52]

December 21: Congress voted to grant Mary one year's Presidential salary— $25,000.00.

1866

May 22: Mary purchased a home at 375 West Washington Street (old number) in Chicago between what was then Willard and Elizabeth Streets. She lived there briefly.

September 6: Mary visited Lincoln's grave in Oak Ridge Cemetery. At the St. Nicholas Hotel, Mary was interviewed by Lincoln's former law partner, William H. Herndon.

1867

March: Mary first wrote to Elizabeth Keckly about selling her jewelry.

May 1: Mary rented her Chicago home and moved to the Clifton House owned by Joshua Bunell. Tad began to attend the Chicago Academy.[53]

June 8: By this date, Mary had sold her furniture and many personal items to John Alston.[54]

June–August 13: Mary traveled to Racine, Wisconsin in search of a school for Tad. For fifty-one days, she resided at Congress Hall, a prominent resort.[55]

September: Mary traveled to New York under the assumed name of "Mrs. Clark" and tried to sell pieces of her wardrobe and jewelry.[56]

October 13: Mary was boarding with Daniel Cole, a contractor at 460 West Washington Street.[57]

November: Lincoln's estate was finally settled, and Judge David Davis was given legal guardianship of Tad, thus controlling Tad's share of the estate. Davis gave Tad an allowance of $100 per month.

1868

January 12: Mary had moved to the Clifton House in Chicago.

Spring: Elizabeth Keckly's book *Behind the Scenes* was published and became the first "tell-all" glimpse of an employee's look at the private lives of public figures. Mary was mortified at the inclusion of private letters and candid conversations within its pages. This breach of friendship ended the relationship between the two women.

June: Mary traveled to Springfield to visit Lincoln's Tomb and meet with John Todd Stuart regarding the completion of the monument.

July 23: Mary and Tad had traveled to a health resort in Cresson, Pennsylvania in the Alleghany Mountains.[58]

August 19: Mary was in Altoona, a railroad town in central Pennsylvania. Mary and Tad remained in Altoona until they left for Washington in late September.

September 24: Robert Todd Lincoln married Mary Eunice Harlan in Washington, D.C. Mary attended her son's wedding wearing a plain black mourning dress. She sat away from the other guests, and did not attend any of the social festivities associated with the wedding.[59] After the wedding, Mary traveled to Baltimore and registered at Barnum's City Hotel. Tad remained in Washington until September 29.

October 1: Mary and Tad sailed from Baltimore aboard the *City of Baltimore* bound for Europe.

October 15: They docked at Southampton England, and then traveled to Bremen, Germany. From there, Mary and Tad went to Frankfurt-am-Main. Tad was enrolled in Dr. Johann Heinrich Hohagen's Educational Institute and Business School. Mary rented a room at Hôtel d' Angleterre, but later moved to the Hotel de Holland.

1869

January 14: Senator Oliver P. Morton (Indiana) introduced a bill requesting an annual pension for Mary. It was denied.

February–mid March: Mary traveled to Nice, France due to the cold temperatures in Germany. In route, she traveled to Baden, Germany for a couple of days where she visited a castle said to be haunted by the "White Lady."

March 3: Congress rejected a bill to grant Mary a pension.

March 5: Senator Charles Sumner introduced another pension bill which was sent back to the committee and was stuck there for over a year.

March 19: Mary left Nice, France and return to Frankfurt-am-Main.

July: Mary and Tad traveled for seven weeks visiting Paris and London on their way to Scotland to visit with Reverend James Smith who had been their minister in Springfield. They saw several cities in Scotland. On the return journey to Germany, they traveled to Brussels.

August 17: Mary and Tad returned to Frankfurt.

August 30–September: Mary visited Kronberg, Germany a region in the Taunus Mountains.

October: Mary had returned to Frankfurt-am-Main.

October 15: Mary "Mamie" Todd Lincoln was born in Chicago.

1870

February 12: Mary was in Florence, Italy.

March 22: Mary and Tad were in Frankfurt-am-Main. Tad was in school.

May 2: A bill was introduced to grant Mary a $3,000 per year pension. It passed the House but failed in the Senate.

May 19: Tad had finished his education at Hohagen's Institute and was enrolled in a school at Oberursel for two months. Mary went to visit for a "day or two."[60]

May–June: Mary was in Marienbad, Bohemia.

July 14: Congress passed a bill granting Mary a $3,000 annual pension. President Grant signed the bill the same day.

July 16: Mary was in Innsbruck, Austria vacationing with Tad.

August: Mary was once again in Frankfurt-am-Main.

September: Mary and Tad embarked on a journey to England. Her first stop was London, but by September 7, she was in York.

September 10–November 7: Mary was in Leamington, England.

November–December: Mary was in Russell Square, London, England. According to Mary's niece, Louisa Keys, it was during this stay in London that Mary attended St. James's Court.

1871

January–early February: Mary and Tad were in London. Tad was in school.

February: Mary travel to Italy visiting Milan, Lake Como, Genoa, Florence, and Venice.

February 12: Mary arrived in Florence, Italy.

March: Mary was in Frankfurt-am-Main, Germany.

April 29: Mary and Tad boarded the *Russia* in Liverpool headed for the United States. General Philip H. Sheridan was also on aboard.

May 9: Mary and Tad went to a reception for General Sheridan.

May 11: Mary and Tad arrived in New York where they stayed at the Everett House.[61]

May 15: Mary and Tad left New York City for Chicago where they stayed with Robert and his family on Wabash Avenue for a short while. Soon, Mary and her youngest son had moved to the Clifton House.

July 15: Thomas "Tad" Lincoln died of "compression of the heart." His funeral was held at the home of Robert Todd Lincoln. He was taken to Springfield for burial.

October 8–10: Mary was in Chicago during the Great Chicago Fire.

1872

July 6–mid-August: Mary stayed at a spa in Waukesha, Wisconsin. A letter to Norman Williams stated she was "going up to a wild part of the country, North—in Wis." She also traveled to the cities of Madison and Baraboo.[62]

1873

December 15: From Chicago, Mary wrote to her cousin, John Todd Stuart, stating she had been in Canada for months.

December 25: Mary gave Mary Swing an inscribed two-volume set of Longfellow's poems.

1874

January 1: Mary gave Elizabeth Swing an inscribed volume of Tennyson.[63]

January 4: Mary attended the first services held at the Fourth Presbyterian Church after it was rebuilt following the devastating Chicago Fire.

March 12: Mary wrote to Elizabeth Swing and sent a gift of chains and lockets to her daughters, Mary and Helen.

April 6: Mary sold her home on Washington Street. By this time, she was living at the Grand Central Hotel on LaSalle Street in Chicago.

October 22: Mary attended the wedding of Mary Swing to Jewett E. Ricker, Sr. at the Fourth Presbyterian Church in Chicago, Illinois. Mary's gift to the bride included a "going away" hat, items for her trousseau, a set of silver ice cream spoons, and a pair of gold bracelets. Mary helped the bride dress for the wedding.[64]

1875

February 20: Mary was visiting St. Augustine, Florida.

March: Mary had been in Florida and stayed until mid-month.

March 12: Believing Robert to be seriously ill, Mary sent a telegram to Robert's physician pleading the necessity of medical assistance.

April: Mary was registered at the Grand Pacific Hotel in Chicago.

May 18: Dr. Ralph N. Isham examined Mary and determined that she should be placed in a hospital to be treated for insanity.

May 19: A petition for trial was filed in Cook County, Illinois against Mary Lincoln. Just a few hours later, Mary was found guilty of insanity by a jury consisting of twelve jurors.

May 20: Robert was appointed conservator of his mother's estate, and Mary was placed under the care of Dr. R. J. Patterson at Bellevue Place, a private sanitarium in Batavia, Illinois.

September 11: Mary was released from Bellevue and allowed to return to Springfield to live with her sister Elizabeth Edwards.

1876

June 15: A second trial was held to determine Mary's sanity. The jury determined that Mary was now sane and able to conduct her own affairs.

June 19: Mary wrote a seething letter to Robert Lincoln demanding that he return everything she had ever given to him and his wife.[65]

September: Mary left Springfield with her great-nephew Lewis E. Baker as her escort. They traveled first to Kentucky to visit Mammoth Cave and Lexington. They went to Philadelphia for the Centennial celebration, and finally to New York. There, Mary boarded the ship *Labrador* destined for France.[66]

October 17: Mary arrived in Havre, France.[67]

October 18: Mary sailed to Bordeaux on the *Columbia*. She made her headquarters at Hotel de la Paix, Place Royale in Pau, France.

1877

Mary remained in Pau, France throughout the year.

November: Mary shipped a trunk of woolen garments to her sister Frances Wallace who was struggling financially. The clothing was worth several hundred dollars.[68]

1878

March: Mary left Pau to visit Naples, Italy.[69]

April: Mary spent two weeks in Sorrento, Italy before returning briefly to Naples.

May: Mary was in Rome at the Hotel d'Italie.[70]

June 5: Mary arrived in Marseilles, France.[71]

June 24: Mary was in Vichy, France.

July: Mary returned to Pau.

1879

July: Mary spent ten days on the seashore of St. Jean de Luz, France.[72]

July: Three days of her trip were spent at Biarritz, France, just twenty-two miles from the Spanish boarder.

August–September: Mary traveled to the Pyrenees but returned to Pau frequently to receive mail and conduct business.

December: Mary injured herself in an accident while hanging a picture over a mantel.

1880

January: Mary made a short visit to Avignon, France.[73]

March: Mary was in Marseilles, France.[74]

April: Mary returned to Avignon.[75]

June: Mary returned to Pau.

October: Preparing to leave France, Mary was in Bordeaux.

October 16: Mary left LeHavre, France on the *Am'érique* to return to America.

October 27: Mary was met at the New York harbor by her great-nephew Lewis Baker. The two went immediately to the Clarendon Hotel.[76]

November 3: Mary returned to Springfield to live with her sister Elizabeth Edwards. The Edwards still lived on South Second Street.

1881

May 1881: Robert brought his daughter "Mamie" to visit her grandmother.

October: Mary was registered at Miller's Hotel in New York. She had traveled there to be examined by several doctors including Dr. Lewis Sayre, an orthopedist and her general physician; Dr. Meredith Clymer, a neurologist; Dr. Hermann Knapp, an ophthalmologist; and Dr. William Puncoast, a surgeon.[77]

1882

January: A bill is introduced in Congress to increase Mary's pension to $5,000 per year and to award her another $15,000.

February: Mary moved from Miller's Hotel to the Grand Central Hotel.[78]

March 22: Mary left New York to return to Springfield.[79]

July 16: Surrounded by family members, Mary died at the home of her sister Elizabeth Edwards.

July 19: Mary's funeral was held at the First Presbyterian Church. She was interred in the Lincoln Tomb.

NOTES

Introduction

1. For years, historians spelled Elizabeth's surname "Keckley." Recent research by Jennifer Fleischer has proven that Elizabeth used the spelling "Keckly" and that spelling is used throughout this book.

1. Mary Grows Up in the Bluegrass

1. Elizabeth Humphreys Norris to Emilie Todd Helm, letter, September 28, 1895.

2. Coleman, *The Squire's Sketches of Lexington* (65).

3. Fayette County Kentucky Records, Deed Book 8, Lexington, Kentucky, 133; Helm, *True Story of Mary*, 16; Stevens, Richard E., ed., "Lexington Kentucky 1806 Occupations Directory," University of Delaware, http://www.math.udel.edu/~rstevens/datasets.html, row 5 (access date February 11, 2018); Deese, *Lexington Kentucky* 61.

4. Esvelt, *Descendants of David Todd.*

5. Baker, *Mary Todd Lincoln*, 18-19.

6. Untitled document, Todd Lineage, Box 1, J-L, William H. Townsend Collection, University of Kentucky, Lexington, Kentucky.

7. Helm, *True Story of Mary*, 17; Edwards, *Historic Sketches of the Edwards and Todd Families*, 11.

8. Kentucky 1860 Census Records, Woodford County, 930; Wilson and Davis, *Herndon's Informants*, 357.

9. U.S. Census 1850, Springfield, Sangamon County, Illinois, III, 103B, 119, 120B.

10. DAR application #94011, located in the Mary G. Townsend Murphy Collection (private).

11. *Kittochtinny Magazine* , 2–3, 74–75; Helm, *True Story of Mary Lincoln*, 11.

12. Cyrus Parker Jones's Funeral Notices Scrap Book, 1806–1887, Special Collections, Kentucky Room, Lexington Public Library, Lexington, Kentucky.

13. Hardin, "The Brown Family of Liberty Hall," 84; McCreary, *The Kentucky Todds in Lexington Cemetery*, 26; Todd Family Papers of Emily Todd Helm, Mary G. Townsend Murphy Collection private).

14. *Kittochtinny Magazine*, 1–3.

15. Ellison, "Todds of the Bluegrass," 6; Sexton, "The Clark's Grant," *Hoosier Journal of Ancestry* 6, no. 1 (January 1979): 3; no. 2 (April 1979): 4–6; Fayette County Will Book E.

16. Fayette County Kentucky Records, Will Book C.

17. "Muster Roll of Capt. Robert S. Todd's Company for 1811," Mary G. Townsend Murphy Collection (private).

18. *Journal of the House of Representatives of the Commonwealth of Kentucky,* 5; Collins, and Collins, *Collin's Historical Sketches of Kentucky,* 170; Helm, *True Story of Mary,* 14–15.

19. Baker, *Mary Todd Lincoln,* 24.

20. Helm, *True Story of Mary Lincoln,* 97–98; Deposition of Mary Lincoln, October 1852, William H. Townsend Collection, Box 1, J-3, King Library, University of Kentucky, Lexington.

21. Helm, *True Story of Mary Lincoln,* 5.

22. Evans, *Mrs. Abraham Lincoln,* 103.

23. Helm, *True Story of Mary Lincoln,* 1–5; Evans, *Mrs. Abraham Lincoln,* 103.

24. *Kittchtinny Magazine,* 72–74.

25. Ranck, *History of Lexington, Kentucky,* 282.

26. Second Presbyterian Church, www.2preslex.org/about/our-history.

27. Transylvania University websites: http://www2.transy.edu/about/disciples.htm; www.transy.edu/about/our-history.

28. Coleman, *The Squire's Sketches of Lexington,* 37.

29. Elizabeth L. Humphreys Norris to Emilie Todd Helm, letter, September 28, 1895, Manuscript Department, SC 1980, ALPL, Springfield, IL; Townsend, *Lincoln and the Bluegrass,* 51.

30. Runyon, *The Mentelles,* 15–17, 65, 69.

31. Italics indicate a woman's maiden name.

32. *Kentucky Gazette,* July 25, 1798; Townsend, *The Boarding School of Mary Todd Lincoln,* 5–7.

33. "Mary Lincoln Juvenile/Educational Biography." National First Ladies Library, http://www.firstladies.org/curriculum/educational-biography.aspx?biography=17 (accessed March 10, 2019).

34. Miller, "Women in the Vanguard," 311.

35. Elizabeth L. Humphreys Norris to Emilie Todd Helm, letter, September 28, 1895, Manuscript Department, SC1980, ALPL, Springfield, IL.

36. Helm, *True Story of Mary,* 52.

37. *Lexington Intelligencer,* March 6, 1838; Townsend, *Lincoln in the Bluegrass,* 58.

38. Neff, "The Education of Destitute, Homeless Children," 21.

39. Evans, *Mrs. Abraham Lincoln,* 83–86.

40. Runyon, *The Mentelles,* 185.

41. Townsend, *Lincoln in the Bluegrass,* 59; Runyon, *The Mentelles,* 182.

42. Elizabeth L. Humphreys Norris to Emilie Todd Helm, letter, September 28, 1895, Manuscript Department, SC 1980, ALPL, Springfield, IL; Wilson, and Davis, eds., *Herndon's Informants*, 357; Evans, *Mrs. Abraham Lincoln*, 86.

43. Bradford, *Education*, 8–9; *Kentucky Gazette*, September 7, 1827; Helm, *True Story of Mary*, 34.

44. Ralley, "Cousin and Childhood Friend Tells of Days When she and Martyr's Wife Were Girls Together," *Lexington Herald*, February 14, 1909.

45. Wright, *Lexington*, 30.

46. Helm, *True Story of Mary*, 27–30; Elizabeth Humphreys Norris to Emilie Todd Helm, letter, September 28, 1895, Elizabeth Humphreys Norris Letters, SC1980, Manuscript Department, Abraham Lincoln Presidential Library and Museum, Springfield, Illinois.

47. Helm, *True Story of Mary*, 44, 53.

48. Helm, *True Story of Mary*, 33.

49. Helm, *True Story of Mary*, 33.

50. Helm, *True Story of Mary*, 104.

2. Wife, Mother, and Friend

1. Mary Lincoln to Emilie Todd Helm, September 20, 1857, in Turner and Turner, *Mary Todd Lincoln*, 50.

2. Schwartz, "Mary Todd's 1835 Visit to Springfield, Illinois,", 42–45.

3. Power, *History of the Early Settlers of Sangamon County*, 278.

4. Wilson and, *Herndon's Informants*, 357; Esvelt, Todd Family Genealogical Records.

5. Mrs. John Todd Stuart to Elizabeth Stuart, letter, January 21, 1855, Stuart-Hay Family Papers, Manuscript Department, Abraham Lincoln Presidential Library and Museum, Springfield, IL.

6. James C. Conkling to Mercy Levering, letter, September 21, 1840, Conkling Family Papers, 1838–1920, Abraham Lincoln Presidential Library and Museum, Springfield, IL.

7. Helm, *True Story of Mary*, 81.

8. Raymond, "Some Incidents in the Life of Mrs. Benjamin S. Edwards."

9. Matilda Edwards to Nelson Edwards, November 30, 1840, in Randall, *Biography of a Marriage*, 4.

10. Mary Lincoln to Mary Jane Welles, December 6, 1865, in Turner and Turner, *Mary Todd Lincoln*, 295.

11. Ralley, Mrs. Mary Bradley, *Lexington Herald*, February 14, 1909, "Cousin and Childhood Friend of Mary Todd Lincoln Tell of Days When She and Martyr's Wife Were Girls Together"; Miller, *Lincoln and His World*, vol. 3, 446.

12. Stuart, "Some Recollections, 111.

13. Raymond, "Some Incidents in the Life of Mrs. Benjamin S. Edwards,", 3.

14. "A Story of the Early Days in Springfield—And a Poem," *Journal of the Illinois State Historical Society* 16, nos. 1–2 (April–July 1923): 141-46; Emerson, *Lincoln's Lover*, 1–2; Randall, *Biography of a Marriage*, 6.

15. Goltz, *Incidents in the Life of Mary Todd Lincoln*, 49; Stuart, "Some Recollections," 123; Raymond, "Some Incidents," 7.

16. Mary Lincoln to Mercy Ann Levering, July 23, 1840, in Turner and Turner, *Mary Todd Lincoln*, 18.

17. Miller, *Prairie Politician*, 449; Mary Lincoln to Mercy Ann Levering, July 23, 1840, in Turner and Turner, *Mary Todd Lincoln*, 18.

18. Mary Lincoln to Mercy Ann Levering, June 1841, in Turner and Turner, *Mary Todd Lincoln*, 26.

19. Kunhardt Jr., Kunhardt III, and Kunhardt, *Lincoln: An Illustrated Biography*, 56; McCreary, *Fashionable First Lady*, 7; Brown, "Springfield Society Before the Civil War,", 481; Helm, *True Story of Mary*, 74.

20. Wilson and Davis, *Herndon's Informants*, 444.

21. Helm, *True Story of Mary*, 64.

22. Helm, *True Story of Mary*, 81–82.

23. Wilson and Davis, *Herndon's Informants*, 443.

24. North Todd Gentry to Miss Kate Helm, letter, December 1, 1927, Helm Correspondence, F Box 2, Folder K. Helm Correspondence, 1926–1927, William Townsend Collection, King Library, University of Kentucky; Miller, *Prairie Politician*, 448; Miers, *Lincoln Day by Day*, 139.

25. Basler et al., *The Collected Works of Abraham Lincoln*, vol. 1, 282.

26. Evans, *Mrs. Abraham Lincoln*, 117.

27. Warren, "One Hundredth Anniversary of the Lincoln-Todd Marriage,".

28. "Lincoln's Marriage," Newspaper Interview with Mrs. Frances Wallace, September 2, 1895.

29. Wilson and Davis, *Herndon's Informants*, 443.

30. Wilson and Davis, *Herndon's Informants*, 592.

31. Wilson and Davis, *Herndon's Informants*, 623.

32. Helm, *True Story of Mary*, 88-89.

33. Stevens, *A Reporter's Lincoln*, 73-80; Randall, *Biography of a Marriage*, 47.

34. Helm, *True Story of Mary*, 82.

35. Stuart, "Some Recollections," 120.

36. Wilson and Davis, *Herndon's Informants*, 477.

37. Miller, *Prairie Politician*, 450.

38. Julia Jayne Trumbull to Julia Trumbull, letter, November 18, 1846, Lyman Trumbull Family Papers, Case 26, Drawer 5, Folder 44, Abraham Lincoln Presidential Library, Springfield, Illinois.

39. Keckly, *Behind the Scenes*, 231–235; Wilson and Davis, *Herndon's Informants*, 623.

40. Randall, *Biography of a Marriage*, 64.

41. Brown, "Springfield Society Before the Civil War," 480.

42. Wilson, *Honor's Voice*, 284–285.

43. Herndon and Weik, *Herndon's Life of Lincoln*, 191.

44. Linder, *Reminiscence of the Early Bench and Bar of Illinois*, 65–67.

45. Stuart, "Some Recollections," 112; Mary Lincoln to Mary Jane Welles, December 6, 1865, in Turner and Turner, *Mary Todd Lincoln*, 295–296; Mary Lincoln to Francis Bicknell Carpenter, December 8, 1865, in Turner and Turner, *Mary Todd Lincoln*, 297–300.

46. Helm, *True Story of Mary*, 94–95.

47. Raymond, "Some Incidents," 5–6.

48. Raymond, "Some Incidents," 6; "Lincoln's Marriage: Newspaper Interview with Mrs. Frances Wallace, September 2, 1895."

49. Helm, *True Story of Mary*, 95; McCreary, *Fashionable First Lady*, 10.

50. Rankin, *Personal Recollections of Abraham Lincoln*, 168.

51. Wilson and Davis, *Herndon's Informants*, 624.

52. Helm, *True Story of Mary*, 95.

53. Herndon, and Weik, *Herndon's Life of Lincoln*, 180.

54. Wilson, and Davis, *Herndon's Informants*, 597.

55. Miller, *The Rise to National Prominence*, 335–336,

56. Miller, *The Rise to National Prominence*, 722–223.

57. Helm, *True Story of Mary*, 110, 116.

58. Wilson and Davis, *Herndon's Informants*, 443.

59. Abraham Lincoln to Mary Lincoln, April 16, 1848, in Basler et al. *The Collected Works of Abraham Lincoln*, vol. 1, 465–466.

60. Mary Lincoln to Abraham Lincoln, May 1848, in Turner and Turner, *Mary Todd Lincoln*, 38.

61. Helm, *True Story of Mary*, 110–111.

62. C. E. L., "A Kindly Word for Abraham Lincoln's Widow," 1.

63. Mary Lincoln to Francis Bicknell Carpenter, December 8, 1865, in Turner and Turner, *Mary Todd Lincoln*, 297–300; Mary Lincoln to Oliver S. Halsted, Jr., May 29, 1865, in Turner and Turner, *Mary Todd Lincoln*, 236.

64. Mary Lincoln to Sally Orne, December 12, 1869, in Turner and Turner, *Mary Todd Lincoln*, 534.

65. Evans, *Mrs. Abraham Lincoln*, 155; Keckly, *Behind the Scenes*, 235; Helm, *True Story of Mary*, 106; Randall, *Biography of a Marriage*, 81–82.

66. Townsend, *Lincoln and Liquor*, 100–101.

67. Wilson, *Lincoln among His Friends*, 87; Carl Sandburg to William H. Townsend, letter, April 12, 1933, Sandburg Correspondence, Box B-4, Folder 17, William H. Townsend Collection, University of Kentucky, Lexington, Kentucky.

68. Mary Lincoln to Henry C. Deming, December 16, 1867, in Turner and Turner, *Mary Todd Lincoln*, 464.

69. Wilson and Davis, *Herndon's Informants*, xiii–xv.

70. Wilson and Davis, *Herndon's Informants*, 452–453.

71. Baker, "Parallel Lives," 6; Springen, "Hellcat or Helpmatehttps://www.newsweek.com/hellcat-or-helpmate-look-mary-todd-lincoln-100149 (accessed April 5, 2019).

72. Williams, and Burkhimer, *The Mary Lincoln Enigma*, 221.

73. Baker, "Parallel Lives," 7.

74. Wilson and Rodney, *Herndon's Informants*, 443.

75. Mary Lincoln to Emilie Todd Helm, November 23, 1856, in Turner and Turner, *Mary Todd Lincoln*, 46.

76. Wilson, *Lincoln among His Friends*, 84–89.

77. Basler, "Lease Contract," *Collected Works of Abraham Lincoln*, vol. 1, 406–407; Findley, *A. Lincoln*, 61.

78. James Cornelius, Curator, Lincoln Collection ALPLM, email to Donna McCreary, August 10, 2016; Helm, *True Story of Mary*, 99; Findley, *A. Lincoln*, 61–63; Randall, *Biography of a Marriage*, 104–105.

79. Helm, *True Story of Mary*, 101–102.

80. Helm, *True Story of Mary*, 99–100.

81. Findley, *A. Lincoln*, 68.

82. Second Presbyterian Church, Lexington, Kentucky, www.2preslex.org/about/our-history/ (accessed August 15, 2016).

83. Townsend, *Lincoln and the Bluegrass*, 140; Findley, *Lincoln*, 68.

84. Townsend, *Lincoln and His Wife's Hometown*, 162; Busey, *Personal Reminiscences*, 25–28; Theodore Weld to Angeliana Grimké Weld, January 1, 1842, in Randall, *Biography of a Marriage*, 108.

85. Mary Lincoln to Caleb B. Smith, May 31, 1861, in Turner and Turner, *Mary Todd Lincoln*, 87.

86. Findley, *A. Lincoln*, 69, 92.

87. Findley, *A. Lincoln*, 79.

88. Abraham Lincoln to Mary Lincoln, April 16, 1848, in Basler et al., *The Collected Works*, vol. 1, 465–466.

89. Mary Lincoln to Abraham Lincoln, May 1848, in Turner and Turner, *Mary Todd Lincoln*, 37–38.

90. Abraham Lincoln to Mary Lincoln, June 12, 1848, in Basler et al., *The Collected Works*, vol. 1, 478.

91. *Lexington Observer and Reporter*, August 9, 1848; Townsend, *Lincoln and the Bluegrass*, 153.

92. Miers, *Lincoln Day by Day*, vol. 1, 319, 321–322.

93. Roberts, "We All Knew Abr'ham," 25–28; Busey, *Personal Reminiscences*, 28.

94. Herndon and Weik, *Herndon's Life of Lincoln*, 246–247.

95. Mier, *Lincoln Day by Day*, vol 2, 22–23; *Illinois Journal*, September 26, 1849; *Illinois Journal*, September 23, 1849.

96. Basler, et al., *The Collected Works*, vol. 2, 305.

97. Helm, *True Story of Mary*, 107–108.

98. Mary Lincoln to Emilie Todd Helm, November 23, 1856, in Turner and Turner, *Mary Todd Lincoln*, 46.

99. Blumenthal, *All the Powers of Earth*, 419–420.

100. Emerson, *Giant in the Shadows*, 32.

101. Krause, Boston, and Stowell, *Now They Belong to the Ages*, 23.

102. Neely and McMurtry, *The Insanity File*, 157.

103. Miller, *Prairie Politician*, 37–38.

104. Pratt, *The Personal Finances of Abraham Lincoln*, 84.

105. Abraham Lincoln to John D. Johnston, letter, January 12, 1851, *The Collected Works* vol. 2, 96–97; Mary Lincoln to Rhoda White, May 2, 1868, in Turner and Turner, *Mary Todd Lincoln*, 475; Clinton, *Mrs. Lincoln*, 90.

106. Stuart, "Some Recollections," 110.

107. Mary Lincoln to Hannah Shearer, January 1, 1860, in Turner and Turner, *Mary Todd Lincoln*, 61–62.

108. Sorensen, *The Illinois State Library*, 37.

109. Emerson, *Giant in the Shadows*, 33–36, 38, 47; Helm, *True Story of Mary*, 108; Paull and Hart, *Lincoln's Springfield Neighborhood*, 12, 119; James Cornelius to Donna McCreary, email, May 12, 2017.

110. Basler et al., *The Collected Works*, vol. 1, 391.

111. Wilson and Davis, eds., *Herndon's Informants*, 597.

112. Mary Lincoln to Alexander Williamson, June 15, 1865, in Turner and Turner, *Mary Todd Lincoln*, 251.

113. Wilson and Davis, *Herndon's Informants*.

114. Hertz, *The Hidden Lincoln*, 129.

115. Barker, *Lincoln's Marriage*.

116. Bayne, *Tad Lincoln's Father*, 47.

117. Paull and Hart, *Lincoln's Springfield Neighborhood*, 100.

118. "Took Tea at Mrs. Lincoln's," 63.

119. Williams and Burkhimer, *The Mary Lincoln Enigma*, 186.

120. Cunnington and Cunnington, *The History of Underclothes*, 148.

121. Williams and Burkhimer, *The Mary Lincoln Enigma*, 187.

122. Pratt, "The Lincolns Go Shopping," 66–81; *John Irwin and Co. Ledgers 1* (July 3, 1844), 10.

123. Arnold, *The Life of Abraham Lincoln*, 83.

124. Mary Lincoln to Hannah Shearer, June 26, 1859, in Turner and Turner, *Mary Todd Lincoln*, 56.

125. Wilson, *Lincoln among His Friends*, 86; Paul and Hart, *Lincoln's Springfield Neighborhood*, 54.

126. Mary Lincoln to Abraham Lincoln, May 1848, in Turner and Turner, *Mary Todd Lincoln*, 36–37.

127. Helm, *True Story of Mary*, 108, 223.

128. Menz, *Lincoln Home Historic Furnishing Report*.

129. Helm, *True Story of Mary*, 98.

130. Wilson and Davis, *Herndon's Informants*, 451.

131. Paull and Hart, *Lincoln's Springfield Neighborhood*, 142.

132. Lincoln Home Chronology, www.nps.gov/liho/historyculture/homechronology.

133. Brown, "Springfield Society Before the Civil War," 477.

134. *New York Evening Post*, May 23, 1860.

135. Paull and Hart, *Lincoln's Springfield Neighborhood*, 137.

136. Mary Lincoln to Abraham Lincoln, letter, May 1848, Mary Lincoln Letters, Abraham Lincoln Presidential Library and Museum, Springfield, Illinois.

137. The Lincoln Home National Historic Site, Frequently Asked Questions.

138. Scruggs, *Lincoln's Hired Girls*, 3.

139. Hale, *Early American Cookery*, 125.

140. Hale, *Early American Cookery*, 125.

141. Mary Lincoln to Emilie Todd Helm, November 23, 1856, in Turner and Turner, *Mary Todd Lincoln*, 46.

142. Scruggs, *Lincoln's Hired Girls*, 4–5.

143. Mary Lincoln to Mary Brayman, June 17, 1861, in Turner and Turner, *Mary Todd Lincoln*, 90.

144. Paull and Hart, *Lincoln's Springfield Neighborhood*, 178; Scruggs, *Lincoln's Hired Girls*, 4.

145. Wilson and Davis, *Herndon's Informants*, 407.

146. *St. Louis Post–Dispatch*, November 25, 1894, "She Nursed Bob Lincoln"; Paull and Hart, *Lincoln's Springfield Neighborhood*, 100.

147. Scruggs, *Lincoln's Hired Girls*, 5.

148. Scruggs, *Lincoln's Hired Girls*, 8.

149. Scruggs, *Lincoln's Hired Girls*, 6.

150. Temple, *By Square & Compass*, 132.

151. Temple, *By Square & Compass*, 131–132; Mary Lincoln to Hannah Shearer, October 2, 1859, in Turner and Turner, *Mary Todd Lincoln*, 59.

152. Ostendorf and Oleksy, *Lincoln's Unknown Private Life*, 69.

153. Ostendorf and Oleksy, *Lincoln's Unknown Private Life*, 12; Paull and Hart, *Lincoln's Springfield Neighborhood*, 103.

154. Paull and Hart, *Lincoln's Springfield Neighborhood*, 99.

155. Mary Lincoln to Mary Brayman, June 17, 1861, in Turner and Turner, *Mary Todd Lincoln*, 90.

156. Paull and Hart, *Lincoln's Springfield Neighborhood*, 85.

157. Paull and Hart, *Lincoln's Springfield Neighborhood*, 86; Scruggs, *Lincoln's Hired Girls*, 11.

158. Paull and Hart, *Lincoln's Springfield Neighborhood*, 86–88.

159. Scruggs, *Lincoln's Hired Girls*, 11.

160. Searcher, *Lincoln's Journey to Greatness*, 42; Mary Lincoln to Mary Brayman, June 17, 1861, in Turner and Turner, *Mary Todd Lincoln*, 90; Paull and Hart, *Lincoln's Springfield Neighborhood*, 108.

161. Paull and Hart, *Lincoln's Springfield Neighborhood*, 107.

162. Wilson and Davis, *Herndon's Informants*, 596–97.

163. Paull and Hart, *Lincoln's Springfield Neighborhood*, 98.

164. Paull and Hart, *Lincoln's Springfield Neighborhood*, 103.

165. Scruggs, *Lincoln's Hired Girls*, 13.

166. Paull and Hart, *Lincoln's Springfield Neighborhood*, 109.

167. Paull and Hart, *Lincoln's Springfield Neighborhood*, 82.

168. Paull and Hart, *Lincoln's Springfield Neighborhood*, 149.

169. Paull and Hart, *Lincoln's Springfield Neighborhood*, 153.

170. Paull and Hart, *Lincoln's Springfield Neighborhood*, 153.

3. Assailed from All Sides

1. Sword, *Southern Invincibility*, 94.

2. Emerson, *Giant in the Shadows*, 52.

3. Mercie A. Conkling to Clinton L. Conkling, letter, February 12, 1861, in Hart, *Letters of Springfield Ladies*, 20.

4. Searcher, *Lincoln's Journey to Greatness*, 43.

5. Searcher, *Lincoln's Journey to Greatness*, 114.

6. Searcher, *Lincoln's Journey to Greatness*, 188.

7. Grimsley, "Six Months in the White House," 43.

8. Emerson, *Giant in the Shadows*, 54.

9. *Cincinnati Commercial*, February 16, 1861.

10. *New York Times*, February 25, 1861; *New York World*, February 27, 1861

11. Emerson, *Giant in the Shadows*, 60–61; Epstein, *The Lincolns*, 296–297.

12. Searcher, *Lincoln's Journey to Greatness*, 264.

13. Conroy, *Lincoln's White House*, 33.

14. Eskew and Adams, *Willard's of Washington*, 266.

15. Carr and Carr, *The Willard Hotel*, 31.

16. Grimsley, "Six Months in the White House," 45.

17. Carr and Carr, *The Willard Hotel*, 31.

18. Grimsley, "Six Months in the White House," 46.

19. Kunhardt Jr. et al., *Lincoln*, 147; *Frank Leslie's Illustrated Newspaper*, March 23, 1861, 285.

20. *Frank Leslie's Illustrated Newspaper*, March 23, 1861, 285.

21. *New York World*, March 5, 1861, 5; *Frank Leslie's Illustrated Newspaper*, March 23, 1861, 285.

22. Her book, *Behind the Scenes,* was published under the name "Keckley" and historians have used this spelling ever since. However, more recent research by Jennifer Fleischer reveals that Elizabeth signed her name using the spelling "Keckly." Fleischer observed the signature on a war pension application for Keckly's son after his death at the Battle of Wilson's Creek in 1861. Keckly signed her name using the same spelling in other documents. For clarification and respect for the subject, the spelling "Keckly" is used throughout. Fleischer, *Mrs. Lincoln and Mrs. Keckly,* 7.

23. Keckley (sic), *Behind the Scenes,* 79; LTC Eugene Eckel McLean Memorial, www.findagrave.com, Memorial #10605823; Miers, *Lincoln Day by Day,* 23.

24. Bayne, *Tad Lincoln's Father,* 43–50.

25. Burlingame, *At Lincoln's Side,* 187.

26. Gernsheim, *Victorian and Edwardian Fashion,* 42.

27. *Frank Leslie's Illustrated Newspaper,* February 22, 1862, 209.

28. *The Pall Mall Gazette,* Monday, November 15, 1880.

29. Bayne, *Tad Lincoln's Father,* 169.

30. *Frank Leslie's Illustrated Newspaper,* February 22, 1862, 214.

31. Elizabeth Edwards to Julie Edwards Baker, letter, March 2, 1862, Elizabeth Todd Edwards Letters, Manuscript Department, SC 445, Abraham Lincoln Presidential Library and Museum, Springfield, Illinois.

32. Emerson, *Mary Lincoln's Insanity Case,* 3.

33. Pitch, *"They Have Killed Papa Dead!,"* 232, 441.

34. Gernsheim, *Victorian and Edwardian Fashion,* 31.

35. Grimsley, "Six Months in the White House," 58.

36. "Tribute to the Dead from Mrs. Jane Grey Swisshelm," *Chicago Daily Tribune,* July 20, 1882, 7.

37. Conroy, *Lincoln's White House,* 33.

38. Burlingame, *Inside the White House in War Times,* 26.

39. Conroy, *Lincoln's White House,* 33; Grimsley, "Six Months in the White House," 47, 58.

40. Conroy, *Lincoln's White House,* 34–35.

41. Burlingame, *Inside the White House in War Times,* 183.

42. Cole and McDonough, *Witness to the Young Republic,* 382; Burlingame, *Lincoln: A Life,* 280; Conroy, *Lincoln's White House,* 125–126.

43. Burlingame, *Inside the White House in War Times,* 182–183.

44. Pratt and East, "Mrs. Lincoln Refurbishes the White House," 17.

45. Inventory of books owned by Mary Lincoln located at the Abraham Lincoln Presidential Library and Museum, Springfield, IL. May 1, 2012.

46. Pratt, and East, "Mrs. Lincoln Refurbishes the White House," 17.

47. *Frank Leslie's Illustrated Newspaper,* February 22, 1862.

48. Baker, *Mary Todd Lincoln,* 190–191.

49. Baker, *Mary Todd Lincoln*, 191; Conway, *Lincoln's White House*, 103; Cole and McDonough, *Witness to the Young Republic*, 375.

50. Tripler, *Eunice Tripler*, 138–140.

51. Keckly, *Behind the Scenes*, 85.

52. Burlingame, *At Lincoln's Side*, 188.

53. Leech, *Reveille in Washington 1860–1865*, 301.

54. Tripler, *Eunice Tripler*, 143.

55. James B. Swain to John Hay, partial letter, February 21, 1889, Lincoln Collection, Spiritualism Folder, L2, C126a, Abraham Lincoln Presidential Library and Museum, Springfield, Illinois.

56. Dowdey and Manarin, *The Wartime Papers of Robert E. Lee*, 10–11.

57. Burlingame, *At Lincoln's Side*, 1; Carpenter, *Six Months at the White House with Abraham Lincoln*, 131.

58. Steers, *Lincoln Legends*, 80–88.

59. Helm, *True Story of Mary*, 220–222.

60. Michelle L. Hamilton, *I Would Still Be Drowned in Tears*, 26–27.

61. Helm, *True Story of Mary*, 25-6.

62. Helm, *True Story of Mary*, 77. Mary, who was proud of her Scottish ancestry, probably either misspoke or was misquoted. "Scottish" refers to those whose relatives immigrated from Scotland while "scotch" is the name for whisky that is distilled in Scotland.

63. Hamilton, *I Would Still Be Drowned in Tears*, 35–36; Wilson and Davis, *Herndon's Informant*, 173.

64. McMurtry, "Lincoln's Attendance at Spiritualistic Séances," 2; Dr. James Cornelius to Donna McCreary, email, September 20, 2017.

65. Mary Lincoln to Charles Sumner, July 4, 1865, in Turner and Turner, *Mary Todd Lincoln*, 256.

66. Helm, *True Story of Mary*, 226-27. Alexander "Alec" Todd was one of Mary's half-brothers. A Confederate, he was killed at the Battle of Baton Rouge, Louisiana, less than six months after Willie's death.

67. Mary Lincoln to Sally Orne, November 20, 1869, in Turner and Turner, *Mary Todd Lincoln*, 525.

68. Burlingame, *At Lincoln's Side*, 2–3.

69. Grimsley, "Six Months in the White House," 51.

70. Pratt, *Concerning Mr. Lincoln*, 84.

71. Helm, *True Story of Mary*, 211–212; *New York Herald*, July 11, 1863; Basler, et al., *The Collected Works*, vol 6, 323; Randall, *Biography of a Marriage*, 324.

72. Helm, *True Story of Mary*, 241–242.

73. Mary Lincoln to Daniel E. Sickles, September 31, 1862, in Turner and Turner, *Mary Todd Lincoln*, 133,

74. Mary Lincoln to Abraham Lincoln, November 2, 1862, in Turner and Turner, *Mary Todd Lincoln*, 139–40.

75. Keckly, *Behind the Scenes*, 131–132.

76. Interview with Ian Hunt, Chief of Acquisitions and Research, July 14, 2017, Abraham Lincoln Presidential Library and Museum, Springfield, Illinois.

77. *Sacramento Union*, May 8, 1863, as quoted in Randall, *Biography of a Marriage*, 322.

78. Williams and Burkhimer, *The Mary Lincoln Enigma*, 230.

79. Randall, *Biography of a Marriage*, 372–375; Keckly, *Behind the Scenes*, 165–167.

80. Burlingame, *Inside the White House in War Times*, 32; Pratt, and East, "Mrs. Lincoln Refurbishes the White House," 31–32.

81. Bayne, *Tad Lincoln's Father*, 78.

82. Bayne, *Tad Lincoln's Father*, 107.

83. Grimsley, "Six Months in the White House," 62.

84. Grimsley, "Six Months in the White House," 70–71; "Mrs. Lincoln Arrived, Metropolitan on Sept. 2," *New York Tribune*, September 5, 1861; Helm, *True Story of Mary*, 119.

85. Mike Ressler to Colonel Albert C. Jerman, letter, July 22, 1998, Mary Polka file, United States Marine Band Library, Marine Barracks, Washington DC.

86. Washington, *They Knew Lincoln*, 77–78.

87. Conroy, *Lincoln's White House*, 103.

88. Keckly, *Behind the Scenes*, 90; Mary Lincoln to Elizabeth Keckly, December 26, December 27, 1867 (2 letters), in Turner and Turner, *Mary Todd Lincoln*, 466; Mary Lincoln to Elizabeth Keckly, January 12, January 15, 1868 (2 letters), in Turner and Turner, *Mary Todd Lincoln*, 468–469.

89. Mary Lincoln to Alexander Williamson, December 1, 1865, in Turner and Turner, *Mary Todd Lincoln*, 290-91.

90. Burlingame, *At Lincoln's Side*, 187.

91. Cornelius and Knorowski, *Under Lincoln's Hat*, 30.

92. Pinsker, *Lincoln's Sanctuary*, 68, 88.

93. Washington, *They Knew Lincoln*, 77–78.

94. Washington, *They Knew Lincoln*, 119.

95. Baker, *Mary Todd Lincoln*, 190; Holzer, *Lincoln President-Elect*, 234.

96. Bayne, *Tad Lincoln's Father*, 111.

97. Grimsley, "Six Months in the White House," 56.

98. Burlingame, *Inside the White House in War Times*, 48, 182.

99. Bayne, *Tad Lincoln's Father*, 173; The White House Historical Association Facebook post, March 31, 2017.

100. Mary Lincoln to Mrs. Agen, August 10, 1864, in Turner and Turner, *Mary Todd Lincoln*, 179.

4. *The Darkest Night of All*

1. Miers, *Lincoln Day by Day*, vol. 3, 327; Bogar, *Backstage at the Lincoln Assassination*, 103–104.

2. Bogar, *Backstage at the Lincoln Assassination*, 103.

3. Bogar, *Backstage at the Lincoln Assassination*, 329-30.

4. Dr. Henry Anson to Mrs. Anson, letter, April 19, 1865, Lincoln Collection, photocopy, Abraham Lincoln Presidential Library and Museum, Springfield, Illinois.

5. Bogar, *Backstage at the Lincoln Assassination*, 3; Good, *We Saw Lincoln Shot*, 22.

6. Pitch, *"They Have Killed Papa Dead!,"* 117.

7. Good, *We Saw Lincoln Shot*, 22.

8. Bogar, *Backstage at the Lincoln Assassination*, 79; Emerson, *Giant in the Shadows*, 101.

9. Bogar, *Backstage at the Lincoln Assassination*, 6-7.

10. Miers, *Lincoln Day by Day*, vol 3, 330; Emerson, *Giant in the Shadows*, 103.

11. Pitch, *"They Have Killed Papa Dead!,"* 150; Cole and McDonough, *Witness to the Young Republic*, 469–472; Turner and Turner, *Mary Todd Lincoln*, 222.

12. Keckly, *Behind the Scenes*, 184-9.

13. Pitch, *"They Have Killed Papa Dead!,"* 147.

14. Meirs, *Lincoln Day by Day*, vol. 3, 330.

15. Tanner, "Lincoln's Death Tragic Moment in Nation's Life."

16. Keckly, *Behind the Scenes*, 191-92.

17. Turner and Turner, *Mary Todd Lincoln*, 223; Emerson, *Giant in the Shadows*, 108.

18. Cole and McDonough, *Witness to the Young Republic*, 471.

19. Searcher, *The Farewell to Lincoln*, 68; Cole and McDonough, *Witness to the Young Republic*, 471.

20. Pitch, *"They Have Killed Papa Dead!,"* 232.

21. Swanson, *Manhunt*, 18–19.

22. Mary Lincoln to Sally Orne, March 15, 1866 in Turner and Turner, *Mary Todd Lincoln*, 345.

23. Mary Lincoln to Francis Bicknell Carpenter, November 15, 1865, in Turner and Turner, *Mary Todd Lincoln*, 284-5.

24. Mary Lincoln to Edward Lewis Baker, Jr., April 11, 1877, in Turner and Turner, *Mary Todd Lincoln*, 632.

5. *Widowhood and Exile*

1. Keckly, *Behind the Scenes*, 193; Emerson, *Giant in the Shadows*, 107; Turner and Turner, *Mary Todd Lincoln*, 224.

2. Mary Lincoln to Sally Orne, March 15, 1866, in Turner and Turner, *Mary Todd Lincoln*, 345.

3. Keckly, *Behind the Scenes*, 191.

4. Gerry, *Through Five Administrations*, 71.

5. Keckly, *Behind the Scenes*, 203-204.

6. Gerry, *Through Five Administrations*, 69–70.

7. Cole and McDonough, *Witness to the Young Republic*, 479.

8. Peterson, *Lincoln in American Memory*, 8.

9. Mary Lincoln to James Smith, December 17, 1866, in Turner and Turner, *Mary Todd Lincoln*, 400.

10. Cole and McDonough, *Witness to the Young Republic*, 478.

11. Gerry, *Through Five Administrations*, 70.

12. Emerson, *Giant in the Shadows*, 111.

13. Arnold, *The Life of Abraham Lincoln*. 435.

14. Mary Lincoln to Richard J. Oglesby, June 10, 1865, in Turner and Turner, *Mary Todd Lincoln*, 244.

15. Turner and Turner, *Mary Todd Lincoln*, 244.

16. Turner and Turner, *Mary Todd Lincoln*, 245.

17. J. B. S. Todd to John Todd Stuart, telegraph, April 31, 1865, Manuscript Department, Todd & Smith Letters, SC913-2, Abraham Lincoln Presidential Library and Museum, Springfield, Illinois.

18. Emerson, *Giant in the Shadows*, 111–113.

19. Coleand McDonough, *Witness to the Young Republic*, 478.

20. Keckly, *Behind the Scenes*, 208.

21. Keckly, *Behind the Scenes*, 203.

22. Keckly, *Behind the Scenes*, 207.

23. Cole and McDonough, *Witness to the Young Republic*, 498.

24. Keckly, *Behind the Scenes*, 147–150.

25. Keckly, *Behind the Scenes*, 204; Baker, *Mary Todd Lincoln*, 258; Turner and Turner, *Mary Todd Lincoln*, 247.

26. Mary Lincoln to Sally Orne, August 31, 1865, in Turner and Turner, *Mary Todd Lincoln*, 269–271.

27. Mary Lincoln to Alexander Williamson, September 9, 1865, in Turner and Turner, *Mary Todd Lincoln*, 272–273; Mary Lincoln to Alexander Williamson, November 26, 1865, in Turner and Turner, *Mary Todd Lincoln*, 286; Mary Lincoln to Alexander Williamson, November 28, 1865, in Turner and Turner, *Mary Todd Lincoln*, 287.

28. Mary Lincoln to Noah Brooks, May 11, 1866, in Turner and Turner, *Mary Todd Lincoln*, 362–363.

29. James Y. Smith to unknown, April 26, 1865, Library of Congress, www.loc.gov/item/scsm0007221, January 7, 2020.

30. Mary Lincoln to Alexander Williamson, February 20, 1866, in Turner and Turner, *Mary Todd Lincoln*, 338–339.

31. Robert Todd Lincoln David Davis, telegraph, April 15, 1865, Robert Todd Lincoln Papers, Abraham Lincoln Presidential Library and Museum, Springfield, Illinois.

32. Pratt, *The Personal Finances of Abraham Lincoln*, 131–141; Mayoras and Mayoras, "Are You Better Prepared Than Abraham Lincoln Was?"

33. Turner and Turner, *Mary Todd Lincoln*, 499, 555, 572.

34. Pitch, *"They Have Killed Papa Dead!,"* 231.

35. Mary Lincoln to Rhoda White, June 8, 1871, in Turner and Turner, *Mary Todd Lincoln*, 590.

36. Gernon, *The Lincolns in Chicago*, 47–48, 53.

37. Evans, *Mrs. Abraham Lincoln*, 191.

38. Mary Lincoln to Leonard Sweet, September 13, 1867, as quoted in Randall, *Biography of a Marriage*, 408.

39. Keckly, *Behind the Scenes*, 269–270.

40. "Disgraceful," *The Conservative*, Clarksburg, WV, November 9, 1867.

41. McCreary, *Fashionable First Lady*, 127–133.

42. Birmingham, *Our Crowd*, 148.

43. Mary Lincoln to David Davis, December 15, 1868, in Turner and Turner, *Mary Todd Lincoln*, 496; F.W. Bogen to Charles Sumner as quoted in Randall, *Biography of a Marriage*, 417.

44. Mary Lincoln to Eliza Slataper, December 13, 1868, in Turner and Turner, *Mary Todd Lincoln*, 493–496.

45. Randall, *Biography of a Marriage*, 417.

46. Mary Lincoln to Eliza Slataper, August 21, 1869, in Turner and Turner, *Mary Todd Lincoln*, 512–513.

47. Mary Lincoln to Rhoda White, August 30, 1969, in Turner and Turner *Mary Todd Lincoln*, 515-517; Mary Lincoln to Sally Orne, October 18, 1869, in Turner and Turner, *Mary Todd Lincoln*, 519.

48. Temple, "Mary Todd Lincoln's Travels," 193.

49. Mary Lincoln to Rhoda White, August 30, 1869, in Turner and Turner, *Mary Todd Lincoln*, 517.

50. *The State Journal-Register*, May 3, 1976, 21; Guinon, Barbara. Todd-Keyes Family Genealogical Records. Private Collection. Petersburg, IL.

51. Elizabeth Edwards to Robert Todd Lincoln, letter, October 29, 1876, Insanity File Collection, Lincoln Financial Foundation Collection, Allen County Library, Fort Wayne, Indiana.

52. Williams and Burkhimer, *The Mary Lincoln Enigma*, 163–166.

53. Turner and Turner, *Mary Todd Lincoln*, 479–486. Mary usually wrote her location at the top of her letters, thus making a timeline of her travels easier to construct.

54. Mary Lincoln to John Todd Stuart, December 15, 1873, in Turner and Turner, *Mary Todd Lincoln*, 603.

55. Mary Todd Lincoln to Edward Swift Isham, March 12, 1875 (two telegrams on the same date), Insanity File Collection, Lincoln Foundation Collection. Allen County Public Library, Fort Wayne, Indiana.

56. Elizabeth Edwards to Robert Todd Lincoln, letter, October 29, 1876, Insanity File Collection, Lincoln Financial Foundation Collection, Allen County Library, Fort Wayne, Indiana.

57. Evans, *Mrs. Abraham Lincoln*, 307.

58. Mary Lincoln to Eliza Henry, August 31, 1865, in Turner and Turner, *Mary Todd Lincoln*, 271–272; Mary Lincoln to William H. Herndon, August 28, 1866, in Turner and Turner, *Mary Todd Lincoln*, 384; Mary Lincoln to Richard J. Oglesby, June 5, 1965, in Turner and Turner, *Mary Todd Lincoln*, 244.

59. Mary Lincoln to Sally Orne, August 31, 1865 in Turner and Turner, *Mary Todd Lincoln*, 269; Mary Lincoln to Mary Jane Welles, July 11, 1865, in Turner and Turner, *Mary Todd Lincoln*, 257; Mary Lincoln to Mary Ann Foote, March 27, 1866, in Turner and Turner, *Mary Todd Lincoln*, 347.

60. Olivia Borderave, "The Wife of Abraham Lincoln Lived Four Years in Pau," *La Republique*, January 31, 2013.

61. Spiritualism Folder, Drawer 4A, Denominational Contacts. Lincoln Financial Collection, Fort Wayne, Indiana.

62. Bernhardt, *Memories of My Life*, 370.

63. Lachman, *The Last of the Lincolns*, 273; Emerson, *Giant in the Shadows*, 225.

64. *Daily Illinois State Register*, August 4, 1881, p. 2.

65. Ann Smith to Emilie Todd Helm, letter, June 19 (no year, but probably 1881), Mary G. Townsend Murphy Collection (private).

66. Kunhardt, "An Old Lady's Lincoln Memories," 57–60.

67. Mary Lincoln to Jacob Bunn, December 12, 1876, in Turner and Turner, *Mary Todd Lincoln*, 622–623. Note: The "Daily Galignani of Paris" Mary referenced was *Galignani's Messenger*, a French newspaper printed in English from 1814 to 1904.

68. Mary Lincoln to Sally Orne, December 24, 1865, in Turner and Turner, *Mary Todd Lincoln*, 311–312.

69. Mary Lincoln to Mary Jane Welles, December 29, 1865, in Turner and Turner, *Mary Todd Lincoln*, 315–317.

70. Mary Lincoln to Alexander Williamson, September 7, 1866, in Turner and Turner, *Mary Todd Lincoln*, 385–386.

71. Raimbouville, *Vichy and Its Medicinal Properties*.

72. Evans, *Mrs. Abraham Lincoln*, 342.

73. Mary Lincoln to Edward Lewis Baker, letter, October 4, 1879, in Turner and Turner, *Mary Todd Lincoln*, 690; Mary Lincoln to Edward Lewis Baker, letter, January 16, 1880, *Mary Todd Lincoln*, 693.

74. "Dust to Dust," *Chicago Tribune*, July 20, 1882.

75. Ann Todd Smith to Emily Todd Helm, letter, July 17, 1882, Mary G. Townsend Murphy Collection.

76. Ann Todd Smith to Emily Todd Helm, letter, July 17, 1882, Mary G. Townsend Murphy Collection.

77. Wilson and Davis, *Herndon's Informants,* 671; Emerson, *The Madness of Mary Lincoln,* 132.

78. Mary Lincoln, obituary, *Chicago Times* and *Chicago Tribune,* July 17, 1882

79. Barton, *The Women Lincoln Loved,* 367.

80. Bell, "Mary Todd Lincoln—a Profile," 4–11.

81. Neely and McMurtry, *The Insanity File,* 123.

82. Neely, "Mary Todd Lincoln (1818–1882)," 1.

83. Temple, *Abraham Lincoln: From Skeptic to Prophet,* 399.

84. Neely, "Mary Todd Lincoln (1818–1882)," 1.

85. Mary Lincoln to Charles Sumner, July 4, 1865, in Turner and Turner, *Mary Todd Lincoln,* 256.

6. The Issue of Sanity

1. Mary Lincoln to Robert Todd Lincoln, June 19, 1876, in Turner and Turner, *Mary Todd Lincoln,* 615–616.

2. Neely and McMurtry, *The Insanity File,* ix.

3. Mary Lincoln to Robert Todd Lincoln, June 19, 1876, in Turner and Turner, *Mary Todd Lincoln,* 615–616.

4. McCreary, *Fashionable First Lady,* ix.

5. Emerson, *Giant in the Shadows,* 165.

6. Emerson, *Giant in the Shadows,* 164–165; Emerson, *The Madness of Mary Lincoln,* 50–51.

7. Neely and McMurtry, *The Insanity File,* 23.

8. Emerson, *The Madness of Mary Lincoln,* 59–60.

9. The *Tribune* and the *Chicago Inter-Ocean* both reported seventeen witnesses. The *Chicago Times* listed eighteen.

10. Emerson, *The Madness of Mary Lincoln,* 58; Ross, "Mary Todd Lincoln, Patient at Bellevue Place, Batavia," 8–9.

11. Verdict of the Jury, May 19, 1875, Chicago Historical Society, Lincoln Collection, 1876, Box 236, Folder 306.

12. *New York Times,* May 21, 1875.

13. Neely and McMurtry, *The Insanity File,* 37.

14. Ross, "Mary Todd Lincoln, Patient at Bellevue Place, Batavia," 5, 26, 34.

15. Neely and McMurtry, *The Insanity File,* 58.

16. Ross, "Mary Todd Lincoln, Patient at Bellevue Place, Batavia," 30.

17. *Chicago Times,* August 24, 1875.

18. Dr. R. J. Patterson to Robert Todd Lincoln, September 7, 1875, in Emerson, *Giant in the Shadows,* 177.

19. Elizabeth Edwards to Robert Todd Lincoln, letter, September 15, 1875, folder 16, box 2, Insanity File; Elizabeth Edwards to Robert Todd Lincoln, November 5, 1875, folder 16, box 2, Insanity File, Lincoln Financial Foundation Collection. Allen County Public Library, Fort Wayne, Indiana.

20. *Chicago Daily Tribune*, June 16, 1876, 8.

21. Pritchard, *The Dark Days of Abraham Lincoln's Widow*, 93; Neely and Mc-Murtry, *The Insanity File*, 122.

7. Family Relationships

1. Helm, *True Story of Mary*, 94.

2. Eskew and Adams, *Willard's of Washington*, 51; Grimsley, "Six Months in the White House," 48.

3. Elizabeth Todd Grimsley to John Todd Stuart, Letter, March 20–21, 1861, Special Collections, Manuscript Department, SC608, Abraham Lincoln Presidential Library and Museum.

4. Sword, *Southern Invincibility*, 43.

5. Elizabeth Todd Grimsley to John Todd Stuart, letter, March 20–21, 1861, Special Collections, Manuscript Department, SC608, Abraham Lincoln Presidential Library and Museum.

6. Elizabeth Todd Edwards to Julia Edwards Baker, April 9, 1862, in Hart, *Letters of Springfield Ladies*, 100-101; Elizabeth Todd Edwards to Julia Edwards Baker, April 26, 1862, in Hart, *Letters of Springfield Ladies*, 101–102.

7. Helm, *True Story of Mary*, 231.

8. Helm, *True Story of Mary*, 222–231; Keckly, *Behind the Scenes*, 135–136.

9. Helm, *True Story of Mary*, 222.

10. Mary Lincoln to Elizabeth Todd Grimsley, letter, September 29, 1861, in Turner and Turner, *Mary Todd Lincoln*, 105–106.

11. Elizabeth Todd Edwards to Edward Lewis Baker, letter, August 26, 1860, in Hart, *Lincoln's Springfield: Letters of Springfield Ladies*, 91.

12. *Daily Intelligence*, Wheeling, West Virginia, November 22, 1860, p 1, col. 3.

13. Elizabeth Todd Edwards to Julia Edwards Baker, February 10, 1861, in Hart, *Letters of Springfield Ladies*, 97.

14. Mary Lincoln to Abraham Lincoln, letter, May (unknown) 1848, in Turner and Turner, *Mary Todd Lincoln*, 37.

15. Helm, *True Story of Mary*, 17–18.

16. Baker, *Mary Todd Lincoln*, 26.

17. Helm, *True Story of Mary*, 81.

18. Helm, *True Story of Mary*, 82.

19. "Lincoln's Marriage" Newspaper Interview with Mrs. Frances Wallace, Springfield, Illinois, September 2, 1895. Lincoln Collection, Abraham Lincoln Presidential Library and Museum, Springfield, Illinois.

20. "Lincoln's Marriage."

21. Kunhardt, "An Old Lady's Lincoln Memories,", 57.

22. Robert Smith Todd to Ninian Edwards, letter, December 1, 1846, Manuscript Department, Folder SC1549, Abraham Lincoln Presidential Library and Museum, Springfield, Illinois.

23. Helm, *True Story of Mary*, 100.

24. Helm, *True Story of Mary*, 106, 120.

25. Mary Lincoln to Sarah Bush Lincoln, December 19, 1867, in Turner and Turner, *Mary Todd Lincoln*, 464–465.

26. Bayne, *Tad Lincoln's Father*, 153.

27. Emerson, *Giant in the Shadows*, 225.

28. Mr. Craig's name appears as "Charles" in the notes of Basler, *The Collected Works* 7:84, December 21, 1863. However, Mr. Craig's first name as engraved on his tombstone and in Cyrus Parker Jones's Funeral Notices is "John."

29. Basler et al., *The Collected Works*, vol. 7, 83.

30. Sword, *Southern Invincibility*, 48; Baker, *Mary Todd Lincoln*, 103.

31. Berry, *House of Abraham*, vii.

32. Mary Lincoln to Edward Lewis Baker, Jr., October 7, 1880, in Turner and Turner, *Mary Todd Lincoln*, 704.

33. Keckly, Elizabeth, *Behind the Scenes*, 135–136.

34. Townsend, *Lincoln and the Bluegrass*, 333. The Minié ball was a conical shaped bullet with a hollow base. Developed by Claude-Étienne Minié in 1849, the minié was the primary bullet of choice during the Civil War. Its shape made it easier to load a rifle during combat.

35. Townsend, *Lincoln and the Bluegrass*, 332–333.

8. Slavery and African Americans

1. Clinton, "Epilogue," in Williams and Burkhimer, *The Mary Lincoln Enigma*, 354.

2. Townsend, *Lincoln and the Bluegrass*, 185, 374; *Lexington Observer & Reporter*, October 20, 1849, December 2, 1854, 2; Berry, *House of Abraham*, 19.

3. Fayette County, Deed Book, Book M, 118.

4. George R. C. Todd v. Elizabeth L. Todd et al. (File 1389, Fayette Circuit Court); Townsend, *Lincoln and the Bluegrass*, 204–205.

5. Helm, *True Story of Mary*, 25.

6. Elizabeth L. Humphreys Norris to Emilie Todd Helm, letter (no date), Manuscript Department, Folder SC 1980, Elizabeth L. Norris Collection, Abraham Lincoln Presidential Library and Museum, Springfield, Illinois.

7. Helm, *True Story of Mary*, 22–23.

8. King, "Famous Dishes from the Old Kentucky Home," 143–144.

9. George R. C. Todd v. Elizabeth L. Todd et al. (File 1389, Fayette Circuit Court); Townsend, *Lincoln and the Bluegrass*, 205; www.mtlhouse.org/slavery (accessed 05/22/2021).

10. Helm, *True Story of Mary*, 35–36.

11. Helm, *True Story of Mary*, 23, 36.

12. Helm, *True Story of Mary*, 41.

13. Affidavit of Mrs. E. L. Todd, George R. C. Todd v. Elizabeth L. Todd et al. (File 1389, Fayette Circuit Court); Townsend, *Lincoln and the Bluegrass*, 205

14. Townsend, *Lincoln and the Bluegrass*, 205; untitled document (no date), Todd Lawsuit, William H. Townsend Collection, Box 1, J-3, King Library, University of Kentucky, Lexington, Kentucky.

15. Helm, *True Story of Mary*, 46.

16. Elizabeth L. Norris to Emilie Todd Helm, letter, July 18, 1985, Manuscript Department, Folder SC 1980, Elizabeth L. Norris Collection, Abraham Lincoln President Library and Museum, Springfield, Illinois.

17. Helm, *True Story of Mary*, 23, 39.

18. Helm, *True Story of Mary*, 40.

19. Affidavits of William S. McChesney, Mrs. E.L Todd, George R. C. Todd, and Thomas S. Redd, George R. C. Todd v. Elizabeth L. Todd, et al. (File 1389, Fayette Circuit Court); Order Book 36, Fayette Circuit Court, 539, 548; Townsend, *Lincoln and the Bluegrass*, 205.

20. Helm, *True Story of Mary*, 38-9.

21. Townsend, *Lincoln and the Bluegrass*, 128.

22. Elizabeth Humphreys Norris to Emilie Todd Helm, letter, July 18, 1895, Manuscript Department, Folder SC 1980, Elizabeth L. Norris Collection, Abraham Lincoln Presidential Library and Museum, Springfield, Illinois.

23. Townsend, *Lincoln and the Bluegrass*, 127.

24. Townsend, *Lincoln and the Bluegrass*, 180.

25. Townsend, *Lincoln and the Bluegrass*, 176–191; liberianfo.co/prd/presidents/Alfred-f-russell/; pantheon.world/profile/person/Alfred_Francis_Russell. (April 5, 2020).

26. Fayette County Deed Book 17, 194.

27. Helm, *True Story of Mary*, 22-3.

28. Helm, *True Story of Mary*, 4, 47; Baker, *Mary Todd Lincoln*, 30.

29. Main Street Baptist Church, Lexington, Kentucky, www.mainstreetbaptistchurchlexky.org.

30. Townsend, *Lincoln and the Bluegrass*, 164.

31. Helm, *True Story of Mary*, 40.

32. Townsend, *Lincoln and the Bluegrass*, 165–167.

33. Estate settlement of R.S. Todd. Kentucky Historical Society. Microfilm 82-0014, Box 12, Folder 425, Drawers 1–3.

34. Hart, "Springfield's African Americans," 42–44.

35. Esvelt, Terry. Todd Family Genealogical records. Private Collection.

36. Helm, *True Story of Mary*, 103.

37. Neely and McMurtry, *The Insanity File*, 174.

38. Gerry, *Through Five Administrations*, 17–18.

39. Miers, *Lincoln Day by Day*, vol. III, 269; Washington D.C. *Evening Star*, July 2, 1864, p. 2.

40. Carpenter, *Six Months at the White House with Abraham Lincoln*, 196.

41. Washington D.C. *Evening Star*, August 5, 1864, p. 3; *Weekly National Intelligencer*, August 11, 1864, p. 4.

42. Carpenter, *Six Months at the White House with Abraham Lincoln*, 199–201.

43. Helm, *True Story of Mary*, 34–35.

44. Helm, *True Story of Mary*, 35.

45. Mary Lincoln to Emilie Todd Helm, November 23, 1856, in Turner and Turner, *Mary Todd Lincoln*, 46.

46. Turner and Turner, *Mary Todd Lincoln*, 46.

47. Mary Lincoln to Elizbeth Keckly, October 29, 1867, in Turner and Turner, *Mary Todd Lincoln*, 447.

48. Dirck, "Mary Lincoln, Race and Slavery," in Williams and Burkhimer, *The Mary Lincoln Enigma*, 49.

49. Keckly, *Behind the Scenes*, 113–114.

50. Mary Lincoln to Abraham Lincoln, November 3, 1862, in Turner and Turner, *Mary Todd Lincoln*, 141.

51. Keckly, *Behind the Scenes*, 116.

52. Keckly, *Behind the Scenes*, 88–90.

53. Keckly, *Behind the Scenes*, 203.

9. *Personality and Habits*

1. Wilson and Davis, *Herndon's Informants*, 443.

2. Snively and Davidson, "James M. Davidson," 187.

3. Cornelius, "A Photographer, a Teacher, and Two Musicians."

4. Temple, "Alexander Williamson—Tutor to the Lincoln Boys," 16.

5. Bayne, *Tad Lincoln's Father*, 37–41.

6. Neely and McMurtry, *The Insanity File*, 155–156.

7. Helm, *True Story of Mary*, 21.

8. Mary Lincoln to Mercy Ann Levering, December 15, 1840, in Turner and Turner, *Mary Todd Lincoln*, 20.

9. Lincoln's Marriage, Newspaper Interview with Mrs. Frances Wallace.

10. Mary Lincoln to Abraham Lincoln, May 1848, in Turner and Turner, *Mary Todd Lincoln*, 37.

11. Susan Haake to Donna McCreary, email, July 8, 2010.

12. The Zouaves were light infantry regiments of the French Army that were linked to North Africa. Their uniforms were fashioned after the Algerian Berber style of clothing and colors. Traditionally, the soldiers wore baggy red trousers; an

embroidered sleeveless vest; a short, opened, embellished jacket; headgear; and a long sash.

13. Bayne, *Tad Lincoln's Father*, 132-38.

14. Rankin, *Personal Recollections of Lincoln*, 158–159.

15. Scripps, *Life of Abraham Lincoln*, quoted in Evans, *Mrs. Abraham Lincoln*, 9–10.

16. Wilson and Davis, *Herndon on Lincoln*, 20.

17. Burlingame, *At Lincoln's Side*, 19–20.

18. Cole and McDonough, *Witness to the Young Republic*, 479.

19. Helm, *True Story of Mary*, 103.

20. Mary Lincoln to Edward Lewis Baker, Jr., October 4, 1879, in Turner and Turner, *Mary Todd Lincoln*, 690.

21. Turner and Turner, *Mary Todd Lincoln*, 690; Mary Lincoln to Edward Lewis Baker, Jr., January 16, 1880, in Turner and Turner, *Mary Todd Lincoln*, 694.

22. Gerry, *Through Five Administrations*, 6.

23. C. E. L., "A Kindly Word for Abraham Lincoln's Widow,".

24. Mary Lincoln to Abraham Lincoln, November 2, 1862, in Turner and Turner, *Mary Todd Lincoln*, 140.

25. Evans, *Mrs. Abraham Lincoln*, 339.

26. Evans, *Mrs. Abraham Lincoln*, 339–340.

27. Mary Lincoln to Mary Harlan Lincoln, March 22, 1869, in Turner and Turner, *Mary Todd Lincoln*, 506.

28. Helm, *True Story of Mary*, 116.

29. Helm, *True Story of Mary*, 21–22.

10. Beyond the Grave

1. "Mary Todd Lincoln (1818–1882)," 2; "Dust to Dust," *Chicago Tribune*, July 20, 1882, 7.

2. Emerson, *The Madness of Mary Lincoln*, 135–137.

3. Russo and Mann, *Images of America, Oak Ridge Cemetery*, 28–43.

4. Russo and Mann, *Images of America, Oak Ridge Cematary*, 39.

5. Russo and Mann, *Images of America, Oak Ridge Cematary*, 30.

6. Robert T. Lincoln to Hon. O. M. Hatch, letter, September 10, 1890, Robert Todd Lincoln Collection, Abraham Lincoln Library and Museum, Springfield, Illinois.

7. Swick and McCreary, "His Own Place in the Sun," 3–6.

8. For more information and examples of Mary's signature, see *Mary Todd Lincoln, Her Life and Letters* by Justin and Linda Turner.

9. Rogstad, *Companionship in Granite*, 13.

10. Rogstad, *Companionship in Granite*, 12.

11. Mike Moore, "Mary Todd Lincoln Statue Is Missing a Nose," *The Journal Express*, August 4, 2009.

12. Volkmann, *Lincoln in Sculpture*, 29.

13. Interview with Iris LaRue, curator, Lincoln Museum, Hodgenville, Kentucky, May 28, 2013.

14. *The Illustrated Buffalo Express*, "Announcing the New Mary Lincoln Candy and Coffee Shop," February 26, 1922.

15. Menz, Katherine B., *Lincoln Home Historic Furnishing Report*.

16. Menz, Katherine B., *Lincoln Home Historic Furnishing Report*.

17. Menz, Katherine B., *Lincoln Home Historic Furnishing Report*.

18. Temple, *By Square & Compass*, 177–178.

19. Temple, *By Square & Compass*, 205.

20. Temple, *By Square & Compass*, 206.

21. J. M. Spencer to Robert Todd Lincoln, letter, January 11, 1912, Robert Todd Lincoln papers, Folder: Sayre College Memorial to MTL, 1910–1914, Abraham Lincoln Presidential Library and Museum, Springfield, Illinois.

22. J. M. Spencer to Robert Todd Lincoln, letter, January 11, 1912.

23. Henry Watterson was a former member of the U.S. House of Representatives from Kentucky. He was a journalist and the successful editor of the *Louisville Journal*. He successfully merged his paper with the *Louisville Courier* thus creating the *Courier-Journal*. Watterson served in the Confederate army during the Civil War and afterward was a leader in the Democratic Party.

24. Robert Sterling Yard to Robert Todd Lincoln, letter, March 31, 1914. Robert Todd Lincoln Papers, Folder: Sayre College Memorial to MLT, 1910–1914, Abraham Lincoln Presidential Library and Museum, Springfield, Illinois.

25. Emerson, "Mary Lincoln," 180–235.

26. Mary Harlan Lincoln to Katherine Helm, letter, October 27 (no year), Mary G. Townsend Murphy Collection.

27. Katherine Helm to Mary Harlan Lincoln, letter (no date), Mary G. Townsend Murphy Collection.

28. Katherine Helm to Emilie Todd Helm, letter (no date), Mary G. Townsend Murphy Collection.

29. Otis L. Wiese to Katherine Helm, letter, Feb. 1, 1928, Special Collection, William H. Townsend Collection Box 3, Folder J2, K. Helm Correspondence, 1928, University of Kentucky Library, Lexington, Kentucky.

30. Mary Harlan Lincoln to Emilie Todd Helm, letter, May 18, 1924, Mary G. Townsend Murphy Collection.

31. Mary Harlan Lincoln to Katherine Helm, letter (no date), Mary G. Townsend Murphy Collection.

32. McCreary, *Fashionable First Lady*, 153–155; Harlan-Lincoln House Collection at Iowa Wesleyan College, Mt. Pleasant Iowa.

33. Stuart, "Some Recollections of the Early Days," 118.

34. King, *Four Marys and a Jessie*, 132–133; Emerson, *Giant in the Shadows*, 330–331.

35. King, *Four Marys and a Jessie*, 146.

36. King, *Four Marys and a Jessie*, 144, 150.

37. Emerson, *Giant in the Shadows*, 353.

38. Infant Beckwith, www.findagrave.com Memorial #74209593.

39. Emerson, *Giant in the Shadows*, 363.

40. Emerson, *Giant in the Shadows*, 396.

41. Katherine Helm to Mary Harlan Lincoln, letter, 1927, Mary G. Townsend Murphy Collection.

42. Emerson, *Giant in the Shadows*, 419; King, *Four Marys and a Jessie*, 208–209.

43. Mary Harlan Lincoln to Jessie Lincoln Randolph, letter, September 29, 1934, Friends of Hildene Archives Collection, Manchester, Vermont.

44. King, *Four Marys and a Jessie*, 194–195, 1997.

45. Obituary, "R. Beckwith, 81, President Lincoln's Great-Grandson," *Los Angeles Times*, December 27, 1985.

46. Robert Todd Lincoln "Bud" Beckwith memorial, www.findagrave, Memorial #20697070 (accessed August 21, 2020).

47. Mercie A. Conkling to Clinton L. Conkling, July 19, 1862, in Hart, *Letters of Springfield Ladies*, 67.

Appendix 1

1. Helm, *True Story of Mary*, 13–14; *The Kittochtinny Magazine*, January 1905, 88; Kleber, *The Kentucky Encyclopedia*, 888.

2. Naomi Keith Sexton, "The Clark's Grant," 6, no.1 (January 1979): 1–5; no. 2 (April 1979): 4; no. 3 (July 1979): 4–6, Indiana Collection, vertical file, Charlestown-Clark County Public Library, Charlestown, IN; Wright, John D. Jr., *Lexington: Heart of the Bluegrass*, 4.

3. Roseann Reinemuth Hogan, *Kentucky Ancestry*, 227.

4. *The Kittochtinny Magazine*, January 1905, 180; Cyrus Parker Jones Funeral Notes, Kentucky Room, Lexington Public Library; Levi O. Todd, Todd family Bible, unpublished pages.

5. Parker Family Papers 1780–1811. Filson Club, Louisville, Kentucky.

6. Green, *Historic Families of Kentucky*, 274.

7. Fayette County Will Book S, 576.

8. Todd Family Papers of Emily Todd Helm, Mary G. Townsend Murphy Collection.

9. *Journal of the House of Representatives of the Commonwealth of Kentucky*, 5; Collins and Collins, *Collin's Historical Sketches of Kentucky*, 170; Helm, *True Story of Mary*, 14–15.

10. Todd family Bible. The original Bible, which was owned by Levi W. Todd, has been lost, but the genealogy pages were copied by Dr. Wayne Temple.

11. Todd Family Papers of Emily Todd Helm, William Townsend Manuscript Collection, box 1, J–L, Todd Lineage, King Library, University of Kentucky.

12. Todd Family Papers of Emily Todd Helm, Mary G. Townsend Murphy Collection.

13. Todd Family Papers of Emily Todd Helm, Mary G. Townsend Murphy Collection.

14. Todd Family Papers of Emily Todd Helm, Mary G. Townsend Murphy Collection. "City Brevities," *Evening Courier*, Madison, Indiana, February 16, 1874. Betsy's tombstone lists her death date as February 14, 1874, as does her obituary in the *Evening Courier*, but other obituaries state the date of death as February 16, 1874.

15. Hardin, "The Brown Family of Liberty Hall," 84.

16. "City Brevities," *Evening Courier*, Madison, Indiana. February 16, 1874.

17. Edwards, *Historic Sketches*, 11.

18. Helm, *True Story of Mary*, 17.

19. "Memorial for Ninian Edwards, #19958;" https://www.findagrave.com, January 29, 2001; Memorial for Elvira Lane Edwards, #36130579, https://www.findagrave.com. April 21, 2009.

20. Power, *History of the Early Settlers of Sangamon County*, 278.

21. Todd Family Papers of Emily Todd Helm, Mary G. Townsend Murphy Collection; Obituary, *Illinois State Register*, Springfield, IL, August 15, 1899.

22. Interview with Judith Winkleman, Lincoln Home National Historic Site ranger, May 1997.

23. Todd Family Papers of Emily Todd Helm, William Townsend Manuscript Collection, box 1, J-L, Todd Lineage, King Library, University of Kentucky; Oak Ridge Cemetery Interment Records, vol. 3, p. 83.

24. Todd Family records of Emily Todd Helm, William Townsend Manuscript Collection, box 1, J-L, Todd Lineage, King Library, University of Kentucky.

25. Williams, *Williams' Lexington (KY) Directory, City Guide, and Business Mirror.*

26. Summons of Levi O. Todd, July 12, 1859. William H. Townsend Collection, Box 8, Miscellaneous, King Library, University of Kentucky.

27. Helm Papers, box 12, folder 425, drawers 1–3, 82-0014, King Library, University of Kentucky; Levi O. Todd obituary, *Daily National Intelligencer*, November 3, 1864; Levi O. Todd obituary, *National Unionist* (Lexington, Kentucky), October 28, 1864.

28. Lexington Cemetery Burial Records, Lexington, Kentucky.

29. Todd Family Papers of Emily Todd Helm, Mary G. Townsend Murphy Collection.

30. Cyrus Parker Jones Funeral Notes.

31. Todd Family Papers of Emily Todd Helm, Mary G. Townsend Murphy Collection.

32. Julia M. Trumbull to her sister-in-law Julia Trumbull, letter, November 18, 1846, Lyman Trumbull Family Papers, case 26, drawer 5, folder 44, Abraham Lincoln Presidential Library and Museum, Springfield, Illinois.

33. Obituary, *Illinois Journal*, June 13, 1860, 2; Oak Ridge Cemetery Records, Illinois Digital Archives, www.idaillinois.org, April 22, 2017.

34. Interview with Judy Winkleman.

35. Ann Todd Smith to Emilie Todd Helm, letter, April 20 (no year but probably 1888), Mary G. Townsend Murphy Collection.

36. Todd Family Papers of Emily Todd Helm, Mary G. Townsend Murphy Collection; Obituary, *The Barnwell People*, May 3, 1900, 3.

37. Waring, *A History of Medicine in South Carolina*, 1825–.

38. "Lincoln's Brother-in-Law was a Confederate Soldier," *Camden Chronicle*, January 12, 1923.

39. Strater, *The Life and Times of a Rebel Surgeon*.

40. Todd Family Papers of Emily Todd Helm, Mary G. Townsend Murphy Collection.

41. Todd Family Papers of Emily Todd Helm, Mary G. Townsend Murphy Collection.

42. *Frankfort (KY) Roundabout*, Saturday, March 19, 1904, 1.

43. Todd Family Papers of Emily Todd Helm, Mary G. Townsend Murphy Collection, private, Lexington, Kentucky.

44. David H. Todd to Emilie Todd Helm, letter, April 15 (no year), Helm Papers, Box H, Folder 425, drawers 1–3, Kentucky Historical Society, Frankfort, Kentucky; Colonel Field to David Todd, letter (no date), Letter, April 15 (no year), Helm Papers, Box H, Folder 425, Drawers 1-3, Kentucky Historical Society, Frankfort, Kentucky.

45. Berry, *House of Abraham*, 43-44, 116; Todd Family Papers of Emily Todd Helm, Mary G. Townsend Murphy Collection; "Miner Descent: Stephen Minor's Children—Unionist Slave Owners," https://minerdescent.com/2013/01/25/stephen-minor-children-unionist-slave-owners/, accessed 5/25/21.

46. Todd Family Papers of Emily Todd Helm, Mary G. Townsend Murphy Collection.

47. Katherine Helm Correspondence, 1928, William H. Townsend Collection, box 3, folder J-Z, King Library, University of Kentucky, Lexington, Kentucky.

48. Todd Family Papers of Emily Todd Helm, Mary G. Townsend Murphy Collection.

49. 1860 Federal Census, Dallas County, Alabama.

50. There is debate about the spelling of Emilie's name. According to a letter written by Emilie's daughter (Elodie Helm Lewis to Gerald McMurtry, letter, June 13, 1942) Emilie was named after her Uncle Alexander Humphreys' wife Emilie Parret of New Orleans. Emilie used several variations of her first name and her

middle name including, Emily, Emilie, Emile, Perret, Perrit, and Perit. The author has chosen the spelling based on the name of the aunt.

51. Todd Family Papers of Emily Todd Helm, Mary G. Townsend Murphy Collection.

52. Helm, *True Story of Mary Lincoln*, 221.

53. *Madison Courier*, July 18, 1866; Holwager, *A History of Christ Episcopal Church*.

54. Todd Family Papers of Emily Todd Helm, Mary G. Townsend Murphy Collection.

55. Unknown author to Emily Todd Helm, letter (no date), Todd Family Papers, The Lincoln Museum, Fort Wayne, Indiana; Charles D. Brandenburg to Emily Todd Helm, letter, June 12, 1892, Helm Papers, Box 12, Folder 425, Drawers 1–3, Kentucky Historical Society, Frankfort, Kentucky.

56. Todd Family Papers of Emily Todd Helm, Mary G. Townsend Murphy Collection.

57. Neely, "A View of Lincoln from a House Divided," 2.

58. Todd Family Papers of Emily Todd Helm, Mary G. Townsend Murphy Collection.

59. Swick and McCreary, "His Own Place in the Sun," 3–6.

60. Mary Lincoln to Abraham Lincoln, May 1848, in Turner and Turner, *Mary Todd Lincoln*, 37.

61. Edward Baker's original tombstone from Hutchinson Cemetery is located at the Abraham Lincoln Presidential Museum in Springfield, Illinois; Oak Ridge Cemetery Records, vol. 1, 27.

62. Bayne, *Tad Lincoln's Father*, 8.

63. Keckly, *Behind the Scenes*, 106–110.

64. Bayne, *Tad Lincoln's Father*, 8; Grimsley, "Six Months in the White House," 48–49.

65. "Memorial for Edwards Lewis Baker," no. 34511085, Find-a-grave.com, https://www.findagrave.com/memorial/34511085/edward-lewis-baker (accessed February 19, 2019.

66. Edwards, *Historic Sketches*, 20.

67. Todd Family Files, drawer 2, Lincoln Museum, Fort Wayne, Indiana.

68. Elizabeth Todd Grimsley to John Todd Stuart, letter, May 24, 1861, Manuscript Department SC608, ALPLM; Grimsley, "Six Months in the White House," 58–59.

69. Esvelt, Descendants of David Todd.

70. *The Kittochtinny Magazine*, January 1905, 89.

71. Evans, *Mrs. Abraham Lincoln*, 89.

72. "Memorial for Anna Maria Parker Dickson," no. 18082106, Find-a-grave.com, https://www.findagrave.com/memorial/18082106?search=true (accessed February 19, 2019).

73. Miers, *Lincoln Day by Day*, vol. 1, 153.

74. Todd family Bible (originally owned by Levi Todd, now lost); Todd Family Papers, Barbara Guinon Collection, private, Petersburg, Illinois.

75. "Mrs. Louisa Keys Dies at Residence," May 30, 1943. Todd Family Files, drawer 2, Lincoln Museum, Fort Wayne, Indiana; Elizabeth Todd Edwards to Robert Todd Lincoln, letter, October 29, 1876, Lincoln Collection, Allen County Public Library, Fort Wayne, Indiana.

76. Esvelt, *Descendants of David Todd.*

77. Emily Todd Helm DAR application #94011, Todd Family Papers of Emily Todd Helm, Mary G. Townsend Murphy Collection, private, Lexington, Kentucky; Esvelt, *Descendants of David Todd.*

78. Sanders, *History of Walnut Hill Presbyterian Church,* 11.

79. Esvelt, *Descendants of David Todd.*

80. Esvelt, *Descendants of David Todd.*

81. Esvelt, *Descendants of David Todd.*

82. Emily Todd Helm DAR application #94011, Todd Family Papers of Emily Todd Helm, Mary G. Townsend Murphy Collection, private, Lexington, Kentucky; Esvelt, *Descendants of David Todd.*

83. Esvelt, *Descendants of David Todd.*

84. Esvelt, *Descendants of David Todd.*

85. Esvelt, *Descendants of David Todd.*

86. Esvelt, *Descendants of David Todd.*

87. "Cousin and Childhood Friend Tell of Days When She and Martyr's Wife Were Girls Together," *Herald,* February 14, 1909; U.S. Civil War Soldier Records and Profiles, 1861–1865; "Death of Robert Woodrow," *The News-Herald* (Hillsboro, OH), October 29, 1896, 5.

Appendix 2

1. *The Biographical Encyclopedia of Kentucky,* 638.

2. Margaretta Brown to Amelia Mason, letter, February 15, 1836, Brown Family Papers Collection (Knox Brown Papers), Filson Club, Louisville, KY.

3. Townsend, *Lincoln and the Bluegrass,* 52–53.

4. Brandon Fisher to Donna McCreary, email, July 20, 2014.

5. Helm, *True Story of Mary,* 31–32.

6. Townsend, *Lincoln and the Bluegrass,* 52–53.

7. Helm, *True Story of Mary,* 30; Clay, *The Life of Cassius Marcellus Clay,* 47, 64–68, 542.

8. Wright, *Lexington: Heart of the Bluegrass,* 59.

9. Helm, *True Story of Mary,* 30; Townsend, *Lincoln and the Bluegrass,* 292–293; Mary Lincoln to Jeremiah T. Boyle, August 21, 1862, in Turner and Turner, *Mary Todd Lincoln,* 131.

10. Helm, *True Story of Mary,* 2–5.

11. "The Diary of Mrs. William M. Black," *Journal of Illinois State Historical Society*, vol. 48 (1955): 59–64.

12. Mary Lincoln to Elizabeth Dale Black, September 17, 1853, in Turner and Turner, *Mary Todd Lincoln*, 42.

13. Mary Lincoln to Mercy Ann Levering, December 15(?), 1840, in Turner and Turner, *Mary Todd Lincoln*, 21.

14. Paull and Hart, *Lincoln's Springfield Neighborhood*, 135–138; Mary Lincoln to Mary Brayman, June 17, 1861, in Turner and Turner, *Mary Todd Lincoln*, 90.

15. Mary Lincoln to Mercy Levering Conkling, July 29, 1864, in Turner and Turner, *Mary Todd Lincoln*, 12.

16. Chenery, William Todd, "Mary Todd Lincoln Should Be Remembered for Many Kind Acts," *Illinois State Register*, February 27, 1939; Paull and Hart, *Lincoln's Springfield Neighborhood*, 54–55.

17. Paull and Hart, *Lincoln's Springfield Neighborhood*, 126; Mary Lincoln to Jesse K. Dubois, June 19, 1868, in Turner and Turner, *Mary Todd Lincoln*, 477; "Memorial for Adelia Morris DuBois," no. 24248506, Find-a-grave.com, https://www.findagrave.com/memorial/24248506/adelia-dubois, (accessed February 23, 2019).

18. Raymond, *Some Incidents in the Life of Mrs. Benjamin S. Edwards*.

19. Mary Lincoln to Noah Brooks, May 11, 1866, in Turner and Turner, *Mary Todd Lincoln*, 362-3.

20. Mary Lincoln to Mercy Ann Levering, June 1841, in Turner and Turner, *Mary Todd Lincoln*, 26; Mary Lincoln to Edward Lewis Baker, Jr., June 12, 1880, in Turner and Turner, *Mary Todd Lincoln*, 699.

21. Cornelius, "A Photographer, a Teacher, and Two Musicians."

22. Paull and Hart, *Lincoln's Springfield Neighborhood*, 58; Mary Lincoln to Mrs. Samuel H. Melvin, April 27, 1861, in Turner and Turner, *Mary Todd Lincoln*, 85–86.

23. Mary Lincoln to Elizabeth Dale Black, September 17, 1853, in Turner and Turner, *Mary Todd Lincoln*, 42; "The Diary of Mrs. William M. Black," 61.

24. Wallace, *Past and Present of the City of Springfield and Sangamon County, Illinois*, 723.

25. Mary Lincoln to Mercy Ann Levering, June (no date) 1841, in Turner and Turner, *Mary Todd Lincoln*, 28.

26. Mary Lincoln to Hannah Shearer, April 24, 1859, in Turner and Turner, *Mary Todd Lincoln*, 54–55.

27. "Diary of Mrs. William M. Black,"61; Paull and Hart, *Lincoln's Springfield Neighborhood*, 53; Turner and Turner, *Mary Todd Lincoln*, 127–128.

28. Grimsley, "Six Months in the White House," 64; Mary Lincoln to Rhoda White, August 30, 1869, in Turner and Turner, *Mary Todd Lincoln*, 515-517; Mary Lincoln to Rev. James Smith, June 8, 1870, in Turner and Turner, *Mary Todd Lincoln*, 566–568.

29. Mary Lincoln to Mercy Ann Levering, December 15, 1840, in Turner and Turner, *Mary Todd Lincoln*, 20.

30. A. G. Henry to Mrs. Henry, Letter, February 18, 1863, Special Collections, ALPL, Springfield, IL.

31. Mary Lincoln to Anson G. Henry, July 26, 1865, in Turner and Turner, *Mary Todd Lincoln*, 264. A "whited Sepulchre" refers to someone who is inwardly evil but professes to be virtuous. The phrase comes from the King James Bible, Matthew 23:27.

32. Wilson and Davis, *Herndon's Informants*, 623, 646; Mary Lincoln to Mercy Ann Levering, June 1841, in Turner and Turner, *Mary Todd Lincoln*, 27; Helm, *True Story of Mary*, 81.

33. Helm, *True Story of Mary*, 81.

34. Mary Lincoln to Mercy Ann Levering, July 23, 1840, in Turner and Turner, *Mary Todd Lincoln*, 18.

35. Mary Lincoln to Mercy Ann Levering, December 15, 1840, in Turner and Turner, *Mary Todd Lincoln*, 21; Mary Lincoln to Mercy Ann Levering, June 1841, in Turner and Turner, *Mary Todd Lincoln*, 26.

36. Swain, "Little Known Victims of the Lincoln Assassination."

37. Fleischer, *Mrs. Lincoln and Mrs. Keckly*, 7.

38. Mary Lincoln to Elizabeth Blair Lee, July 11, 1865, in Turner and Turner, *Mary Todd Lincoln*, 259.

39. Sally Orne to Robert T. Lincoln, letter, August 8, 1875, Robert Lincoln Collection, folder 1843–1926, 1906–62, Chicago Historical Society.

40. Turner, "The Mary Lincoln Letters to Mrs. Felician Slataper," 12.

41. Jane Grey Swisshelm to Emilie Todd Helm, letter (no date), Mary G. Townsend Murphy Collection; Swisshelm, Jane Grey, "Tribute to the Dead," *Chicago Daily Tribune*, July 20, 1882.

42. Cole and McDonough, *Witness to the Young Republic*, 470–471.

43. Turner and Turner, *Mary Todd Lincoln*, 585.

44. Staudenraus, *Mr. Lincoln's Washington*, 29.

45. Mary Lincoln to Charles Sumner, September 7, 1870, in Turner and Turner, *Mary Todd Lincoln*, 576–577.

46. Clemmer, *Memorial Sketch of Elizabeth Emerson Atwater*, 21.

47. Shipman, *The Phrenological Journal and Life Illustrated*, 127; Helm, *True Story of Mary*, 269–274.

Appendix 3

1. Schwartz, Thomas F. "Mary Todd's 1835 Visit to Springfield, Illinois." *Journal of the Abraham Lincoln Association*, vol. 26, no. 1 (Winter 2005), 42-5.

2. Evans, *Mrs. Abraham Lincoln*, 83–6.

3. Brown, "Springfield Society before the Civil War," 477–500.

4. Miller, *Lincoln and His World: Volume I, The Early Years*, 447; North Todd Gentry to Katherine Helm, letter, December 1, 1927, William H. Townsend Collection, F box 2, K. Helm Correspondence, 1926–1926, King Library, University of Kentucky.

5. Miller, *Lincoln and His World: Volume I, The Early Years*, 448.

6. Findley, *A. Lincoln*, 62; Strozier and Soini, *Your Friend Forever*, 213.

7. Miers, *Lincoln Day by Day*, vol. 1, 319.

8. Miers, *Lincoln Day by Day*, 321.

9. Miers, *Lincoln Day by Day*, 322.

10. Miers, *Lincoln Day by Day*, vol. 2, 23.

11. Virginia Stuart to her daughter Elizabeth Stuart, letter, January 28, 1855, Manuscript Department, Stuart/Hay Family Papers, Abraham Lincoln Presidential Library and Museum, Springfield, Illinois.

12. Mary Lincoln to Emilie Todd Helm, February 16, 1857, in Turner and Turner, *Mary Todd Lincoln*, 48.

13. Mary Lincoln to Emilie Todd Helm, September 20, 1857, in Turner and Turner, *Mary Todd Lincoln*, 49–50; Miers, *Lincoln Day by Day*, vol. 2, 198.

14. Mary Lincoln to Hannah Shearer, June 27, 1859, in Turner and Turner, *Mary Todd Lincoln*, 56–57.

15. Mary Lincoln to Hannah Shearer, January 1, 1860, in Turner and Turner, *Mary Todd Lincoln*, 61–62.

16. Turner and Turner, *Mary Todd Lincoln*, 61–62.

17. Strozier and Soini, *Your Friend Forever*, 223.

18. Searcher, *Lincoln's Journey to Greatness*, 72–73.

19. Searcher, *Lincoln's Journey to Greatness*, 96.

20. Searcher, *Lincoln's Journey to Greatness*, 130.

21. Linnabery, "Niagara Discoveries."

22. Searcher, *Lincoln's Journey to Greatness*, 182–210.

23. Searcher, *Lincoln's Journey to Greatness*, 248.

24. Searcher, *Lincoln's Journey to Greatness*, 264-266; Miers, *Lincoln Day by Day*, vol. III, 22.

25. Todd, "Six Months in the White House," 58.

26. Todd, "Six Months in the White House," 48; Elizabeth Todd Grimsley to John Todd Stuart, Letter, March 20, 1861, Manuscript Department SC608, ALPLM, Springfield; Temple, "Mary Todd Lincoln's Travels," 182-185.

27. *New York Tribune*, June 20, 1861.

28. *New York Tribune*, June 22, 1861.

29. Miers, *Lincoln Day by Day*, vol. III, 52.

30. *New York Tribune*, August 16, 1861

31. Jeannie H. James and Wayne C. Temple, "Mrs. Lincoln's Clothing," *Lincoln Herald*, vol. 62-63 (Summer 1960), 60; McCreary, *Fashionable First Lady*, 54.

32. Linnabery, "Niagara Discoveries."

33. Miers, *Lincoln Day by Day*, vol. III, 71.

34. *National Republican*, November 4, 1861, p. 1, col. 1.

35. Bogar, *Backstage at the Lincoln Assassination*, 20.

36. *Chicago Daily Tribune*, June 20, 1862, p. 7, col. 2.

37. Temple, "Mary Todd Lincoln's Travels," 185–186.

38. Temple, "Mary Todd Lincoln's Travels," 187–88.

39. Hennessy, "Lincoln Wins Back His Army," 38.

40. Hennessy, "Lincoln Wins Back His Army," 38-40; Miers, *Lincoln Day by Day*, vol. 3, 178.

41. Pinsker, *Lincoln's Sanctuary*, 105; Miers, *Lincoln Day by Day*, vol. III, 194–196.

42. Pinsker, *Lincoln's Sanctuary*, 106.

43. Temple, "Mary Todd Lincoln's Travels," 189.

44. Temple, "Mary Todd Lincoln's Travels," 189.

45. Benjamin Hardin Helm, tombstone inscription, Helm Cemetery, Elizabethtown, Kentucky.

46. Pinsker, *Lincoln's Sanctuary*, 106.

47. Mary Lincoln to Mrs. Agen, August 10, 1864, in Turner and Turner, *Mary Todd Lincoln*, 179.

48. James and Temple, "Mrs. Lincoln's Clothing," 63.

49. Mary Lincoln to Abram Wakeman, March 20, 1865, in Turner and Turner, *Mary Todd Lincoln*, 205.

50. Temple, "Mary Todd Lincoln's Travels," 191-3.

51. Gernon, *The Lincolns in Chicago*, 47-8.

52. Mary Lincoln to Mary Jane Wells, December 29, 1865, in Turner and Turner, *Mary Todd Lincoln*, 317.

53. Gernon, *The Lincolns in Chicago*, 53.

54. Gernon, *The Lincolns in Chicago*, 54

55. Rogstad, "New Letters Tell of Mary Lincoln's 51 Days in Racine, Wisconsin," 5–6.

56. Keckly, *Behind the Scenes*, 347–348; McCreary, *Fashionable First Lady*, 127–135.

57. Gernon, *The Lincolns in Chicago*, 53.

58. Turner, "The Mary Lincoln Letters to Mrs. Felician Slataper," 13.

59. James and Temple, "Mrs. Lincoln's Clothing," 64; McCreary, *Fashionable First Lady*, 136.

60. Mary Lincoln to Mary Harlan Lincoln, May 19, 1870, in Turner, and Turner, *Mary Todd Lincoln*, 559.

61. Turner and Turner, *Mary Todd Lincoln*, 585.

62. Mary Lincoln to Norman Williams, August 8, 1872, in Turner and Turner, *Mary Todd Lincoln*, 599-600; "Odd Wisconsin: President's Widow Consulted

Milwaukee Psychic," *Wisconsin State Journal*. August 6, 2014, www.host.madison
.com/news/local/odd-wisconsin-president-s-widow-consulted-milwaukee-psychic
/article.

63. Ricker, "Mary Lincoln and the Swings," 6.

64. Ricker, "Mary Lincoln and the Swings," 8.

65. Mary Todd Lincoln to Robert Todd Lincoln, June 19, 1876, in Turner and
Turner, *Mary Todd Lincoln*, 615–616.

66. Elizabeth Edwards to Robert Todd Lincoln, letter, October 29, 1876, Lincoln
Collection, insanity file, Allen County Public Library, Fort Wayne, Indiana.

67. Mary Lincoln to Edwards Lewis Baker, Jr., October 17, 1876, in Turner and
Turner, *Mary Todd Lincoln*, 617–618.

68. Mary Lincoln to Jacob Bunn, November 7, 1877, in Turner and Turner, *Mary
Todd Lincoln*, 654.

69. Mary Lincoln to Jacob Bunn, March 22, 1878, in Turner and Turner, *Mary
Todd Lincoln*, 665.

70. Mary Lincoln to Jacob Bunn, May 22, 1878, in Turner and Turner, *Mary
Todd Lincoln*, 667.

71. Mary Lincoln to Jacob Bunn, June 5, 1878, in Turner and Turner, *Mary Todd
Lincoln*, 667–668.

72. Mary Lincoln to Edward Lewis Baker, Jr., August 3, 1879, in Turner and
Turner, *Mary Todd Lincoln*, 686–688.

73. Mary Lincoln to Edward Lewis Baker, Jr., January 16, 1880, in Turner and
Turner, *Mary Todd Lincoln*, 694.

74. Mary Lincoln to Jacob Bunn, March 5, 1880, in Turner and Turner, *Mary
Todd Lincoln*, 696.

75. Mary Lincoln to Jacob Bunn, April 26, 1880, in Turner and Turner, *Mary
Todd Lincoln*, 697.

76. Mary Lincoln to Edward Lewis Baker, Jr., October 7, 1880, in Turner and
Turner, *Mary Todd Lincoln*, 703.

77. Hirschhorn and Feldman, "Mary Lincoln's Final Illness," 511–542.

78. Mary Lincoln to Noyes W. Miner, February 21, 1882, in Turner and Turner,
Mary Todd Lincoln, 714.

79. Mary Lincoln to Edward Lewis Baker, Jr., March 21, 1882, in Turner and
Turner, *Mary Todd Lincoln*, 716.

BIBLIOGRAPHY

Archives and Collections

Brown Family Papers, Filson Club, Louisville, KY.

Conkling Family Papers, 1838–1920. Abraham Lincoln Presidential Library and Museum, Springfield, IL.

Cyrus Parker Jones Funeral Notices Scrap Book, 1806–1887. Special Collections, Kentucky Room, Lexington Public Library, Lexington, KY.

Edwards, Elizabeth Parker Todd. Letters. Abraham Lincoln Presidential Library and Museum, Springfield, IL.

Esvelt, Terry. Todd Family Genealogical Records. Private Collection.

Fayette County Kentucky, Circuit Court File 1389. *George R. C. Todd v. Elizabeth L. Todd.* Lexington, KY.

Fayette County Kentucky, Deed Book M. Court Records. Lexington, KY.

Fayette County Kentucky, Order Book 36, Fayette Circuit Court Records. Lexington, KY.

Fayette County Kentucky Will Books C and E. Court Records. Lexington, KY.

Guinon, Barbara. Todd-Keyes Family Genealogical Records. Private Collection. Petersburg, IL.

Helm, Emilie Todd. Papers. Special Collections, Kentucky Historical Society, Frankfort, KY.

Hildene, the Lincoln Family Home. Archives Friends of Hildene Inc., Manchester, VT.

Hill, Mary Miner. Memoirs. Manuscript Department, Abraham Lincoln Presidential Library and Museum, Springfield, IL.

Irwin, John and Co. Ledgers 1. Springfield, Illinois.

Lexington Cemetery Records. Lexington, KY.

Lincoln, Abraham. Collection. Abraham Lincoln Presidential Library and Museum, Springfield, IL.

——, Collection. Lincoln Foundation Collection. Allen County Public Library, Fort Wayne, IN.

Lincoln, Abraham, Library and Museum, Harrogate, TN.

Lincoln Home National Historic Site, Springfield, IL.

Lincoln, Mary Todd, House. Lexington, KY.

Lincoln, Mary Todd. Insanity File. Lincoln Financial Foundation Collection. Allen County Public Library, Fort Wayne, IN.

———, Letters. Abraham Lincoln Presidential Library and Museum, Springfield, IL.

Lincoln, Robert Todd, Papers. Abraham Lincoln Presidential Library and Museum, Springfield, IL.

———, Papers, Chicago History Museum.

Murphy, Mary Genevieve Townsend, Collection. Private Collection, Lexington, KY.

Norris, Elizabeth L. Humphreys Letters. Manuscript Division. Abraham Lincoln Presidential Library and Museum, Springfield, IL.

Oak Ridge Cemetery Interment Records, vols 1 & 2. Abraham Lincoln Presidential Library and Museum, Springfield, IL.

Parker Family Papers 1780–1811. Filson Club, Louisville, Kentucky.

Stuart-Hay Family Papers. Manuscript Division. Abraham Lincoln Presidential Library and Museum, Springfield, IL.

Todd Family Bible, originally owned by Levi O. Todd, copies owned by Dr. Wayne Temple.

Todd Family Files, Lincoln Financial Foundation Collection. Allen County Public Library, Fort Wayne, IN.

Todd, John B. S. Papers. Manuscript Division. Abraham Lincoln Presidential Library and Museum, Springfield, IL.

Todd, Robert Smith. Estate Settlement, Kentucky Historical Society, Frankfort, KY.

Todd, Robert Smith Collection, Abraham Lincoln Presidential Library and Museum, Springfield, IL.

Townsend, William H., Collection. Special Collections, University of Kentucky Library, Lexington, KY.

Transylvania University. Academic Index, Medical Department Students, years 1846–47. Lexington, KY.

Trumbull, Lyman. Papers. Manuscript Division. Abraham Lincoln Presidential Library and Museum, Springfield, IL.

United States Marine Band Library, Department of the Navy, Marine Barracks, Washington DC.

Winkelman, Judith. Interview with author, May 1997.

Newspapers

Barnwell People, The (Barnwell, South Carolina)
Camden Chronicle (Camden, South Carolina)
Chicago Daily Tribune
Chicago Times

Evening Courier (Madison, Indiana)
Frank Leslie's Illustrated Newspaper
Frankfort Roundabout (Kentucky)
Illinois State Journal
Illinois State Register
Illustrated Buffalo Express (Buffalo, New York)
Journal Times, The. (Racine, WI)
Kentucky Gazette
Lexington Herald (Kentucky)
Lexington Intelligencer (Kentucky)
Lockport Union-Sun & Journal (New York)
Los Angeles Times
Madison Courier (Indiana)
New York Evening Post
New York Herald
New York Semi-Weekly
New York Tribune
Pall Mall Gazette, The (London, England)
Sacramento Union
St. Louis Post-Dispatch
Washington, D.C. Evening Star
Weekly National Intelligencer

Books, Journals, and Pamphlets

Arnold, Isaac N. *The Life of Abraham Lincoln.* Chicago: Jensen, McClurg, 1885, Reprint 1909.

Baker, Jean H. *Mary Todd Lincoln: A Biography.* New York: W. W. Norton, 1987.
——— "Parallel Lives: Abraham and Mary Lincoln," Speech, Fifty-eighth Annual Lincoln Dinner, Lincoln Shrine, Redlands, California, February 12, 1990.

Barker, Harry Ellsworth. *Lincoln's Marriage: Newspaper Interview with Mrs. Frances Wallace, Springfield, Illinois, September 2, 1895* (pamphlet). Springfield, Illinois: 1917.

Barton, William E. *The Women Lincoln Loved.* Indianapolis, IN: Bobbs-Merrill Company, 1927.

Basler, Roy P., ed., and Dolores Pratt and Lloyd A. Dunlap, asst. eds. *The Collected Works of Abraham Lincoln 1809–1865.* 9 vols. New Brunswick, NJ: Rutgers University Press, 1953–1955.

Bayne, Julia Taft. *Tad Lincoln's Father.* Boston: Little Brown, 1931.

Bell, Patricia. "Mary Todd Lincoln–a Profile," *Civil War Times Illustrated*, vol. 7, no. 7, (November 1968): 4–11.

Bernhardt, Sarah. *Memories of My Life.* New York: D. Appleton, 1907.

Berry, Stephen. *House of Abraham: Lincoln & The Todds, A Family Divided by War*. New York: Houghton Mifflin, 2007.

The Biographical Encyclopedia of Kentucky of the Dead and Living Men of the Nineteenth Century, vol. 1. Cincinnati, OH: J. M. Armstrong, 1878.

Birmingham, Stephen, *Our Crowd: The Great Jewish Families of New York*. New York: Dell Publishing, 1967.

Blumenthal, Sidney. *All the Powers of Earth: The Political Life of Abraham Lincoln*. New York: Simon & Schuster, 2019.

Bogar, Thomas A. *Backstage at the Lincoln Assassination: The Untold Story of the Actors and Stagehands at Ford's Theatre*. Washington, DC: Regnery History, 2013.

Bradford, J. E., *Education in the Ohio Valley Prior to 1840*, issue 6. Columbus, OH: F. J. Heer Print Company, 1916.

Brown, Caroline Owsley. "Springfield Society before the Civil War." *Journal of the Illinois State Historical Society*, vol. 15, no. 1–2 (April–July 1922): 477–500.

Burlingame, Michael. *At Lincoln's Side: John Hay's Civil War Correspondence and Selected Writings*. Carbondale: Southern Illinois University Press, 2000.

———"The Mary Lincoln Enigma: Historians on America's Most Controversial First Lady," Civil War Book Review: vol. 15: iss. 2, 2013, DOI: 10.31390/cwbr .15.2.12. Available at: https://digitalcommons.lsu.edu/cwbr/vol15/iss2/10.

——— *Inside the White House in War Times: Memoirs and Reports of Lincoln's Secretary by William O. Stoddard*. Lincoln: University of Nebraska Press, 2000.

——— *Lincoln: A Life*. Baltimore, MD: John Hopkins University Press, 2008.

Busey, Samuel, MD, LLD. *Personal Reminiscences and Recollections of Forty-six Years Membership in the Medical Society of the District of Columbia and Residence in this City, with Biographical Sketches of Many of the Deceased Members*. Washington DC: Dornan Printer, 1895.

Carpenter, Francis B. *Six Months at the White House with Abraham Lincoln: The Story of a Picture*. New York: Hurd and Houghton, 1866.

Carr, Richard Wallace, and Mary Pinak Carr. *The Willard Hotel: An Illustrated History*. Washington DC: Dicmar Trading Co., 1986.

Clay, Cassius Marcellus. *The Life of Cassius Marcellus Clay: Memoirs, Writings and Speeches showing His Conduct in the Overthrow of American Slavery, The Salvation of the Union, and the Restoration of the Autonomy of the States*. Cincinnati, OH: J. Fletcher Brennan & Co., 1886.

Clemmer, Mary. *Memorial Sketch of Elizabeth Emerson Atwater: Written for her Friends*. Buffalo, NY: Courier Company, 1879.

Clinton, Catherine. *Mrs. Lincoln: A Life*. New York: Harper Collins, 2009.

Cole, Donald B. and John J. McDonough eds. *Witness to the Young Republic: A Yankee's Journal, 1828–1870, Benjamin Brown French*. Hanover, NH: University Press of New England, 1989.

Coleman, J. Winston, Jr. *The Squire's Sketches of Lexington*. Lexington, KY: Henry Clay Press, 1972.

Collins, Lewis and Richard H. Collins, *Collin's Historical Sketches of Kentucky: History of Kentucky, Revised, Enlarged, Four-fold, and Brought Down to the Year 1874 by His Son*. Frankfort: Kentucky Historical Society, 1966.

Conroy, James B. *Lincoln's White House: The People's House in Wartime*. Lanham, MD: Rowman & Littlefield, 2016.

Cornelius, James M. "A Photographer, a Teacher, and Two Musicians," Springfield, IL: unpublished manuscript, July 31, 2013.

Cornelius, James M. and Carol Knorowski, Abraham Lincoln Presidential Library Foundation. *Under Lincoln's Hat: 100 Objects That Tell the Story of His Life and Legacy*. Guilford, CT: Lyons Press, 2016.

Cunnington, C. Willett and Phyllis Cunnington. *The History of Underclothes*. New York: Dover, 1992.

Deese, Wynelle. *Lexington Kentucky: Changes in the Early Twentieth Century*. Chicago: Arcadia Publishing, 1998.

Dowdey, Clifford and Louis H. Manarin, eds. *The Wartime Papers of Robert E. Lee*. New York: Bramhall House, 1961.

DuPont, M. Kay. *Loving Mr. Lincoln: The Personal Diaries of Mary Todd Lincoln*. Atlanta, GA: Jedco Press, 2003.

Edwards, Georgie Hortense. *Historic Sketches of the Edwards & Todd Families and Their Descendants, 1523–1895*. Springfield, IL: H. W. Rokkee Printer & Binder, 1895.

Ellison, Betty. "Todds of the Bluegrass." Woodford County Historical Society publication, September 1989.

Emerson, Jason, *Giant in the Shadows: The Life of Robert T. Lincoln*. Carbondale: Southern Illinois University Press, 2012.

——— *Lincoln's Lover: Mary Lincoln in Poetry*. Kent, OH: The Kent State University Press, 2018.

——— "Mary Lincoln: An Annotated Bibliography," *Journal of the Illinois State Historical Society*, vol. 103, no 2 (Summer 2010): 180–235.

——— *Mary Lincoln's Insanity Case: A Documentary History*. Champaign: University of Illinois Press, 2015.

——— *The Madness of Mary Lincoln*. Carbondale: Southern Illinois University Press, 2007.

Epstein, Daniel Mark. *The Lincolns*. New York: Ballantine Books, 2009.

Eskew, Garnett Laidlaw, assisted by B. P. Adams. *Willard's of Washington: The Epic of a Capital Caravansary*. New York: Coward–McCann, 1954.

Evans, W. A. *Mrs. Abraham Lincoln: A Study of Her Personality and Her Influence on Lincoln*. Carbondale: Southern Illinois University Press, 2010.

Findley, Paul. *A. Lincoln: The Crucible of Congress, The Years Which Forged His Greatness.* New York: Crown Publishers, 1979.

Fleischer, Jennifer. *Mrs. Lincoln and Mrs. Keckly: The Remarkable Story of the Friendship Between a First Lady and a Former Slave.* New York: Broadway, 2003.

Gernon, Blaine Brooks, *The Lincolns in Chicago.* Chicago: Ancarthe Publishers, 1934.

Gernsheim, Alison. *Victorian and Edwardian Fashion: A Photographic Survey.* New York: Dover Publications, 1981.

Gerry, Margarita Spaulding, ed. *Through Five Administrations: Reminiscences of Colonel William H. Crook, Bodyguard to President Lincoln.* New York: Harper & Brothers, 1910.

Green, Thomas Marshall. *Historic Families of Kentucky.* Baltimore: Southern Book Company, 1959.

Goltz, Carlos W. *Incidents in the Life of Mary Todd Lincoln.* Sioux City, IA: Deitch and Lamar, 1928.

Good, Timothy S. *We Saw Lincoln Shot: One Hundred Eyewitness Accounts.* Jackson: University Press of Mississippi, 1995.

Grimsley, Elizabeth Todd. "Six Months in the White House." *Journal of the Illinois State Historical Society,* vol. XIX, no. 3–4, (October 1926–January 1927).

Hale, Sarah Josepha. *Early American Cookery: The Good Housekeeper, 1841.* Mineola, New York: Dover Publication, Reprint edition, 1996.

Hamilton, Michelle L. *"I Would Still Be Drowned in Tears": Spiritualism in Abraham Lincoln's White House.* LaMesa, CA: Vanderblümen Publications, 2013.

Hardin, Bayless. "The Brown Family of Liberty Hall." *The Club History Quarterly,* vol. 16, no. 2 (April 1942): 75–87.

Hart, Richard E. "Springfield's African Americans as a Part of the Lincoln Community," *Journal of the Abraham Lincoln Association,* vol. 20, issue 1 (Winter 1999): 35–54.

——— *Lincoln's Springfield: Letters of Springfield Ladies.* Springfield, IL: Spring Creek Series, 2019.

Helm, Emilie Todd. "Mary Todd Lincoln: Reminiscences and Letters of the Wife of President Lincoln." *McClure's Magazine* (September 1898): 476–480.

Helm, Katherine. *The True Story of Mary, Wife of Lincoln: Containing the Recollections of Mary Lincoln's Sister Emilie (Mrs. Ben Hardin Helm), Extracts from Her War-Time Diary, Numerous Letters and Other Documents now First Published.* New York: Harper and Brothers, 1928.

Hennessy, John. "Lincoln Wins Back His Army." *Civil War Times Illustrated,* February 2001, 34–42.

Herndon, William Henry and Jesse W. Weik. *Herndon's Life of Lincoln: The History and Personal Recollections of Abraham Lincoln.* New York: Da Capo Press, 1983.

Hertz, Emanuel. *The Hidden Lincoln: From the Letters and Papers of William H. Herndon.* New York: Blue Ribbon Books, 1940.

Hirschhorn, Norbert and Robert G. Feldman. "Mary Lincoln's Final Illness: A Medical and Historical Reappraisal," *Journal of the History of Medicine*, vol. 54, issue 4 (October 1, 1999) Oxford: Oxford University Press, 511–542.

Hogan, Roseann Reinemuth. *Kentucky Ancestry: A Guide to Genealogical and Historical Research.* Salt Lake City, UT: Ancestry, 1992.

Holwager, Georgia R. *A History of Christ Episcopal Church: Madison, Indiana, July 15, 1835–July 15, 1985.* Printed privately, 1985.

Holzer, Harold. *Lincoln President-Elect: Abraham Lincoln and the Great Secession Winter 1860–1861.* New York: Simon & Schuster, 2008.

Journal of the House of Representatives of the Commonwealth of Kentucky. Frankfort, KY: Kendall and Russell, Printers for the State, 1821.

James, Jeannie H. and Wayne C. Temple. "Mrs. Lincoln's Clothing," *Lincoln Herald,* vol. 62–63 (Summer 1960).

Keckly, Elizabeth. *Behind the Scenes* or *Thirty Years a Slave, and Four Years in the White House.* 1868. Reprint, New York: The New York Printing Company, 1989.

Kleber, John E., editor. *The Kentucky Encyclopedia.* Lexington: University Press of Kentucky, 1992.

King, C. J. *Four Marys and a Jessie: The Story of the Lincoln Women.* Manchester, VT: Friends of Hildene, Inc, 2005.

King, Caroline B. "Famous Dishes from the Old Kentucky Home," *The Ladies' Home Journal* (May 1923), 143–144.

Kittochtinny Magazine: A Tentative Record of Local History and Genealogy West of the Susquehanna, vol. 1, no. 2. Chambersburg, PA: G.O. Seilhamer, January 1905.

Krause, Susan, Kelley A. Boston, and Daniel W. Stowell, *Now They Belong to the Ages: Abraham Lincoln and His Contemporaries in Oak Ridge Cemetery.* Springfield: Papers of Abraham Lincoln, Illinois Historic Preservation Agency, 2005.

Kunhardt. Dorothy Meserve. "An Old Lady's Lincoln Memories." *Life,* February 9, 1959, 57–59.

Kunhardt, Philip B., Jr., Philip B. Kunhardt III, and Peter W. Kunhardt. *Lincoln: An Illustrated Biography.* New York: Random House, 1992.

Lachman, Charles. *The Last of the Lincolns: The Rise and Fall of a Great American Family.* New York: Union Square Press, 2008.

Leech, Margaret. *Reveille in Washington 1860-1865.* New York: Harper and Brothers. 1941.

L, C. E. (probably Charles Edwards Lester). "A Kindly Word for Abraham Lincoln's Widow." *Christian Register* 101, no. 36 (September 7, 1872).

Lincoln Log. www.lincolnlog.org.

Lincoln Home Chronology. www.nps.gov/liho/historyculture/homechronology.

"Lincoln's Marriage, Newspaper Interview with Mrs. Frances Wallace, September 2, 1895." Springfield, IL: Privately Printed. 1917. Lincoln Collection, ALPL.

Linder, General Usher F. *Reminiscence of the Early Bench and Bar of Illinois*. Chicago: Chicago Legal News Company, 1879.

Linnabery, Ann Marie. "Niagara Discoveries" 'A. Lincoln and Family' Visited Niagara Falls. *Lockport Union-Sun & Journal*, (April 15, 2017).

Mayoras, Danielle and Andy Mayoras. "Are You Better Prepared Than Abraham Lincoln Was?" *Forbes*, December 4, 2012. http://www.forbes.com/sites/trialandheirs/2012/12/04/are-you-better-prepared-than-abraham-lincoln-was/.

McCreary, Donna D. *Fashionable First Lady: The Victorian Wardrobe of Mary Lincoln*. Charlestown, IN: Lincoln Presentations, 2007.

———. *Lincoln's Table: A President's Culinary Journey from Cabin to Cosmopolitan*, Charlestown, IN: Lincoln Presentations, 2008.

———. *The Kentucky Todds in Lexington Cemetery*. Charlestown, IN: Lincoln Presentations, 2012.

McMurtry, Dr. R. Gerald, ed. "Lincoln's Attendance at Spiritualistic Séances." *Lincoln Lore*. no. 1499 (January 1963): 2–3.

McWaid, Maureen. "113 Days of Madness." *Old Fox River* 1, no. 1 (1993): 4–8.

Menz, Katherine B. *Lincoln Home Historic Furnishing Report*, November 1, 1983. Harpers Ferry Center, National Park Service, U.S. Department of Interior.

Miers, Earl Schenck. *Lincoln Day by Day: A Chronology, 1809–1865*. Dayton, OH: Morningside House, 1991.

Miller, Page Putnam. "Women in the Vanguard of the Sunday School Movement," *Journal of Presbyterian History*, vol. 38, no. 4 (Winter 1980): 311–325.

Miller, Richard Lawrence. *Lincoln and His World: Volume 1, The Early Years: Birth to Illinois Legislature*. Mechanicsburg, PA: Stockpole Books, 2006.

Miller, Richard Lawrence. *Lincoln and His World: Volume 2, Prairie Politician 1834–1842*. Jefferson, NC: McFarland and Company, 2011.

———. *Volume 3, The Rise to National Prominence, 1843–1853*. Jefferson, NC: McFarland and Company, 2008.

Neely, Mark E. Jr., ed. "A View of Lincoln from a House Divided," *Lincoln Lore*, no. 1651 (September 1975):1–4.

———. "Mary Todd Lincoln (1818–1882)," *Lincoln Lore*, no. 1725 (November 1981): 1–3.

Neely, Mark E. Jr. and R. Gerald McMurtry. *The Insanity File: The Case of Mary Todd Lincoln*. Carbondale: Southern Illinois University Press, 1986.

Neff, Charlotte. "The Education of Destitute, Homeless Children in Nineteenth Century Ontario." *Journal of Family History*, vol. 29, no. 1 (January 2004), 3–46.

"Odd Wisconsin: President's widow consulted Milwaukee psychic," *Wisconsin State Journal*, (August 6, 2014) Wisconsin Historical Society, www.wisconsinhistory.org, www.host.madison.com/news/local/odd-wisconsin-president-s-widow-consulted-milwaukee-psychic/article.

Ostendorf, Lloyd and Walter Oleksy, eds. *Lincoln's Unknown Private Life: An Oral History by His Housekeeper Mariah Vance 1850–1860*. Mamaroneck, NY: Hastings House Book Publishing, 1995.

Paull, Bonnie E, & Richard E. Hart. *Lincoln's Springfield Neighborhood*. Mt. Pleasant, SC: Arcadia Publishing and History Press, 2015.

Peterson, Merrill D. *Lincoln in American Memory*. New York: Oxford University Press, 1994.

Pinsker, Matthew. *Lincoln's Sanctuary Abraham Lincoln and the Soldiers' Home*. New York: Oxford University Press, 2003.

Pitch, Anthony S. *"They Have Killed Papa Dead!"* Hanover, NH: Steerforth Press, 2008.

Power, John Carroll. *History of the Early Settlers of Sangamon County: Centennial Record*. Springfield, IL: Edwin A. Wilson & Co, 1876.

Pratt, Henry E. *Concerning Mr. Lincoln: In Which Abraham Lincoln Is Pictured as He Appeared to Letter Writers of His Time*. Springfield, IL: The Abraham Lincoln Association, 1944.

———— "The Lincolns Go Shopping," *Journal of the Illinois State Historical Society*, vol. 48, no. 1 (Spring 1955), 66–81.

———— *The Personal Finances of Abraham Lincoln*, Chicago, IL: Lakeside Press, 1943.

Pratt, Harry E. and Ernest E. East, "Mrs. Lincoln Refurbishes the White House," *Lincoln Herald*, vol. 47, no. 1 (February 1946).

Pritchard, Myra Helmer, edited and annotated by Jason Emerson. *The Dark Days of Abraham Lincoln's Widow: As Revealed by Her Own Letters*. Carbondale: Southern Illinois University Press, 2011.

Raimbouville, E. De. *Vichy and Its Medicinal Properties*. New York: Louis Weiss & Co, Printers, no date.

Ralley, Mary Bradley, Mrs., "Cousin and Childhood Friend of Mary Todd Lincoln Tells of Days When She and Martyr's Wife Were Girls Together," *Lexington Herald*, February 14, 1909.

Ranck, George Washington. *History of Lexington, Kentucky: Its Early Annals and Recent Progress*. Cincinnati, OH: Robert Clarke, 1872.

Randall, Ruth Painter. *Mary Lincoln: Biography of a Marriage*. Boston: Little, Brown, 1953.

Rankin, Henry B. *Personal Recollections of Abraham Lincoln*. New York: G.P. Putnam's Sons, 1916.

Raymond, Mary Edwards. "Some Incidents in the Life of Mrs. Benjamin S. Edwards," 1909. Sangamon Valley Collection, biography E26r. Main Lincoln Library, Springfield, Illinois: no known publisher.

Ricker, Ann. "Mary Lincoln and the Swings," *For the People: A Newsletter of the Abraham Lincoln Association*, vol. 2, no 1 (Spring 2000), 1–2, 6, 8.

Roberts, Octavia. "We All Knew Abr'ham," *Abraham Lincoln Quarterly*, vol. 4, no. 3 (March 1946), 17–28.

Rogstad, Steven K. *Companionship in Granite: Celebrating the Abraham and Mary Todd Lincoln Monument–an Address.* Racine, WI: Kenson, 1998.

———"New Letters Tell of Mary Lincoln's 51 Days in Racine, Wisconsin," *For the People: A Newsletter of the Abraham Lincoln Association,* vol. 22, no. 3 (Fall 2020), Springfield, Illinois, 5–6.

Ross, Rodney A. "Mary Todd Lincoln, Patient at Bellevue Place, Batavia." *Journal of the Illinois State Historical Society,* vol. 63, no. 1 (Spring 1970): 5–34.

Runyon, Randolph Paul. *The Mentelles: Mary Todd Lincoln, Henry Clay, and the Immigrant Family who Educated Antebellum Kentucky.* Lexington: University Press of Kentucky, 2018.

Russo, Edward J. and Curtis R. Mann. *Images of America, Oak Ridge Cemetery.* Mt. Pleasant, SC: Arcadia Publishing, 2009.

Sanders, Robert Stuart. *History of Walnut Hill Presbyterian Church.* Frankfort: Kentucky Historical Society, 1956.

Schwartz, Thomas F. "Mary Todd's 1835 Visit to Springfield, Illinois." *Journal of the Abraham Lincoln Association* Vol. 26, no. 1 (Winter 2005): 42–45.

Scruggs, Camesha. *Lincoln's Hired Girls: A Look into African American, Irish, and Portuguese Hired Help in the Lincoln Home from 1844-1861.* Springfield, IL: Lincoln Home National Historic Site, unpublished document, 2008.

Searcher, Victor. *Lincoln's Journey to Greatness.* Philadelphia, PA: John C. Winston, 1960.

——— *The Farewell to Lincoln.* Nashville, TN: Abingdon Press, 1965.

Sexton, Naomi Keith. "The Clark's Grant," *Hoosier Journal of Ancestry* no. 1 (January 1979): 3-5, no. 2 (April 1979): 4-6, no. 3 (July 1979): 4. Indiana Collection, vertical file. Charlestown-Clark County Public Library, Charlestown, IN.

Shipman, Alice Davidson. *The Phrenological Journal and Life Illustrated,* vol. 77, no. 8. Philadelphia, PA: Fowler and Wells, 1883.

Snively, E. A. and J. M. Dempster Davidson, "James M. Davidson: Born May 22, 1828: Died September 29, 1894, *Journal of the Illinois State Historical Society,* vol. 9, no. 2 (July 1916): 184–194.

Sorensen, Mark W. *The Illinois State Library: 1818-1870.* Illinois Periodicals Online: www.lib.niu.edu/1999/index.html, 1999.

Springen, Karen. "Hellcat or Helpmate: A Look at Mary Todd Lincoln," *Newsweek,* https://www.newsweek.com/hellcat-or-helpmate-look-mary-todd-lincoln-100149, September 18, 2007 (accessed April 5, 2019).

Staudenraus, P. J. ed. *Mr. Lincoln's Washington: The Civil War Dispatches of Noah Brooks.* South Brunswick, NJ: Thomas Yoseloff Ltd, 1967.

Steers, Edward. *Lincoln Legends: Myths, Hoaxes, and Confabulations Associated with Our Greatest President.* Lexington: University Press of Kentucky, 2007.

Stevens, Richard E., ed. "Lexington Kentucky 1806 Occupations Directory," University of Delaware, http://www.math.udel.edu/~rstevens/datasets.html (accessed February 11, 2018).

Stevens, Walter Barlow. *A Reporter's Lincoln.* Saint Louis: Missouri Historical Society, 1916.

Strater, Terrance. *The Life and Times of a Rebel Surgeon, Dr. George Rodgers Clark Todd, Brother of Mary Todd Lincoln.* Unpublished manuscript, 1998.

Strozier, Charles B. with Wayne Soini. *Your Friend Forever, A. Lincoln: The Enduring Friendship of Abraham Lincoln and Joshua Speed.* New York: Columbia University Press, 2016.

Stuart, Emily Huntington. "Some Recollections of the Early Days in Springfield and Reminiscences of Abraham Lincoln and Other Celebrities Who Lived in That Little Town in My Youth." Paper presented to the Teachers' Federation in Chicago, Illinois, Society, Daughters of the American Revolution genealogy records, 1940–1941, Springfield, IL: The Society, 1918

Swain, Claudia. "Little Known Victims of the Lincoln Assassination." *Boundary Stones,* https://blogs.weta.org/boundarystones/2013/02/22/little-known-victims-lincoln-assassination, February 22, 2013.

Swanson, James L. *Manhunt: The 12-Day Chase for Lincoln's Killer.* New York: William Morrow, An Imprint of Harper Collins Publishers, 2006.

Swick, Gerald D., and Donna D. McCreary. "His Own Place in the Sun." *Lincoln Lore.* no. 1853 (Summer 1998): 3–6.

Sword, Wiley. *Southern Invincibility: A History of the Confederate Heart.* New York: St. Martin's Press, 1999.

Temple Wayne C. *Abraham Lincoln: From Skeptic to Prophet.* Mahomet, Il: Mayhaven Publishing, Inc., 1995.

———— "Alexander Williamson—Tutor to the Lincoln Boys," *Address at Annual Meeting, Lincoln Fellowship of Wisconsin,* Historical Bulletin 26, 1971.

———— *By Square & Compass: Saga of the Lincoln Home.* Mahomet, IL: Mayhaven Publishing, Revised Edition, 2002.

———— "Mary Todd Lincoln's Travels." *Journal of the Illinois State Historical Society* Vol. 52, no. 1, Sesquicentennial (Spring 1959): 180–194.

"Took Tea at Mrs. Lincoln. The Diary of Mrs. William M. Black." *Journal of the Illinois State Historical Society* 48, no. 1 (Spring 1955) 59–64.

Townsend, William H. *The Boarding School of Mary Todd Lincoln.* Lexington, KY: privately printed, 1941.

———— *Lincoln and the Bluegrass: Slavery and Civil War in Kentucky.* Lexington: University Press of Kentucky, 1989.

———— *Lincoln and His Wife's Hometown.* Indianapolis, IN: Bobb-Merrill, 1929.

———— *Lincoln and Liquor.* New York: The Press of the Pioneers, Inc, 1934.

Tripler, Eunice. *Eunice Tripler: Some Notes of Her Personal Recollections.* New York: The Grafton Press, 1910.

Turner, Justin. "The Mary Lincoln Letters to Mrs. Felician Slataper." *Journal of the Illinois State Historical Society* vol. 49. no. 1 (Spring 1956): 7–33.

Turner, Justin G. and Linda Levitt Turner. *Mary Todd Lincoln: Her Life and Letters.* New York: Alfred A. Knoph, 1972.

Volkmann, Carl. *Lincoln in Sculpture.* Springfield: Illinois State Historical Society, 2009.

Wallace, Joseph M. A, ed. *Past and Present of the City of Springfield and Sangamon County, Illinois.* Chicago: S. J. Clarke, 1904.

Waring, Dr. Joseph I. *A History of Medicine in South Carolina.* St. Andrews: South Carolina Medical Association, 1964.

Warren, Dr. Louis A. "Servants in the White House." *Lincoln Lore,* no. 440 (September 13, 1937): one page.

———"One Hundredth Anniversary of the Lincoln-Todd Marriage." *Lincoln Lore,* no. 707 (October 26, 1942): one page.

Washington, John E. *They Knew Lincoln.* New York: E.P. Dutton, 1942.

Williams, C. S. *Williams' Lexington (KY) Directory, City Guide, and Business Mirror.* vol. 1, 1859–1860. Lexington, KY: Hitchcock and Searles, 1859.

Williams, Frank J. and Michael Burkhimer, eds. *The Mary Lincoln Enigma.* Carbondale: Southern Illinois University Press, 2012.

Wilson, Douglas L. *Honor's Voice: The Transformation of Abraham Lincoln.* New York: Vintage Books, 1999.

Wilson, Douglas L. and Rodney O. Davis, eds. *Herndon's Informants: Letters, Interviews, and Statements about Abraham Lincoln.* Chicago: University of Illinois Press, 1998.

——— *Herndon on Lincoln: Letters, William H. Herndon.* Knox College Lincoln Studies Center. Urbana: University of Illinois Press. 2016.

Wilson, Rufus Rockwell, ed. *Lincoln among His Friends: A Sheaf of Intimate Memories.* Caldwell, ID: Caxton Printers, 1942.

Wright, John D. Jr. *Lexington: Heart of the Bluegrass, an Illustrated History.* Lexington, KY: Lexington-Fayette County Historic Commission, 1982.

INDEX

Lincoln, Thomas (Abraham's father), 151

Lincoln, Thomas "Tad" (son), 49, 52, 71, 97, 99–100, 104, 105, 107, 123–127, 176, 178, 232

Lincoln, William Wallace "Willie" (son), 49, 51, 52, 71, 79, 90, 94, 97, 99–100, 145, 154, 176, 231–232, 241–242

Lincoln and the Bluegrass (Townsend), 164

Lincoln/Douglas debates, 48

Lincoln-Douglas Triangle, The (Bauer), 35, 201

Lincoln Home (Springfield, Illinois), 196, 197–198

Lincoln Monument Association, 197, 235

Lincoln Museum (Fort Wayne, Indiana), 1–2

Lincoln's Christmas (author's performance), 1

Lincoln's Mary and the Babies, 29

Lincoln's Table (McCreary), xi

Lincoln Tomb, 186–187

linens, household, 55

liquor consumption, 38–39, 67, 95

literature, love of, 83, 178–179

Logan, America T. Bush, 234

Logan, David, 234

Logan, Sarah (Briggs), 217

Logan, Stephen Trigg (cousin), 23, 27–28, 143, 149, 234, 244

Loving Mr. Lincoln (Dupont), 178

Lucretia (enslaved woman), 164

Ludlum, Cornelius, 42, 44

Lyle, Madelon, 193

Lyles, Martha "Mattie" Belton (Todd), 225–226

Madame Alexander Doll Convention, 195

Madame Alexander Dolls, 194

Madison, Dolley, 93

Madison, Dolly Todd, 146

Madness of Mary Lincoln, The (Emerson), 201

Main Street Baptist Church, 165

Mammy Sally, 88

"manure dinner," 85

Marsh, Charlotte Dawson, 52, 241

Marsh, William, 241

Martin de Crastos, Justina, 65

Mary, the Widow of Lincoln (author's performance), 1

Mary, Wife of Lincoln (Helm), 8, 201

Mary Jane (enslaved woman), 161

Mary Lincoln Candy Company, 192–193

"Mary Lincoln Polka," 96

Mary Lincoln's Coterie, 210

Mary Todd Lincoln, An Appreciation (Morrow), 189

Mary Todd Lincoln: A Biography (Baker), x

Mary Todd Lincoln: Her Life and Letters (Turner & Turner), 201

Mary Todd Lincoln House, 6–7, 197

Matheny, James H., 35

McChord, James, 13

McClellan, General George B., 92

McClernand, General John A., 133

McDowell, Dr. Ephraim, 146

McDowell, Elizabeth (Porter), 219

McKee, Alexander, 32

McLean, Eugene, 76

McLean, John, 76

McLean, Margaret Foster Sumner, 76, 245

McMurtry, R. Gerald, x, 136

Meissen porcelain, 177

Melvin, Samuel (Dr.), 68, 241

Melvin, Sarah, 241

Mentelle, August Waldermarde, 15, 16

Merriman, Dr., 33

Merryman, Dr. Elias H., 25

migraine headaches, 181–182

Miller, Richard, 36

Miner, Reverend Noyes W., 242

Mitchell, Cornelia, 99

Monroe, President James, 235

Moore, Mary Tyler, 210

Moore, Mrs. Thomas B., 72

Morrow, Honoré Willsie, 189

DONNA D. MCCREARY, a writer, lecturer, and performer, wrote *Lincoln's Table: Victorian Recipes from Kentucky, Indiana, and Illinois to the White House* and an essay in Frank J. Williams and Michael Burkhimer's edited collection, *The Mary Lincoln Enigma* (SIU Press, 2012). Under her own imprint, Lincoln Presentations, she published *Fashionable First Lady: The Victorian Wardrobe of Mary Lincoln, The Kentucky Todds in Lexington Cemetery*, and an expanded edition of her recipe book, *Lincoln's Table: A President's Culinary Journey from Cabin to Cosmopolitan*. McCreary lectures at Lincoln sites, museums, and libraries throughout the Midwest, and from 1992 to 2012 she portrayed Mary Lincoln. She is a co-founder of Mary Lincoln's Coterie.